BUTLER'S LIVES OF THE SAINTS

WITH REFLECTIONS FOR EVERY DAY IN THE YEAR

REV. ALBAN BUTLER

DOVER PUBLICATIONS, INC.
MINEOLA, NEW YORK

Bibliographical Note

This Dover edition, first published in 2005, is an unabridged republication of the edition published by Benziger Brothers, Inc., New York, in 1894. The life of St. Catherine Laboure, as well as the appendix and index have been reprinted from the Benziger edition published in 1955.

Library of Congress Cataloging-in-Publication Data

Butler, Alban, 1711–1773.
    [Lives of the saints]
    Butler's lives of the saints : with reflections for every day in the year / Alban Butler.—Dover ed.
       p. cm.
    Includes index.
    Rev. ed. of: Lives of the saints. New York : Benziger Brothers, 1894.
    ISBN 0-486-44399-X (pbk.)
    1. Christian saints—Biography. 2. Devotional calendars—Catholic Church. 3. Catholic Church—Prayer books and devotions—English. 4. Christian saints—Prayer books and devotions—English. I. Title.

BX4655.3.B88 2005
282'.092'2—dc22
[B]
                                      2005049691

Manufactured in the United States of America
Dover Publications, Inc., 31 East 2nd Street, Mineola, N.Y. 11501

THE MOVABLE FEASTS.

MOVABLE FEASTS are so called because they have no fixed place in the calendar; their celebration happening sooner or later, year by year, according as the feast of Easter itself occurs at a different period. The latter feast is always celebrated on the Sunday which accompanies or follows the first full moon after the spring equinox. As the movable feasts afford useful lessons, we ought to take them fully to heart

ADVENT.

THE time of Advent cannot exactly be considered festal, nor can it be classed among the movable feasts; and yet the first day of Advent is, in another sense, *movable,* inasmuch as it happens always on the fourth Sunday before Christmas—which festival itself falls on different days of the week. Advent means *coming,* and the four weeks whereof it consists represent the four thousand years which preceded the *coming* of the Son of God into this world. Formerly, Advent-time was observed by fasting, abstinence, and mortification, but not in a manner so rigorous as that of Lent. Notwithstanding the alleviations which the Church has thought well to introduce in the course of time, Advent has still remained a period of recollection and prayer. The true Christian ought to take advantage thereof, and by pious yearnings entreat for the *coming* of the Son of God into his heart by grace, and into the world at large by the spreading of the Gospel.

Reflection.—"All the days in which I am now in warfare I await until my change come. Thou shalt call me, and I will answer Thee."

3

QUINQUAGESIMA SUNDAY.—THE FORTY HOURS' DEVOTION.

QUINQUAGESIMA SUNDAY is the third day preceding Ash Wednesday. That holy season is approaching when the Church denies herself her songs of joy in order the more forcibly to remind us, her children, that we are living in a Babylon of spiritual danger, and to excite us to regain that genuine Christian spirit which everything in the world around us is striving to undermine. If we are obliged to take part in the amusements of the few days before Lent, let it be with a heart deeply imbued with the maxims of the Gospel. But, as a substitute for frivolous amusements and dangerous pleasures, the Church offers a feast surpassing all earthly enjoyments, and a means whereby we can make some amends to God for the insults offered to His divine majesty. The Lamb that taketh away the sins of the world is exposed upon our altars. On this His throne of mercy He receives the homage of those who come to adore Him and acknowledge Him for their King; He accepts the repentance of those who come to tell Him how grieved they are at having followed any other master; and He offers Himself again to His Eternal Father as a propitiation for those sinners who yet treat His favors with indifference. It was the pious Cardinal Gabriel Paleotti, Archbishop of Bologna, who, in the sixteenth century, first originated the admirable devotion of the *Forty Hours.* His object in this solemn *exposition* of the Most Blessed Sacrament was to offer to the divine majesty some compensation for the sins of man, and, at the very time when the world was busiest in deserving His anger, to appease it by the sight of His own Son, the Mediator between heaven and earth. Pope Benedict XIV. granted many indulgences to all the faithful of the Papal States who, during these days, should visit Our Lord in this mystery of His love, and should pray for the pardon of sinners. This favor, at first so restricted, afterwards was extended by Pope Clement XIII. to the universal Church. Thus the *Forty Hours' Devotion* has spread throughout the whole world and become one of the most solemn expressions of Catholic piety.

Reflection.—Let us then go apart, for at least one short hour, from the dissipation of earthly enjoyments, and, kneeling in the presence of our Jesus, merit the grace to keep our hearts innocent and detached.

ASH WEDNESDAY.

MAN, drawn from the dust, must return to it, and all that he does meanwhile, with the exception of what good he may achieve, is but dust and vanity; the good alone survives. Such are the truths which the Church wishes to engrave in the memory, but still more in the hearts, of her children, by the sprinkling of ashes on this first day of Lent. This custom dates from the first centuries of the Church, and was then observed, not toward all the faithful without distinction, but toward public sinners who had submitted themselves to canonical penance, to obtain thereby reconciliation with the Church and admission to a share in the divine Eucharist. The bishop imposed on them the obligation of wearing the hair-shirt and penitent garb, placing ashes on their head, and then excluding them from the church until the day of Easter. Meanwhile, they had to remain humbly prostrate at the church-porch, imploring the prayers of those who, more happy than they, might assist at the divine mysteries within the sacred building. The custom of putting ashes on the head in token of penitence is even more ancient than Christianity; the Jews practised it, and the holy King David tells us that he had submitted to the observance. It may be said rather to date from the first ages of the world; for the holy man Job, long before even the time of Moses, followed the custom. Nothing is, in fact, more calculated to lead the sinner to enter into himself than the remembrance of his last end. Nothing is better fitted to beat down pride and put a check on futile projects and guilty purposes than the terrible and sad memento, " Remember that thou art but dust! " Empires, riches, honors, and dignities, resplendent palaces, triumphal cars, fair adornments, beauty, strength, and power, all crumble away, and their very possessor is but a ruin, and, ere a few days have sped, will have dwindled into dust.

Reflection.—Bear ever in mind, then, men and sinners, that "you are dust, and unto dust you shall return."

THE FIVE WOUNDS OF OUR LORD.

YE that delight in decking your head with costly and superb adornments, who love to cumber your hands with gold and precious jewels, who revel in luxury and in soft garments, approach and see to what a condition Jesus Christ, your Captain and Saviour, is reduced. His head is crowned with thorns and streaming with blood, and every base indignity heaped thereon by ruffian executioners; His feet and hands are pierced by nails, His side gaping with a wide-open wound. Such are the mournful accents uttered by the Church on the first Friday of Lent, two days after she has strewed ashes on the heads of the faithful. "For you it is," she exclaims, "that the Son of God, the Word made flesh, has undergone these heart-rending affronts, with intent to expiate your evil-doings, and to teach you that the idol of your body, which you deck out with so much care and eager delight, deserves, on the contrary, naught but affliction and suffering. How can you, while wreathing yourselves with flowers, venture to tread in the footsteps of a Master Who bears a thorny crown? And with what mind do you propose becoming the disciples of such a Master? That forehead made lustrous with borrowed splendor, those limbs delicately clad and brilliantly adorned, will first become the food of the grave-worm, and afterward the prey of that fire that quencheth not, if you strive not to bend them down to that lowliness which is native to them, to the state of subjection for which they were created, and to the penitence they have merited by reason of sin."

Reflection.—May the contemplation of the wounds of Our Saviour engrave deeply in our mind the maxim uttered by His own divine lips: "If any man will come after Me, let him deny himself, take up his cross, and follow Me."

THE MOST PRECIOUS BLOOD OF OUR LORD JESUS CHRIST.

THE Church, inspired by the Holy Ghost, has established a special feast in honor of the Most Precious Blood of Our Lord. This saving blood was first shed at the circumcision of the divine Infant; it was next poured out in the bloody sweat of agony in the Garden of Olives; again it flowed under the cruel blows of the savage soldiery; then when the crown of thorns was pressed into His temples; and finally when "one of the soldiers with a spear opened His side, and there came out blood and water." St. Augustine, explaining these words of St. John, points out that the Evangelist does not use the words *struck* or *wounded,* but says distinctly, "one of the soldiers with a spear *opened* His side," that we may understand thereby that the gate of life was opened, and from that sacred side issued all those sacraments of the Church without which we can never hope to gain eternal life. This precious blood was symbolized by the victim of the Old Law; but while these latter sacrifices served only to purify the outer man, the blood of Jesus Christ, by virtue of its infinite efficacy, washes us free from all sin, provided we avail ourselves of the means established by our divine Saviour in His Church for the application of its infinite merits.

Reflection.—Let us haste, then, to profit by the graces offered us. Let us wash away the stains of sin in the Sacrament of Penance, and nourish ourselves with the most blessed body and blood of the holy Eucharist. Let us ever be attentive at Mass, where this adorable blood mystically pours forth again upon the altar to plead our cause before the throne of divine justice.

THE SEVEN DOLORS OF THE BLESSED VIRGIN.

EVE, when placed by the hand of God in a garden of delights, received but one precept to be obeyed so as to be forever happy — a precept easy of accomplishment, the non-observance whereof should needs be inexcusable, inasmuch as neither urgent want nor strong inclination led to its violation; there was conjoined, moreover, the assurance of death following inevitably upon the transgression of the precept. But the serpent, kindling with jealousy and hate, came to tempt her. She gazed on the forbidden fruit, gathered thereof, and carried it to her husband, and together they ate, incurring the fatal loss, and involving mankind in their downfall. Mary, preceded by the God made man, went toiling with Him up the arid steep of Calvary, in order to accomplish the most heart-rending of all sacrifices. Eve had rebelled; Mary surrendered her will. Eve had yielded to the enticing voice of the tempter; Mary heard the voice of the same demon of jealousy and hate, uttering by the mouth of the impious Jews blasphemies and maledictions, but she was not frightened from her purpose. Eve, in her disobedience, stretched forth her hand toward the tree of the knowledge of good and evil; Mary, in her submission to the designs of God, stretches forth hers to the tree of the cross. Eve had sacrificed to her caprice the spouse through whom she had received being; Mary assists at the sacrifice of the Son to Whom she has given being. Eve was born of man without the agency of a mother; Mary gave birth to the Man-God without the intervention of a spouse. Eve, after her disobedience, became the mother, in the order of nature, of a race accursed; Mary, through her submission, has become, in the order of grace, the Mother of a race sanctified.

These points of resemblance and contrast offer themselves spontaneously to the mind, provided we ponder somewhat over the remembrance celebrated by the Church on the Friday in Holy Week, under the title of " The Seven Dolors of the Blessed Virgin." A mother's heart can alone comprehend the agony of torture endured by this Mother at the foot of the cross whereon her Son was immolated; we do not attempt to describe, nor are any mere human lips, indeed, able to express it.

Reflection.—Let us adore this divine and mysterious abyss of charity, in whose depth our salvation was worked out at the price of so much suffering; and let us bear in mind what we have cost that Mother to whose guardianship we were made over even from the sublime height of the cross.

THE MOST HOLY CROWN OF THORNS OF OUR LORD JESUS CHRIST.

THE Most Holy Crown of Thorns, consecrated by the head and the blood of our divine Saviour, has always been looked upon as one of the most precious of relics.

Having been carried to Constantinople, it was there carefully kept, during the reign of the French emperors, up to the beginning of the thirteenth century. At that time the emperor, Baldwin II., was sorely pressed by the Saracens and Greeks, and, considering Constantinople as no longer secure, he sent the precious relic to his cousin, St. Louis, who accepted it with delight. St. Louis, in requital, afterward voluntarily paid off a large sum which the emperor had borrowed from the Venetians. In 1239 the sacred treasure was carried in a sealed case, with great devotion, by holy men, to France. St. Louis, accompanied by many prelates and his entire court, met it five leagues beyond Sens. The pious king, with his brother, Robert of Artois, both barefooted, carried it into that city to the Cathedral of St. Stephen, accompanied by a numerous procession. Two years after, it was taken to Paris, where it was received with great solemnity and placed in the *Holy Chapel,* which St. Louis built for its reception. Every year, on the 11th of August, the transfer of this relic from Venice to Paris is celebrated in the *Holy Chapel.*

PALM SUNDAY.

ESSONS without end, at once lofty and hallowing, might be deduced from the triumphant entry of Jesus Christ into Jerusalem, celebrated by the Church on this day; we limit ourselves, however, to considering the event under one aspect merely, in order to draw therefrom a moral lesson for our spiritual instruction. Jesus Christ enters Jerusalem, and the people forthwith improvise a triumph all the more noble because it has cost neither blood nor tears, and so much the more touching because it is spontaneous. The whole town is in commotion, the roadway is strewn with branches and covered with the garments of the bystanders, every mouth resounding with acclamations and blessings and praise. Jesus Christ is proclaimed the Son of David, the King of the nation, and the Messias. Ere a few days are sped, the very people that had applauded now clamor for His death, curse and insult Him, and assist at His degrading death with fiendish cries of triumph.

Even thus pass away the glories of the world, its joys, its possessions, even life itself. To-day at the height of greatness, to-morrow in the deepest abasement; but yesterday the idol of a nation, to-day the object of its hate; now surrounded with prosperity, and, yet a little while, borne down by misfortune; one day full of life and vigor, and the next consigned to the tomb.

Foolish, then, are they who would account as of any value, or would cling to, things perishable! What bitter awakenings have not such poor deluded beings to expect, and what chagrin and tearful disappointments do they not create for themselves! The Christian who places the aim of his hopes and the centre of his affections at a higher range is both wiser and more happy. Prosperity does not blind nor inebriate him, since he knows it to be capricious and changeful; adverse fortune does not overwhelm him, because he was prepared for it and awaited it with calmness. The unforeseen alone affords any ground for fear; and to the faithful Christian there is nothing that is unforeseen.

Reflection.—The recommendation given by the great Apostle may be aptly brought to mind: " And they that weep be as though they wept not; and they that rejoice, as though they rejoiced not; and they that use this world, as though they used it not; for the fashion of this world passeth away."

MAUNDY THURSDAY.

ON Thursday, the eve of the Passion, Jesus Christ took bread, and, having blessed it, broke and distributed it to His apostles, saying to them, " Take and eat: THIS IS MY BODY, which shall be delivered for you." Then taking the chalice, He blessed and gave it to them, saying, " Drink ye all of this; for this is the chalice of My blood, which shall be shed for you." He thereafter added, " This do in remembrance of Me." These words, in all their precision, simplicity, and clearness, contain the institution of the adorable Sacrament of the Eucharist, an irrefragable proof of the Real Presence of Jesus Christ in this sacrament, and the demonstration of His perpetuity in the Church. But, rather than indulge in reasoning, let us set forth briefly the principal effect. Jesus Christ, before instituting it, had said that this sacrament would communicate life eternal to those receiving it; and this, in one aspect at least, and so far as it is given to man to understand the mysteries of God, is comprehensible. Sin had implanted in man the germ of death and vice. By reason of his disobedience man had become incapable of good, or even of a holy thought, as the great Apostle tells us. Now, in God is the source of being, life, good, virtue, and all excellence. God, by communicating Himself substantially to man by means of this august sacrament, implants the germ of immortality and virtue. Man, if limited to his own powers, could not even think out a useful way of becoming virtuous, for whence should he take the principle of virtue and the means of putting it in practice? He would consequently have to incur eternal loss, since salvation without virtue is a thing utterly impossible. But once pervaded with the principle of grace by an intimate union with God, he has only to let it develop and to cultivate the good seed sown in him. Thus does the diamond, of itself colorless and dim, absorb the light when exposed thereto, becoming a sparkling centre of light and shining with a radiant lustre. The more vivid the light, the more brightly will the diamond shine, if it be pure. In like manner, the more man launches himself into the divine substance, the more will he therewith be inundated by Holy Communion; the more potent, also, will his life become in virtues strong and manifold, and, consequently, in sure claims to salvation.

Reflection.—With what respect, love, and ardor ought we not to receive this divine food, " which maketh to live forever " !

GOOD FRIDAY.

JESUS CHRIST was nailed to the cross about midday, expired thereon in the afternoon, and was taken down in the evening toward sunset, or the sixth hour. According to the language of St. Paul, thus did He, by His blood, pacify heaven and earth. If this form of expression convey not simply the reconciliation of heaven with the earth, it veils a mystery impenetrable to feeble reason. But this very reconciliation is in itself the greatest mystery; for man always vainly tries to explain it by recurring to comparisons and considerations of human conception merely, which are vastly insufficient from the fact of their being human. And what matters it, after all, whether we understand or not so great a mystery? Enough for us that it has produced its effect, and that we are able to adore it in gratitude and love. That philosophy should rail at what it does not fathom is sheer foolishness. Incredulity may scoff at what it does not recognize; it concerns it, however, to know whether reason be on its side. Let heresy explain, after human fashion, things divine; as for us Christians, let us fix our gaze on the Mediator between God and man, raised aloft between heaven and earth, with arms outstretching in order to enfold the universe, with head downbent to give to the world the kiss of peace and reconciliation, after having, at the cost of His blood, purchased peace; and let us humble our whole being in heartfelt thanksgiving and love. Let us reverently imprint our lips on this cross, the instrument of our salvation; let us bend down trembling before the just God, Who takes such noble revenge for our guilt. By our works let us make some return for the price we have cost; by our penitence and tears let us apply to ourselves the merit of His redemption, and henceforth live only for heaven, since we have been made heirs to heaven.

Reflection.—The cross, " to the Jews indeed a stumbling-block, and to the Gentiles foolishness," is, withal, the instrument of Christ's power and of the wisdom of God.

HOLY SATURDAY.

THREE hours after Jesus Christ had uttered His last sigh on the cross, two of His disciples, Nicodemus and Joseph of Arimathea, went to ask Pilate for the body, that they might give it burial. Having obtained it, they embalmed it according to the custom of the Jews, and deposited it not far from the place of Calvary, in a tomb hewn in the rock, wherein no one had yet been laid. Pilate caused the entrance to be sealed up, and placed a guard over it, lest the body should be taken away. The Saviour thus remained from nightfall on the Friday till the first rays of dawn on the Sunday. He had Himself said that He was to pass this time in the tomb, and had quoted as an example the abiding of the prophet Jonas for the same space of time in the whale's belly. It was then a real death that was associated with these signs and precautions, and the sacrifice had been consummated and was irrevocable. Well might we then marvel at such excess of love, covering ourselves with confusion at the thought of how feebly we love Him Who hath so greatly loved us, and of how little we do for Him Who hath accomplished so much for us. But we should enter upon another consideration. With Jesus Christ died also the ancient world with its hideous worship; the synagogue with its symbols and mysteries; and the man of sin, the old Adam, with its concupiscences — yea, even death itself, which had been inflicted on man in punishment for sin. With Jesus Christ died sin, and sin was placed in the tomb with Him; for, according to the beautiful expression of the Apostle, the Saviour fastened the sins of men to the cross.

Now the cross itself was buried on the spot where Christ had suffered, as was the custom among the Jews, and as was fully shown by the finding thereof in conjunction with those of the two thieves, three centuries later, by St. Helen; whence it follows that among us Christians, the disciples, that is, of Christ, and regenerated by His death, there ought never to lurk any shadow of Jewish superstition or pagan morals, any remnant of the old Adam or man of sin. Concupiscences, disorderly passions, and love of the world should no longer exist but as the memory of a time that is no more.

Reflection.—" For we are buried together with Him by baptism unto death; that as Christ is risen from the dead by the glory of His Father, so we also may walk in newness of life. For if we have been planted together in the likeness of His death, we shall be also of His resurrection, knowing this, that the old man is crucified with Him, that the body of sin may be destroyed, and that we may serve sin no longer."

EASTER SUNDAY.

THE resurrection of the dead is one of the most consoling truths of Christianity. To die forever would be the most terrible of all destinies. The plant and the animal, unendowed with reason, die, never to live again; but they have not, at least, any apprehension as to what death is. To die is to them one of the thousand accidents bound up with life; to the plant it is as nothing, and for the animal without reason a merely transitory pang, death itself being but the affair of a moment. For man, on the contrary, death has terrors which precede it, anguish accompanying it, and apprehensions consequent upon it. The most strongly attempered spirit shudders on reflecting that it must incur death; the most selfish man has attachments which he with difficulty severs; the most determined unbeliever experiences doubts as to the shadowy *To-morrow* of death. Man would then be the most pitiable among all beings were Religion not at hand to say to him, " The grave is a place of momentary rest; you will come forth thence one day. The God that gave being to your limbs will restore them; the Resurrection of Jesus Christ gives thereof an assured pledge."

This confidence in the future resurrection is a subject of the greatest joy to the children of God, the groundwork of their faith, the mainspring of their hope, and the most lasting comfort amid the evils of this life. For if Christ had not risen, says the apostle St. Paul, in vain would we believe in Him. He would be convicted of having been an impostor, and His apostles of being mad; His death would not have availed us anything, and we should still be dwelling in the bonds of sin. Those dying in Jesus Christ would perish, and, our hope in Him not extending beyond the present life, we should be the most unfortunate of men, inasmuch as, after having had, as our portion in this life, sufferings and afflictions, we should not be able to console ourselves with the expectation of future good. But Jesus Christ having come forth living from the tomb, His doctrine is confirmed by His Resurrection; it establishes the certitude of His mission in His character as Son of God, the efficacy of the sacrifice He offered on the cross, the divinity of His priesthood, the rewards of the other life, and the glorified resurrection of the flesh.

Reflection.—We shall one day rise again; but let us range by the side of such a consoling expectation that terrible warning of the prophet Daniel, " Many of those that sleep in the dust of the earth shall awake, some unto life everlasting, and others unto reproach eternal."

THE ASCENSION.

THE mystery which the Church honors on this day is at the same time that of the triumph of Jesus Christ and the hallowed hope of His disciples. The Saviour, after having accomplished His mission on earth, ascends to heaven to put His manhood in possession of the glory due to it, and to prepare for us an abiding-place. He ascends thither as our King, Liberator, Chief, and Mediator: our King, because He has purchased us at the cost of His blood; our Liberator, because He has conquered death and sin, and has ransomed us from the thraldom of Satan; our Chief, because He wishes that we should follow in His footsteps, and that we should be where He is, even as He has Himself declared; our Mediator, because we can have access to the Father only through Him. He ascends thither as our High Priest, in order to offer unceasingly to God the blood which He has shed for us in His character of man, and to obtain for us through the merits of His sacrifice the remission of our sins.

Let us, then, by means of faith, follow Him in His Ascension to heaven, and abide there henceforth in heart and spirit. Let us remember that heaven is wholly ours, as our inheritance; and, amid the temptations and miseries of this life, let us think often of this home of peace, of glory, and of bliss eternal.

We must not flatter ourselves, however, that without earnest efforts on our part we shall have any share in the kingdom of Jesus Christ. There are many mansions in the house of our heavenly Father, but there are not many roads leading thither. Jesus Christ has traced out for us the way of humiliation and suffering, and it is the only one that conducts to eternal peace. If the hardships of the journey and the sight of our own weakness strike us with dread, we should gather energy by leaning on the promises of the God-man. He will be with us even unto the end, and if we love Him all will become easy.

Reflection.—Let us cherish hope: " Christ being come, a High Priest of the good things to come, hath entered into the holy of holies, by His own blood having obtained eternal redemption."

WHIT-SUNDAY.

FIFTY days after Easter the apostles and disciples of Jesus Christ were assembled in an upper chamber, engaged in prayer, according to the recommendation of the divine Master, and awaiting the accomplishment of the promise He had made to them, of sending them a Comforting Spirit, the Paraclete, Who should teach them all things. Lo! a great noise, as of a rushing tempest, was suddenly heard, the house was rocked to and fro, and tongues of fire were seen resting on the head of each one. At once all were changed into new men, their minds being endowed with full understanding of the Scriptures and of the wonders they had hitherto witnessed without comprehending, and their souls were filled with strength from on high; thenceforth they belonged no more to themselves, but to the work of the Gospel. From that time forth this divine Spirit has not ceased to pour Himself forth upon the Church to enlighten, confirm, protect, and guide; He has not ceased communicating Himself to each of the faithful individually, either by means of the sacraments or by grace, whenever He has found hearts well disposed.

The Fathers of the Church and all theologians are of one mind in recognizing, in the workings of the Holy Ghost in the hearts of the faithful, seven chief gifts: *Wisdom, Understanding, Counsel, Fortitude, Knowledge, Piety,* and *the Fear of the Lord.* The gift of Wisdom helps us to judge healthily of all things concerning our last end; the gift of Understanding, to apprehend the truths revealed, and to submit our hearts thereto; the gift of Counsel, to choose in all things the part best fitted for the sanctification of our souls; the gift of Fortitude, to resist temptations and overcome dangers; the gift of Knowledge, to discern the best means of sanctifying ourselves; the gift of Piety, or Godliness, causes us to love religion and the practices having reference to divine worship; the gift of the Fear of the Lord turns us aside from sin and from whatever may displease God.

Reflection.—" They that are according to the flesh mind the things that are of the flesh; but they that are accord-

ing to the Spirit mind the things that are of the Spirit.
For the wisdom of the flesh is death; but the wisdom of
the Spirit is life and peace."

TRINITY SUNDAY.

THE Holy Trinity is one only God in three Persons, the
Father, the Son, and the Holy Ghost, equal in all
things and co-eternal.   The Father gives being to the Son,
and the Holy Ghost proceeds from the Father and the
Son: the most adorable, truly, of all mysteries, and likewise the most impenetrable!   St. Anselm has endeavored
to explain it from a single point of view only, and has
accomplished this in a masterly yet necessarily insufficient
manner.   The Father, he says, cannot exist a single instant
without knowing Himself, because, in God, to know is
to exist, even as to will is to act.   This knowledge personified is "the Word," His Son.   The Son is, then, co-
eternal with the Father.   The Father and the Son cannot exist a single instant without loving each other; their
mutual love is, again, personified, because in God to love is
still to exist, God being love itself.   This third Person, thus
co-eternal with the other two Persons, is the Holy Ghost.
But the inhabitants with God can alone understand these
wonders, and they understand because they see them.

The free-thinker, surrounded by the mysteries of nature,
and who is to himself a complete mystery, is not willing to
admit of any in religion.   "I only wish to believe," he
says, "what I understand"!   The poor fool would not believe much were he taken at his word.   He would neither
believe in the food he takes, seeing that he could not explain how it imparts nourishment, nor in the light of the
sun, since he does not apprehend how it brings him into
relation with distant objects, nor even in his own arguments, since he does not comprehend how his mind evokes
and gives them shape.

Literally speaking, there exist no mysteries, there are
only truths; but truth becomes a mystery to him who does
not understand it.   Writing is a mystery to one who knows
not how to read; it ceases to be so to any one who has re-

ceived instruction. According as we educate the soul and widen the measure of knowledge, mysteries begin to disappear in proportion; therefore is it that there are no mysteries in heaven, because the angels and the blessed behold with open gaze the objects whereof we now possess but the mysterious definition. To deserve to behold them one day in their heavenly company, one condition is requisite, namely, to adore them meanwhile with steadfast and perfect faith in the word of God, which proposes them for our belief. In the realm of nature a mystery is a truth not understood, which one believes withal because one sees it. In the sphere of religion a mystery is a truth not understood, which one believes because God has revealed it.

Reflection.—Wherefore rebel against the word of God? Is it not " as if the clay should rebel against the potter, and the work should say to the worker thereof, Thou understandest not " ?

CORPUS CHRISTI.

ILL the thirteenth century the Church had not thought of establishing a special festival in honor of the Blessed Sacrament, being satisfied with celebrating on Holy Thursday the institution of this divine mystery. At that period, however, as heresiarchs dared to attack the Real Presence of Jesus Christ in the Eucharist, and numerous miracles and special revelations had occurred to concentrate the attention of the Christian world on this dogma, Pope Urban IV. decreed, in 1244, that a special feast should be instituted, which, by its solemnity and pomp, should be as a protestation in favor of the unwavering faith of the Church, and should, at the same time, offer an honorable reparation for the blasphemies of impious men. But this pontiff happening to die soon after, the Bull had not all the effect intended, and it was only after the Council of Vienna, held in 1332, that the feast of the Blessed Sacrament, or Corpus Christi, was definitively established throughout the Catholic world. The holy Council of Trent newly approved in a formal and earnest

manner both the worship itself and its attendant pomp.
The feast of Corpus Christi is, then, a solemn act of faith
in the Real Presence of Jesus Christ in the Blessed
Eucharist; and this belief, to which the Church attaches
an importance of the highest moment, is the very groundwork of Catholicity, or rather is the very essence of all
Christianity; for if Jesus Christ be not present really and
corporeally under the elements of bread and wine, as He
has Himself formally told us, His word is no longer reliable,
He is no longer God, and there remains of religion naught
save a beautiful but sterile philosophy, which each one can
remodel after his own mind.   If it be allowable, as Protestants contend, to interpret in a purely allegorical sense
words of such clearness that there are not, throughout the
whole of the Gospel, any more positive or precise, it is per-
missible to interpret everything at will, and the Gospel
remains an enigma, the solution whereof is nowhere to be
found.   It is furthermore the intention of the Church to
make an avowal of her love and gratitude to Our Saviour
Jesus Christ, and to offer reparation for all the profanations
and sacrileges to which this adorable sacrament has been
exposed.

Reflection.—O weak-hearted and lukewarm Christians!
O ye infidels, unbelievers, and heretics of all ages! " if
you did but know the gift of God, you would perhaps have
asked of Him, and He would have given you living
water ! "

LIVES OF THE SAINTS.

January 1.—THE CIRCUMCISION OF OUR LORD.

CIRCUMCISION was a sacrament of the Old Law, and the first legal observance required by Almighty God of the descendants of Abraham. It was a sacrament of initiation in the service of God, and a promise and engagement to believe and act as He had revealed and directed. The law of circumcision continued in force until the death of Christ, and Our Saviour being born under the law, it *became Him,* Who came to teach mankind obedience to the law of God, *to fulfil all justice,* and to submit to it. Therefore He was circumcised that He might *redeem them that were under the law,* by freeing them from the servitude of it; and that those who were in the condition of servants before might be set at liberty, and *receive the adoption of sons* in Baptism, which, by Christ's institution, succeeded to circumcision. On the day that the divine Infant was circumcised, He received the name of Jesus, which signifies SAVIOUR, which had been given Him by the angel before He was conceived. That name, so beautiful, so glorious, the divine Child does not wish to bear for one moment without fulfilling its meaning; even at the moment of His circumcision He showed Himself a SAVIOUR by shedding for us that blood a single drop of which is more than sufficient for the ransom and salvation of the whole world.

Reflection.—Let us profit by the circumstance of the new year, and of the wonderful renewal wrought in the world by the great mystery of this day, to renew in our hearts an increase of fervor and of generosity in the service of God. May this year be one of fervor and of progress! It will go by rapidly, like that which has just ended. If God permits us to see its end, how glad and happy we shall be to have passed it holily!

January 2.—ST. FULGENTIUS, Bishop.

IN spite of family troubles and delicate health, Fulgentius was appointed at an early age procurator of his province at Carthage. This success, however, did not satisfy his heart. Levying the taxes proved daily more distasteful, and when he was twenty-two, St. Austin's treatise on the Psalms decided him to enter religion. After six years of peace, his monastery was attacked by Arian heretics, and Fulgentius himself driven out destitute to the desert. He now sought the solitude of Egypt, but finding that country also in schism, he turned his steps to Rome. There the splendors of the imperial court only told him of the greater glory of the heavenly Jerusalem, and at the first lull in the persecution he resought his African cell. Elected bishop in 508, he was summoned forth to face new dangers, and was shortly after banished by the Arian king, Thrasimund, with fifty-nine orthodox prelates, to Sardinia. Though the youngest of the exiles, he was at once the mouthpiece of his brethren and the stay of their flocks. By his books and letters, which are still extant, he confounded both Pelagian and Arian heresiarchs, and confirmed the Catholics in Africa and Gaul. An Arian priest betrayed Fulgentius to the Numidians, and ordered him to be scourged. This was done. His hair and beard were plucked out, and he was left naked, his body one bleeding sore. Even the Arian bishop was ashamed of this brutality, and offered to punish the priest if the Saint would prosecute him. But Fulgentius replied, " A Christian must not seek revenge in this world. God knows how to right His servants' wrongs. If I were to bring the punishment of man on that priest, I should lose my own reward with God. And it would be a scandal to many little ones that a Catholic and a monk, however unworthy he

be, should seek redress from an Arian bishop." On
Thrasimund's death the bishops returned to their flocks,
and Fulgentius, having reëstablished discipline in his see,
retired to an island monastery, where after a year's preparation he died in peace in the year 533.

Reflection.—Each year may bring us fresh changes and
trials; let us learn from St. Fulgentius to receive all that
happens as from the hand of God, and appointed for our
salvation.

ST. MACARIUS OF ALEXANDRIA.

ⅯACARIUS when a youth left his fruit-stall at Alexandria to join the great St. Antony. The patriarch, warned by a miracle of his disciple's sanctity,
named him the heir of his virtues. His life was one long
conflict with self. " I am tormenting my tormentor," replied he to one who met him bent double with a basket
of sand in the heat of the day. " Whenever I am slothful
and idle, I am pestered by desires for distant travel."
When he was quite worn out he returned to his cell. Since
sleep at times overpowered him, he kept watch for twenty
days and nights; being about to faint, he entered his cell
and slept, but henceforth slept only at will. A gnat stung
him; he killed it. In revenge for this softness he remained
naked in a marsh till his body was covered with noxious
bites and he was recognized only by his voice. Once
when thirsty he received a present of grapes, but passed
them untouched to a hermit who was toiling in the heat.
This one gave them to a third, who handed them to a
fourth; thus the grapes went the round of the desert
and returned to Macarius, who thanked God for his
brethren's abstinence. Macarius saw demons assailing
the hermits at prayer. They put their fingers into the
mouths of some, and made them yawn. They closed the
eyes of others, and walked upon them when asleep. They
placed vain and sensual images before many of the
brethren, and then mocked those who were captivated by
them. None vanquished the devils effectually save those
who by constant vigilance repelled them at once. Maca-

rius visited one hermit daily for four months, but never
could speak to him, as he was always in prayer; so he
called him an "angel on earth." After being many years
Superior, Macarius fled in disguise to St. Pachomius, to
begin again as his novice; but St. Pachomius, instructed
by a vision, bade him return to his brethren, who loved
him as their father. In his old age, thinking nature
tamed, he determined to spend five days alone in prayer.
On the third day the cell seemed on fire, and Macarius
came forth. God permitted this delusion, he said, lest he
be ensnared by pride. At the age of seventy-three he was
driven into exile and brutally outraged by the Arian heretics. He died A. D. 394.

Reflection.—Prayer is the breath of the soul. But St.
Macarius teaches us that mind and body must be brought
to subjection before the soul is free to pray.

January 3.—ST. GENEVIEVE, Virgin.

GENEVIEVE was born at Nanterre, near Paris. St. Germanus, when passing through, specially noticed a
little shepherdess, and predicted her future sanctity. At
seven years of age she made a vow of perpetual chastity. After the death of her parents, Paris became her
abode; but she often travelled on works of mercy, which,
by the gifts of prophecy and miracles, she unfailingly performed. At one time she was cruelly persecuted: her
enemies, jealous of her power, called her a hypocrite and
tried to drown her; but St. Germanus having sent her
some blessed bread as a token of esteem, the outcry ceased,
and ever afterwards she was honored as a Saint. During
the siege of Paris by Childeric, king of the Franks, Genevieve went out with a few followers and procured corn for
the starving citizens. Nevertheless Childeric, though a
pagan, respected her, and at her request spared the lives of
many prisoners. By her exhortations again, when Attila
and his Huns were approaching the city, the inhabitants,
instead of taking flight, gave themselves to prayer and
penance, and averted, as she had foretold, the impending
scourge. Clovis, when converted from paganism by his

holy wife, St. Clotilda, made Genevieve his constant adviser, and, in spite of his violent character, made a generous and Christian king. She died within a few weeks of that monarch, in 512, aged eighty-nine.

A pestilence broke out at Paris in 1129, which in a short time swept off fourteen thousand persons, and, in spite of all human efforts, daily added to its victims. At length, on November 26th, the shrine of St. Genevieve was carried in solemn procession through the city. That same day but three persons died, the rest recovered, and no others were taken ill. This was but the first of a series of miraculous favors which the city of Paris has obtained through the relics of its patron Saint.

Reflection.—Genevieve was only a poor peasant girl, but Christ dwelt in her heart. She was anointed with His Spirit, and with power; she went about doing good, and God was with her.

January 4.—ST. TITUS, Bishop.

TITUS was a convert from heathenism, a disciple of St. Paul, one of the chosen companions of the Apostles in his journey to the Council of Jerusalem, and his fellow-laborers in many apostolic missions. From the Second Epistle which St. Paul sent by the hand of Titus to the Corinthians we gain an insight into his character and understand the strong affection which his master bore him. Titus had been commissioned to carry out a twofold office needing much firmness, discretion, and charity. He was to be the bearer of a severe rebuke to the Corinthians, who were giving scandal and were wavering in their faith; and at the same time he was to put their charity to a further test by calling upon them for abundant alms for the church at Jerusalem. St. Paul meanwhile was anxiously awaiting the result. At Troas he writes, " I had no rest in my spirit, because I found not Titus, my brother." He set sail to Macedonia. Here at last Titus brought the good news. His success had been complete. He reported the sorrow, the zeal, the generosity of the Christians, till the Apostle could not contain his joy, and sent back to them his faith-

ful messenger with the letter of comfort from which we
have quoted. Titus was finally left as a bishop in Crete,
and here he, in turn, received the epistle which bears his
name, and here at last he died in peace.

The mission of Titus to Corinth shows us how well the
disciple caught the spirit of his master. He knew how to
be firm and to inspire respect. The Corinthians, we are
told, " received him with fear and trembling." He was
patient and painstaking. St. Paul " gave thanks to God,
Who had put such carefulness for them in the heart of
Titus." And these gifts were enhanced by a quickness to
detect and call out all that was good in others, and by a
joyousness which overflowed upon the spirit of St. Paul
himself, who " abundantly rejoiced in the joy of Titus."

Reflection.—Saints win their empire over the hearts of
men by their wide and affectionate sympathy. This was
the characteristic gift of St. Titus, as it was of St. Paul, St.
Francis Xavier, and many others.

ST. GREGORY, Bishop.

ST. GREGORY was one of the principal senators of Autun,
and continued from the death of his wife a widower
till the age of fifty-seven, at which time, for his singular
virtues, he was consecrated Bishop of Langres, which see
he governed with admirable prudence and zeal thirty-three
years, sanctifying his pastoral labors by the most profound
humility, assiduous prayer, and extraordinary abstinence
and mortification. An incredible number of infidels were
converted by him from idolatry, and worldly Christians
from their disorders. He died about the beginning of
the year 541, but some days after the Epiphany. Out of
devotion to St. Benignus, he desired to be buried near that
Saint's tomb at Dijon; this was executed by his virtuous
son Tetricus, who succeeded him in his bishopric.

January 5.—ST. SIMEON STYLITES.

ONE winter's day, about the year 401, the snow lay thick around Sisan, a little town in Cilicia. A shepherd boy, who could not lead his sheep to the fields on account of the cold, went to the church instead, and listened to the eight Beatitudes, which were read that morning. He asked how these blessings were to be obtained, and when he was told of the monastic life a thirst for perfection arose within him. He became the wonder of the world, the great St. Simeon Stylites. He was warned that perfection would cost him dear, and so it did. A mere child, he began the monastic life, and therein passed a dozen years in superhuman austerity. He bound a rope round his waist till the flesh was putrefied. He ate but once in seven days, and, when God led him to a solitary life, kept fasts of forty days. Thirty-seven years he spent on the top of pillars, exposed to heat and cold, day and night adoring the majesty of God. Perfection was all in all to St. Simeon; the means nothing, except in so far as God chose them for him. The solitaries of Egypt were suspicious of a life so new and so strange, and they sent one of their number to bid St. Simeon come down from his pillar and return to the common life. In a moment the Saint made ready to descend; but the Egyptian religious was satisfied with this proof of humility. " Stay," he said, " and take courage; your way of life is from God."

Cheerfulness, humility, and obedience set their seal upon the austerities of St. Simeon. The words which God put into his mouth brought crowds of heathens to baptism and of sinners to penance. At last, in the year 460, those who watched below noticed that he had been motionless three whole days. They ascended, and found the old man's body still bent in the attitude of prayer, but his soul was with God. Extraordinary as the life of St. Simeon may appear, it teaches us two plain and practical lessons: First, we must constantly renew within ourselves an intense desire for perfection. Secondly, we must use with fidelity and courage the means of perfection God points out.

Reflection.—St. Augustine says: "This is the business of our life: by effort and by toil, by prayer and supplication, to advance in the grace of God, till we come to that height of perfection in which with clean hearts we may behold God."

January 6.—THE EPIPHANY OF OUR LORD.

THE word Epiphany means "manifestation," and it has passed into general acceptance throughout the universal Church, from the fact that Jesus Christ *manifested* to the eyes of men His divine mission on this day first of all, when a miraculous star revealed His birth to the kings of the East, who, in spite of the difficulties and dangers of a long and tedious journey through deserts and mountains almost impassable, hastened at once to Bethlehem to adore Him and to offer Him mystical presents, as to the King of kings, to the God of heaven and earth, and to a Man withal feeble and mortal. The second manifestation was when, going out from the waters of the Jordan after having received Baptism from the hands of St. John, the Holy Ghost descended on Him in the visible form of a dove, and a voice from heaven was heard, saying, "This is My beloved Son, in Whom I am well pleased." The third manifestation was that of His divine power, when at the marriage-feast of Cana He changed the water into wine, at the sight whereof His disciples believed in Him. The remembrance of these three great events, concurring to the same end, the Church has wished to celebrate in one and the same festival.

Reflection.—Admire the almighty power of this little Child, Who from His cradle makes known His coming to the shepherds and magi — to the shepherds by means of His angel, to the magi by a star in the East. Admire the docility of these kings. Jesus is born; behold them at His feet! Let us be little, let us hide ourselves, and the divine strength will be granted to us. Let us be docile and quick in following divine inspirations, and we shall then become wise of the wisdom of God, powerful in His almighty power.

January 7.—ST. LUCIAN, Martyr.

ST. LUCIAN was born at Samosata in Syria. Having lost his parents in his youth, he distributed all his worldly goods, of which he inherited an abundant share, to the poor, and withdrew to Edessa, to live near a holy man named Macarius, who imbued his mind with a knowledge of the Holy Scriptures, and led him to the practice of the Christian virtues. Having become a priest, his time was divided between the external duties of his holy state, the performance of works of charity, and the study of sacred literature. He revised the books of the Old and New Testaments, expunging the errors which had found their way into the text either through the negligence of copyists or the malice of heretics, thus preparing the way for St. Jerome, who shortly after was to give to the world the Latin translation known as "The Vulgate." Having been denounced as a Christian, Lucian was thrown into prison and condemned to the torture, which was protracted for twelve whole days. Some Christian visited him in prison, on the feast of the Epiphany, and brought bread and wine to him; while bound and chained down on his back, he consecrated the divine mysteries upon his own breast, and communicated the faithful who were present. He finished his glorious career in prison, and died with the words, " I am a Christian," on his lips.

Reflection.—If we would keep our faith pure, we must study its holy truths. We cannot detect falsehood till we know and love the truth; and to us the truth is not an abstraction, but a Person, Jesus Christ, God and Man.

January 8.—ST. APOLLINARIS, THE APOLOGIST, Bishop.

CLAUDIUS APOLLINARIS, Bishop of Hierapolis in Phrygia, was one of the most illustrious prelates of the second age. Notwithstanding the great encomiums bestowed on him by Eusebius, St. Jerome, Theodoret, and others, but little is known of his actions; and his writings, which then were held in great esteem, seem now to be all lost. He wrote many able treatises against the heretics, and pointed out, as St. Jerome testifies, from what philosophical sect each heresy derived its errors. Nothing rendered his name so illustrious, however, as his noble apology for the Christian religion which he addressed to the Emperor Marcus Aurelius, about the year 175, soon after the miraculous victory that prince had obtained over the Quadi by the prayers of the Christians. St. Apollinaris reminded the emperor of the benefit he had received from God through the prayers of his Christian subjects, and implored protection for them against the persecution of the pagans. Marcus Aurelius published an edict in which he forbade any one, under pain of death, to accuse a Christian on account of his religion; by a strange inconsistency, he had not the courage to abolish the laws then in force against the Christians, and, as a consequence, many of them suffered martyrdom, though their accusers were also put to death. The date of St. Apollinaris' death is not known; the Roman Martyrology mentions him on the 8th of January.

Reflection.—"Therefore I say unto you, all things whatsoever you ask when you pray, believe that you shall receive: and they shall come unto you."

January 9.—SS. JULIAN and BASILISSA, Martyrs.

ST. JULIAN and St. Basilissa, though married, lived, by mutual consent, in perpetual chastity; they sanctified themselves by the most perfect exercises of an ascetic life, and employed their revenues in relieving the poor and the sick. For this purpose they converted their house into a kind of hospital, in which they sometimes entertained a thousand poor people. Basilissa attended those of her sex, in separate lodgings from the men; these were taken care of by Julian, who from his charity is named the Hospitalarian. Egypt, where they lived, had then begun to abound with examples of persons who, either in the cities or in the deserts, devoted themselves to the most perfect exercises of charity, penance, and mortification. Basilissa, after having stood seven persecutions, died in peace; Julian survived her many years and received the crown of a glorious martyrdom, together with Celsus, a youth, Antony, a priest, Anastasius, and Marcianilla, the mother of Celsus. Many churches and hospitals in the East, and especially in the West, bear the name of one or other of these martyrs. Four churches at Rome, and three out of five at Paris, which bear the name of St. Julian, were originally dedicated under the name of St. Julian, the Hospitalarian and martyr. In the time of St. Gregory the Great, the skull of St. Julian was brought out of the East into France, and given to Queen Brunehault; she gave it to the nunnery which she founded at Étampes; part of it is at present in the monastery of Morigny, near Étampes, and part in the church of the regular canonesses of St. Basilissa at Paris.

Reflection.—God often rewards men for works that are pleasing in His sight by giving them grace and opportunity to do other works higher still. St. Augustine said, " I have never seen a compassionate and charitable man die a bad death."

January 10.—ST. WILLIAM, Archbishop.

ILLIAM BERRUYER, of the illustrious family of the ancient Counts of Nevers, was educated by Peter the Hermit, Archdeacon of Soissons, his uncle by the mother's side. From his infancy William learned to despise the folly and emptiness of the world, to abhor its pleasures, and to tremble at its dangers. His only delight was in exercises of piety and in his studies, in which he employed his whole time with indefatigable application. He was made canon, first of Soissons and afterwards of Paris; but he soon resolved to abandon the world, and retired into the solitude of Grandmont, where he lived with great regularity in that austere Order until finally he joined the Cistercians, then in wonderful odor of sanctity. After some time he was chosen Prior of the Abbey of Pontigny, and afterwards became Abbot of Chaalis. On the death of Henri de Sully, Archbishop of Bourges, William was chosen to succeed him. The announcement of this new dignity which had fallen on him overwhelmed him with grief, and he would not have accepted the office had not the Pope and his General, the Abbot of Citeaux, commanded him to do so. His first care in his new position was to conform his life to the most perfect rules of sanctity. He redoubled all his austerities, saying it was incumbent on him now to do penance for others as well as for himself. He always wore a hair-shirt under his religious habit, and never added to his clothing in winter or diminished it in summer; he never ate any flesh-meat, though he had it at his table for strangers. When he drew near his end, he was, at his request, laid on ashes in his hair-cloth, and in this posture expired on the 10th of January, 1209. His body was interred in his cathedral, and, being honored by many miracles, was taken up in 1217, and in the year following William was canonized by Pope Honorius III.

Reflection.—The champions of faith prove the truth of their teaching no less by the holiness of their lives than by the force of their arguments. Never forget that to convert others we must first see to our own souls.

January 11.—ST. THEODOSIUS, THE CENOBI-ARCH.

THEODOSIUS was born in Cappadocia in 423. The example of Abraham urged him to leave his country, and his desire to follow Jesus Christ attracted him to the religious life. He placed himself under Longinus, a very holy hermit, who sent him to govern a monastery near Bethlehem. Unable to bring himself to command others, he fled to a cavern, where he lived in penance and prayer. His great charity, however, forbade him to refuse the charge of some disciples, who, few at first, became in time a vast number, and Theodosius built a large monastery and three churches for them. He became eventually Superior of the religious communities of Palestine. Theodosius accommodated himself so carefully to the characters of his subjects that his reproofs were loved rather than dreaded. But once he was obliged to separate from the communion of the others a religious guilty of a grave fault. Instead of humbly accepting his sentence, the monk was arrogant enough to pretend to excommunicate Theodosius in revenge. Theodosius thought not of indignation, nor of his own position, but meekly submitted to this false and unjust excommunication. This so touched the heart of his disciple that he submitted at once and acknowledged his fault. Theodosius never refused assistance to any in poverty or affliction; on some days the monks laid more than a hundred tables for those in want. In times of famine Theodosius forbade the alms to be diminished, and often miraculously multiplied the provisions. He also built five hospitals, in which he lovingly served the sick, while by assiduous spiritual reading he maintained himself in perfect recollection. He successfully opposed the Eutychian heresy in Jerusalem, and for this was banished by the emperor. He suffered a long and painful malady, and refused to pray to be cured, calling it a salutary penance for his former successes. He died at the age of a hundred and six.

Reflection.—St. Theodosius, for the sake of charity, sacrificed all he most prized — his home for the love of God, and his solitude for the love of his neighbor. Can ours be true charity if it costs us little or nothing?

January 12.—ST. AELRED, Abbot.

"ONE thing thou lackest." In these words God called Aelred from the court of a royal Saint, David of Scotland, to the silence of the cloister. He left the king, the companions of his youth, and a friend most dear, to obey the call. The conviction that in the world his soul was in danger alone enabled him to break such ties. Long afterwards the bitterness of the parting remained fresh in his soul, and he declared that, "though he had left his dear ones in the body to serve his Lord, his heart was ever with them." He entered the Cistercian Order, and even there his yearning for sympathy showed itself in a special attraction to one among the brethren named Simon. This holy monk had left the world in his youth, and ap-

peared as one deaf and dumb, so absorbed was he in God.
One day Aelred, forgetting for the moment the rule of
perpetual silence, spoke to him.   At once he prostrated
himself at his feet in token of his fault; but Simon's look
of pain and displeasure haunted him for many a year, and
taught him to let no human feeling disturb for one moment
his union with God.   A certain novice once came to Aelred, saying that he must return to the world.   But
Aelred had begged his soul of God, and answered,
" Brother, ruin not thyself; nevertheless thou canst not,
even though thou wouldst."   However, he would not listen, and wandered among the hills, thinking all the while
he was going far from the abbey.   At sunset he found
himself before a convent strangely like Rieveaux, and so it
was.   The first monk he met was Aelred, who fell on his
neck, saying, " Son, why hast thou done so with me?   Lo!
I have wept for thee with many tears, and I trust in God
that, as I have asked of Him, thou shalt not perish."   The
world does not so love its friends.   At the command of his
superiors Aelred composed his great works, the *Spiritual
Friendship* and the *Mirror of Charity*.   In the latter he
says that true love of God is only to be obtained by joining
ourselves in all things to the Passion of Christ.   He died
in 1167, founder and Abbot of Rieveaux, the most austere
monastery in England, and Superior of some three hundred monks.

Reflection.—When a man has given himself to God,
God gives back friendship with all His other gifts a hun-
dredfold.   Friends are then loved no longer for themselves
only, but for God, and that with a love lively and tender;
for God can easily purify feeling.   It is not feeling, but
self-love, which corrupts friendship.

January 13.—ST. VERONICA OF MILAN.

VERONICA'S parents were peasants of a village near
Milan.   From her childhood she toiled hard in the
house and the field, and accomplished cheerfully every
menial task.   Gradually the desire for perfection grew
within her; she became deaf to the jokes and songs of her

companions, and sometimes, when reaping and hoeing, would hide her face and weep. Knowing no letters, she began to be anxious about her learning, and rose secretly at night to teach herself to read. Our Lady told her that other things were necessary, but not this. She showed Veronica three mystical letters which would teach her more than books. The first signified purity of intention; the second, abhorrence of murmuring or criticism; the third, daily meditation on the Passion. By the first she learned to begin her daily duties for no human motive, but for God alone; by the second, to carry out what she had thus begun by attending to her own affairs, never judging her neighbor, but praying for those who manifestly erred; by the third she was enabled to forget her own pains and sorrows in those of her Lord, and to weep hourly, but silently, over the memory of His wrongs. She had constant ecstasies, and saw in successive visions the whole life of Jesus, and many other mysteries. Yet, by a special grace, neither her raptures nor her tears ever interrupted her labors, which ended only with death. After three years' patient waiting she was received as a lay-sister in the convent of St. Martha at Milan. The community was extremely poor, and Veronica's duty was to beg through the city for their daily food. Three years after receiving the habit she was afflicted with secret but constant bodily pains, yet never would consent to be relieved of any of her labors, or to omit one of her prayers. By exact obedience she became a living copy of the rule, and obeyed with a smile the least hint of her Superior. She sought to the last the most hard and humbling occupations, and in their performance enjoyed some of the highest favors ever granted to a Saint. She died in 1497, on the day she had foretold, after a six months' illness, aged fifty-two years, and in the thirtieth of her religious profession.

Reflection.—When Veronica was urged in sickness to accept some exemption from her labors, her one answer was, " I must work while I can, while I have time." Dare we, then, waste ours?

January 14.—ST. HILARY OF POITIERS.

S̪T. HILARY was a native of Poitiers in Aquitaine.
Born and educated a pagan, it was not till near
middle age that he embraced Christianity, moved thereto
mainly by the idea of God presented to him in the Holy
Scriptures. He soon converted his wife and daughter,
and separated himself rigidly from all un-Catholic company. In the beginning of his conversion St. Hilary would
not eat with Jews or heretics, nor salute them by the way;
but afterwards, for their sake, he relaxed this severity.
He entered Holy Orders, and in 353 was chosen bishop of
his native city. Arianism, under the protection of the
Emperor Constantius, was just then in the height of its
power, and St. Hilary found himself called upon to support
the orthodox cause in several Gallic councils, in which
Arian bishops formed an overwhelming majority. He was
in consequence accused to the emperor, who banished him
to Phrygia. He spent his three years and more of exile in
composing his great works on the Trinity. In 359 he attended the Council of Seleucia, in which Arians, semi-
Arians, and Catholics contended for the mastery. With
the deputies of the council he proceeded to Constantinople,
and there so dismayed the heads of the Arian party that
they prevailed upon the emperor to let him return to Gaul.
He traversed Gaul, Italy, and Illyria, wherever he came
discomfiting the heretics and procuring triumph of ortho-
doxy. After seven or eight years of missionary travel he
returned to Poitiers, where he died in peace in 368.

Reflection.—Like St. Hilary, we, too, are called to a
lifelong contest with heretics; we shall succeed in proportion as we combine hatred of heresy with compassion for
its victims.

January 15.—ST. PAUL, the First Hermit.

ST. PAUL was born in Upper Egypt, about the year 230, and became an orphan at the age of fifteen. He was very rich and highly educated. Fearing lest the tortures of a terrible persecution might endanger his Christian perseverance, he retired into a remote village. But his pagan brother-in-law denounced him, and St. Paul, rather than remain where his faith was in danger, entered the barren desert, trusting that God would supply his wants. And his confidence was rewarded; for on the spot to which Providence led him he found the fruit of the palm-tree for food, and its leaves for clothing, and the water of a spring for drink. His first design was to return to the world when the persecution was over; but, tasting great delights in prayer and penance, he remained the rest of his life, ninety years, in penance, prayer, and contemplation. God revealed his existence to St. Antony, who sought him for three days. Seeing a thirsty she-wolf run through an opening in the rocks, Antony followed her to look for water, and found Paul. They knew each other at once, and praised God together. When St. Antony visited him, a raven brought him a loaf, and St. Paul said, " See how good God is! For sixty years this bird has brought me half a loaf every day; now thou art come, Christ has doubled the provision for His servants." Having passed the night in prayer, at dawn of day Paul told Antony that he was about to die, and asked to be buried in the cloak given to Antony by St. Athanasius. Antony hastened to fetch it, and on his way back saw Paul rise to heaven in glory. He found his dead body kneeling as if in prayer, and two lions came and dug his grave. Paul died in his one hundred and thirteenth year.

Reflection.—We shall never repent of having trusted in God, for He cannot fail those who lean on Him; nor shall we ever trust in ourselves without being deceived.

January 16.—ST. HONORATUS, Archbishop.

ST. HONORATUS was of a consular Roman family settled in Gaul. In his youth he renounced the worship of idols, and gained his elder brother, Venantius, to Christ. Convinced of the hollowness of the things of this world, they wished to renounce it with all its pleasures, but a fond pagan father put continual obstacles in their way. At length, taking with them St. Caprais, a holy hermit, for their director, they sailed from Marseilles to Greece, with the intention to live there unknown in some desert. Venantius soon died happily at Methone, and Honoratus, being also sick, was obliged to return with his conductor. He first led a hermitical life in the mountains near Frejus. Two small islands lie in the sea near that coast; on the smaller, now known as St. Honoré, our Saint settled, and, being followed by others, he there founded the famous monastery of Lerins, about the year 400. Some of his followers he appointed to live in community; others, who seemed more perfect, in separate cells as anchorets. His rule was chiefly borrowed from that of St. Pachomius. Nothing can be more amiable than the description St. Hilary has given of the excellent virtues of this company of saints, especially of the charity, concord, humility, compunction, and devotion which reigned among them under the conduct of our holy abbot. He was, by compulsion, consecrated Archbishop of Arles in 426, and died, exhausted with austerities and apostolical labors, in 429.

Reflection.—The soul cannot truly serve God while it is involved in the distractions and pleasures of the world. St. Honoratus knew this, and chose to be a servant of Christ his Lord. Resolve, in whatever state you are, to live absolutely detached from the world, and to separate yourself as much as possible from it.

January 17.—ST. ANTONY, Patriarch of Monks.

ST. ANTONY was born in the year 251, in Upper Egypt. Hearing at Mass the words, " If thou wilt be perfect, go, sell what thou hast, and give to the poor," he gave away all his vast possessions. He then begged an aged hermit to teach him the spiritual life. He also visited various solitaries, copying in himself the principal virtue of each. To serve God more perfectly, Antony entered the desert and immured himself in a ruin, building up the door so that none could enter. Here the devils assaulted him most furiously, appearing as various monsters, and even wounding him severely; but his courage never failed, and he overcame them all by confidence in God and by the sign of the cross. One night, whilst Antony was in his solitude, many devils scourged him so terribly that he lay as if dead. A friend found him thus, and believing him dead carried him home. But when Antony came to himself he persuaded his friend to carry him, in spite of his wounds, back to his solitude. Here, prostrate from weakness, he defied the devils, saying, " I fear you not; you cannot separate me from the love of Christ." After more vain assaults the devils fled, and Christ appeared to Antony in glory. His only food was bread and water, which he never tasted before sunset, and sometimes only once in two, three, or four days. He wore sackcloth and sheepskin, and he often knelt in prayer from sunset to sunrise. Many souls flocked to him for advice, and after twenty years of solitude he consented to guide them in holiness — thus founding the first monastery. His numerous miracles attracted such multitudes that he fled again into solitude, where he lived by manual labor. He expired peacefully at a very advanced age. St. Athanasius, his biographer, says that the mere knowledge of how St. Antony lived is a good guide to virtue.

Reflection.—The more violent were the assaults of temptation suffered by St. Antony, the more firmly did he grasp his weapons, namely, mortification and prayer. Let us imitate him in this if we wish to obtain victories like his.

January 18.—ST. PETER'S CHAIR AT ROME.

ST. PETER having triumphed over the devil in the East, the latter pursued him to Rome in the person of Simon Magus. He who had formerly trembled at the voice of a poor maid now feared not the very throne of idolatry and superstition. The capital of the empire of the world, and the centre of impiety, called for the zeal of the Prince of Apostles. God had established the Roman Empire, and extended its dominion beyond that of any former monarchy, for the more easy propagation of His Gospel. Its metropolis was of the greatest importance for this enterprise. St. Peter took that province upon himself, and, repairing to Rome, there preached the faith and established his ecclesiastical chair. That St. Peter preached in Rome, founded the Church there, and died there by martyrdom under Nero, are facts the most incontestable, by the testimony of all writers of different countries who lived near that time; persons of unquestionable veracity, and who could not but be informed of the truth in a point so interesting and of its own nature so public and notorious. This is also attested by monuments of every kind; by the prerogatives, rights, and privileges which that church enjoyed from those early ages in consequence of this title. It was an ancient custom observed by churches to keep an annual festival of the consecration of their bishops. The feast of the Chair of St. Peter is found in ancient martyrologies. Christians justly celebrate the founding of this mother-church, the centre of Catholic communion, in thanksgiving to God for His mercies to His Church, and to implore His future blessings.

Reflection.—As one of God's greatest mercies to His Church, let us earnestly beg of Him to raise up in it zealous pastors, eminently replenished with His Spirit, with which He animated His apostles.

January 19.—ST. CANUTUS, King, Martyr.

St. Canutus, King of Denmark, was endowed with excellent qualities of both mind and body. It is hard to say whether he excelled more in courage or in conduct and skill in war; but his singular piety eclipsed all his other endowments. He cleared the seas of pirates, and subdued several neighboring provinces which infested Denmark with their incursions. The kingdom of Denmark was elective till the year 1660, and, when the father of Canutus died, his eldest brother, Harold, was called to the throne. Harold died after reigning for two years, and Canutus was chosen to succeed him. He began his reign by a successful war against the troublesome, barbarous enemies of the state, and by planting the faith in the conquered provinces. Amid the glory of his victories he humbly prostrated himself at the foot of the crucifix, laying there his diadem, and offering himself and his kingdom to the King of kings. After having provided for the peace and safety of his country, he married Eltha, daughter of Robert, Earl of Flanders, who proved a spouse worthy of him. His next concern was to reform abuses at home. For thus purpose he enacted severe but necessary laws for the strict administration of justice, and repressed the violence and tyranny of the great, without respect to persons. He countenanced and honored holy men, and granted many privileges and immunities to the clergy. His charity and tenderness towards his subjects made him study by all possible ways to make them a happy people. He showed a royal munificence in building and adorning churches, and gave the crown which he wore, of exceeding great value, to a church in his capital and place of residence, where the kings of Denmark are yet buried. To the virtues which constitute a great king, Canutus added those which prove the great saint. A rebellion having sprung up in his kingdom, the king was surprised at church by the rebels. Perceiving his danger, he confessed his sins at the foot of the altar, and received Holy Communion. Stretching out his arms before the altar, the Saint fervently recommended his soul to his Creator; in this posture he was struck by a javelin thrown through a window, and fell a victim for Christ's sake.

Reflection.—The soul of a man is endowed with many noble powers, and feels a keen joy in their exercise; but the keenest joy we are capable of feeling consists in prostrating all our powers of mind and heart in humblest adoration before the majesty of God.

January 20.—ST. SEBASTIAN, Martyr.

ST. SEBASTIAN was an officer in the Roman army, esteemed even by the heathen as a good soldier, and honored by the Church ever since as a champion of Jesus Christ. Born at Narbonne, Sebastian came to Rome about the year 284, and entered the lists against the powers of evil. He found the twin brothers Marcus and Marcellinus in prison for the faith, and, when they were near yielding to the entreaties of their relatives, encouraged them to despise flesh and blood, and to die for Christ. God confirmed his words by miracle: light shone around him while he spoke; he cured the sick by his prayers; and in this divine strength he led multitudes to the faith, among them the Prefect of Rome, with his son Tiburtius. He saw his disciples die before him, and one of them came back from heaven to tell him that his own end was near. It was in a contest of fervor and charity that St. Sebastian found the occasion of martyrdom. The Prefect of Rome, after his conversion, retired to his estates in Campania, and took a great number of his fellow-converts with him to this place of safety. It was a question whether Polycarp the priest or St. Sebastian should accompany the neophytes. Each was eager to stay and face the danger at Rome, and at last the Pope decided that the Roman church could not spare the services of Sebastian. He continued to labor at the post of danger till he was betrayed by a false disciple. He was led before Diocletian, and, at the emperor's command, pierced with arrows and left for dead. But God raised him up again, and of his own accord he went before the emperor and conjured him to stay the persecution of the Church. Again sentenced, he was at last beaten to death by clubs, and crowned his labors by the merit of a double martyrdom.

Reflection.—Your ordinary occupations will give you opportunities of laboring for the faith. Ask help from St. Sebastian. He was not a priest nor a religious, but a soldier.

January 21.—ST. AGNES, Virgin, Martyr.

T. AGNES was but twelve years old when she was led to the altar of Minerva at Rome and commanded to obey the persecuting laws of Diocletian by offering incense. In the midst of the idolatrous rites she raised her hands to Christ, her Spouse, and made the sign of the life-giving cross. She did not shrink when she was bound hand and foot, though the gyves slipped from her young hands, and the heathens who stood around were moved to tears. The bonds were not needed for her, and she hastened gladly to the place of her torture. Next, when the judge saw that pain had no terrors for her, he inflicted an insult worse than death: her clothes were stripped off, and she had to stand in the street before a pagan crowd; yet even this did not daunt her. " Christ," she said, " will guard His own." So it was. Christ showed, by a miracle, the value which He sets upon the custody of the eyes. Whilst the crowd turned away their eyes from the spouse of Christ, as she stood exposed to view in the street, there was one young man who dared to gaze at the innocent child with immodest eyes. A flash of light struck him blind, and his companions bore him away half dead with pain and terror.

Lastly, her fidelity to Christ was proved by flattery and offers of marriage. But she answered, " Christ is my Spouse: He chose me first, and His I will be." At length the sentence of death was passed. For a moment she stood erect in prayer, and then bowed her neck to the sword. At one stroke her head was severed from her body, and the angels bore her pure soul to Paradise.

Reflection.—Her innocence endeared St. Agnes to Christ, as it has endeared her to His Church ever since. Even as penitents we may imitate this innocence of hers in our own degree. Let us strictly guard our eyes, and Christ, when He sees that we keep our hearts pure for love of Him, will renew our youth and give us back the years which the canker-worm has wasted.

January 22.—ST. VINCENT, Martyr.

VINCENT was archdeacon of the church at Saragossa. Valerian, the bishop, had an impediment in his speech; thus Vincent preached in his stead, and answered in his name when both were brought before Dacian, the president, during the persecution of Diocletian. When the bishop was sent into banishment, Vincent remained to suffer and to die. First of all, he was stretched on the rack; and, when he was almost torn asunder, Dacian, the president, asked him in mockery " how he fared now." Vincent answered, with joy in his face, that he had ever prayed to be as he was then. It was in vain that Dacian struck the executioners and goaded them on in their savage work. The martyr's flesh was torn with hooks; he was bound in a chair of red-hot iron; lard and salt were rubbed into his wounds; and amid all this he kept his eyes raised to heaven, and remained unmoved. He was cast into a solitary dungeon, with his feet in the stocks; but the angels of Christ illuminated the darkness, and assured Vincent that he was near his triumph. His wounds were now tended to prepare him for fresh torments, and the faithful were permitted to gaze on his mangled body. They came in troops, kissed the open sores, and carried away as relics cloths dipped in his blood. Before the tortures could recommence, the martyr's hour came, and he breathed forth his soul in peace.

Even the dead bodies of the saints are precious in the sight of God, and the hand of iniquity cannot touch them. A raven guarded the body of Vincent where it lay flung upon the earth. When it was sunk out at sea the waves cast it ashore; and his relics are preserved to this day in

the Augustinian monastery at Lisbon, for the consolation
of the Church of Christ.

Reflection.—Do you wish to be at peace amidst suffering and temptation? Then make it your principal endeavor to grow in habits of prayer and in union with
Christ. Have confidence in Him. He will make you
victorious over your spiritual enemies and over yourself.
He will enlighten your darkness and sweeten your sufferings, and in your solitude and desolation He will draw
nigh to you with His holy angels.

January 23.—ST. RAYMUND OF PENNAFORT.

BORN A. D. 1175, of a noble Spanish family, Raymund,
at the age of twenty, taught philosophy at Barcelona with marvellous success. Ten years later his rare
abilities won for him the degree of Doctor in the University of Bologna, and many high dignities. A tender
devotion to our blessed Lady, which had grown up with
him from childhood, determined him in middle life to
renounce all his honors and to enter her Order of St. Dominic. There, again, a vision of the Mother of Mercy instructed him to coöperate with his penitent St. Peter
Nolasco, and with James, King of Aragon, in founding the
Order of Our Lady of Ransom for the Redemption of Captives. He began this great work by preaching a crusade
against the Moors, and rousing to penance the Christians,
enslaved in both soul and body by the infidel. King James
of Aragon, a man of great qualities, but held in bond by a
ruling passion, was bidden by the Saint to put away the
cause of his sin. On his delay, Raymund asked for leave
to depart from Majorca, since he could not live with sin.
The king refused, and forbade, under pain of death, his
conveyance by others. Full of faith, Raymund spread his
cloak upon the waters, and, tying one end to his staff as a
sail, made the sign of the cross and fearlessly stepped upon
it. In six hours he was borne to Barcelona, where, gathering up his cloak dry, he stole into his monastery. The
king, overcome by this miracle, became a sincere penitent
and the disciple of the Saint till his death. In 1230,

Gregory IX. summoned Raymund to Rome, made him his confessor and grand penitentiary, and directed him to compile " The Decretals," a collection of the scattered decisions of the Popes and Councils. Having refused the archbishopric of Tarragona, Raymund found himself in 1238 chosen third General of his Order; which post he again succeeded in resigning, on the score of his advanced age. His first act when set free was to resume his labors among the infidels, and in 1256 Raymund, then eighty-one, was able to report that ten thousand Saracens had received Baptism. He died A. D. 1275.

Reflection.—Ask St. Raymund to protect you from that fearful servitude, worse than any bodily slavery, which even one sinful habit tends to form.

January 24.—ST. TIMOTHY, Bishop, Martyr.

TIMOTHY was a convert of St. Paul. He was born at Lystra in Asia Minor. His mother was a Jewess, but his father was a pagan; and though Timothy had read the Scriptures from his childhood, he had not been circumcised as a Jew. On the arrival of St. Paul at Lystra the youthful Timothy, with his mother and grandmother, eagerly embraced the faith. Seven years later, when the Apostle again visited the country, the boy had grown into manhood, while his good heart, his austerities and zeal had won the esteem of all around him; and holy men were prophesying great things of the fervent youth. St. Paul at once saw his fitness for the work of an evangelist. Timothy was forthwith ordained, and from that time became the constant and much-beloved fellow-worker of the Apostle. In company with St. Paul he visited the cities of Asia Minor and Greece — at one time hastening on in front as a trusted messenger, at another lingering behind to confirm in the faith some recently founded church. Finally, he was made the first Bishop of Ephesus; and here he received the two epistles which bear his name, the first written from Macedonia and the second from Rome, in which St. Paul from his prison gives vent to his longing desire to see his " dearly beloved son," if possible, once more before his death. St. Timothy himself, not many years after the death of St. Paul, won his martyr's crown at Ephesus. As a child Timothy delighted in reading the sacred books, and to his last hour he would remember the parting words of his spiritual father, " *Attende lectioni* — Apply thyself to reading."

Reflection.—St. Paul, in writing to Timothy, a faithful and well-tried servant of God, and a bishop now getting on in years, addresses him as a child, and seems most anxious about his perseverance in faith and piety. The letters abound in minute personal instructions for this end. It is therefore remarkable what great stress the Apostle lays on the avoiding of idle talk, and on the application to holy reading. These are his chief topics. Over and over again he exhorts his son Timothy to " avoid tattlers and busybodies ; to give no heed to novelties ; to shun profane and vain babblings, but to hold the form of sound words ; to be an example in word and conversation ; to attend to reading, to exhortation, and to doctrine."

January 25.—THE CONVERSION OF ST. PAUL.

THE great apostle Paul, named Saul at his circumcision, was born at Tarsus, the capital of Silicia, and was by privilege a Roman citizen, to which quality a great distinction and several exemptions were granted by the laws of the empire. He was early instructed in the strict observance of the Mosaic law, and lived up to it in the most scrupulous manner. In his zeal for the Jewish law, which he thought the cause of God, he became a violent persecutor of the Christians. He was one of those who combined to murder St. Stephen, and in the violent persecution of the faithful which followed the martyrdom of the holy deacon, Saul signalized himself above others. By virtue of the power he had received from the high priest, he dragged the Christians out of their houses, loaded them with chains, and thrust them into prison. In the fury of his zeal he applied for a commission to take up all Jews at Damascus who confessed Jesus Christ, and bring them bound to Jerusalem, that they might serve as examples for

the others.   But God was pleased to show forth in him His
patience and mercy.   While on his way to Damascus, he
and his party were surrounded by a light from heaven,
brighter than the sun, and suddenly struck to the ground.
And then a voice was heard saying, " Saul, Saul, why dost
thou persecute Me ? "   And Saul answered, " Who art
Thou, Lord ? " and the voice replied, " I am Jesus, Whom
thou dost persecute."   This mild expostulation of Our
Redeemer, accompanied with a powerful interior grace,
cured Saul's pride, assuaged his rage, and wrought at
once a total change in him.   Wherefore, trembling and
astonished, he cried out, " Lord, what wilt Thou have me
to do ? "   Our Lord ordered him to arise and to proceed on
his way to the city, where he should be informed of what
was expected from him.   Saul, arising from the ground,
found that, though his eyes were open, he saw nothing.
He was led by hand into Damascus, where he was lodged
in the house of a Jew named Judas.   To this house came
by divine appointment a holy man named Ananias, who,
laying his hands on Saul, said, " Brother Saul, the Lord
Jesus, Who appeared to thee on thy journey, hath sent me
that thou mayest receive thy sight and be filled with the
Holy Ghost."   Immediately something like scales fell from
Saul's eyes, and he recovered his sight.   Then he arose
and was baptized ; he stayed some few days with the disciples at Damascus, and began immediately to preach in
the synagogues that Jesus was the Son of God.   Thus a
blasphemer and a persecutor was made an apostle, and
chosen as one of God's principal instruments in the conversion of the world.

Reflection.—Listen to the words of the " Imitation of
Christ," and let them sink into your heart :   " He who
would keep the grace of God, let him be grateful for grace
when it is given, and patient when it is taken away.   Let
him pray that it may be given back to him, and be careful
and humble, lest he lose it."

January 26.—ST. POLYCARP, Bishop, Martyr.

ST. POLYCARP, Bishop of Smyrna, was a disciple of St.
John. He wrote to the Philippians, exhorting them
to mutual love and to hatred of heresy. When the
apostate Marcion met St. Polycarp at Rome, he asked the
aged Saint if he knew him. "Yes," St. Polycarp answered, "I know you for the first-born of Satan." These
were the words of a Saint most loving and most charitable, and specially noted for his compassion to sinners.
He hated heresy, because he loved God and man so much.
In 167, persecution broke out in Smyrna. When Polycarp heard that his pursuers were at the door, he said,
"The will of God be done;" and meeting them, he begged
to be left alone for a little time, which he spent in prayer
for "the Catholic Church throughout the world." He was
brought to Smyrna early on Holy Saturday; and, as he
entered, a voice was heard from heaven, "Polycarp, be
strong." When the proconsul besought him to curse
Christ and go free, Polycarp answered, "Eighty-six years
I have served Him, and He never did me wrong; how can
I blaspheme my King and Saviour?" When he threatened him with fire, Polycarp told him this fire of his lasted
but a little, while the fire prepared for the wicked lasted
forever. At the stake he thanked God aloud for letting
him drink of Christ's chalice. The fire was lighted, but
it did him no hurt; so he was stabbed to the heart, and
his dead body was burnt. "Then," say the writers of his
acts, "we took up the bones, more precious than the richest jewels or gold, and deposited them in a fitting place, at
which may God grant us to assemble with joy to celebrate
the birthday of the martyr to his life in heaven!"

Reflection.—If we love Jesus Christ, we shall love the
Church and hate heresy, which rends His mystical body,
and destroys the souls for which He died. Like St. Polycarp, we shall maintain our constancy in the faith by love
of Jesus Christ, Who is its author and its finisher.

January 27.—ST. JOHN CHRYSOSTOM.

T. John was born at Antioch in 344. In order to break with a world which admired and courted him, he in 374 retired for six years to a neighboring mountain. Having thus acquired the art of Christian silence, he returned to Antioch, and there labored as priest, until he was ordained Bishop of Constantinople in 398. The effect of his sermons was everywhere marvellous. He was very urgent that his people should frequent the holy sacrifice, and in order to remove all excuse he abbreviated the long Liturgy until then in use. St. Nilus relates that St. John Chrysostom was wont to see, when the priest began the holy sacrifice, " many of the blessed ones coming down from heaven in shining garments, and with bare feet, eyes intent, and bowed heads, in utter stillness and silence, assisting at the consummation of the tremendous mystery." Beloved as he was in Constantinople, his denunciations of vice made him numerous enemies. In 403 these procured his banishment; and although he was almost immediately recalled, it was not more than a reprieve. In 404 he was banished to Cucusus in the deserts of Taurus. In 407 he was wearing out, but his enemies were impatient. They hurried him off to Pytius on the Euxine, a rough journey of nigh 400 miles. He was assiduously exposed to every hardship, cold, wet, and semi-starvation, but nothing could overcome his cheerfulness and his consideration for others. On the journey his sickness increased, and he was warned that his end was nigh. Thereupon, exchanging his travel-stained clothes for white garments, he received Viaticum, and with his customary words, " Glory be to God for all things. Amen," passed to Christ.

Reflection.—We should try to understand that the most productive work in the whole day, both for time and eternity, is that involved in hearing Mass. St. John Chrysostom felt this so keenly that he allowed no consideration of venerable usage to interfere with the easiness of hearing Mass.

January 28.—ST. CYRIL OF ALEXANDRIA.

ST. CYRIL became Patriarch of Alexandria in 412. Having at first thrown himself with ardor into the party politics of the place, God called him to a nobler conflict. In 428, Nestorius, Bishop of Constantinople, began to deny the unity of Person in Christ, and to refuse to the Blessed Virgin the title of " Mother of God." He was strongly supported by disciples and friends throughout the East. As the assertion of the divine maternity of Our Lady was necessary to the integrity of the doctrine of the Incarnation, so, with St. Cyril, devotion to the Mother was the necessary complement of his devotion to the Son. St. Cyril, after expostulating in vain, accused Nestorius to Pope Celestine. The Pope commanded retraction, under pain of separation from the Church, and intrusted St. Cyril with the conduct of the proceedings. The appointed day, June 7, 431, found Nestorius and Cyril at Ephesus, with over 200 bishops. After waiting twelve days in vain for the Syrian bishops, the council with Cyril tried Nestorius, and deposed him from his see. Upon this the Syrians and Nestorians excommunicated St. Cyril, and complained of him to the emperor as a peace-breaker. Imprisoned and threatened with banishment, the Saint rejoiced to confess Christ by suffering. In time it was recognized that St. Cyril was right, and with him the Church triumphed. Forgetting his wrongs, and careless of controversial punctilio, Cyril then reconciled himself with all who would consent to hold the doctrine of the Incarnation intact. He died in 444.

Reflection.—The Incarnation is the mystery of God's dwelling within us, and therefore should be the dearest object of our contemplation. It was the passion of St. Cyril's life; for it he underwent toil and persecution, and willingly sacrificed credit and friends.

January 29.—ST. FRANCIS OF SALES.

FRANCIS was born of noble and pious parents, near
Annecy, 1566, and studied with brilliant success at
Paris and Padua. On his return from Italy he gave up
the grand career which his father had marked out for
him in the service of the state, and became a priest.
When the Duke of Savoy had resolved to restore the
Church in the Chablais, Francis offered himself for the
work, and set out on foot with his Bible and breviary and
one companion, his cousin Louis of Sales. It was a work
of toil, privation, and danger. Every door and every
heart was closed against him. He was rejected with insult and threatened with death. But nothing could daunt
or resist him, and ere long the Church burst forth into a
second spring. It is stated that he converted 72,000 Cal-
vinists. He was then compelled by the Pope to become
Coadjutor Bishop of Geneva, and succeeded to the see
in 1602. At times the exceeding gentleness with which
he received heretics and sinners almost scandalized his
friends, and one of them said to him, " Francis of Sales
will go to Paradise, of course; but I am not so sure of the
Bishop of Geneva: I am almost afraid his gentleness will
play him a shrewd turn." " Ah," said the Saint, " I
would rather account to God for too great gentleness than
for too great severity. Is not God all love? God the
Father is the Father of mercy; God the Son is a Lamb;
God the Holy Ghost is a Dove — that is, gentleness itself.
And are you wiser than God? " In union with St. Jane
Frances of Chantal he founded at Annecy the Order of the
Visitation, which soon spread over Europe. Though poor,
he refused provisions and dignities, and even the great see
of Paris. He died at Avignon, 1622.

Reflection.—" You will catch more flies," St. Francis
used to say, " with a spoonful of honey than with a hundred barrels of vinegar. Were there anything better or
fairer on earth than gentleness, Jesus Christ would have
taught it us; and yet He has given us only two lessons to
learn of Him — meekness and humility of heart."

January 30.—ST. BATHILDES, Queen.

ST. BATHILDES was an Englishwoman, who was carried over whilst yet young into France, and there sold for a slave, at a very low price, to Erkenwald, mayor of the palace under King Clovis II. When she grew up, her master was so much taken with her prudence and virtue that he placed her in charge of his household. The renown of her virtues spread through all France, and King Clovis II. took her for his royal consort. This unexpected elevation produced no alteration in a heart perfectly grounded in humility and the other virtues; she seemed to become even more humble than before. Her new station furnished her the means of being truly a mother to the poor; the king gave her the sanction of his royal authority for the protection of the Church, the care of the poor, and the furtherance of all religious undertakings. The death of her husband left her regent of the kingdom. She at once forbade the enslavement of Christians, did all in her power to promote piety, and filled France with hospitals and religious houses. As soon as her son Clotaire was of an age to govern, she withdrew from the world and entered the convent of Chelles. Here she seemed entirely to forget her worldly dignity, and was to be distinguished from the rest of the community only by her extreme humility, her obedience to her spiritual superiors, and her devotion to the sick, whom she comforted and served with wonderful charity. As she neared her end, God visited her with a severe illness, which she bore with Christian patience until, on the 30th of January, 680, she yielded up her soul in devout prayer.

Reflection.— In all that we do, let God and His holy will be always before our eyes, and our only aim and desire be to please Him.

January 31.—ST. MARCELLA, Widow.

ST. MARCELLA, whom St. Jerome called the glory of the Roman women, became a widow in the seventh month after her marriage. Having determined to consecrate the remainder of her days to the service of God, she rejected the hand of Cerealis, the consul, uncle of Gallus Cæsar, and resolved to imitate the lives of the ascetics of the East. She abstained from wine and flesh-meat, employed all her time in pious reading, prayer, and visiting the churches, and never spoke with any man alone. Her example was followed by many who put themselves under her direction, and Rome was in a short time filled with monasteries. When the Goths under Alaric plundered Rome in 410, our Saint suffered severely at the hands of the barbarian, who cruelly scourged her in order to make her reveal the treasures which she had long before distributed in charity. She trembled only, however, for the innocence of her dear spiritual daughter, Principia, and falling at the feet of the cruel soldiers, she begged with many tears that they would offer no insult to that pure virgin. God moved them to compassion, and they conducted our Saint and her pupil to the Church of St. Paul, to which Alaric had granted the right of sanctuary, with that of St. Peter. St. Marcella, who survived this but a short time, closed her eyes by a happy death, in the arms of St. Principia, about the end of August, 410.

February 1.—ST. BRIDGID, Abbess, and Patroness of Ireland.

NEXT to the glorious St. Patrick, St. Bridgid, whom we may consider his spiritual daughter in Christ, has ever been held in singular veneration in Ireland. She was born about the year 453, at Fochard in Ulster. During her infancy, her pious father saw in a vision men clothed in white garments pouring a sacred unguent on her head, thus prefiguring her future sanctity. While yet very young, Bridgid consecrated her life to God, bestowed

everything at her disposal on the poor, and was the edification of all who knew her. She was very beautiful, and
fearing that efforts might be made to induce her to break
the vow by which she had bound herself to God, and to bestow her hand on one of her many suitors, she prayed that
she might become ugly and deformed. Her prayer was
heard, for her eye became swollen, and her whole countenance so changed that she was allowed to follow her
vocation in peace, and marriage with her was no more
thought of. When about twenty years old, our Saint
made known to St. Mel, the nephew and disciple of St.
Patrick, her intention to live only to Jesus Christ, and he
consented to receive her sacred vows. On the appointed
day the solemn ceremony of her profession was performed
after the manner introduced by St. Patrick, the bishop
offering up many prayers, and investing Bridgid with a
snow-white habit, and a cloak of the same color. While
she bowed her head on this occasion to receive the veil, a
miracle of a singularly striking and impressive nature occurred: that part of the wooden platform adjoining the
altar on which she knelt recovered its original vitality, and
put on all its former verdure, retaining it for a long time
after. At the same moment Bridgid's eye was healed, and
she became as beautiful and as lovely as ever.

Encouraged by her example, several other ladies made
their vows with her, and in compliance with the wish of
the parents of her new associates, the Saint agreed to
found a religious residence for herself and them in the
vicinity. A convenient site having been fixed upon by the
bishop, a convent, the first in Ireland, was erected upon it;
and in obedience to the prelate Bridgid assumed the superiority. Her reputation for sanctity became greater every
day; and in proportion as it was diffused throughout the
country the number of candidates for admission into the
new monastery increased. The bishops of Ireland, soon
perceiving the important advantages which their respective
dioceses would derive from similar foundations, persuaded
the young and saintly abbess to visit different parts of the
kingdom, and, as an opportunity offered, introduce into
each one the establishment of her institute.

While thus engaged in a portion of the province of Con-

naught, a deputation arrived from Leinster to solicit the
Saint to take up her residence in that territory; but the
motives which they urged were human, and such could
have no weight with Bridgid.   It was only the prospect of
the many spiritual advantages that would result from compliance with the request that induced her to accede, as she
did, to the wishes of those who had petitioned her.   Taking with her a number of her spiritual daughters, our
Saint journeyed to Leinster, where they were received with
many demonstrations of respect and joy.   The site on
which Kildare now stands appearing to be well adapted for
a religious institute, there the Saint and her companions
took up their abode.   To the place appropriated for the
new foundation some lands were annexed, the fruits of
which were assigned to the little establishment.   This do-
nation indeed contributed to supply the wants of the community, but still the pious sisterhood principally depended
for their maintenance on the liberality of their benefactors.
Bridgid contrived, however, out of their small means to
relieve the poor of the vicinity very considerably; and
when the wants of these indigent persons surpassed her
slender finances, she hesitated not to sacrifice for them the
movables of the convent.   On one occasion our Saint, imitating the burning charity of St. Ambrose and other great
servants of God, sold some of the sacred vestments that she
might procure the means of relieving their necessities.
She was so humble that she sometimes attended the cattle
on the land which belonged to her monastery.

The renown of Bridgid's unbounded charity drew multitudes of the poor to Kildare; the fame of her piety attracted thither many persons anxious to solicit her prayers
or to profit by her holy example.   In course of time the
number of these so much increased that it became necessary to provide accommodation for them in the neighborhood of the new monastery, and thus was laid the foundation and origin of the town of Kildare.

The spiritual exigencies of her community, and of those
numerous strangers who resorted to the vicinity, having
suggested to our Saint the expediency of having the local-
ity erected into an episcopal see, she represented it to the
prelates, to whom the consideration of it rightly belonged.

Deeming the proposal just and useful, Conlath, a recluse of eminent sanctity, illustrious by the great things which God had granted to his prayers, was, at Bridgid's desire, chosen the first bishop of the newly erected diocese. In process of time it became the ecclesiastical metropolis of the province to which it belonged, probably in consequence of the general desire to honor the place in which St. Bridgid had so long dwelt.

After seventy years devoted to the practice of the most sublime virtues, corporal infirmities admonished our Saint that the time of her dissolution was nigh. It was now half a century since, by her holy vows, she had irrevocably consecrated herself to God, and during that period great results had been attained; her holy institute having widely diffused itself throughout the Green Isle, and greatly advanced the cause of religion in the various districts in which it was established. Like *a river of peace,* its progress was steady and silent; it fertilized every region fortunate enough to receive its waters, and caused it to put forth spiritual flowers and fruits with all the sweet perfume of evangelical fragrance. The remembrance of the glory she had procured to the Most High, as well as the services rendered to dear souls ransomed by the precious blood of her divine Spouse, cheered and consoled Bridgid in the infirmities inseparable from old age. Her last illness was soothed by the presence of Nennidh, a priest of eminent sanctity, over whose youth she had watched with pious solicitude, and who was indebted to her prayers and instructions for his great proficiency in sublime perfection. The day on which our abbess was to terminate her course, February 1, 523, having arrived, she received from the hands of this saintly priest the blessed body and blood of her Lord in the divine Eucharist, and, as it would seem, immediately after her spirit passed forth, and went to possess Him in that heavenly country where He is seen *face to face* and enjoyed without danger of ever losing Him. Her body was interred in the church adjoining her convent, but was some time after exhumed, and deposited in a splendid shrine near the high altar.

In the ninth century, the country being desolated by the Danes, the remains of St. Bridgid were removed in order to secure them from irreverence; and, being transferred to Down-Patrick, were deposited in the same grave with those of the glorious St. Patrick. Their bodies, together with that of St. Columba, were translated afterwards to the cathedral of the same city, but their monument was destroyed in the reign of King Henry VIII. The head of St. Bridgid is now kept in the church of the Jesuits at Lisbon.

Reflection.— Outward resemblance to Our Lady was St. Bridgid's peculiar privilege; but all are bound to grow like her in interior purity of heart. This grace St. Bridgid has obtained in a wonderful degree for the daughters of her native land, and will never fail to procure for all her devout clients.

ST. IGNATIUS, Bishop, Martyr.

T. Ignatius, Bishop of Antioch, was the disciple of St. John. When Domitian persecuted the Church, St. Ignatius obtained peace for his own flock by fasting and prayer. But for his part he desired to suffer with Christ, and to prove himself a perfect disciple. In the year 107, Trajan came to Antioch, and forced the Christians to choose between apostasy and death. "Who art thou, poor devil," the emperor said when Ignatius was brought before him, "who settest our commands at naught?" "Call not him 'poor devil,'" Ignatius answered, "who bears God within him." And when the emperor questioned him about his meaning, Ignatius explained that he bore in his heart Christ crucified for his sake. Thereupon the emperor condemned him to be torn to pieces by wild beasts at Rome. St. Ignatius thanked God, Who had so honored him, "binding him in the chains of Paul, His apostle."

He journeyed to Rome, guarded by soldiers, and with no fear except of losing the martyr's crown. He was devoured by lions in the Roman amphitheatre. The wild beasts left nothing of his body, except a few bones, which were reverently treasured at Antioch, until their removal to the Church of St. Clement at Rome, in 637. After the martyr's death, several Christians saw him in vision standing before Christ, and interceding for them.

Reflection.— Ask St. Ignatius to obtain for you the grace of profiting by all you have to suffer, and rejoicing in it as a means of likeness to your crucified Redeemer.

February 2.—THE PURIFICATION, COMMONLY CALLED CANDLEMAS-DAY.

THE law of God, given by Moses to the Jews, ordained that a woman, after childbirth, should continue for a certain time in a state which that law calls unclean, during which she was not to appear in public, nor presume to touch anything consecrated to God. This term was of forty days upon the birth of a son, and double that time for a daughter. On the expiration of the term, the mother was to bring to the door of the tabernacle, or Temple, a lamb and a young pigeon, or turtle-dove, as an offering to God. These being sacrificed to Almighty God by the priest, the woman was cleansed of the legal impurity and reinstated in her former privileges.

A young pigeon, or turtle-dove, by way of a sin-offering, was required of all, whether rich or poor; but as the expense of a lamb might be too great for persons in poor circumstances, they were allowed to substitute for it a second dove.

Our Saviour having been conceived by the Holy Ghost, and His blessed Mother remaining always a spotless virgin, it is evident that she did not come under the law; but as the world was, as yet, ignorant of her miraculous conception, she submitted with great punctuality and exactness to every humbling circumstance which the law required. Devotion and zeal to honor God, by every observance prescribed by His law, prompted Mary to perform this act of religion, though evidently exempt from the precept. Being poor herself, she made the offering appointed for the poor; but, however mean in itself, it was made with a perfect heart, which is what God chiefly regards in all that is offered to Him. Besides the law which obliged the mother to purify herself, there was another which ordered that the

first-born son should be offered to God, and that, after its
presentation, the child should be ransomed with a certain
sum of money, and peculiar sacrifices offered on the occasion.

Mary complies exactly with all these ordinances. She
obeys not only in the essential points of the law, but has
strict regard to all the circumstances. She remains forty
days at home; she denies herself, all this time, the liberty
of entering the Temple; she partakes not of things sacred;
and on the day of her purification she walks several miles
to Jerusalem, with the world's Redeemer in her arms. She
waits for the priest at the gate of the Temple, makes her
offerings of thanksgiving and expiation, presents her divine
Son by the hands of the priest to His Eternal Father, with
the most profound humility, adoration, and thanksgiving.
She then redeems Him with five shekels, as the law ap-
points, and receives Him back again as a sacred charge
committed to her special care, till the Father shall again
demand Him for the full accomplishment of man's redemption.

The ceremony of this day was closed by a third mystery
— the meeting in the Temple of the holy persons Simeon
and Anne with Jesus and His parents. Holy Simeon, on
that occasion, received into his arms the object of all his
desires and sighs, and praised God for being blessed with
the happiness of beholding the so-much-longed-for Messias.
He foretold to Mary her martyrdom of sorrow, and that
Jesus brought redemption to those who would accept of it
on the terms it was offered them; but a heavy judgment on
all infidels who should obstinately reject it, and on Christians, also, whose lives were a contradiction to His holy
maxims and example. Mary, hearing this terrible pre-
diction, did not answer one word, felt no agitation of mind
from the present, no dread for the future; but courageously
and sweetly committed all to God's holy will. Anne, also,
the prophetess, who in her widowhood served God with
great fervor, had the happiness to acknowledge and adore
in this great mystery the Redeemer of the world. Simeon,
having beheld Our Saviour, exclaimed: "Now dismiss
Thy servant, O Lord, according to Thy word, because my
eyes have seen Thy salvation."

This feast is called CANDLEMAS, because the Church blesses the candles to be borne in the procession of the day.

Reflection.— Let us strive to imitate the humility of the ever-blessed Mother of God, remembering that humility is the path which leads to abiding peace and brings us near to the consolations of God.

February 3.—ST. BLASE, Bishop and Martyr.

ST. BLASE devoted the earlier years of his life to the study of philosophy, and afterwards became a physician. In the practice of his profession he saw so much of the miseries of life and the hollowness of worldly pleasures, that he resolved to spend the rest of his days in the service of God, and from being a healer of bodily ailments to become a physician of souls. The Bishop of Sebaste, in Armenia, having died, our Saint, much to the gratification of the inhabitants of that city, was appointed to succeed him. St. Blase at once began to instruct his people as much by his example as by his words, and the great virtues and sanctity of this servant of God were attested by many miracles. From all parts the people came flocking to him for the cure of bodily and spiritual ills. Agricolaus, Governor of Cappadocia and the Lesser Armenia, having begun a persecution by order of the Emperor Licinius, our Saint was seized and hurried off to prison. While on his way there, a distracted mother, whose only child was dying of a throat disease, threw herself at the feet of St. Blase and implored his intercession. Touched at her grief, the Saint offered up his prayers, and the child was cured; and since that time his aid has often been effectually solicited in cases of a similar disease. Refusing to worship the false gods of the heathens, St. Blase was first scourged; his body was then torn with hooks, and finally he was beheaded in the year 316.

Reflection.— There is no sacrifice which, by the aid of grace, human nature is not capable of accomplishing. When St. Paul complained to God of the violence of the temptation, God answered, " My grace is sufficient for thee, for power is made perfect in infirmity."

February 4.—St. JANE OF VALOIS.

ORN of the blood royal of France, herself a queen,
Jane of Valois led a life remarkable for its humilia-
tions even in the annals of the Saints. Her father, Louis
XI., who had hoped for a son to succeed him, banished
Jane from his palace, and, it is said, even attempted her
life. At the age of five the neglected child offered her
whole heart to God, and yearned to do some special service
in honor of His blessed Mother. At the king's wish,
though against her own inclination, she was married to the
Duke of Orleans. Towards an indifferent and unworthy
husband her conduct was ever most patient and dutiful.
Her prayers and tears saved him from a traitor's death
and shortened the captivity which his rebellion had
merited. Still nothing could win a heart which was already given to another. When her husband ascended the
throne as Louis XII., his first act was to repudiate by false
representations one who through twenty-two years of cruel
neglect had been his true and loyal wife. At the final sentence of separation, the saintly queen exclaimed, "God be
praised Who has allowed this, that I may serve Him better
than I have heretofore done." Retiring to Bourges, she
there realized her long-formed desire of founding the
Order of the Annunciation, in honor of the Mother of God.
Under the guidance of St. Francis of Paula, the director
of her childhood, St. Jane was enabled to overcome the
serious obstacles which even good people raised against the
foundation of her new Order. In 1501 the rule of the Annunciation was finally approved by Alexander VI. The
chief aim of the institute was to imitate the ten virtues
practised by Our Lady in the mystery of the Incarnation,
the superioress being called "Ancelle," handmaid, in
honor of Mary's humility. St. Jane built and endowed
the first convent of the Order in 1502. She died in heroic
sanctity, 1505, and was buried in the royal crown and
purple, beneath which lay the habit of her Order.

Reflection.— During the lifetime of St. Jane, the An-
gelus was established in France. The sound of the Ave

thrice each day gave her hope in her sorrow, and fostered in her the desire still further to honor the Incarnation. How often might we derive grace from the same beautiful devotion, so enriched by the Church, yet neglected by so many Christians!

February 5.—ST. AGATHA, Virgin, Martyr.

ST. AGATHA was born in Sicily, of rich and noble parents — a child of benediction from the first, for she was promised to her parents before her birth, and consecrated from her earliest infancy to God. In the midst of dangers and temptations she served Christ in purity of body and soul, and she died for the love of chastity. Quintanus, who governed Sicily under the Emperor Decius, had heard the rumor of her beauty and wealth, and he made the laws against the Christians a pretext for summoning her from Palermo to Catania, where he was at the time. " O Jesus Christ! " she cried, as she set out on this dreaded journey, " all that I am is Thine; preserve me against the tyrant."

And Our Lord did indeed preserve one who had given herself so utterly to Him. He kept her pure and undefiled while she was imprisoned for a whole month under charge of an evil woman. He gave her strength to reply to the offer of her life and safety, if she would but consent to sin, " Christ alone is my life and my salvation." When Quintanus turned from passion to cruelty, and cut off her breasts, Our Lord sent the Prince of His apostles to heal her. And when, after she had been rolled naked upon potsherds, she asked that her torments might be ended, her Spouse heard her prayer and took her to Himself.

St. Agatha gave herself without reserve to Jesus Christ; she followed Him in virginal purity, and then looked to Him for protection. And down to this day Christ has shown His tender regard for the very body of St. Agatha. Again and again, during the eruptions of Mount Etna, the people of Catania have exposed her veil for public veneration, and found safety by this means; and in modern times, on opening the tomb in which her body lies waiting for the resurrection, they beheld the skin still entire, and felt the sweet fragrance which issued from this temple of the Holy Ghost.

Reflection.— Purity is a gift of God: we can gain it and preserve it only by care and diligence in avoiding all that may prove an incentive to sin.

THE MARTYRS OF JAPAN.

ABOUT forty years after St. Francis Xavier's death a persecution broke out in Japan, and all Christian rites were forbidden under pain of death. A confraternity of martyrs was at once formed, the object of which was to die for Christ. Even the little children joined it. Peter, a Christian child six years old, was awakened early and told that he was to be beheaded, together with his father. Strong in grace, he expressed his joy at the news, dressed himself in his gayest clothing, and took the hand of the soldier who was to lead him to death. The headless trunk of his father first met his view; calmly kneeling down, he prayed beside the corpse, and, loosening his collar, prepared his neck for the stroke. Moved by this touching scene, the executioner threw down his sabre and fled. None but a brutal slave could be found for the murderous task; with unskilled and trembling hand he hacked the child to pieces, who at last died without uttering a single cry. Christians were branded with the cross, or all but buried alive, while the head and arms were slowly sawn off with blunt weapons. The least shudder under their anguish was interpreted into apostasy. The obstinate were put to the most cruel deaths, but the survivors only envied them. Five noblemen were escorted to the stake by 40,000 Christians with flowers and lights, singing the litanies of Our Lady as they went. In the great martyrdom, at which thousands also assisted, the martyrs sent up a flood of melody from the fire, which only died away as one after another went to sing the new song in heaven. Later on, a more awful doom was invented. The victims were lowered into a sulphurous chasm, called the " mouth of hell," near which no bird or beast could live. The chief of these,

Paul Wiborg, whose family had been already massacred for the faith, was thrice let down; thrice he cried, with a loud voice, " Eternal praise be to the ever-adorable Sacrament of the Altar." The third time he went to his reward.

Reflection.— If mere children face torture and death with joy for Christ, can we begrudge the slight penance He asks us to bear?

February 6.—ST. DOROTHY, Virgin, Martyr.

ST. DOROTHY was a young virgin, celebrated at Cæsarea, where she lived, for her angelic virtue. Her parents seem to have been martyred before her in the Diocletian persecution, and when the Governor Sapricius came to Cæsarea he called her before him, and sent this child of martyrs to the home where they were waiting for her.

She was stretched upon the rack, and offered marriage if she would consent to sacrifice, or death if she refused. But she replied that " Christ was her only Spouse, and death her desire." She was then placed in charge of two women who had fallen away from the faith, in the hope that they might pervert her; but the fire of her own heart rekindled the flame in theirs, and led them back to Christ. When she was set once more on the rack, Sapricius himself was amazed at the heavenly look she wore, and asked her the cause of her joy. "Because," she said, " I have brought back two souls to Christ, and because I shall soon be in heaven rejoicing with the angels." Her joy grew as she was buffeted in the face and her sides burned with plates of red-hot iron. " Blessed be Thou," she cried, when she was sentenced to be beheaded,—" blessed be Thou, O Thou Lover of souls! Who dost call me to Paradise, and invitest me to Thy nuptial chamber."

St. Dorothy suffered in the dead of winter, and it is said that on the road to her passion a lawyer called Theophilus, who had been used to calumniate and persecute the Christians, asked her, in mockery, to send him " apples or roses from the garden of her Spouse." The Saint promised to grant his request, and, just before she died, a little child stood by her side bearing three apples and three roses.

She bade him take them to Theophilus and tell him this was the present which he sought from the garden of her Spouse. St. Dorothy had gone to heaven, and Theophilus was still making merry over his challenge to the Saint when the child entered his room. He saw that the child was an angel in disguise, and the fruit and flowers of no earthly growth. He was converted to the faith, and then shared in the martyrdom of St. Dorothy.

Reflection.— Do you wish to be safe in the pleasures and happy in the troubles of the world? Pray for heavenly desires, and say, with St. Philip, " Paradise, Paradise! "

February 7.—ST. ROMUALD, Abbot.

IN 976, Sergius, a nobleman of Ravenna, quarrelled with a relative about an estate, and slew him in a duel. His son Romuald, horrified at his father's crime, entered the Benedictine monastery at Classe, to do a forty days' penance for him. This penance ended in his own vocation to religion. After three years at Classe, Romuald went to live as a hermit near Venice, where he was joined by Peter Urseolus, Duke of Venice, and together they led a most austere life in the midst of assaults from the evil spirits. St. Romuald founded many monasteries, the chief of which was that at Camaldoli, a wild desert place, where he built a church, which he surrounded with a number of separate cells for the solitaries who lived under his rule. His disciples were hence called Camaldolese. He is said to have seen here a vision of a mystic ladder, and his white-clothed monks ascending by it to heaven. Among his first disciples were Sts. Adalbert and Boniface, apostles of Russia, and Sts. John and Benedict of Poland, martyrs for the faith. He was an intimate friend of the Emperor St. Henry, and was reverenced and consulted by many great men of his time. He once passed seven years in solitude and complete silence.

In his youth St. Romuald was much troubled by temptations of the flesh. To escape them he had recourse to hunting, and in the woods first conceived his love for

solitude. His father's sin, as we have seen, first prompted
him to undertake a forty days' penance in the monastery,
which he forthwith made his home. Some bad example
of his fellow-monks induced him to leave them and adopt
the solitary mode of life. The penance of Urseolus, who
had obtained his power wrongfully, brought him his first
disciple; the temptations of the devil compelled him to his
severe life; and finally the persecutions of others were the
occasion of his settlement at Camaldoli, and the foundation of his Order. He died, as he had foretold twenty
years before, alone, in his monastery of Val Castro, on the
19th of June, 1027.

Reflection.—St. Romuald's life teaches us that, if we
only follow the impulse of the Holy Spirit, we shall easily
find good everywhere, even on the most unlikely occasions. Our own sins, the sins of others, their ill will
against us, or our own mistakes and misfortunes, are
equally capable of leading us, with softened hearts, to the
feet of God's mercy and love.

February 8.—ST. JOHN OF MATHA.

THE life of St. John of Matha was one long course of
self-sacrifice for the glory of God and the good of
his neighbor. As a child, his chief delight was serving
the poor; and he often told them he had come into the
world for no other end but to wash their feet. He studied
at Paris with such distinction that his professors advised
him to become a priest, in order that his talents might
render greater service to others; and, for this end, John
gladly sacrificed his high rank and other worldly advantages. At his first Mass an angel appeared, clad in white,
with a red and blue cross on his breast, and his hands re-
posing on the heads of a Christian and a Moorish captive.
To ascertain what this signified, John repaired to St. Felix
of Valois, a holy hermit living near Meaux, under whose
direction he led a life of extreme penance. The angel
again appeared, and they then set out for Rome, to learn
the will of God from the lips of the Sovereign Pontiff,
who told them to devote themselves to the redemption of

captives. For this purpose they founded the Order of the Holy Trinity. The religious fasted every day, and gathering alms throughout Europe took them to Barbary, to redeem the Christian slaves. They devoted themselves also to the sick and prisoners in all countries. The charity of St. John in devoting his life to the redemption of captives was visibly blessed by God. On his second return from Tunis he brought back one hundred and twenty liberated slaves. But the Moors attacked him at sea, overpowered his vessel, and doomed it to destruction, with all on board, by taking away the rudder and sails, and leaving it to the mercy of the winds. St. John tied his cloak to the mast, and prayed, saying, " Let God arise, and let His enemies be scattered. O Lord, Thou wilt save the humble, and wilt bring down the eyes of the proud." Suddenly the wind filled the small sail, and, without guidance, carried the ship safely in a few days to Ostia, the port of Rome, three hundred leagues from Tunis. Worn out by his heroic labors, John died in 1213, at the age of fifty-three.

Reflection.—Let us never forget that our blessed Lord bade us love our neighbor not only as ourselves, but as He loved us, Who afterwards sacrificed Himself for us.

February 9.— ST. APOLLONIA AND THE MARTYRS OF ALEXANDRIA.

AT Alexandria, in 249, the mob rose in savage fury against the Christians. Metras, an old man, perished first. His eyes were pierced with reeds, and he was stoned to death. A woman named Quinta was the next victim. She was led to a heathen temple and bidden worship. She replied by cursing the false god again and again, and she too was stoned to death. After this the houses of the Christians were sacked and plundered. They took the spoiling of their goods with all joy.

St. Apollonia, an aged virgin, was the most famous among the martyrs. Her teeth were beaten out; she was led outside the city, a huge fire was kindled, and she was told she must deny Christ, or else be burned alive. She was silent for a while, and then, moved by a special inspiration of the Holy Ghost, she leaped into the fire and died in its flames. The same courage showed itself the next year, when Decius became emperor, and the persecution grew till it seemed as if the very elect must fall away. The story of Dioscorus illustrates the courage of the Alexandrian Christians, and the esteem they had for martyrdom. He was a boy of fifteen. To the arguments of the judge he returned wise answers: he was proof against torture. His older companions were executed, but Dioscorus was spared on account of his tender years; yet the Christians could not bear to think that he had been deprived of the martyr's crown, except to receive it afterwards more gloriously. " Dioscorus," writes Dionysius, Bishop of Alexandria at this time, " remains with us, reserved for some longer and greater combat." There were indeed many Christians who came, pale and trembling, to offer the heathen sacrifices. But the judges themselves were struck with horror at the multitudes who rushed to martyrdom. Women triumphed over torture, till at last the judges were glad to execute them at once and put an end to the ignominy of their own defeat.

Reflection.—Many saints, who were not martyrs, have longed to shed their blood for Christ. We, too, may pray for some portion of their spirit; and the least suffering for the faith, borne with humility and courage, is the proof that Christ has heard our prayer.

February 10.—ST. SCHOLASTICA, Abbess.

OF this Saint but little is known on earth, save that she was the sister of the great patriarch St. Benedict, and that, under his direction, she founded and governed a numerous community near Monte Casino. St. Gregory sums up her life by saying that she devoted herself to God from her childhood, and that her pure soul went to God in the likeness of a dove, as if to show that her life had been enriched with the fullest gifts of the Holy Spirit. Her brother was accustomed to visit her every year, for " she could not be sated or wearied with the words of grace

which flowed from his lips." On his last visit, after a day
passed in spiritual converse, the Saint, knowing that her
end was near, said, " My brother, leave me not, I pray you,
this night, but discourse with me till dawn on the bliss of
those who see God in heaven." St. Benedict would not
break his rule at the bidding of natural affection; and then
the Saint bowed her head on her hands and prayed; and
there arose a storm so violent that St. Benedict could not
return to his monastery, and they passed the night in
heavenly conversation. Three days later St. Benedict saw
in a vision the soul of his sister going up in the likeness of
a dove into heaven. Then he gave thanks to God for the
graces He had given her, and for the glory which had
crowned them. When she died, St. Benedict, her spiritual
daughters, and the monks sent by St. Benedict mingled
their tears and prayed, " Alas! alas! dearest mother, to
whom dost thou leave us now? Pray for us to Jesus, to
Whom thou art gone." They then devoutly celebrated
holy Mass, " commending her soul to God;" and her body
was borne to Monte Casino, and laid by her brother in the
tomb he had prepared for himself. " And they bewailed
her many days;" and St. Benedict said, " Weep not, sisters and brothers; for assuredly Jesus has taken her before us to be our aid and defence against all our enemies,
that we may stand in the evil day and be in all things perfect." She died about the year 543.

Reflection.—Our relatives must be loved in and for
God; otherwise the purest affection becomes inordinate
and is so much taken from Him.

February 11.—ST. SEVERINUS, Abbot of Agaunum.

S T. SEVERINUS, of a noble family in Burgundy, was
educated in the Catholic faith, at a time when the
Arian heresy reigned in that country. He forsook the
world in his youth, and dedicated himself to God in
the monastery of Agaunum, which then only consisted of
scattered cells, till the Catholic King Sigismund built
there the great abbey of St. Maurice. St. Severinus was
the holy abbot of that place, and had governed his com-

munity many years in the exercise of penance and charity, when, in 504, Clovis, the first Christian king of France, lying ill of a fever, which his physicians had for two years ineffectually endeavored to remove, sent his chamberlain to conduct the Saint to court; for it was said that the sick from all parts recovered their health by his prayers. St. Severinus took leave of his monks, telling them he should never see them more in this world. On his journey he healed Eulalius, Bishop of Nevers, who had been for some time deaf and dumb; also a leper, at the gates of Paris; and coming to the palace he immediately restored the king to perfect health, by putting on him his own cloak. The king, in gratitude, distributed large alms to the poor and released all his prisoners. St. Severinus, returning toward Agaunum, stopped at Château-Landon in Gatinois, where two priests served God in a solitary chapel, among whom he was admitted, at his request, as a stranger, and was soon greatly admired by them for his sanctity. He foresaw his death, which happened shortly after, in 507. The place is now an abbey of reformed canons regular of St. Austin. The Huguenots scattered the greater part of his relics when they plundered this church.

Reflection.—God loads with His favor those who delight in exercising mercy. "According to thy ability be merciful: if thou hast much, give abundantly; if thou hast little, take care even so to bestow willingly a little."

February 12.—ST. BENEDICT OF ANIAN.

BENEDICT was the son of Aigulf, Governor of Languedoc, and was born about 750. In his early youth he served as cup-bearer to King Pepin and his son Charlemagne, enjoying under them great honors and possessions. Grace entered his soul at the age of twenty, and he resolved to seek the kingdom of God with his whole heart. Without relinquishing his place at court, he lived there a most mortified life for three years; then a narrow escape from drowning made him vow to quit the world, and he entered the cloister of St. Seine. In reward for his heroic austerities in the monastic state, God bestowed upon

him the gift of tears, and inspired him with a knowledge
of spiritual things. As procurator, he was most careful
of the wants of the brethren, and most hospitable to the
poor and to guests. Declining to accept the abbacy, he
built himself a little hermitage on the brook Anian, and
lived some years in great solitude and poverty; but the
fame of his sanctity drawing many souls around him, he
was obliged to build a large abbey, and within a short
time governed three hundred monks. He became the
great restorer of monastic discipline throughout France
and Germany. First, he drew up with immense labor a
code of the rules of St. Benedict, his great namesake,
which he collated with those of the chief monastic founders, showing the uniformity of the exercises in each, and
enforced by his " Penitential " their exact observance;
secondly, he minutely regulated all matters regarding
food, clothing, and every detail of life; and thirdly, by
prescribing the same for all, he excluded jealousies and
insured perfect charity. In a Provincial Council held in
813, under Charlemagne, at which he was present, it was
declared that all monks of the West should adopt the rule
of St. Benedict. He died February 11, 821.

Reflection.—The decay of monastic discipline and its
restoration by St. Benedict prove that none are safe from
loss of fervor, but that all can regain it by fidelity to grace.

February 13.—ST. CATHERINE OF RICCI.

ALEXANDRINA of Ricci was the daughter of a noble
Florentine. At the age of thirteen she entered the
Third Order of St. Dominic in the monastery of Prato,
taking in religion the name of Catherine, after her patron
and namesake of Siena. Her special attraction was to the
Passion of Christ, in which she was permitted miraculously
to participate. In the Lent of 1541, being then twenty-one
years of age, she had a vision of the crucifixion so heart-
rending that she was confined to bed for three weeks, and
was only restored, on Holy Saturday, by an apparition of
St. Mary Magdalene and Jesus risen. During twelve years
she passed every Friday in ecstasy. She received the sa-

cred stigmata, the wound in the left side, and the crown of thorns. All these favors gave her continual and intense suffering, and inspired her with a loving sympathy for the yet more bitter tortures of the Holy Souls. In their behalf she offered all her prayers and penances; and her charity toward them became so famous throughout Tuscany that after every death the friends of the deceased hastened to Catherine to secure her prayers. St. Catherine offered many prayers, fasts, and penances for a certain great man, and thus obtained his salvation. It was revealed to her that he was in purgatory; and such was her love of Jesus crucified that she offered to suffer all the pains about to be inflicted on that soul. Her prayer was granted. The soul entered heaven, and for forty days Catherine suffered indescribable agonies. Her body was covered with blisters, emitting heat so great that her cell seemed on fire. Her flesh appeared as if roasted, and her tongue like red-hot iron. Amid all she was calm and joyful, saying, " I long to suffer all imaginable pains, that souls may quickly see and praise their Redeemer." She knew by revelation the arrival of a soul in purgatory, and the hour of its release. She held intercourse with the Saints in glory, and frequently conversed with St. Philip Neri at Rome without ever leaving her convent at Prato. She died, amid angels' songs, in 1589.

Reflection.—If we truly love Jesus crucified, we must long, as did St. Catherine, to release the Holy Souls whom He has redeemed but has left to our charity to set free.

February 14.—ST. VALENTINE, Priest and Martyr.

VALENTINE was a holy priest in Rome, who, with St. Marius and his family, assisted the martyrs in the persecution under Claudius II. He was apprehended, and sent by the emperor to the prefect of Rome, who, on finding all his promises to make him renounce his faith ineffectual, commanded him to be beaten with clubs, and afterward to be beheaded, which was executed on the 14th of February, about the year 270. Pope Julius I. is said to have built a church near Ponte Mole to his memory, which for a long time gave name to the gate now called Porta del Popolo, formerly Porta Valentini. The greater part of his relics are now in the Church of St. Praxedes. To abolish the heathens' lewd superstitious custom of boys drawing the names of girls, in honor of their goddess Februata Juno, on the 15th of this month, several zealous pastors substituted the names of Saints in billets given on this day.

Reflection.—In the cause of justice and truth, prudence should not be held in account; otherwise prudence is mere human respect. St. Paul says: " The wisdom of the flesh is death."

February 15.—STS. FAUSTINUS and JOVITA, Martyrs.

FAUSTINUS and Jovita were brothers, nobly born, and zealous professors of the Christian religion, which they preached without fear in their city of Brescia, while the bishop of that place lay concealed during the persecution. Their remarkable zeal excited the fury of the heathens against them, and procured them a glorious death for their faith at Brescia in Lombardy, under the Emperor Adrian. Julian, a heathen lord, apprehended them; and the emperor himself, passing through Brescia, when neither threats nor torments could shake their constancy, commanded them to be beheaded. They seem to have suffered about the year 121. The city of Brescia honors them as its chief patrons, possesses their relics, and a very ancient church in that city bears their names.

Reflection.—The spirit of Christ is a spirit of martyrdom — at least of mortification and penance. It is always the spirit of the cross. The more we share in the suffering life of Christ, the greater share we inherit in His spirit, and in the fruit of His death. To souls mortified to their senses and disengaged from earthly things, God gives frequent foretastes of the sweetness of eternal life, and the most ardent desires of possessing Him in His glory. This is the spirit of martyrdom, which entitles a Christian to a happy resurrection and to the bliss of the life to come.

February 16.—BLESSED JOHN DE BRITTO,
Martyr.

ON PEDRO II. of Portugal, when a child, had among his little pages a modest boy of rich and princely parents. Much had John de Britto — for so was he called — to bear from his careless-living companions, to whom his holy life was a reproach. A terrible illness made him turn for aid to St. Francis Xavier, a Saint so well loved by the Portuguese; and when, in answer to his prayers, he recovered, his mother vested him for a year in the dress worn in those days by the Jesuit Fathers. From that time John's heart burned to follow the example of the Apostle of the Indies. He gained his wish. On December 17, 1662, he entered the novitiate of the Society at Lisbon; and eleven years later, in spite of the most determined opposition of his family and of the court, he left all to go to convert the Hindus of Madura. When Blessed John's mother knew that her son was going to the Indies, she used all her influence to prevent him leaving his own country, and persuaded the Papal Nuncio to interfere. "God, Who called me from the world into religious life, now calls me from Portugal to India," was the reply of the future martyr. "Not to answer the vocation as I ought, would be to provoke the justice of God. As long as I live, I shall never cease striving to gain a passage to India." For fourteen years he toiled, preaching, converting, baptizing multitudes, at the cost of privations, hardships, and persecutions. At last, after being seized, tortured, and nearly massacred by the heathens, he was banished from the country. Forced to return to Portugal, John once more broke through every obstacle, and went back again to his labor of love. Like St. John the Baptist, he died a victim to the anger of a guilty woman, whom a convert king had put aside, and, like the Precursor, he was beheaded after a painful imprisonment.

Reflection.—" It is a great honor, a great glory to serve God, and to contemn all things for God.   They will have a great grace who freely subject themselves to God's most holy will."—*The Imitation of Christ.*

ST. ONESIMUS, Disciple of St. Paul.

HE was a Phrygian by birth, slave to Philemon, a person of note of the city of Colossæ, converted to the faith by St. Paul.   Having robbed his master and being obliged to fly, he providentially met with St. Paul, then a prisoner for the faith at Rome, who there converted and baptized him, and sent him with his canonical letter of recommendation to Philemon, by whom he was pardoned, set at liberty, and sent back to his spiritual father, whom he afterwards faithfully served.   That apostle made him, with Tychicus, the bearer of his Epistle to the Colossians, and afterwards, as St. Jerome and other Fathers witness, a preacher of the Gospel and a bishop.   He was crowned with martyrdom under Domitian in the year 95.

Reflection.—With what excess of goodness does God communicate Himself to souls that open themselves to Him!   With what caresses does He often visit them! With what a profusion of graces does He enrich and strengthen them!   In our trials and temptations let us then offer our hearts to God, remembering, as St. Paul says, " To them that love God all things work together unto good."

February 17.—ST. FLAVIAN, Bishop, Martyr.

FLAVIAN was elected Patriarch of Constantinople in 447.   His short episcopate of two years was a time of conflict and persecution from the first.   Chrysaphius, the emperor's favorite, tried to extort a large sum of money from him on the occasion of his consecration.   His fidelity in refusing this simoniacal betrayal of his trust brought on him the enmity of the most powerful man in the empire.

A graver trouble soon arose.   In 448 Flavian had to

condemn the rising heresy of the monk Eutyches, who obstinately denied that Our Lord was in two perfect natures after His Incarnation. Eutyches drew to his cause all the bad elements which so early gathered about the Byzantine court. His intrigues were long baffled by the vigilance of Flavian; but at last he obtained from the emperor the assembly of a council at Ephesus, in August 449, presided over by his friend Dioscorus, Patriarch of Alexandria. Into this "robber council," as it is called, Eutyches entered, surrounded by soldiers. The Roman legates could not even read the Pope's letters; and at the first sign of resistance to the condemnation of Flavian, fresh troops entered with drawn swords, and, in spite of the protests of the legates, terrified most of the bishops into acquiescence.

The fury of Dioscorus reached its height when Flavian appealed to the Holy See. Then it was that he so forgot his apostolic office as to lay violent hands on his adversary. St. Flavian was set upon by Dioscorus and others, thrown down, beaten, kicked, and finally carried into banishment. Let us contrast their ends. Flavian clung to the teaching of the Roman Pontiff, and sealed his faith with his blood. Dioscorus excommunicated the Vicar of Christ, and died obstinate and impenitent in the heresy of Eutyches.

Reflection.—By his unswerving loyalty to the Vicar of Christ, Flavian held fast to the truth and gained the martyr's crown. Let us learn from him to turn instinctively to that one true guide in all matters concerning our salvation.

February 18.—ST. SIMEON, Bishop, Martyr.

ST. SIMEON was the son of Cleophas, otherwise called Alpheus, brother to St. Joseph, and of Mary, sister to the Blessed Virgin. He was therefore nephew both to St. Joseph and to the Blessed Virgin, and cousin to Our Saviour. We cannot doubt but that he was an early follower of Christ, and that he received the Holy Ghost on the day of Pentecost, with the Blessed Virgin and the apostles. When the Jews massacred St. James the Lesser, his brother Simeon reproached them for their atrocious cruelty. St. James, Bishop of Jerusalem, being put to death in the year 62, twenty-nine years after Our Saviour's Resurrection, the apostles and disciples met at Jerusalem to appoint him a successor. They unanimously chose St. Simeon, who had probably before assisted his brother in the government of that Church.

In the year 66, in which Sts. Peter and Paul suffered martyrdom at Rome, the civil war began in Judea, by the seditions of the Jews against the Romans. The Christians in Jerusalem were warned by God of the impending destruction of that city. They therefore departed out of it the same year,— before Vespasian, Nero's general, and afterwards emperor, entered Judea,— and retired beyond Jordan to a small city called Pella, having St. Simeon at their head. After the taking and burning of Jerusalem they returned thither again, and settled themselves amidst its ruins, till Adrian afterwards entirely razed it. The Church here flourished, and multitudes of Jews were converted by the great number of prodigies and miracles wrought in it.

Vespasian and Domitian had commanded all to be put to death who were of the race of David. St. Simeon had escaped their searches; but, Trajan having given the same order, certain heretics and Jews accused the Saint, as being both of the race of David and a Christian, to Atticus, the Roman governor in Palestine. The holy bishop was condemned to be crucified. After having undergone the usual tortures during several days, which, though one hundred and twenty years old, he suffered with so much patience that he drew on him a universal admiration, and that of Atticus in particular, he died in 107. He must have governed the Church of Jerusalem about forty-three years.

Reflection.—We bear the name of Christians, but are full of the spirit of worldlings, and our actions are infected with the poison of the world. We secretly seek ourselves, even when we flatter ourselves that God is our only aim; and whilst we undertake to convert the world, we suffer it to pervert us. When shall we begin to study to crucify our passions and die to ourselves, that we may

lay a solid foundation of true virtue and establish its
reign in our hearts?

February 19.—ST. BARBATUS, Bishop.

ST. BARBATUS was born in the territory of Benevento in
Italy, toward the end of the pontificate of St. Gregory the Great, in the beginning of the seventh century.
His parents gave him a Christian education, and Barbatus
in his youth laid the foundation of that eminent sanctity
which recommends him to our veneration. The innocence,
simplicity, and purity of his manners, and his extraordinary progress in all virtues, qualified him for the service
of the altar, to which he was assumed by taking Holy
Orders as soon as the canons of the Church would allow it.
He was immediately employed by his bishop in preaching,
for which he had an extraordinary talent, and, after some
time, made curate of St. Basil's in Morcona, a town near
Benevento. His parishioners were steeled in their irregu-
larities, and they treated him as a disturber of their peace,
and persecuted him with the utmost violence. Finding
their malice conquered by his patience and humility, and
his character shining still more bright, they had recourse
to slanders, in which their virulence and success were such
that he was obliged to withdraw his charitable endeavors
among them. Barbatus returned to Benevento, where he
was received with joy. When St. Barbatus entered upon
his ministry in that city, the Christians themselves retained many idolatrous superstitions, which even their
duke, Prince Romuald, authorized by his example, though
son of Grimoald, King of the Lombards, who had edified
all Italy by his conversion. They expressed a religious
veneration for a golden viper, and prostrated themselves
before it; they also paid superstitious honor to a tree, on
which they hung the skin of a wild beast; and those ceremonies were closed by public games, in which the skin
served for a mark at which bowmen shot arrows over their
shoulders. St. Barbatus preached zealously against these
abuses, and at length he roused the attention of the people
by foretelling the distress of their city, and the calamities

which it was to suffer from the army of the Emperor
Constans, who, landing soon after in Italy, laid siege to
Benevento.   Ildebrand, Bishop of Benevento, dying during the siege, after the public tranquillity was restored
St. Barbatus was consecrated bishop on the 10th of March,
663.   Barbatus, being invested with the episcopal character, pursued and completed the good work which he
had so happily begun, and destroyed every trace of superstition in the whole state.   In the year 680 he assisted
in a council held by Pope Agatho at Rome, and the year
following in the Sixth General Council held at Constantinople against the Monothelites.   He did not long survive
this great assembly, for he died on the 29th of February,
682, being about seventy years old, almost nineteen of
which he had spent in the episcopal chair.

Reflection.—St. Augustine says: "When the enemy
has been cast out of your hearts, renounce him, not only in
word, but in work; not only by the sound of the lips, but
in every act of your life."

February 20.—ST. EUCHERIUS, Bishop.

T̲HIS Saint was born at Orleans, of a very illustrious
family.   At his birth his parents dedicated him to
God, and set him to study when he was but seven years
old, resolving to omit nothing that could be done toward
cultivating his mind or forming his heart.   His improvement in virtue kept pace with his progress in learning: he
meditated assiduously on the sacred writings, especially on
St. Paul's manner of speaking on the world and its enjoyments as mere empty shadows that deceive us and vanish
away.   These reflections at length sank so deep into his
mind that he resolved to quit the world.   To put this
design in execution, about the year 714 he retired to the
abbey of Jumiége in Normandy, where he spent six or
seven years in the practice of penitential austerities and
obedience.   Suavaric, his uncle, Bishop of Orleans, having
died, the senate and people, with the clergy of that city,
begged permission to elect Eucherius to the vacant see.
The Saint entreated his monks to screen him from the

dangers that threatened him; but they preferred the public
good to their private inclinations, and resigned him for
that important charge. He was consecrated with universal applause in 721. Charles Martel, to defray the
expenses of his wars and other undertakings, often stripped
the churches of their revenues. St. Eucherius reproved
these encroachments with so much zeal that, in the year
737, Charles banished him to Cologne. The extraordinary
esteem which his virtue procured him in that city moved
Charles to order him to be conveyed thence to a strong
place in the territory of Liege. Robert, the governor of
that country, was so charmed with his virtue that he made
him the distributor of his large alms, and allowed him to
retire to the monastery of Sarchinium, or St. Tron's.
Here prayer and contemplation were his whole employment
till the year 743, in which he died, on the 20th of February.

Reflection.—Nothing softens the soul and weakens
piety so much as frivolous indulgence. God has revealed
what high store He sets by " retirement " in these words:
" I will lead her into solitude, and I will speak to her
heart."

February 21.—ST. SEVERIANUS, Martyr, Bishop.

IN the reign of Marcian and St. Pulcheria, the Council
of Chalcedon, which condemned the Eutychian
heresy, was received by St. Euthymius and by a great
part of the monks of Palestine. But Theodosius, an ignorant Eutychian monk, and a man of a most tyrannical
temper, under the protection of the Empress Eudoxia,
widow of Theodosius the Younger, who lived at Jerusalem,
perverted many among the monks themselves, and having
obliged Juvenal, Bishop of Jerusalem, to withdraw, un-
justly possessed himself of that important see, and, in a
cruel persecution which he raised, filled Jerusalem with
blood; then, at the head of a band of soldiers, he carried
desolation over the country. Many, however, had the
courage to stand their ground. No one resisted him with
greater zeal and resolution than Severianus, Bishop of
Scythopolis, and his recompense was the crown of martyr-

dom; for the furious soldiers seized his person, dragged him out of the city, and massacred him, in the latter part of the year 452 or in the beginning of the year 453.

Reflection.—With what floods of tears can we sufficiently bewail so grievous a misfortune, and implore the divine mercy in behalf of so many souls! How ought we to be alarmed at the consideration of so many dreadful examples of God's inscrutable judgments, and tremble for ourselves! "Let him who stands beware lest he fall." "Hold fast what thou hast," says the oracle of the Holy Ghost to every one of us, "lest another bear away thy crown."

February 22.—ST. PETER'S CHAIR AT ANTIOCH.

THAT St. Peter, before he went to Rome, founded the see of Antioch is attested by many Saints. It was just that the Prince of the Apostles should take this city under his particular care and inspection, which was then the capital of the East, and in which the faith took so early and so deep root as to give birth in it to the name of Christians. St. Chrysostom says that St. Peter made there a long stay; St. Gregory the Great, that he was seven years Bishop of Antioch; not that he resided there all that time, but only that he had a particular care over that Church. If he sat twenty-five years at Rome, the date of his establishing his chair at Antioch must be within three years after Our Saviour's Ascension; for in that supposition he must have gone to Rome in the second year of Claudius. In the first ages it was customary, especially in the East, for every Christian to keep the anniversary of his Baptism, on which he renewed his baptismal vows and gave thanks to God for his heavenly adoption: this they called their spiritual birthday. The bishops in like manner kept the anniversary of their own consecration, as appears from four sermons of St. Leo on the anniversary of his accession or assumption to the pontifical dignity; and this was frequently continued after their decease by the people, out of respect for their memory. St. Leo says we ought to celebrate the chair of St.

Peter with no less joy than the day of his martyrdom; for as in this he was exalted to a throne of glory in heaven, so by the former he was installed head of the Church on earth.

Reflection.—On this festival we are especially bound to adore and thank the Divine Goodness for the establishment and propagation of His Church, and earnestly to pray that in His mercy He preserve the same, and dilate its pale, that His name may be glorified by all nations, and by all hearts, to the boundaries of the earth, for His divine honor and the salvation of souls, framed to His divine image, and the price of His adorable blood.

February 23.—ST. PETER DAMIAN.

ST. PETER DAMIAN was born in 988, and lost both parents at an early age. His eldest brother, in whose hands he was left, treated him so cruelly that a younger brother, a priest, moved by his piteous state, sent him to the University of Parma, where he acquired great distinction. His studies were sanctified by vigils, fasts, and prayers, till at last, thinking that all this was only serving God by halves, he resolved to leave the world. He joined the monks at Font-Avellano, then in the greatest repute, and by his wisdom and sanctity rose to be Superior. He was employed on the most delicate and difficult missions, amongst others the reform of ecclesiastical communities, which was effected by his zeal. Seven Popes in succession made him their constant adviser, and he was at last created Cardinal Bishop of Ostia. He withstood Henry IV. of Germany, and labored in defence of Alexander II. against the Antipope, whom he forced to yield and seek for pardon. He was charged, as Papal Legate, with the repression of simony; again, was commissioned to settle discords amongst various bishops, and finally, in 1072, to adjust the affairs of the Church at Ravenna. He was laid low by a fever on his homeward journey, and died at Faenza, in a monastery of his order, on the eighth day of his sickness, whilst the monks chanted matins around him.

Reflection.—The Saints studied, not in order to be accounted learned, but to become perfect. This only is wisdom and true greatness, to account ourselves as ignorant, and to adhere in all things to the teachings and instincts of the Church.

ST. SERENUS, a Gardener, Martyr.

ERENUS was by birth a Grecian. He quitted estate, friends, and country to serve God in celibacy, penance, and prayer. With this design he bought a garden in Sirmium in Pannonia, which he cultivated with his own hands, and lived on the fruits and herbs it produced. One day there came thither a woman, with her two daughters. Serenus, seeing them come up, advised them to withdraw, and to conduct themselves in future as decency required in persons of their sex and condition. The woman, stung at our Saint's charitable remonstrance, retired in confusion, but resolved on revenging the supposed affront. She accordingly wrote to her husband that Serenus had insulted her. He, on receiving her letter, went to the emperor to demand justice, whereupon the emperor gave him a letter to the governor of the province to enable him to obtain satisfaction. The governor ordered Serenus to be immediately brought before him. Serenus, on hearing the charge, answered, " I remember that, some time ago, a lady came into my garden at an unseasonable hour, and I own I took the liberty to tell her it was against decency for one of her sex and quality to be abroad at such an hour." This plea of Serenus having put the officer to the blush for his wife's conduct, he dropped his prosecution. But the governor, suspecting by this answer that Serenus might be a Christian, began to question him, saying, " Who are you, and what is your religion?" Serenus, without hesitating one moment, answered, " I am a Christian. It seemed a while ago as if God rejected me as a stone unfit to enter His building, but He has the goodness to take me now to be placed in it; I am ready to suffer all things for His name, that I may have a part in His kingdom with His Saints." The governor, hearing this, burst into rage and said, "Since you sought to elude by flight the emperor's edicts, and have positively refused to sacrifice to the gods, I condemn you for these crimes to lose your head." The sentence was no sooner pronounced than the Saint was carried off and beheaded, on the 23d of February, in 307.

Reflection.—The garden affords a beautiful emblem of a Christian's continual progress in the path of virtue. Plants always mount upwards, and never stop in their growth till they have attained to that maturity which the Author of nature has prescribed. So in a Christian, everything ought to carry him toward that perfection which the sanctity of his state requires; and every desire of his soul, every action of his life should be a step advancing to this in a direct line.

February 24.—ST. MATTHIAS, Apostle.

AFTER our blessed Lord's Ascension His disciples met together, with Mary His mother and the eleven apostles, in an upper room at Jerusalem. The little company numbered no more than one hundred and twenty souls. They were waiting for the promised coming of the Holy Ghost, and they persevered in prayer. Meanwhile there was a solemn act to be performed on the part of the Church, which could not be postponed. The place of the fallen Judas must be filled up, that the elect number of the apostles might be complete. St. Peter, therefore, as Vicar of Christ, arose to announce the divine decree. That which the Holy Ghost had spoken by the mouth of David concerning Judas, he said, must be fulfilled. Of him it had been written, "His bishopric let another take." A choice, therefore, was to be made of one among those who had been their companions from the beginning, who could bear witness to the Resurrection of Jesus. Two were named of equal merit, Joseph called Barsabas, and Matthias. Then, after praying to God, Who knows the hearts of all men, to show which of these He had chosen, they cast lots, and the lot fell upon Matthias, who was forthwith numbered with the apostles. It is recorded of the Saint, thus wonderfully elected to so high a vocation, that he was above all remarkable for his mortification of the flesh. It was thus that he made his election sure.

Reflection.— Our ignorance of many points in St. Matthias's life serves to fix the attention all the more firmly upon these two — the occasion of his call to the apostolate, and the fact of his perseverance. We then naturally turn in thought to our own vocation and our own end.

February 25.—ST. TARASIUS.

TARASIUS was born at Constantinople about the middle of the eighth century, of a noble family. His mother Eucratia, brought him up in the practice of the most eminent virtues. By his talents and virtue he gained the esteem of all, and was raised to the greatest honors of the empire, being made consul, and afterwards first secretary of state to the Emperor Constantine and the Empress Irene, his mother. In the midst of the court, and in its highest honors, he led a life like that of a religious man. Paul, Patriarch of Constantinople, the third of that name, though he had conformed in some respects to the then reigning heresy, had several good qualities, and was not only beloved by the people for his charity to the poor, but highly esteemed by the whole court for his great prudence. Touched with remorse, he quitted the patriarchal see, and put on a religious habit in the monastery of Florus in Constantinople. Tarasius was chosen to succeed him by the unanimous consent of the court, clergy, and people. Finding it in vain to oppose his election, he declared that he could not in conscience accept of the government of a see which had been cut off from the Catholic communion, except on condition that a general council should be called to compose the disputes which divided the Church at that time in relation to holy images. This being agreed to, he was solemnly declared patriarch, and consecrated soon after, on Christmas Day. The council was opened on the 1st of August, in the Church of the Apostles at Constantinople, in 786; but, being disturbed by the violences of the Iconoclasts, it adjourned, and met again the year following

in the Church of St. Sophia at Nice. The council, having
declared the sense of the Church in relation to the matter
in debate, which was found to be the allowing to holy
pictures and images a relative honor, was closed with the
usual acclamations and prayers for the prosperity of the
emperor and empress; after which, synodal letters were
sent to all the churches, and in particular to the Pope, who
approved the council. The life of this holy patriarch was
a model of perfection to his clergy and people. His table
contained barely the necessaries of life; he allowed himself
very little time for sleep, being always up the first and last
in his family. Reading and prayer filled all his leisure
hours. The emperor having become enamoured of Theo-
dota, a maid of honor to his wife, the Empress Mary, was
resolved to divorce the latter. He used all his efforts to
gain the patriarch over to his desires, but St. Tarasius
resolutely refused to countenance the iniquity. The holy
man gave up his soul to God in peace on the 25th of February, 806, after having sat twenty-one years and two
months.

Reflection.—The highest praise which Scripture pronounces on the holy man Job is comprised in these words,
" He was simple and upright."

February 26.—ST. PORPHYRY, Bishop.

AT the age of twenty-five, Porphyry, a rich citizen of
Thessalonica, left the world for one of the great religious houses in the desert of Sceté. Here he remained
five years, and then, finding himself drawn to a more solitary life, passed into Palestine, where he spent a similar
period in the severest penance, till ill health obliged him to
moderate his austerities. He then made his home in Jerusalem, and in spite of his ailments visited the Holy Places
every day; thinking, says his biographer, so little of his
sickness that he seemed to be afflicted in another body, and
not his own. About this time God put it into his heart to
sell all he had and give to the poor, and then in reward of
the sacrifice restored him by a miracle to perfect health.
In 393 he was ordained priest and intrusted with the care

of the relics of the true cross; three years later, in spite of all the resistance his humility could make, he was consecrated Bishop of Gaza. That city was a hotbed of paganism, and Porphyry found in it an ample scope for his apostolic zeal. His labors and the miracles which attended them effected the conversion of many; and an imperial edict for the destruction of the pagan temples, obtained through the influence of St. John Chrysostom, greatly strengthened his hands. When St. Porphyry first went to Gaza, he found there one temple more splendid than the rest, in honor of the chief god. When the edict went forth to destroy all traces of heathen worship, St. Porphyry determined to put Satan to special shame where he had received special honor. A Christian church was built upon the site, and its approach was paved with the marbles of the heathen temple. Thus every worshipper of Jesus Christ trod the relics of idolatry and superstition underfoot each time he went to assist at the holy Mass. He lived to see his diocese for the most part clear of idolatry, and died in 420.

Reflection.— All superstitious searching into secret things is forbidden by the First Commandment equally with the worship of any false god. Let us ask St. Porphyry for a great zeal in keeping this commandment, lest we be led away, as so many are, by a curious and prying mind.

February 27.—ST. LEANDER, Bishop.

S T. LEANDER was born of an illustrious family at Carthagena in Spain. He was the eldest of five brothers, several of whom are numbered among the Saints. He entered into a monastery very young, where he lived many years and attained to an eminent degree of virtue and sacred learning. These qualities occasioned his being promoted to the see of Seville; but his change of condition made little or no alteration in his method of life, though it brought on him a great increase of care and solicitude. Spain at that time was in possession of the Visigoths. These Goths, being infected with Arianism, established this heresy wherever they came; so that when St. Leander was made bishop it had reigned in Spain a hundred years. This was his great affliction; however, by his prayers to God, and by his most zealous and unwearied endeavors, he became the happy instrument of the conversion of that nation to the Catholic faith. Having converted, among others, Hermenegild, the king's eldest son and heir apparent, Leander was banished by King Leovigild. This pious prince was put to death by his unnatural father, the year following, for refusing to receive Communion from the hands of an Arian bishop. But, touched with remorse not long after, the king recalled our Saint; and falling sick and finding himself past hopes of recovery, he sent for St. Leander, and recommended to him his son Recared. This son, by listening to St. Leander, soon became a Catholic, and finally converted the whole nation of the Visigoths. He was no less successful with respect to the Suevi, a people of Spain, whom his father Leovigild had perverted.

St. Leander was no less zealous in the reformation of manners than in restoring the purity of faith; and he planted the seeds of that zeal and fervor which afterwards produced so many martyrs and Saints. This holy doctor of Spain died about the year 596, on the 27th of February, as Mabillon proves from his epitaph. The Church of Seville has been a metropolitan see ever since the third century. The cathedral is the most magnificent, both as to structure and ornament, of any in all Spain.

February 28.—STS. ROMANUS and LUPICINUS, Abbots.

ROMANUS at thirty-five years of age left his relatives and spent some time in the monastery of Ainay at Lyons, at the great church at the conflux of the Saône and Rhone which the faithful had built over the ashes of the famous martyrs of that city; for their bodies being burned by the pagans, their ashes were thrown into the Rhone, but a great part of them was gathered by the Christians and deposited in this place. Romanus a short time after re-

tired into the forests of Mount Jura, between France and
Switzerland, and fixed his abode at a place called Condate,
at the conflux of the rivers Bienne and Aliere, where he
found a spot of ground fit for culture, and some trees
which furnished him with a kind of wild fruit. Here he
spent his time in praying, reading, and laboring for his
subsistence. Lupicinus, his brother, came to him some
time after in company with others, who were followed by
several more, drawn by the fame of the virtue and miracles
of these two Saints. Their numbers increasing, they built
several monasteries, and a nunnery called La Beaume,
which no men were allowed ever to enter, and where St.
Romanus chose his burial-place. The brothers governed
the monks jointly and in great harmony, though Lupicinus
was the more inclined to severity of the two. Lupicinus
used no other bed than a chair or a hard board; never
touched wine, and would scarcely ever suffer a drop either
of oil or milk to be poured on his pottage. In summer his
subsistence for many years was only hard bread moistened
in cold water, so that he could eat it with a spoon. His
tunic was made of various skins of beasts sewn together,
with a cowl; he used wooden shoes, and wore no stockings
unless when he was obliged to go out of the monastery.
St. Romanus died about the year 460, and St. Lupicinus
survived him almost twenty years.

February 29.—ST. OSWALD, Bishop.

OSWALD was of a noble Saxon family, and was endowed
with a very rare and beautiful form of body and
with a singular piety of soul. He was brought up by his
uncle, St. Odo, Archbishop of Canterbury, and was chosen,
while still young, dean of the secular canons of Winchester,
then very relaxed. His attempt to reform them was a
failure; and he saw, with that infallible instinct which so
often guides the Saints in critical times, that the true
remedy for the corruptions of the clergy was the restoration of the monastic life. He therefore went to France
and took the habit of St. Benedict, but returned, only to
receive the news of Odo's death. He found, however, a

new patron in St. Dunstan, now metropolitan, through whose influence he was nominated to the see of Worcester. To these two Saints, together with Ethelwold of Winchester, the monastic revival of the tenth century is mainly due. Oswald's first care was to deprive of their benefices the disorderly clerics, whom he replaced as far as possible by regulars, and himself founded seven religious houses. Considering that in the hearts of the secular canons there were yet some sparks of virtue, he would not at once expel them, but rather entrapped them by a holy artifice. Adjoining the cathedral he built a church in honor of the Mother of God, causing it to be served by a body of strict religious. He himself assisted at the divine Office in this church, and his example was followed by the people. The canons, finding themselves isolated and their cathedral deserted, chose rather to embrace the religious life than to continue not only to injure their own souls, but to be a mockery to their people by reason of the contrast offered by their worldliness to the regularity of their religious brethren. As Archbishop of York a like success attended St. Oswald's efforts; and God manifested His approval of his zeal by discovering to him the relics of his great predecessor, St. Wilfrid, which he reverently translated to Worcester. He died February 29, 992.

Reflection.— A soul without discipline is like a ship without a helm; she must inevitably strike unawares upon the rocks, founder on the shoals, or float unknowingly into the harbor of the enemy.

March 1.—ST. DAVID, Bishop.

ST. DAVID, son of Sant, Prince of Cardigan and of Non, was born in that country in the fifth century, and from his earliest years gave himself wholly to the service of God. He began his religious life under St. Paulinus, a disciple of St. Germanus, Bishop of Auxerre, who had been sent to Britain by Pope St. Celestine to stop the ravages of the heresy of Pelagius, at that time abbot, as it is said, of Bangor. On the reappearance of that heresy, in the beginning of the sixth century, the bishops

assembled at Brevi, and, unable to address the people
that came to hear the word of truth, sent for St. David
from his cell to preach to them. The Saint came, and
it is related that, as he preached, the ground beneath his
feet rose and became a hill, so that he was heard by an
innumerable crowd. The heresy fell under the sword of
the Spirit, and the Saint was elected Bishop of Caerleon
on the resignation of St. Dubricius; but he removed the
see to Menevia, a lone and desert spot, where he might,
with his monks, serve God away from the noise of the
world. He founded twelve monasteries, and governed his
Church according to the canons sanctioned in Rome. At
last, when about eighty years of age, he laid himself down,
knowing that his hour was come. As his agony closed,
Our Lord stood before him in a vision, and the Saint
cried out: " Take me up with Thee," and so gave up his
soul on Tuesday, March 1, 561.

ST. ALBINUS, Bishop.

ST. ALBINUS was of an ancient and noble family in Brittany, and from his childhood was fervent in every
exercise of piety. He ardently sighed after the happiness
which a devout soul finds in being perfectly disengaged
from all earthly things. Having embraced the monastic
state at Tintillant, near Angers, he shone a perfect model
of virtue, living as if in all things he had been without
any will of his own; and his soul seemed so perfectly governed by the spirit of Christ as to live only for Him. At
the age of thirty-five years he was chosen abbot, in 504,
and twenty-five years afterwards Bishop of Angers. He
everywhere restored discipline, being inflamed with a holy
zeal for the honor of God. His dignity seemed to make
no alteration either in his mortifications or in the constant
recollection of his soul. Honored by all the world, even
by kings, he was never affected with vanity. Powerful in
works and miracles, he looked upon himself as the most
unworthy and most unprofitable among the servants of
God, and had no other ambition than to appear such in
the eyes of others as he was in those of his own humility.

In the third Council of Orleans, in 538, he procured the thirtieth canon of the Council of Epaone to be revived, by which those are declared excommunicated who presume to contract incestuous marriages in the first or second degree of consanguinity or affinity. He died on the 1st of March, in 549.

Reflection.— With whatever virtues a man may be endowed, he will discover, if he considers himself attentively, a sufficient depth of misery to afford cause for deep humility; but Jesus Christ says, " He that humbleth himself shall be exalted."

March 2.—ST. SIMPLICIUS, Pope.

S<small>T.</small> S<small>IMPLICIUS</small> was the ornament of the Roman clergy under Sts. Leo and Hilarius, and succeeded the latter in the pontificate in 468. He was raised by God to comfort and support his Church amidst the greatest storms. All the provinces of the Western Empire, out of Italy, were fallen into the hands of barbarians. The emperors for many years were rather shadows of power than sovereigns, and, in the eighth year of the pontificate of Simplicius, Rome itself fell a prey to foreigners. Italy, by oppressions and the ravages of barbarians, was left almost a desert without inhabitants; and the imperial armies consisted chiefly of barbarians, hired under the name of auxiliaries. These soon saw that their masters were in their power. The Heruli demanded one third of the lands of Italy, and upon refusal chose for their leader Odoacer, one of the lowest extraction, but a resolute and intrepid man, who was proclaimed king of Rome in 476. He put to death Orestes, who was regent of the empire for his son Augustulus, whom the senate had advanced to the imperial throne. Odoacer spared the life of Augustulus, appointed him a salary of six thousand pounds of gold, and permitted him to live at full liberty near Naples. Pope Simplicius was wholly taken up in comforting and relieving the afflicted, and in sowing the seeds of the Catholic faith among the barbarians. The East gave his zeal no less employment and concern. Peter

Cnapheus, a violent Eutychian, was made by the heretics
Patriarch of Antioch; and Peter Mongus, one of the most
profligate men, that of Alexandria. Acacius, the Patriarch of Constantinople, received the sentence of St. Simplicius against Cnapheus, but supported Mongus against
him and the Catholic Church, and was a notorious change-
ling, double-dealer, and artful hypocrite, who often made
religion serve his own private ends. St. Simplicius at
length discovered his artifices, and redoubled his zeal to
maintain the holy faith, which he saw betrayed on every
side, whilst the patriarchal sees of Alexandria and Antioch were occupied by furious wolves, and there was not
one Catholic king in the whole world. The emperor
measured everything by his passions and human views.
St. Simplicius, having sat fifteen years, eleven months, and
six days, went to receive the reward of his labors in 483.
He was buried in St. Peter's on the 2d of March.

Reflection.— " He that trusteth in God shall fare never
the worse," saith the Wise Man in the Book of Ecclesi-
asticus.

March 3.—ST. CUNEGUNDES, Empress.

S T. CUNEGUNDES was the daughter of Siegfried, the first
Count of Luxemburg, and Hadeswige, his pious wife.
They instilled into her from her cradle the most tender
sentiments of piety, and married her to St. Henry, Duke
of Bavaria, who, upon the death of the Emperor Otho III.,
was chosen king of the Romans, and crowned on the 6th
of 'June, 1002. She was crowned at Paderborn on St.
Laurence's day. In the year 1014 she went with her husband to Rome, and received the imperial crown with him
from the hands of Pope Benedict VIII. She had, by St.
Henry's consent, before her marriage made a vow of virginity. Calumniators afterwards made vile accusations
against her, and the holy empress, to remove the scandal
of such a slander, trusting in God to prove her innocence,
walked over red-hot ploughshares without being hurt.
The emperor condemned his too scrupulous fears and cre-
dulity, and from that time they lived in the strictest union

of hearts, conspiring to promote in everything God's honor and the advancement of piety.

Going once to make a retreat in Hesse, she fell dangerously ill, and made a vow to found a monastery, if she recovered, at Kaffungen, near Cassel, in the diocese of Paderborn, which she executed in a stately manner, and gave it to nuns of the Order of St. Benedict. Before it was finished St. Henry died, in 1024. She earnestly recommended his soul to the prayers of others, especially to her dear nuns, and expressed her longing desire of joining them. She had already exhausted her treasures in founding bishoprics and monasteries, and in relieving the poor, and she had therefore little left now to give. But still thirsting to embrace perfect evangelical poverty, and to renounce all to serve God without obstacle, she assembled a great number of prelates to the dedication of her church of Kaffungen on the anniversary day of her husband's death, 1025; and after the gospel was sung at Mass she offered on the altar a piece of the true cross, and then, putting off her imperial robes, clothed herself with a poor habit; her hair was cut off, and the bishop put on her a veil, and a ring as a pledge of her fidelity to her heavenly Spouse. After she was consecrated to God in religion, she seemed entirely to forget that she had been empress, and behaved as the last in the house, being persuaded that she was so before God. She prayed and read much, worked with her hands, and took a singular pleasure in visiting and comforting the sick. Thus she passed the last fifteen years of her life. Her mortifications at length reduced her to a very weak condition, and brought on her last sickness. Perceiving that they were preparing a cloth fringed with gold to cover her corpse after her death, she changed color and ordered it to be taken away; nor could she be at rest till she was promised she should be buried as a poor religious in her habit. She died on the 3d of March, 1040. Her body was carried to Bamberg and buried near that of her husband. She was solemnly canonized by Innocent III. in 1200.

Reflection.— Detachment of the mind, at least, is needful to those who cannot venture on an effectual renuncia-

tion. " So likewise every one of you," saith Jesus Christ,
" that doth not renounce all that he possesseth, cannot be
My disciple."

March 4.—ST. CASIMIR, King.

CASIMIR, the second son of Casimir III., King of Poland
was born A. D. 1458. From the custody of a most
virtuous mother, Elizabeth of Austria, he passed to the
guardianship of a devoted master, the learned and pious
John Dugloss. Thus animated from his earliest years by
precept and example, his innocence and piety soon ripened
into the practice of heroic virtue. At the age of twenty-
five, sick of a lingering illness, he foretold the hour of his
death, and chose to die a virgin rather than take the life
and health which the doctors held out to him in the married state. In an atmosphere of luxury and magnificence
the young prince had fasted, worn a hair-shirt, slept upon
the bare earth, prayed by night, and watched for the opening of the church doors at dawn. He had become so ten-
derly devoted to the Passion of Our Lord that at Mass he
seemed quite rapt out of himself, and his charity to the
poor and afflicted knew no bounds. His love for our
blessed Lady he expressed in a long and beautiful hymn,
familiar to us in our own tongue. The miracles wrought
by his body after death fill a volume. The blind saw, the
lame walked, the sick were healed, a dead girl was raised
to life. And once the Saint in glory led his countrymen
to battle, and delivered them by a glorious victory from
the schismatic Russian hosts.

One hundred and twenty-two years after his death the
Saint's tomb in the cathedral of Vienna was opened, that
the holy body might be transferred to the rich marble
chapel where it now lies. The place was damp, and the
very vault crumbled away in the hands of the workmen;
yet the Saint's body, wrapped in robes of silk, was found
whole and incorrupt, and emitted a sweet fragrance, which
filled the church and refreshed all who were present.
Under his head was found his hymn to Our Lady, which
he had had buried with him. The following night three

young men saw a brilliant light issuing from the open tomb and streaming through the windows of the chapel.

Reflection.— Let the study of St. Casimir's life make us increase in devotion to the most pure Mother of God — a sure means of preserving holy purity.

March 5.—STS. ADRIAN and EUBULUS, Martyrs.

IN the seventh year of Diocletian's persecution, continued by Galerius Maximianus, when Firmilian, the most bloody governor of Palestine, had stained Cæsarea with the blood of many illustrious martyrs, Adrian and Eubulus came out of the country called Magantia to Cæsarea, in order to visit the holy confessors there. At the gates of the city they were asked, as others were, whither they were going, and upon what errand. They ingenuously confessed the truth, and were brought before the president, who ordered them to be tortured and their sides to be torn with iron hooks, and then condemned them to be exposed to wild beasts. Two days after, when the pagans at Cæsarea celebrated the festival of the public Genius, Adrian was exposed to a lion, and not being despatched by that beast, but only mangled, was at length killed by the sword. Eubulus was treated in the same manner two days later. The judge offered him his liberty if he would sacrifice to idols; but the Saint preferred a glorious death, and was the last that suffered in this persecution at Cæsarea, which had now continued twelve years, under three successive governors, Flavian, Urban, and Firmilian. Divine vengeance pursuing the cruel Firmilian, he was that same year beheaded for his crimes, by the emperor's order, as his predecessor Urban had been two years before.

Reflection.— It is in vain that we take the name of Christians, or pretend to follow Christ, unless we carry our crosses after Him. It is in vain that we hope to share in His glory, and in His kingdom, if we accept not the condition. We cannot arrive at heaven by any other road but that which Christ held, Who bequeathed His cross to all His elect as their portion and inheritance in this world.

March 6.—ST. COLETTE, Virgin.

AFTER a holy childhood, Colette joined a society of devout women called the Beguines; but not finding their state sufficiently austere, she entered the Third Order of St. Francis, and lived in a hut near her parish church of Corbie in Picardy. Here she had passed four years of extraordinary penance when St. Francis, in a vision, bade her undertake the reform of her Order, then much relaxed. Armed with due authority, she established her reform throughout a large part of Europe, and, in spite of the most violent opposition, founded seventeen convents of the strict observance. By the same wonderful prudence she assisted in healing the great schism which then afflicted the Church. The Fathers in council at Constance were in doubt how to deal with the three claimants to the tiara — John XXIII., Benedict XIII., and Gregory XII. At this crisis Colette, together with St. Vincent Ferrer, wrote to the Fathers to depose Benedict XIII., who alone refused his consent to a new election. This was done, and Martin V. was elected, to the great good of the Church. Colette equally assisted the Council of Basle by her advice and prayers; and when, later, God revealed to her the spirit of revolt that was rising, she warned the bishops and legates to retire from the council. St. Colette never ceased to pray for the Church, while the devils, in turn, never ceased to assault her. They swarmed round her as hideous insects, buzzing and stinging her tender skin. They brought into her cell the decaying corpses of public criminals, and assuming themselves monstrous forms struck her savage blows; or they would appear in the most seductive guise, and tempt her by many deceits to sin. St. Colette once complained to Our Lord that the demons prevented her from praying. " Cease, then," said the devil to her, " your prayers to the great Master of the Church, and we will cease to torment you; for you torment us more by your prayers than we do you." Yet the virgin of Christ triumphed alike over their threats and their allurements, and said she would count that day the unhappiest of her life in which she suffered nothing for her God. She died

March 6, 1447, in a transport of intercession for sinners and the Church.

Reflection.— One of the greatest tests of being a good Catholic is zeal for the Church and devotion to Christ's Vicar.

March 7.—ST. THOMAS AQUINAS.

ST. THOMAS was born of noble parents at Aquino in Italy, in 1226. At the age of nineteen he received the Dominican habit at Naples, where he was studying. Seized by his brothers on his way to Paris, he suffered a two years' captivity in their castle of Rocca-Secca; but neither the caresses of his mother and sisters, nor the threats and stratagems of his brothers, could shake him in his vocation. While St. Thomas was in confinement at Rocca-Secca, his brothers endeavored to entrap him into sin, but the attempt only ended in the triumph of his purity. Snatching from the hearth a burning brand, the Saint drove from his chamber the wretched creature whom they had there concealed. Then marking a cross upon the wall, he knelt down to pray, and forthwith, being rapt in ecstasy, an angel girded him with a cord, in token of the gift of perpetual chastity which God had given him. The pain caused by the girdle was so sharp that St. Thomas uttered a piercing cry, which brought his guards into the room. But he never told this grace to any one save only to Father Raynald, his confessor, a little while before his death. Hence originated the Confraternity of the " Angelic Warfare," for the preservation of the virtue of chastity. Having at length escaped, St. Thomas went to Cologne to study under Blessed Albert the Great, and after that to Paris, where for many years he taught philosophy and theology. The Church has ever venerated his numerous writings as a treasure-house of sacred doctrine; while in naming him the Angelic Doctor she has indicated that his science is more divine than human. The rarest gifts of intellect were combined in him with the tenderest piety. Prayer, he said, had taught him more than study. His singular devotion to the Blessed Sacra-

ment shines forth in the Office and hymns for Corpus
Christi, which he composed. To the words miraculously
uttered by a crucifix at Naples, "Well hast thou written
concerning Me, Thomas. What shall I give thee as a
reward?" he replied, "Naught save Thyself, O Lord."
He died at Fossa-Nuova, 1274, on his way to the General Council of Lyons, to which Pope Gregory X. had summoned him.

Reflection.— The knowledge of God is for all, but hidden treasures are reserved for those who have ever followed
the Lamb.

March 8.—ST. JOHN OF GOD.

NOTHING in John's early life foreshadowed his future
sanctity. He ran away as a boy from his home in
Portugal, tended sheep and cattle in Spain, and served as
a soldier against the French, and afterwards against the
Turks. When about forty years of age, feeling remorse
for his wild life, he resolved to devote himself to the ransom of the Christian slaves in Africa, and went thither
with the family of an exiled noble, which he maintained
by his labor. On his return to Spain he sought to do
good by selling holy pictures and books at low prices. At
length the hour of grace struck. At Granada a sermon by
the celebrated John of Avila shook his soul to its depths,
and his expressions of self-abhorrence were so extraordinary that he was taken to the asylum as one mad. There he
employed himself in ministering to the sick. On leaving
he began to collect homeless poor, and to support them by
his work and by begging. One night St. John found in
the streets a poor man who seemed near death, and, as was
his wont, he carried him to the hospital, laid him on a bed,
and went to fetch water to wash his feet. When he had
washed them, he knelt to kiss them, and started with awe:
the feet were pierced, and the print of the nails bright with
an unearthly radiance. He raised his eyes to look, and
heard the words, "John, to Me thou doest all that thou
doest to the poor in My name: I reach forth My hand for
the alms thou givest; Me dost thou clothe, Mine are the

feet thou dost wash." And then the gracious vision disappeared, leaving St. John filled at once with confusion and consolation. The bishop became the Saint's patron, and gave him the name of John of God. When his hospital was on fire, John was seen rushing about uninjured amidst the flames until he had rescued all his poor. After ten years spent in the service of the suffering, the Saint's life was fitly closed. He plunged into the river Xenil to save a drowning boy, and died, 1550, of an illness brought on by the attempt, at the age of fifty-five.

Reflection.— God often rewards men for works that are pleasing in His sight by giving them grace and opportunity to do other works higher still. St. John of God used to attribute his conversion, and the graces which enabled him to do such great works, to his self-denying charity in Africa.

March 9.—ST. FRANCES OF ROME.

FRANCES was born at Rome in 1384. Her parents were of high rank. They overruled her desire to become a nun, and at twelve years of age married her to Rorenzo Ponziano, a Roman noble. During the forty years of their married life they never had a disagreement. While spending her days in retirement and prayer, she attended promptly to every household duty, saying, " A married woman must leave God at the altar to find Him in her domestic cares; " and she once found the verse of a psalm in which she had been four times thus interrupted completed for her in letters of gold. Her ordinary food was dry bread. Secretly she would exchange with beggars good food for their hard crusts; her drink was water, and her cup a human skull. During the invasion of Rome, in 1413, Ponziano was banished, his estates confiscated, his house destroyed, and his eldest son taken as a hostage. Frances saw in these losses only the finger of God, and blessed His holy name. When peace was restored Ponziano recovered his estate, and Frances founded the Oblates. After her husband's death, barefoot and with a cord about her neck she begged admission to the community, and was soon elected Superioress. She lived always in the presence of God, and amongst many visions was given constant sight of her angel guardian, who shed such brightness around him that the Saint could read her midnight Office by this light alone. He shielded her in the hour of temptation, and directed her in every good act. But when she was betrayed into some defect, he faded from her sight; and when some light words were spoken before her, he covered his face in shame. She died on the day she had foretold, March 9, 1440.

Reflection.—God has appointed an angel to guard each one of us, to whose warnings we are bound to attend. Let us listen to his voice here, and we shall see him hereafter when he leads us before the throne of God.

March 10.—THE FORTY MARTYRS OF SEBASTE.

THE FORTY MARTYRS were soldiers quartered at Sebaste in Armenia, about the year 320. When their legion was ordered to offer sacrifice they separated themselves from the rest and formed a company of martyrs. After they had been torn by scourges and iron hooks they were chained together and led to a lingering death. It was a cruel winter, and they were condemned to lie naked on the icy surface of a pond in the open air till they were frozen to death. But they ran undismayed to the place of their combat, joyfully stripped off their garments, and with one voice besought God to keep their ranks unbroken. " Forty," they cried, " we have come to combat: grant that forty may be crowned." There were warm baths hard by, ready for any one amongst them who would deny Christ. The soldiers who watched saw angels descending with thirty-nine crowns, and, while he wondered at the deficiency in the number, one of the confessors lost heart, renounced his faith, and, crawling to the fire, died body and soul at the spot where he expected relief. But the soldier was inspired to confess Christ and take his place, and again the number of forty was complete. They remained steadfast while their limbs grew stiff and frozen, and died

one by one.   Among the Forty there was a young soldier
who held out longest against the cold, and when the officers came to cart away the dead bodies they found him
still breathing.   They were moved with pity, and wanted to
leave him alive in the hope that he would still change his
mind.   But his mother stood by, and this valiant woman
could not bear to see her son separated from the band of
martyrs.   She exhorted him to persevere, and lifted his
frozen body into the cart.   He was just able to make a sign
of recognition, and was borne away, to be thrown into the
flames with the dead bodies of his brethren.

Reflection.—All who live the life of grace are one in
Christ.   But besides this there are many special ties — of
religion, of community life, or at least of aspirations in
prayer, and pious works.   Thank God if He has bound you
to others by these spiritual ties; remember the character you
have to support, and pray that the bond which unites you
here may last for eternity.

March 11.—ST. EULOGIUS, Martyr.

T. EULOGIUS was of a senatorian family of Cordova, at
that time the capital of the Moors in Spain.   Our
Saint was educated among the clergy of the Church of St.
Zoilus, a martyr who suffered with nineteen others under
Diocletian.   Here he distinguished himself, by his virtue
and learning, and, being made priest, was placed at the
head of the chief ecclesiastical school at Cordova.   He
joined assiduous watching, fasting, and prayer to his
studies, and his humility, mildness, and charity gained
him the affection and respect of every one.   During the
persecution raised against the Christians in the year 850,
St. Eulogius was thrown into prison and there wrote his
Exhortation to Martyrdom, addressed to the virgins Flora
and Mary, who were beheaded the 24th of November, 851.
Six days after their death Eulogius was set at liberty.   In
the year 852 several others suffered the like martyrdom.
St. Eulogius encouraged all these martyrs to their triumphs, and was the support of that distressed flock.   The
Archbishop of Toledo dying in 858, St. Eulogius was

elected to succeed him; but there was some obstacle that hindered him from being consecrated, though he did not outlive his election two months. A virgin, by name Leocritia, of a noble family among the Moors, had been instructed from her infancy in the Christian religion by one of her relatives, and privately baptized. Her father and mother used her very ill, and scourged her day and night to compel her to renounce the Faith. Having made her condition known to St. Eulogius and his sister Anulona, intimating that she desired to go where she might freely exercise her religion, they secretly procured her the means of getting away, and concealed her for some time among faithful friends. But the matter was at length discovered, and they were all brought before the cadi, who threatened to have Eulogius scourged to death. The Saint told him that his torments would be of no avail, for he would never change his religion. Whereupon the cadi gave orders that he should be carried to the palace and be presented before the king's council. Eulogius began boldly to propose the truths of the Gospel to them. But, to prevent their hearing him, the council condemned him immediately to lose his head. As they were leading him to execution, one of the guards gave him a blow on the face for having spoken against Mahomet; he turned the other cheek, and patiently received a second. He received the stroke of death with great cheerfulness, on the 11th of March, 859. St. Leocritia was beheaded four days after him, and her body thrown into the river Guadalquivir, but taken out by the Christians.

Reflection.—Beg of God, through the intercession of these holy martyrs, the gift of perseverance. Their example will supply you with an admirable rule for obtaining this crowning gift. Remember that you have renounced the world and the devil once for all at your Baptism. Do not hesitate; do not look back; do not listen to suggestions against faith or virtue; but advance, day by day, along the road which you have chosen, to God, Who is your portion forever.

March 12.—ST. GREGORY THE GREAT.

GREGORY was a Roman of noble birth, and while still young was governor of Rome. On his father's death he gave his great wealth to the poor, turned his house on the Cœlian Hill into a monastery, which now bears his name, and for some years lived as a perfect monk. The Pope drew him from his seclusion to make him one of the seven deacons of Rome; and he did great service to the Church for many years as what we now call Nuncio to the imperial court at Constantinople. While still a monk the Saint was struck with some boys who were exposed for sale in Rome, and heard with sorrow that they were pagans. "And of what race are they?" he asked. "They are Angles." "Worthy indeed to be Angels of God," said he. "And of what province?" "Of Deira," was the reply. "Truly must we rescue them from the wrath of God. And what is the name of their king?" "He is called Ella." "It is well," said Gregory; "Alleluia must be sung in their land to God." He at once got leave from the Pope, and had set out to convert the English when the murmurs of the people led the Pope to recall him. Still the Angles were not forgotten, and one of the Saint's first cares as Pope was to send from his own monastery St. Augustine and other monks to England. On the death of Pope Pelagius II., Gregory was compelled to take the government of the Church, and for fourteen years his pontificate was a perfect model of ecclesiastical rule. He healed schisms; revived discipline; saved Italy by converting the wild Arian Lombards who were laying it waste; aided in the conversion of the Spanish and French Goths, who were also Arians; and kindled anew in Britain the light of the Faith, which the English had put out in blood. He set in order the Church's prayers and chant, guided and consoled her pastors with innumerable letters, and preached incessantly, most effectually by his own example. He died A. D. 604, worn out by austerities and toils; and the Church reckons him one of her four great doctors, and reveres him as St. Gregory the Great.

Reflection.—The champions of faith prove the truth of their teaching no less by the holiness of their lives than by the force of their arguments. Never forget that to convert others you must first see to your own soul.

March 13.—ST. EUPHRASIA, Virgin.

EUPHRASIA was the daughter of pious and noble parents. After the death of her father his widow withdrew privately with her little daughter into Egypt, where she was possessed of a very large estate. In that country she fixed her abode near a holy monastery of one hundred and thirty nuns. The young Euphrasia, at seven years of age, begged that she might be permitted to serve God in this monastery. The pious mother on hearing this wept for joy, and not long after presented her child to the abbess, who, taking up an image of Christ, gave it to Euphrasia. The tender virgin kissed it, saying, "By vow I consecrate myself to Christ." Then the mother led her before an image of Our Redeemer, and lifting up her hands to heaven said, "Lord Jesus Christ, receive this child under your special protection. You alone doth she love and seek: to you doth she recommend herself." Then leaving her in the hands of the abbess, she went out of the monastery weeping. Some time after this the good mother fell sick, and soon slept in peace. Upon the news of her death the Emperor Theodosius sent for the noble virgin to come to court, having promised her in marriage to a favorite young senator. But the virgin wrote him refusing the alliance, repeating her vow of virginity, and requesting that her estates should be sold and divided among the poor, and all her slaves set at liberty. The Emperor punctually executed all she desired, a little before his death in 395. St. Euphrasia was a perfect pattern of humility, meekness, and charity. If she found herself assaulted by any temptation, she immediately sought the advice of the abbess, who often enjoined her on such occasions some humbling and painful penitential labor, as sometimes to carry great stones from one place to another; which employment she once, under an obstinate assault, continued thirty days together with wonderful simplicity, till the devil, being vanquished by her humble obedience and chastisement of her body, left her in peace. She was favored with miracles both before and after her death, which happened in the year 410, the thirtieth of her age.

March 14.—ST. MAUD, Queen

THIS princess was daughter of Theodoric, a powerful Saxon count. Her parents placed her very young in the monastery of Erford, of which her grandmother Maud was then abbess. Our Saint remained in that house, an accomplished model of all virtues, till her parents married her to Henry, son of Otho, Duke of Saxony, in 913, who was afterwards chosen king of Germany. He was a pious and victorious prince, and very tender of his subjects. Whilst by his arms he checked the insolence of the Hungarians and Danes, and enlarged his dominions by adding to them Bavaria, Maud gained domestic victories over her spiritual enemies more worthy of a Christian and far greater in the eyes of Heaven. She nourished the precious seeds of devotion and humility in her heart by assiduous prayer and meditation. It was her delight to visit, comfort, and exhort the sick and the afflicted; to serve and instruct the poor, and to afford her charitable succor to prisoners. Her husband, edified by her example, concurred with her in every pious undertaking which she projected. After twenty-three years' marriage God was pleased to call the king to himself, in 936. Maud, during his sickness, went to the church to pour forth her soul in prayer for him at the foot of the altar. As soon as she understood, by the tears and cries of the people, that he had expired, she called for a priest that was fasting to offer the holy sacrifice for his soul. She had three sons: Otho, afterwards emperor; Henry, Duke of Bavaria; and St. Brunn, Archbishop of Cologne. Otho was crowned king of Germany in 937, and emperor at Rome in 962, after his victories over the Bohemians and Lombards. The two oldest sons conspired to strip Maud of her dowry, on the unjust pretence that she had squandered the revenues of the state on the poor. The unnatural princes at length repented of their injustice, and restored to her all that had been taken from her. She then became more liberal in her alms than ever, and founded many churches, with five monasteries. In her last sickness she made her confession to her grandson William, the Archbishop of Mentz, who yet died twelve days before her, on his road home. She again made a public confession before the priests and monks of the place, received a second time the last sacraments, and, lying on a sack-cloth, with ashes on her head, died on the 14th of March in 968.

Reflection.—The beginning of true virtue is most ardently to desire it, and to ask it of God with the utmost assiduity and earnestness. Fervent prayer, holy meditation, and reading pious books, are the principal means by which this virtue is to be constantly improved, and the interior life of the soul to be strengthened.

March 15.—ST. ZACHARY, Pope.

ST. ZACHARY succeeded Gregory III., in 741, and was a man of singular meekness and goodness. He loved the clergy and people of Rome to that degree that he hazarded his life for them on occasion of the troubles which Italy fell into by the rebellion of the Dukes of Spoleto and Benevento against King Luitprand. Out of respect to his sanctity and dignity, that king restored to the Church of Rome all the places which belonged to it, and sent back the captives without ransom. The Lombards were moved to tears at the devotion with which they heard him perform the divine service. The zeal and prudence of this holy Pope appeared in many wholesome regulations which he had made to reform or settle the discipline and peace of several churches. St. Boniface, the Apostle of Germany, wrote to him against a certain priest named Virgilius, that he labored to sow the seeds of discord between him and Odilo, Duke of Bavaria, and taught, besides, many errors. Zachary ordered that Virgilius should be sent to Rome, that his doctrine might be examined. It seems that he cleared himself; for we find this same Virgilius soon after made Bishop of Salzburg. Certain Venetian merchants having bought at Rome many slaves to sell to the Moors in Africa, St. Zachary forbade such an iniquitous traffic, and, paying the merchants their price, gave the slaves their liberty. He adorned Rome with sacred buildings, and with great foundations in favor of the poor and pilgrims, and gave every year a considerable sum to furnish oil for the lamps in St. Peter's Church. He died in 752, in the month of March.

March 16.—STS. ABRAHAM and MARY.

ABRAHAM was a rich nobleman of Edessa. At his parents' desire he married, but escaped to a cell near the city as soon as the feast was over. He walled up the cell-door, leaving only a small window through which he received his food. There for fifty years he sang God's praises and implored mercy for himself and for all men. The wealth which fell to him on his parents' death he gave to the poor. As many sought him for advice and consolation, the Bishop of Edessa, in spite of his humility, ordained him priest. St. Abraham was sent, soon after his ordination, to an idolatrous city which had hitherto been deaf to every messenger. He was insulted, beaten, and three times banished, but he returned each time with fresh zeal. For three years he pleaded with God for those souls, and in the end prevailed. Every citizen came to him for Baptism. After providing for their spiritual needs he went back to his cell more than ever convinced of the power of prayer. His brother died, leaving an only daughter, Mary, to the Saint's care. He placed her in a cell near his own, and devoted himself to training her in perfection. After twenty years of innocence she fell, and fled in despair to a distant city, where she drowned the voice of conscience in sin. The Saint and his friend St. Ephrem prayed earnestly for her during two years. Then he went disguised to seek the lost sheep, and had the joy of bringing her back to the desert a true penitent. She received the gift of miracles, and her countenance after death shone as the sun. St. Abraham died five years before her, about 360. All Edessa came for his last blessing and to secure his relics.

Reflection.—Oh, that we realized the omnipotence of prayer! Every soul was created to glorify God eternally; and it is in the power of every one to add by the salvation of his neighbor to the glory of God. Let us make good use of this talent of prayer, lest our brother's blood be required of us at the last.

March 17.—ST. PATRICK, Bishop, Apostle of Ireland.

IF the virtue of children reflects an honor on their parents, much more justly is the name of St. Patrick rendered illustrious by the innumerable lights of sanctity with which the Church of Ireland shone during many ages, and by the colonies of Saints with which it peopled many foreign countries; for, under God, its inhabitants derived from their glorious apostle the streams of that eminent sanctity by which they were long conspicuous to the whole world. St. Patrick was born towards the close of the fourth century, in a village called Bonaven Taberniæ, which seems to be the town of Kilpatrick, on the mouth of the river Clyde, in Scotland, between Dumbarton and Glasgow. He calls himself both a Briton and a Roman, or of a mixed extraction, and says his father was of a good family named Calphurnius, and a denizen of a neighboring city of the Romans, who not long after abandoned Britain, in 409. Some writers call his mother Conchessa, and say she was niece to St. Martin of Tours.

In his sixteenth year he was carried into captivity by certain barbarians, who took him into Ireland, where he was obliged to keep cattle on the mountains and in the forests, in hunger and nakedness, amidst snow, rain, and ice. Whilst he lived in this suffering condition, God had pity on his soul, and quickened him to a sense of his duty by the impulse of a strong interior grace. The young man had recourse to Him with his whole heart in fervent prayer and fasting; and from that time faith and the love of God acquired continually new strength in his tender soul. After six months spent in slavery under the same master, St. Patrick was admonished by God in a dream to return to his own country, and informed that a ship was then ready to sail thither. He went at once to the sea-coast, though at a great distance, and found the vessel; but could not obtain his passage, probably for want of money. The Saint returned towards his hut, praying as he went; but the sailors, though pagans, called him back and took him on board. After three days' sail they made land, but wandered twenty-seven days through deserts, and were a long while distressed for want of provisions, finding nothing to eat. Patrick had often spoken to the company on the infinite power of God; they therefore asked him why he did not pray for relief. Animated by a strong faith, he assured them that if they would address themselves with their whole hearts to the true God He would hear and succor them. They did so, and on the same day met with a herd of swine. From that time provisions never failed them, till on the twenty-seventh day they came into a country that was cultivated and inhabited.

Some years afterwards he was again led captive, but recovered his liberty after two months. When he was at home with his parents, God manifested to him, by divers visions, that He destined him to the great work of the conversion of Ireland. The writers of his life say that after his second captivity he travelled into Gaul and Italy, and saw St. Martin, St. Germanus of Auxerre, and Pope Celestine, and that he received his mission and the apostolical benediction from this Pope, who died in 432. It is certain that he spent many years in preparing himself for his sacred calling. Great opposition was made against his episcopal consecration and mission, both by his own relatives and by the clergy. These made him great offers in order to detain him among them, and endeavored to affright him by exaggerating the dangers to which he exposed himself amidst the enemies of the Romans and Britons, who did not know God. All these temptations threw the Saint into great perplexities; but the Lord, Whose will he consulted by earnest prayer, supported him, and he persevered in his resolution. He forsook his family, sold his birthright and dignity, to serve strangers, and consecrated his soul to God, to carry His name to the ends of the earth. In this disposition he passed into Ireland, to preach the Gospel, where the worship of idols still generally reigned. He devoted himself entirely to the salvation of these barbarians. He travelled over the whole island, penetrating into the remotest corners, and such was the fruit of his preachings and sufferings that he baptized an infinite number of people. He ordained everywhere clergymen, induced women to live in holy widowhood and continence, consecrated virgins to Christ, and instituted monks. He took nothing from the many thousands whom he baptized, and often gave back the little presents which some laid on the altar, choosing rather to mortify the fervent than to scandalize the weak or the infidels. He gave freely of his own, however, both to pagans and Christians, distributed large alms to the poor in the provinces where he passed, made presents to the kings, judging that necessary for the progress of the Gospel, and maintained and educated many children, whom he trained up to serve at the altar. The happy success of his labors cost him many persecutions.

A certain prince named Corotick, a Christian in name only, disturbed the peace of his flock. This tyrant, having made a descent into Ireland, plundered the country where St. Patrick had been just conferring confirmation on a great number of neophytes, who were yet in their white garments after Baptism. Corotick massacred many, and carried away others, whom he sold to the infidel Picts or Scots. The next day the Saint sent the barbarian a letter entreating him to restore the Christian captives, and at least part of the booty he had taken, that the poor people might not perish for want, but was only answered by railleries. The Saint, therefore, wrote with his own hand a letter. In it he styles himself a sinner and an ignorant man; he declares, nevertheless, that he is established Bishop of Ireland, and pronounces Corotick and the other parricides and accomplices separated from him and from Jesus Christ, Whose place he holds, forbidding any to eat with them, or to receive their alms, till they should have satisfied God by the tears of sincere penance, and restored the servants of Jesus Christ to their liberty. This letter expresses his most tender love for his flock, and his grief for those who had been slain, yet mingled with joy because they reign with the prophets, apostles, and martyrs. Jocelin assures us that Corotick was overtaken by the divine vengeance.

St. Patrick held several councils to settle the discipline of the Church which he had planted. St. Bernard and the tradition of the country testify that St. Patrick fixed his metropolitan see at Armagh. He established some other bishops, as appears by his Council and other monuments. He not only converted the whole country by his preaching and wonderful miracles, but also cultivated this vineyard with so fruitful a benediction and increase from heaven as to render Ireland a most flourishing garden in the Church of God, and a country of Saints.

Many particulars are related of the labors of St. Patrick, which we pass over. In the first year of his mission he attempted to preach Christ in the general assembly of the kings and states of all Ireland, held yearly at Tara, the residence of the chief king, styled the monarch of the whole island, and the principal seat of the Druids, or priests, and their paganish rites. The son of Neill, the chief monarch, declared himself against the preacher; however, Patrick converted several, and, on his road to that place, the father of St. Benignus, his immediate successor in the see of Armagh. He afterwards converted and baptized the kings of Dublin and Munster, and the seven sons of the king of Connaught, with the greatest part of their subjects, and before his death almost the whole island. He founded a monastery at Armagh; another called Domnach-Padraig, or Patrick's Church; also a third, named Sabhal-Padraig; and filled the country with churches and schools of piety and learning, the reputation of which, for the three succeeding centuries, drew many foreigners into Ireland. He died and was buried at Down in Ulster. His body was found there in a church of his name in 1185, and translated to another part of the same church.

Ireland is the nursery whence St. Patrick sent forth his missionaries and teachers. Glastonbury and Lindisfarne, Ripon and Malmesbury, bear testimony to the labors of

Irish priests and bishops for the conversion of England.
Iona is to this day the most venerated spot in Scotland.
Columban, Fiacre, Gall, and many others evangelized the
"rough places" of France and Switzerland. America
and Australia, in modern times, owe their Christianity to
the faith and zeal of the sons and daughters of St. Patrick.

Reflection.—By the instrumentality of St. Patrick the
Faith is now as fresh in Ireland, even in this cold nine-
teenth century, as when it was first planted. Ask him to
obtain for you the special grace of his children — to prefer the loss of every earthly good to the least compromise
in matters of faith.

March 18.—ST. CYRIL OF JERUSALEM.

CYRIL was born at or near the city of Jerusalem, about
the year 315. He was ordained priest by St. Maximus, who gave him the important charge of instructing
and preparing the candidates for Baptism. This charge
he held for several years, and we still have one series of
his instructions, given in the year 347 or 348. They are
of singular interest as being the earliest record of the
systematic teaching of the Church on the creed and sacraments, and as having been given in the church built by
Constantine on Mount Calvary. They are solid, simple,
profound; saturated with Holy Scripture; exact, precise,
and terse; and, as a witness and exposition of the Catholic
faith, invaluable. On the death of St. Maximus, Cyril
was chosen Bishop of Jerusalem. At the beginning of
his episcopate a cross was seen in the air reaching from
Mount Calvary to Mount Olivet, and so bright that it
shone at noonday. St. Cyril gave an account of it to the
emperor; and the faithful regarded it as a presage of
victory over the Arian heretics. While Cyril was bishop,
the apostate Julian resolved to falsify the words of Our
Lord by rebuilding the Temple at Jerusalem. He employed the power and resources of a Roman emperor; the
Jews thronged enthusiastically to him and gave munificently. But Cyril was unmoved. "The word of God

abides," he said; "one stone shall not be laid on another."
When the attempt was made, a heathen writer tells us
that horrible flames came forth from the earth, rendering
the place inaccessible to the scorched and scared workmen.
The attempt was made again and again, and then abandoned in despair. Soon after, the emperor perished mis-
erably in a war against the Persians, and the Church had
rest. Like the other great bishops of his time, Cyril was
persecuted, and driven once and again from his see; but
on the death of the Arian Emperor Valens he returned to
Jerusalem. He was present at the second General Council at Constantinople, and died in peace in 386, after a
troubled episcopate of thirty-five years.

Reflection.—"As a stout staff," says St. John Chrysostom, "supports the trembling limbs of a feeble old man,
so does faith sustain our vacillating mind, lest it be tossed
about by sinful hesitation and perplexity."

March 19.—ST. JOSEPH, Spouse of the Blessed Virgin and Patron of the Universal Church.

ST. JOSEPH was by birth of the royal family of David,
but was living in humble obscurity as a carpenter
when God raised him to the highest sanctity, and fitted
him to be the spouse of His Virgin Mother, and foster-
father and guardian of the Incarnate Word. Joseph, says
the Holy Scripture, was a just man; he was innocent and
pure, as became the husband of Mary; he was gentle and
tender, as one worthy to be named the father of Jesus; he
was prudent and a lover of silence, as became the master
of the holy house; above all, he was faithful and obedient
to divine calls. His conversation was with angels rather
than with men. When he learned that Mary bore within
her womb the Lord of heaven, he feared to take her as
his wife; but an angel bade him fear not, and all doubts
vanished. When Herod sought the life of the divine Infant, an angel told Joseph in a dream to fly with the Child
and His Mother into Egypt. Joseph at once arose and
obeyed. This sudden and unexpected flight must have
exposed Joseph to many inconveniences and sufferings in

so long a journey with a little babe and a tender virgin,
the greater part of the way being through deserts and
among strangers; yet he alleges no excuses, nor inquires at
what time they were to return. St. Chrysostom observes
that God treats thus all His servants, sending them frequent trials to clear their hearts from the rust of self-love,
but intermixing seasons of consolation. "Joseph," says
he, "is anxious on seeing the Virgin with child; an angel
removes that fear. He rejoices at the Child's birth, but a
great fear succeeds: the furious king seeks to destroy the
Child, and the whole city is in an uproar to take away His
life. This is followed by another joy, the adoration of the
Magi; a new sorrow then arises: he is ordered to fly into
a foreign unknown country, without help or acquaintance."
It is the opinion of the Fathers that upon their entering
Egypt, at the presence of the child Jesus, all the oracles of
that superstitious country were struck dumb, and the
statues of their gods trembled and in many places fell to
the ground. The Fathers also attribute to this holy visit
the spiritual benediction poured on that country, which
made it for many ages most fruitful in Saints. After the
death of King Herod, of which St. Joseph was informed in
another vision, God ordered him to return with the Child
and His Mother into the land of Israel, which our Saint
readily obeyed. But when he arrived in Judea, hearing
that Archelaus had succeeded Herod in that part of the
country, and apprehensive that he might be infected with
his father's vices, he feared on that account to settle there,
as he would otherwise probably have done for the education
of the Child; and therefore, being directed by God in
another vision, he retired into the dominions of Herod
Antipas, in Galilee, to his former habitation in Nazareth.
St. Joseph, being a strict observer of the Mosaic law, in
conformity to its direction annually repaired to Jerusalem
to celebrate the Passover. Our Saviour, now in the twelfth
year of His age, accompanied His parents thither. Having
performed the usual ceremonies of the feast, they were returning with many of their neighbors and acquaintances
towards Galilee; and never doubting but that Jesus was
with some of the company, they travelled on for a whole

day's journey before they discovered that He was not with
them. But when night came on and they could hear no
tidings of Him among their kindred and acquaintance,
they, in the deepest affliction, returned with the utmost
speed to Jerusalem. After an anxious search of three days
they found Him in the Temple, discoursing with the
learned doctors of the law, and asking them such questions
as raised the admiration of all that heard Him, and made
them astonished at the ripeness of His understanding; nor
were His parents less surprised on this occasion. When
His Mother told Him with what grief and earnestness they
had sought Him, and asked, " Son, why hast Thou thus
dealt with us? behold Thy Father and I sought Thee in
great affliction of mind," she received for answer, " How is
it that you sought Me? did you not know that I must be
about My Father's business? " But though thus staying
in the Temple unknown to His parents, in all other things
He was obedient to them, returning with them to Nazareth,
and there living in all dutiful subjection to them. As no
further mention is made of St. Joseph, he must have died
before the marriage of Cana and the beginning of our
divine Saviour's ministry. We cannot doubt that he had
the happiness of Jesus and Mary attending at his death,
praying by him, assisting and comforting him in his last
moments; whence he is particularly invoked for the great
grace of a happy death and the spiritual presence of Jesus
in that hour.

Reflection.— St. Joseph, the shadow of the Eternal
Father upon earth, the protector of Jesus in His home at
Nazareth, and a lover of all children for the sake of the
Holy Child, should be the chosen guardian and pattern of
every true Christian family.

March 20.—ST. WULFRAN, Archbishop.

H IS father was an officer in the armies of King Dagobert, and the Saint spent some years in the court
of King Clotaire III. and of his mother, St. Bathildes, but
occupied his heart only on God, despising worldly great-

ness as empty and dangerous, and daily advancing in
virtue. His estate of Maurilly he bestowed on the Abbey
of Fontenelle, or St. Vandrille, in Normandy. He was
chosen and consecrated Archbishop of Sens in 682, which
diocese he governed two years and a half with great zeal
and sanctity. A tender compassion for the blindness of
the idolaters of Friesland, and the example of the English
zealous preachers in those parts, moved him to resign his
bishopric, with proper advice, and after a retreat at Fontenelle to enter Friesland in quality of a poor missionary
priest. He baptized great multitudes, among them a son
of King Radbod, and drew the people from the barbarous
custom of sacrificing men to idols. On a certain occasion,
one Ovon having been selected as a victim of a sacrifice to
the heathen gods, St. Wulfran earnestly begged his life of
King Radbod; but the people ran tumultuously to the
palace, and would not suffer what they called a sacrilege.
After many words they consented, but on condition that
Wulfran's God should save Ovon's life. The Saint betook
himself to prayer; the man, after hanging on the gibbet
two hours, and being left for dead, fell to the ground by
the breaking of the cord; being found alive he was given to
the Saint, and became a monk and priest at Fontenelle.
Wulfran also miraculously rescued two children from being
drowned in honor of the idols. Radbod, who had been an
eye-witness to this last miracle, promised to become a
Christian; but as he was going to step into the baptismal
font he asked where the great number of his ancestors and
nobles were in the next world. The Saint replied that hell
is the portion of all who die guilty of idolatry; at which
the prince refused to be baptized, saying he would go with
the greater number. This tyrant sent afterwards to St.
Willibrord to treat with him about his conversion, but
before the arrival of the Saint was found dead. St. Wulfran retired to Fontenelle that he might prepare himself
for death, and expired there on the 20th of April, 720.

Reflection.— In every age the Catholic Church is a missionary church. She has received the world for her inheritance, and in our own days many missioners have
watered with their blood the lands in which they labored.

Help the propagation of the faith by alms, and above all by prayers. You will quicken your own faith and gain a part in the merits of the glorious apostolate.

March 21.—ST. BENEDICT, Abbot.

ST. BENEDICT, blessed by grace and in name, was born of a noble Italian family about 480. When a boy he was sent to Rome, and there placed in the public schools. Scared by the licentiousness of the Roman youth, he fled to the desert mountains of Subiaco, and was directed by the Holy Spirit into a cave, deep, craggy, and almost inaccessible. He lived there for three years, unknown to any one save the holy monk Romanus, who clothed him with the monastic habit and brought him food. But the fame of his sanctity soon gathered disciples round him. The rigor of his rule, however, drew on him the hatred of some of the monks, and one of them mixed poison with the abbot's drink; but when the Saint made the sign of the cross on the poisoned bowl, it broke and fell in pieces to the ground. After he had built twelve monasteries at Subiaco, he removed to Monte Casino, where he founded an abbey in which he wrote his rule and lived until death. By prayer he did all things: wrought miracles, saw visions, and prophesied. A peasant, whose boy had just died, ran in anguish to St. Benedict, crying out, " Give me back my son! " The monks joined the poor man in his entreaties; but the Saint replied, " Such miracles are not for us to work, but for the blessed apostles. Why will you lay upon me a burden which my weakness cannot bear? " Moved at length by compassion he knelt down and, prostrating himself upon the body of the child, prayed earnestly. Then rising, he cried out, " Behold not, O Lord, my sins, but the faith of this man, who desireth the life of his son, and restore to the body that soul which Thou hast taken away." Hardly had he spoken when the child's body began to tremble, and taking it by the hand he restored it alive to its father. Six days before his death he ordered his grave to be opened, and fell ill of a fever. On the sixth day he requested to be borne into the chapel, and, having received the body and blood of Christ, with hands uplifted, and leaning on one of his disciples, he calmly expired in prayer on the 21st of March, 543.

Reflection.— The Saints never feared to undertake any work, however arduous, for God, because, distrusting self, they relied for assistance and support wholly upon prayer.

March 22.—ST. CATHARINE OF SWEDEN,
Virgin.

ST. CATHARINE was daughter of Ulpho, Prince of Nericia in Sweden, and of St. Bridget. The love of God seemed almost to prevent in her the use of her reason. At seven years of age she was placed in the nunnery of Risburgh, and educated in piety under the care of the holy abbess of that house. Being very beautiful, she was, by her father, contracted in marriage to Egard, a young nobleman of great virtue; but the virgin persuaded him to join with her in making a mutual vow of perpetual chastity. By her discourses he became desirous only of heavenly graces, and, to draw them down upon his soul more abundantly, he readily acquiesced in the proposal. The happy couple, having but one heart and one desire, by a holy emulation excited each other to prayer, mortification, and works of charity. After the death of her father, St. Catharine, out of devotion to the Passion of Christ and to the relics of the martyrs, accompanied her mother in her pilgrimages and practices of devotion and penance. After her mother's death at Rome, in 1373, Catharine returned to Sweden, and died abbess of Vadzstena, or Vatzen, on the 24th of March in 1381. For the last twenty-five years of her life she every day purified her soul by a sacramental confession of her sins.

Reflection.— Whoever has to dwell in the world stands in need of great prudence; the Holy Scripture itself assures us that " the knowledge of the holy is prudence."

March 23.—STS. VICTORIAN AND OTHERS,
Martyrs.

HUNERIC, the Arian king of the Vandals in Africa, succeeded his father Genseric in 477. He behaved himself at first with moderation towards the Catholics, but in 480 he began a grievous persecution of the clergy and holy virgins, which in 484 became general, and vast numbers of Catholics were put to death. Victorian, one of the principal lords of the kingdom, had been made governor of Carthage, with the Roman title of Proconsul. He was the wealthiest subject of the king, who placed great confidence in him, and he had ever behaved with an inviolable fidelity. The king, after he had published his cruel edicts, sent a message to the proconsul, promising, if he would conform to his religion, to heap on him the greatest wealth and the highest honors which it was in the power of a prince to bestow. The proconsul, who amidst the glittering pomps of the world perfectly understood its emptiness, made this generous answer: "Tell the king that I trust in Christ. His Majesty may condemn me to any torments, but I shall never consent to renounce the Catholic Church, in which I have been baptized. Even if there were no life after this, I would never be ungrateful and perfidious to God, Who has granted me the happiness of knowing Him, and bestowed on me His most precious graces." The tyrant became furious at this answer, nor can the tortures be imagined which he caused the Saint to endure. Victorian suffered them with joy, and amidst them finished his glorious martyrdom. The Roman Martyrology joins with him on this day four others who were crowned in the same persecution. Two brothers, who were apprehended for the faith, had promised each other, if possible, to die together; and they begged of God, as a favor, that they might both suffer the same torments. The persecutors hung them in the air with great weights at their feet. One of them, under the excess of pain, begged to be taken down for a little ease. His brother, fearing that this might move him to deny his faith, cried out from the rack, " God forbid, dear brother, that you should ask such

a thing. Is this what we promised to Jesus Christ?"
The other was so wonderfully encouraged that he cried out,
"No, no; I ask not to be released; increase my tortures,
exert all your cruelties till they are exhausted upon me."
They were then burned with red-hot plates of iron, and tormented so long that the executioners at last left them, saying, "Everybody follows their example! no one now em-
braces our religion." This they said chiefly because, notwithstanding these brothers had been so long and so grievously tormented, there were no scars or bruises to be seen
upon them. Two merchants of Carthage, who both bore
the name of Frumentius, suffered martyrdom about the
same time. Among many glorious confessors at that time,
one Liberatus, an eminent physician, was sent into banishment with his wife. He only grieved to see his infant
children torn from him. His wife checked his tears by
these words: "Think no more of them: Jesus Christ Himself will have care of them and protect their souls." Whilst
in prison she was told that her husband had conformed.
Accordingly, when she met him at the bar before the judge,
she upbraided him in open court for having basely abandoned God; but discovered by his answer that a cheat had
been put upon her to deceive her into her ruin. Twelve
young children, when dragged away by the persecutors,
held their companions by the knees till they were torn away
by violence. They were most cruelly beaten and scourged
every day for a long time; yet by God's grace every one of
them persevered in the faith to the end of the persecution.

March 24.—ST. SIMON, Infant Martyr.

"HAIL, flowers of the martyrs!" the Church sings in
her Office of the Holy Innocents, who were the first
to die for Christ; and in every age mere children and
infants have gloriously confessed His name. In 1472 the
Jews in the city of Trent determined to vent their hate
against the Crucified by slaying a Christian child at the
coming Passover; and Tobias, one of their number, was
deputed to entrap a victim. He found a bright, smiling
boy named Simon playing outside his home, with no one
guarding him. Tobias patted the little fellow's cheek, and

coaxed him to take his hand. The boy, who was not two years old, did so; but he began to call and cry for his mother when he found himself being led from home. Then Tobias gave him a bright coin to look at, and with many kind caresses silenced his grief, and conducted him securely to his house. At midnight on Holy Thursday the work of butchery began. Having gagged his mouth, they held his arms in the form of a cross, while they pierced his tender body with awls and bodkins in blasphemous mockery of the sufferings of Jesus Christ. After an hour's torture the little martyr lifted his eyes to heaven and gave up his innocent soul. The Jews cast his body into the river; but their crime was discovered and punished, while the holy relics were enshrined in St. Peter's Church at Trent, where they have worked many miracles.

WILLIAM OF NORWICH is another of these children martyrs. His parents were simple country folk, but his mother was taught by a vision to expect a Saint in her son. As a boy he fasted thrice a week and prayed constantly, and he was only an apprentice twelve years of age, at a tanner's in Norwich, when he won his crown. A little before Easter, 1137, he was enticed into a Jew's house, and was there gagged, bound, and crucified in hatred of Christ. Five years passed before the body was found, when it was buried as a saintly relic in the cathedral churchyard. A rose-tree planted hard by flowered miraculously in midwinter, and many sick persons were healed at his shrine.[1]

Reflection.— Learn from the infant martyrs that, however weak you may be, you still can suffer for Christ's sake.

March 25.—THE ANNUNCIATION OF THE BLESSED VIRGIN MARY.

THIS great festival takes its name from the happy tidings brought by the angel Gabriel to the Blessed Virgin, concerning the Incarnation of the Son of God. It commemorates the most important embassy that was ever

---

[1] It must not be thought that these singular and extraordinary instances establish the charge that the slaying of Christian children is part of the Jewish ritual. This accusation against the Jews has been proved to be false.

known: an embassy sent by the King of kings, performed by one of the chief princes of His heavenly court; directed, not to the great ones of this earth, but to a poor, unknown virgin, who, being endowed with the most angelic purity of soul and body, being withal perfectly humble and devoted to God, was greater in His eyes than the mightiest monarch in the world. When the Son of God became man, He could have taken upon Him our nature without the cooperation of any creature; but He was pleased to be born of a woman. In the choice of her whom He raised to this most sublime of all dignities, He pitched upon the one who, by the riches of His grace and virtues, was of all others the most holy and the most perfect. The design of this embassy of the archangel is to give a Saviour to the world, a victim of propitiation to the sinner, a model to the just, a son to this Virgin, remaining still a virgin, and a new nature to the Son of God, the nature of man, capable of suffering pain and anguish in order to satisfy God's justice for our transgressions.

When the angel appeared to Mary and addressed her, the Blessed Virgin was troubled: not at the angel's appearance, says St. Ambrose, for heavenly visions and a commerce with the blessed spirits had been familiar to her; but what alarmed her, he says, was the angel's appearing in human form, in the shape of a young man. What might add to her fright on the occasion was his addressing her in words of praise. Mary, guarded by her modesty, is in confusion at expressions of this sort, and dreads the least appearance of deluding flattery. Such high commendations make her cautious how she answers, till in silence she has more fully considered of the matter: " She revolved in her mind," says St. Luke, " what manner of salutation this should be." Ah, what numbers of innocent souls have been corrupted for want of using the like precautions!

The angel, to calm her, says: " Fear not, Mary, for thou hast found favor before God." He then informs her that she is to conceive and bring forth a Son Whose name shall be Jesus, Who shall be great, and the Son of the Most High, and possessed of the throne of David, her illustrious ancestor. Mary, out of a just concern to know how she may comply with the will of God without prejudice to her vow of virginity, inquires, "How shall this be?" Nor does she give her consent till the heavenly messenger acquaints her that it is to be a work of the Holy Ghost, who, in making her fruitful, will not intrench in the least upon her virginal purity.

In submission, therefore, to God's will, without any further inquiries, she expresses her assent in these humble but powerful words: "Behold the handmaid of the Lord; be it done to me according to Thy word." What faith and confidence does her answer express! what profound humility and perfect obedience!

Reflection.— From the example of the Blessed Virgin in this mystery, how ardent a love ought we to conceive of purity and humility! The Holy Ghost is invited by purity to dwell in souls, but is chased away by the filth of the contrary vice. Humility is the foundation of a spiritual life. By it Mary was prepared for the extraordinary graces and all virtues with which she was enriched, and for the eminent dignity of Mother of God.

March 26.—ST. LUDGER, Bishop.

S T. LUDGER was born in Friesland about the year 743. His father, a nobleman of the first rank, at the child's own request, committed him very young to the care of St. Gregory, the disciple of St. Boniface, and his successors in the government of the see of Utrecht. Gregory educated him in his monastery and gave him the clerical tonsure. Ludger, desirous of further improvement, passed over into England, and spent four years and a half under Alcuin, who was rector of a famous school at York. In 773 he returned home, and St. Gregory dying in 776, his successor, Alberic, compelled our Saint to receive the holy order of priesthood, and employed him for several years in preaching the Word of God in Friesland, where he converted great numbers, founded several monasteries, and built many churches. The pagan Saxons ravaging the country, Ludger travelled to Rome to consult Pope Adrian II. what course to take, and what he thought God required

of him. He then retired for three years and a half to
Monte Casino, where he wore the habit of the Order and
conformed to the practice of the rule during his stay, but
made no religious vows. In 787, Charlemagne overcame
the Saxons and conquered Friesland and the coast of the
Germanic Ocean as far as Denmark. Ludger, hearing this,
returned into East Friesland, where he converted the
Saxons to the Faith, as he also did the province of West-
phalia. He founded the monastery of Werden, twenty-
nine miles from Cologne. In 802, Hildebald, Archbishop
of Cologne, not regarding his strenuous resistance, ordained
him Bishop of Munster. He joined in his diocese five can-
tons of Friesland which he had converted, and also
founded the monastery of Helmstad in the duchy of
Brunswick.

Being accused to the Emperor Charlemagne of wasting
his income and neglecting the embellishment of churches,
this prince ordered him to appear at court. The morning
after his arrival the emperor's chamberlain brought him
word that his attendance was required. The Saint, being
then at his prayers, told the officer that he would follow
him as soon as he had finished them. He was sent for
three several times before he was ready, which the courtiers represented as a contempt of his Majesty, and the emperor, with some emotion, asked him why he had made
him wait so long, though he had sent for him so often.
The bishop answered that though he had the most profound
respect for his Majesty, yet God was infinitely above him;
that whilst we are occupied with Him, it is our duty to
forget everything else. This answer made such an impression on the emperor that he dismissed him with honor
and disgraced his accusers. St. Ludger was favored with
the gifts of miracles and prophecy. His last sickness,
though violent, did not hinder him from continuing his
functions to the very last day of his life, which was Passion Sunday, on which day he preached very early in the
morning, said Mass towards nine, and preached again before night, foretelling to those that were about him that
he should die the following night, and fixing upon a place
in his monastery of Werden where he chose to be interred.
He died accordingly on the 26th of March, at midnight.

Reflection.—Prayer is an action so sublime and super-natural that the Church in her Canonical Hours teaches us to begin it by a fervent petition of grace to perform it well. What an insolence and mockery is it to join with this petition an open disrespect and a neglect of all necessary precautions against distractions! We ought never to appear before God, to tender Him our homages or supplications, without trembling, and without being deaf to all creatures and shutting all our senses to every object that can distract our minds from God.

March 27.—ST. JOHN OF EGYPT.

TILL he was twenty-five, John worked as a carpenter with his father. Then feeling a call from God, he left the world and committed himself to a holy solitary in the desert. His master tried his spirit by many unreasonable commands, bidding him roll the hard rocks, tend dead trees, and the like. John obeyed in all things with the simplicity of a child. After a careful training of sixteen years he withdrew to the top of a steep cliff to think only of God and his soul. The more he knew of himself, the more he distrusted himself. For the last fifty years, therefore, he never saw women, and seldom men. The result of this vigilance and purity was threefold: a holy joy and cheerfulness which consoled all who conversed with him; perfect obedience to superiors; and, in return for this, authority over creatures, whom he had forsaken for the Creator. St. Augustine tells us of his appearing in a vision to a holy woman, whose sight he had restored, to avoid seeing her face to face. Devils assailed him continually, but John never ceased his prayer. From his long communings with God, he turned to men with gifts of healing and prophecy. Twice each week he spoke through a window with those who came to him, blessing oil for their sick and predicting things to come. A deacon came to him in disguise, and he reverently kissed his hand. To the Emperor Theodosius he foretold his future victories and the time of his death. The three last days of his life John gave wholly to God: on the third he was found on his knees as if in prayer, but his soul was with the blessed. He died in 394.

Reflection.— The Saints examine themselves by the perfections of God, and do penance. We judge our conduct by the standard of other men, and rest satisfied with it. Yet it is by the divine holiness alone that we shall be judged when we die.

March 28.—ST. GONTRAN, King.

ST. GONTRAN was the son of King Clotaire, and grandson of Clovis I. and St. Clotildis. Being the second son, whilst his brothers Charibert reigned at Paris, and Sigebert in Ostrasia, residing at Metz, he was crowned king of Orleans and Burgundy in 561, making Chalons his capital. When compelled to take up arms against his ambitious brothers and the Lombards, he made no other use of his victories, under the conduct of a brave general called Mommol, than to give peace to his dominions. The crimes in which the barbarous manners of his nation involved him he effaced by tears of repentance. The prosperity of his reign, both in peace and war, condemns those who think that human policy cannot be modelled by the maxims of the Gospel, whereas nothing can render a government more flourishing. He always treated the pastors of the Church with respect and veneration. He was the protector of the oppressed, and the tender parent of his subjects. He gave the greatest attention to the care of the sick. He fasted, prayed, wept, and offered himself to God night and day as a victim ready to be sacrificed on the altar of His justice, to avert His indignation which he believed he himself had provoked and drawn down upon his innocent people. He was a severe punisher of crimes in his officers and others, and, by many wholesome regulations, restrained the barbarous licentiousness of his troops; but no man was more ready to forgive offences against his own person. With royal magnificence he built and endowed many churches and monasteries. This good king died on the 23rd of March in 593, in the sixty-eighth year of his age, having reigned thirty-one years and some months.

Reflection.— There is no means of salvation more reliable than the practice of mercy, since Our Lord has said it: " Blessed are the merciful, for they shall find mercy."

March 29.—STS. JONAS, BARACHISIUS, and their Companions, Martyrs.

KING SAPOR, of Persia, in the eighteenth year of his reign, raised a bloody persecution against the Christians, and laid waste their churches and monasteries. Jonas and Barachisius, two brothers of the city Beth-Asa, hearing that several Christians lay under sentence of death at Hubaham, went thither to encourage and serve them. Nine of that number received the crown of martyrdom. After their execution, Jonas and Barachisius were apprehended for having exhorted them to die. The president entreated the two brothers to obey the king of Persia, and to worship the sun, moon, fire, and water. Their answer was, that it was more reasonable to obey the immortal King of heaven and earth than a mortal prince. Jonas was beaten with knotty clubs and with rods, and next set in a frozen pond, with a cord tied to his foot. Barachisius had two red-hot iron plates and two red-hot hammers applied under each arm, and melted lead dropped into his nostrils and eyes; after which he was carried to prison, and there hung up by one foot. Despite these cruel tortures, the two brothers remained steadfast in the Faith. New and more horrible torments were then devised under which at last they yielded up their lives, while their pure souls winged their flight to heaven, there to gain the martyr's crown, which they had so faithfully won.

Reflection.— Those powerful motives which supported the martyrs under the sharpest torments ought to inspire us with patience, resignation, and holy joy under sickness and all crosses or trials. Nothing is more heroic in the practice of Christian virtue, nothing more precious in the sight of God, than the sacrifice of patience, submission, constant fidelity, and charity in a state of suffering.

March 30.—ST. JOHN CLIMACUS.

JOHN made, while still young, such progress in learning that he was called the Scholastic. At the age of sixteen he turned from the brilliant future which lay before him, and retired to Mt. Sinai, where he put himself under the direction of a holy monk. Never was novice more fervent, more unrelaxing in his efforts for self-mastery. After four years he took the vows, and an aged abbot foretold that he would some day be one of the greatest lights of the Church. Nineteen years later, on the death of his director, he withdrew into a deeper solitude, where he studied the lives and writings of the Saints, and was raised to an unusual height of contemplation. The fame of his holiness and practical wisdom drew crowds around him for advice and consolation. For his greater profit he visited the solitudes of Egypt. At the age of seventy-five he was chosen abbot of Mt. Sinai, and there " he dwelt in the mount of God, and drew from the rich treasure of his heart priceless riches of doctrine, which he poured forth with wondrous abundance and benediction." He was induced by a brother abbot to write the rules by which he had guided his life; and his book called the *Climax, or Ladder of Perfection,* has been prized in all ages for its wisdom, its clearness, and its unction. At the end of four years he would no longer endure the honors and distractions of his office, and retired to his solitude, where he died, in 605.

Reflection.—" Cast not from thee, my brother," says the *Imitation of Christ,* " the sure hope of attaining to the spiritual life; still hast thou the time and the means."

March 31.—ST. BENJAMIN, Deacon, Martyr.

ISDEGERDES, Son of Sapor III., put a stop to the cruel persecutions against the Christians in Persia, which had been begun by Sapor II., and the Church had enjoyed twelve years' peace in that kingdom, when in 420 it was disturbed by the indiscreet zeal of Abdas, a Christian bishop, who burned down the Pyræum, or Temple of Fire, the great divinity of the Persians. King Isdegerdes thereupon demolished all the Christian churches in Persia, put to death Abdas, and raised a general persecution against the Church, which continued forty years with great fury. Isdegerdes died the year following, in 421. But his son and successor, Varanes, carried on the persecution with greater inhumanity. The very recital of the cruelties he exercised on the Christian strikes us with horror. Among the glorious champions of Christ was St. Benjamin, a deacon. The tyrant caused him to be beaten and imprisoned. He had lain a year in the dungeon, when an ambassador from the emperor obtained his release on condition that he should never speak to any of the courtiers about religion. The ambassador passed his word in his behalf that he would not; but Benjamin, who was a minister of the Gospel, declared that he should miss no opportunity of announcing Christ. The king, being informed that he still preached the Faith in his kingdom, ordered him to be apprehended, caused reeds to be run in between the nails and the flesh, both of his hands and feet, and to be thrust into other most tender parts, and drawn out again, and this to be frequently repeated with violence. Lastly, a knotty stake was thrust into his bowels, to rend and tear them, in which torment he expired in the year 424.

Reflection.— We entreat you, O most holy martyrs, who cheerfully suffered most cruel torments for God our Saviour and His love, on which account you are now most intimately and familiarly united to Him, that you pray to the Lord for us miserable sinners, covered with filth, that He infuse into us the grace of Christ, that it may enlighten our souls that we may love Him.

April 1.—ST. HUGH, Bishop.

IT was the happiness of this Saint to receive from his cradle the strongest impressions of piety by the example and care of his illustrious and holy parents. He was born at Chateau-neuf, in the territory of Valence in Dauphiné, in 1053. His father, Odilo, who served his

country in an honorable post in the army, labored by all
the means in his power to make his soldiers faithful servants of their Creator, and by severe punishments to re-
strain vice.   By the advice of his son, St. Hugh, he afterwards became a Carthusian monk, and died at the age of
a hundred, having received Extreme Unction and Viaticum
from the hands of his son.   Our Saint likewise assisted, in
her last moments, his mother, who had for many years,
under his direction, served God in her own house, by
prayer, fasting, and plenteous alms-deeds.   Hugh, from
the cradle, appeared to be a child of benediction.   He went
through his studies with great applause, and having chosen
to serve God in an ecclesiastical state, he accepted a canonry
in the cathedral of Valence.   His great sanctity and learning rendered him an ornament of that church, and he was
finally made Bishop of Grenoble.   He set himself at once
to reprove vice and to reform abuses, and so plentiful was
the benediction of Heaven upon his labors that he had the
comfort to see the face of his diocese in a short time
exceedingly changed.   After two years he privately resigned his bishopric, presuming on the tacit consent of the
Holy See, and, putting on the habit of St. Bennet, he
entered upon a novitiate in the austere abbey of Casa-Dei
in Auvergne.   There he lived a year, a perfect model of
all virtues to that house of Saints, till Pope Gregory VII.
commanded him, in virtue of holy obedience, to resume his
pastoral charge.

He earnestly solicited Pope Innocent II. for leave to
resign his bishopric, that he might die in solitude, but was
never able to obtain his request.   God was pleased to purify
his soul by a lingering illness before He called him to Himself.   Some time before his death he lost his memory for
everything but his prayers.   He closed his penitential
course on the 1st of April in 1132, wanting only two
months of being eighty years old, of which he had been
fifty-two years bishop.   Miracles attested the sanctity of
his happy death, and he was canonized by Innocent II. in
1134.

Reflection.— Let us learn from the example of the
Saints to shun the tumult of the world as much as our

circumstances will allow, and give ourselves up to the exercises of holy solitude, prayer, and pious reading.

April 2.—ST. FRANCIS OF PAULA.

AT the age of fifteen Francis left his poor home at Paula in Calabria, to live as a hermit in a cave by the sea-coast.   In time disciples gathered round him, and with them, in 1436, he founded the " Minims," so called to show that they were the least of monastic Orders.   They observed a perpetual Lent, and never touched meat, fish, eggs, or milk.   Francis himself made the rock his bed; his best garment was a hair-shirt, and boiled herbs his only fare.   As his body withered his faith grew powerful, and he " did all things in Him Who strengthened him."   He cured the sick, raised the dead, averted plagues, expelled evil spirits, and brought sinners to penance.   A famous preacher, instigated by a few misguided monks, set to work to preach against St. Francis and his miracles.   The Saint took no notice of it, and the preacher, finding that he made no way with his hearers, determined to see this poor hermit and confound him in person.   The Saint received him kindly, gave him a seat by the fire, and listened to a long exposition of his own frauds.   He then quietly took some glowing embers from the fire, and closing his hands upon them unhurt, said, " Come, Father Anthony, warm yourself, for you are shivering for want of a little charity." Father Anthony, falling at the Saint's feet, asked for pardon, and then, having received his embrace, quitted him, to become his panegyrist and attain himself to great perfection.   When the avaricious King Ferdinand of Naples offered him money for his convent, Francis told him to give it back to his oppressed subjects, and softened his heart by causing blood to flow from the ill-gotten coin. Louis XI. of France, trembling at the approach of death, sent for the poor hermit to ward off the foe whose advance neither his fortresses nor his guards could check.   Francis went by the Pope's command, and prepared the king for a holy death.   The successors of Louis showered favors on the Saint, his Order spread throughout Europe, and his

name was reverenced through the Christian world. He
died at the age of ninety-one, on Good Friday, 1507, with
the crucifix in his hand, and the last words of Jesus on his
lips, " Into Thy hands, O Lord, I commend my spirit."

Reflection.— Rely in all difficulties upon God. That
which enabled St. Francis to work miracles will in proportion do wonders for yourself, by giving you strength and
consolation.

April 3.—ST. RICHARD OF CHICHESTER.

RICHARD was born, 1197, in the little town of Wyche,
eight miles from Worcester, England. He and his
elder brother were left orphans when young, and Richard
gave up the studies which he loved, to farm his brother's
impoverished estate. His brother, in gratitude for Richard's successful care, proposed to make over to him all
his lands; but he refused both the estate and the offer of
a brilliant marriage, to study for the priesthood at Oxford. In 1235 he was appointed, for his learning and
piety, chancellor of that University, and afterwards, by
St. Edmund of Canterbury, chancellor of his diocese. He
stood by that Saint in his long contest with the king, and
accompanied him into exile. After St. Edmund's death
Richard returned to England to toil as a simple curate, but
was soon elected Bishop of Chichester in preference to the
worthless nominee of Henry III. The king in revenge refused to recognize the election, and seized the revenues of
the see. Thus Richard found himself fighting the same
battle in which St. Edmund had died. He went to Lyons,
was there consecrated by Innocent IV. in 1245, and returning to England, in spite of his poverty and the king's hostility, exercised fully his episcopal rights, and thoroughly
reformed his see. After two years his revenues were restored. Young and old loved St. Richard. He gave all he
had, and worked miracles, to feed the poor and heal the
sick; but when the rights or purity of the Church were
concerned he was inexorable. A priest of noble blood pol-
luted his office by sin; Richard deprived him of his bene-
fice, and refused the king's petition in his favor. On the

other hand, when a knight violently put a priest in prison, Richard compelled the knight to walk round the priest's church with the same log of wood on his neck to which he had chained the priest; and when the burgesses of Lewes tore a criminal from the church and hanged him, Richard made them dig up the body from its unconsecrated grave, and bear it back to the sanctuary they had violated. Richard died in 1253, while preaching, at the Pope's command, a crusade against the Saracens.

Reflection.— As a brother, as chancellor, and as bishop, St. Richard faithfully performed each duty of his state without a thought of his own interests. Neglect of duty is the first sign of that self-love which ends with the loss of grace.

April 4.—ST. ISIDORE, Archbishop.

ISIDORE was born of a ducal family, at Carthagena in Spain. His two brothers, Leander, Archbishop of Seville, Fulgentius, Bishop of Ecija, and his sister Florentina, are Saints. As a boy he despaired at his ill success in study, and ran away from school. Resting in his flight at a roadside spring, he observed a stone, which was hollowed out by the dripping water. This decided him to return, and by hard application he succeeded where he had failed. He went back to his master, and with the help of God became, even as a youth, one of the most learned men of the time. He assisted in converting Prince Recared, the leader of the Arian party; and with his aid, though at the constant peril of his own life, he expelled that heresy from Spain. Then, following a call from God, he turned a deaf ear to the entreaties of his friends, and embraced a hermit's life. Prince Recared and many of the nobles and clergy of Seville went to persuade him to come forth, and represented the needs of the times, and the good he could do, and had already done, among the people. He refused, and, as far as we can judge, that refusal gave him the necessary opportunity of acquiring the virtue and the power which afterwards made him an illustrious Bishop and Doctor of the Church. On the death of his brother Leander he was called to fill the vacant see. As a teacher, ruler, founder, and reformer, he labored not only in his own diocese, but throughout Spain, and even in foreign countries. He died in Seville on April 4, 636, and within sixteen years of his death was declared a Doctor of the Catholic Church.

Reflection.— The strength of temptation usually lies in the fact that its object is something flattering to our pride, soothing to our sloth, or in some way attractive to the meaner passions. St. Isidore teaches us to listen neither to the promptings of nature nor the plausible advice of friends when they contradict the voice of God.

April 5.—ST. VINCENT FERRER.

THIS wonderful apostle, the " Angel of the Judgment," was born at Valencia in Spain, in 1350, and at the age of eighteen professed in the Order of St. Dominic. After a brilliant course of study he became master of sacred theology. For three years he read only the Scriptures, and knew the whole Bible by heart. He converted the Jews of Valencia, and their synagogue became a church. Grief at the great schism then afflicting the Church reduced him to the point of death; but Our Lord Himself in glory bade him go forth to convert sinners, " for My judgment is nigh." This miraculous apostolate lasted twenty-one years. He preached throughout Europe, in the towns and villages of Spain, Switzerland, France, Italy, England, Ireland, Scotland. Everywhere tens of thousands of sinners were reformed; Jews, infidels, and heretics were converted. Stupendous miracles enforced his words. Twice each day the " miracle bell " summoned the sick, the blind, the lame to be cured. Sinners the most obdurate became Saints; speaking only his native Spanish, he was understood in all tongues. Processions of ten thousand penitents followed him in perfect order. Convents, orphanages, hospitals, arose in his path. Amidst all, his humility remained profound, his prayer constant. He always prepared for preaching by prayer. Once, however, when a person of high rank was to be present at his sermon he neglected prayer for study. The nobleman was not particularly struck by the discourse which had been thus carefully worked up; but coming again to hear the Saint, unknown to the latter, the second sermon made a deep impression on his soul. When St. Vincent heard of the difference, he remarked that in the first sermon it was Vincent who had preached, but in the second, Jesus Christ. He fell ill at Vannes in Brittany, and received the crown of everlasting glory in 1419.

Reflection.—"Whatever you do," said St. Vincent, "think not of yourself, but of God." In this spirit he preached, and God spoke by him; in this spirit, if we listen, we shall hear the voice of God.

April 6.—ST. CELESTINE, Pope.

S T. CELESTINE was a native of Rome, and upon the demise of Pope Boniface he was chosen to succeed him, in September 422, by the wonderful consent of the whole city. His first official act was to confirm the condemnation of an African bishop who had been convicted of grave crimes. He wrote also to the bishops of the provinces of Vienne and Narbonne in Gaul, to correct several abuses, and ordered, among other things, that absolution or reconciliation should never be refused to any dying sinner who sincerely asked it; for repentance depends not so much on time as on the heart. He assembled a synod at Rome in 430, in which the writings of Nestorius were examined, and his blasphemies in maintaining in Christ a divine and a human person were condemned. The Pope pronounced sentence of excommunication against Nestorius, and deposed him. Being informed that Agricola, the son of a British bishop called Saverianus, who had been married before he was raised to the priesthood, had spread the seeds of the Pelagian heresy in Britain, St. Celestine sent thither St. Germanus of Auxerre, whose zeal and conduct happily prevented the threatening danger. He also sent St. Palladius, a Roman, to preach the Faith to the Scots, both in North Britain and in Ireland, and many authors of the life of St. Patrick say that apostle likewise received his commission to preach to the Irish from St. Celestine, in 431.

This holy Pope died on the 1st of August, in 432, having reigned almost ten years.

Reflection.— Vigilance is truly needful to those to whom the care of souls has been confided. "Blessed are the servants whom the Lord at His coming shall find watching."

April 7.—ST. HEGESIPPUS, a Primitive Father.

HE was by birth a Jew, and belonged to the Church of Jerusalem, but travelling to Rome, he lived there nearly twenty years, from the pontificate of Anicetus to that of Eleutherius, in 177, when he returned into the East, where he died at an advanced age, probably at Jerusalem, in the year of Christ 180, according to the chronicle of Alexandria. He wrote in the year 133 a History of the Church in five books, from the Passion of Christ down to his own time, the loss of which work is extremely regretted. In it he gave illustrious proofs of his faith, and showed the apostolical tradition, and that though certain men had disturbed the Church by broaching heresies, yet down to his time no episcopal see or particular church had fallen into error. This testimony he gave after having personally visited all the principal churches, both of the East and the West.

BLESSED HERMAN JOSEPH OF STEINFELD.

HERMAN from his earliest years was a devoted client of the Mother of God. As a little child he used to spend all his playtime in the church at Cologne before an image of Mary, where he received many favors. One bitter winter day, as little Herman was coming barefooted into church, his heavenly Mother appearing to him, asked him lovingly why his feet were bare in such cold weather. "Alas! dear Lady," he said, "it is because my parents are so poor." She pointed to a stone, telling him to look beneath it; there he found four silver pieces wherewith to buy shoes. He did not forget to return and thank her. She enjoined him to go to the same spot in all his wants, and disappeared. Never did the supply fail him; but his comrades, moved by a different spirit, could find nothing. Once Our Lady stretched out her hand, and took an apple which the boy offered her in pledge of his love. Another time he saw her high up in the tribune, with the Holy Child and St. John; he longed to join them, but saw no way of doing so; suddenly he found himself placed by their side, and holding sweet converse with the Infant Jesus. At the age of twelve he entered the Premonstratensian house at Steinfeld, and there led an angelic life of purity and prayer. His fellow-novices, seeing what graces he received from Mary, called him Joseph; and when he shrank from so high an honor, Our Lady in a vision took him as her spouse, and bade him bear the name. Jealously she reproved the smallest faults in her betrothed, and once appeared to him as an old woman, to upbraid him for some slight want of devotion. As her dowry, she conferred on him the most cruel sufferings of mind and body, which were especially severe on the great feasts of the Church. But with the cross Mary brought him the grace to bear it bravely, and thus his heart was weaned from earthly things, and he was made ready for his early and saintly death, which took place about the year 1230.

Reflection.— Do not approach our Blessed Mother with set prayers only. Be intimate with her; confide in her; commend to her every want and every project, small as well as great. It is a childlike reliance and a trustful appeal which she delights to reward.

April 8.—ST. PERPETUUS, Bishop.

S T. PERPETUUS was the eighth Bishop of Tours from St. Gatian, and governed that see above thirty years, from 461 to 491, when he died on the 8th of April. During all that time he labored by zealous sermons, many synods, and wholesome regulations, to lead souls to virtue. St. Perpetuus had a great veneration for the Saints, and respect for their relics, adorned their shrines, and enriched their churches. As there was a continual succession of miracles at the tomb of St. Martin, Perpetuus finding the

church built by St. Bricius too small for the concourse of
people that resorted thither, directed its enlargement.
When the building was finished, the good bishop solem-
nized the dedication of this new church, and performed the
translation of the body of St. Martin, on the 4th of July in
473. Our Saint made and signed his last will, which is
still extant, on the 1st of March, 475, fifteen years before
his death. By it he remits all debts that were owing to
him; and having bequeathed to his church his library and
several farms, and settled a fund for the maintenance of
lamps, and the purchase of sacred vessels, as occasion might
require, he declares the poor his heirs. He adds most
pathetic exhortations to concord and piety; and bequeaths
to his sister, Fidia Julia Perpetua, a little gold cross, with
relics; he leaves legacies to several other friends and priests,
begging of each a remembrance of him in their prayers.
His ancient epitaph equals him to the great St. Martin.

Reflection.— The smart of poverty, says a spiritual
writer, is allayed even more by one word of true sympathy
than by the alms we give. Alms coldly and harshly given
irritate rather than soothe. Even when we cannot give,
words of kindness are as a precious balm; and when we can
give, they are the salt and seasoning of our alms.

April 9.—ST. MARY OF EGYPT.

AT the tender age of twelve, Mary left her father's
house that she might sin without restraint, and for
seventeen years she lived in shame at Alexandria. Then
she accompanied a pilgrimage to Jerusalem, and entangled
many in grievous sin. She was in that city on the Feast of
the Exaltation of the Holy Cross, and went with the crowd
to the church which contained the precious wood. The
rest entered and adored; but Mary was invisibly held back.
In that instant her misery and pollution burst upon her.
Turning to the Immaculate Mother, whose picture faced
her in the porch, she vowed thenceforth to do penance if
she might enter and stand like Magdalen beside the Cross.
Then she entered in. As she knelt before Our Lady on
leaving the church, a voice came to her which said, " Pass

over Jordan, and thou shalt find rest." She went into the
wilderness, and there, in 420, forty-seven years after, the
Abbot Zosimus met her. She told him that for seventeen
years the old songs and scenes had haunted her; ever
since, she had had perfect peace. At her request he brought
her on Holy Thursday the sacred body of Christ. She
bade him return again after a year, and this time he found
her corpse upon the sand, with an inscription saying,
" Bury here the body of Mary the sinner."

Reflection.—Blessed John Colombini was converted to
God by reading St. Mary's life. Let us, too, learn from
her not to be content with confessing and lamenting our
sins, but to fly from what leads us to commit them.

ST. JOHN THE ALMONER.

S T. JOHN was married, but when his wife and two children died he considered it a call from God to lead a
perfect life. He began to give away all he possessed in
alms, and became known throughout the East as the Al-
moner. He was appointed Patriarch of Alexandria; but
before he would take possession of his see he told his servants to go over the town and bring him a list of his lords
— meaning the poor. They brought word that there were
seventy-five hundred of them, and these he undertook to
feed every day. On Wednesday and Friday in every week
he sat on a bench before the church, to hear the complaints
of the needy and aggrieved; nor would he permit his servants to taste food until their wrongs were redressed. The
fear of death was ever before him, and he never spoke an
idle word. He turned those out of church whom he saw
talking, and forbade all detractors to enter his house. He
left seventy churches in Alexandria, where he had found
but seven. A merchant received from St. John five pounds
weight of gold to buy merchandise. Having suffered shipwreck and lost all, he had again recourse to John, who
said, " Some of your merchandise was ill-gotten," and
gave him ten pounds more; but the next voyage he lost
ship as well as goods. John then said, " The ship was
wrongfully acquired. Take fifteen pounds of gold, buy

corn with it, and put it on one of my ships." This time the merchant was carried by the winds without his own knowledge to England, where there was a famine; and he sold the corn for its weight in tin, and on his return he found the tin changed to finest silver. St. John died in Cyprus, his native place, about the year 619.

Reflection.—What sacrifices can we make for the poor which will seem enough, when we reflect that mercy to them is our only means of repaying Jesus Christ, Who sacrificed His life for us?

April 10.—ST. BADEMUS, Martyr.

BADEMUS was a rich and noble citizen of Bethlapeta in Persia, who founded a monastery near that city, which he governed with great sanctity. He conducted his religious in the paths of perfection with sweetness, prudence, and charity. To crown his virtue, God permitted him, with seven of his monks, to be apprehended by the followers of King Sapor, in the thirty-sixth year of his persecution. He lay four months in a dungeon, loaded with chains, during which lingering martyrdom he every day received a number of stripes. But he triumphed over his torments by the patience and joy with which he suffered them for Christ. At the same time, a Christian lord named Nersan, Prince of Aria, was cast into prison because he refused to adore the sun. At first he showed some resolution; but at the sight of tortures his constancy failed him, and he promised to conform. The king, to try if his change was sincere, ordered Bademus to be introduced into the prison of Nersan, which was a chamber in the royal palace, and sent word to Nersan that if he would despatch Bademus, he should be restored to his liberty and former dignities. The wretch accepted the condition; a sword was put into his hand, and he advanced to plunge it into the breast of the abbot. But being seized with a sudden terror, he stopped short, and remained some time without being able to lift up his arm to strike. He had neither courage to repent, nor heart to accomplish his crime. He strove, however, to harden himself, and continued with a trembling hand to aim at the sides of the martyr. Fear, shame, remorse, and respect for the martyr made his strokes forceless and unsteady; and so great was the number of the martyr's wounds, that the bystanders were in admiration at his invincible patience. After four strokes, the martyr's head was severed from the trunk. Nersan a short time after, falling into public disgrace, perished by the sword. The body of St. Bademus was reproachfully cast out of the city by the infidels, but was secretly carried away and interred by the Christians. His disciples were released from their chains four years afterward, upon the death of King Sapor. St. Bademus suffered on the 10th of April in the year 376.

Reflection.—Oh! what ravishing delights does the soul taste which is accustomed, by a familiar habit, to converse in the heaven of its own interior with the Three Persons of the adorable Trinity! Worldlings wonder how holy solitaries can pass their whole time buried in the most profound solitude and silence. But those who have had any experience of this happiness are surprised, with far greater reason, how it is possible that any souls which are created to converse eternally with God should here live in constant dissipation, seldom entertaining a devout thought of Him Whose charms and sweet conversation eternally ravish all the blessed.

April 11.—ST. LEO THE GREAT.

LEO was born at Rome. He embraced the sacred ministry, was made archdeacon of the Roman Church by St. Celestine, and under him and Sixtus III. had a large share in governing the Church. On the death of Sixtus, Leo was chosen Pope, and consecrated on St. Michael's day, 440, amid great joy. It was a time of terrible trial. Vandals and Huns were wasting the provinces of the empire, and Nestorians, Pelagians, and other heretics wrought more grievous havoc among souls. Whilst Leo's zeal made head against these perils, there arose the new heresy of Eutyches, who confounded the two natures of Christ. At once the vigilant pastor proclaimed the true doctrine of the

Incarnation in his famous " tome; " but fostered by the
Byzantine court, the heresy gained a strong hold amongst
the Eastern monks and bishops.   After three years of unceasing toil, Leo brought about its solemn condemnation by
the Council of Chalcedon, the Fathers all signing his tome,
and exclaiming, " Peter hath spoken by Leo."   Soon after,
Attila with his Huns broke into Italy, and marched through
its burning cities upon Rome.   Leo went out boldly to meet
him, and prevailed on him to turn back.   Astonished to
see the terrible Attila, the " Scourge of God," fresh from
the sack of Aquileia, Milan, Pavia, with the rich prize of
Rome within his grasp, turn his great host back to the
Danube at the Saint's word, his chiefs asked him why he
had acted so strangely.   He answered that he saw two
venerable personages, supposed to be Sts. Peter and Paul,
standing behind Leo, and impressed by this vision he withdrew.   If the perils of the Church are as great now as in
St. Leo's day, St. Peter's solicitude is not less.   Two years
later the city fell a prey to the Vandals; but even then
Leo saved it from destruction.   He died A. D. 461, having
ruled the Church twenty years.

Reflection.—Leo loved to ascribe all the fruits of his
unsparing labors to the glorious chief of the apostles, who,
he often declared, lives and governs in his successors.

April 12.—ST. JULIUS, Pope.

S̄T. JULIUS was a Roman, and chosen Pope on the 6th of
February in 337.   The Arian bishops in the East
sent to him three deputies to accuse St. Athanasius, the
zealous Patriarch of Alexandria.   These accusations, as the
order of justice required, Julius imparted to Athanasius,
who thereupon sent his deputies to Rome; when, upon an
impartial hearing, the advocates of the heretics were confounded and silenced upon every article of their accusation.
The Arians then demanded a council, and the Pope assembled one in Rome in 341.   The Arians instead of appearing held a pretended council at Antioch in 341, in which
they presumed to appoint one Gregory, an impious Arian,
Bishop of Alexandria, detained the Pope's legates beyond

the time mentioned for their appearance; and then wrote
to his Holiness, alleging a pretended impossibility of their
appearing, on account of the Persian war and other im-
pediments. The Pope easily saw through these pretences,
and in a council at Rome examined the cause of St.
Athanasius, declared him innocent of the things laid to
his charge by the Arians, and confirmed him in his see.
He also acquitted Marcellus of Ancyra, upon his orthodox
profession of faith. He drew up and sent by Count Gabian
to the Oriental Eusebian bishops, who had first demanded
a council and then refused to appear in it, an excellent
letter, which is looked upon as one of the finest monuments of ecclesiastical antiquity. Finding the Eusebians
still obstinate, he moved Constans, Emperor of the West, to
demand the concurrence of his brother Constantius in the
assembling of a general council at Sardica in Illyricum.
This was opened in May 347, and declared St. Athanasius
and Marcellus of Ancyra orthodox and innocent, deposed
certain Arian bishops, and framed twenty-one canons of
discipline. St. Julius reigned fifteen years, two months,
and six days, dying on the 12th of April, 352.

April 13.—ST. HERMENEGILD, Martyr.

LEOVIGILD, King of the Visigoths, had two sons, Hermenegild and Recared, who reigned conjointly with
him. All three were Arians, but Hermenegild married a
zealous Catholic, the daughter of Sigebert, King of France,
and by her holy example was converted to the faith. His
father, on hearing the news, denounced him as a traitor,
and marched to seize his person. Hermenegild tried to
rally the Catholics of Spain in his defence, but they were
too weak to make any stand, and, after a two years' fruit-
less struggle, he surrendered on the assurance of a free
pardon. When safely in the royal camp, the king had him
loaded with fetters and cast into a foul dungeon at Seville.
Tortures and bribes were in turn employed to shake his
faith, but Hermenegild wrote to his father that he held the
crown as nothing, and preferred to lose sceptre and life
rather than betray the truth of God. At length, on Easter

night, an Arian bishop entered his cell, and promised him his father's pardon if he would but receive Communion at his hands. Hermenegild indignantly rejected the offer, and knelt with joy for his death-stroke. The same night a light streaming from his cell told the Christians who were watching near that the martyr had won his crown, and was keeping his Easter with the Saints in glory.

Leovigild on his death-bed, though still an Arian, bade Recared seek out St. Leander, whom he had himself cruelly persecuted, and, following Hermenegild's example, be received by him into the Church. Recared did so, and on his father's death labored so earnestly for the extirpation of Arianism that he brought over the whole nation of the Visigoths to the Church. "Nor is it to be wondered," says St. Gregory, "that he came thus to be a preacher of the true faith, seeing that he was brother of a martyr, whose merits did help him to bring so many into the lap of God's Church."

Reflection.—St. Hermenegild teaches us that constancy and sacrifice are the best arguments for the Faith, and the surest way to win souls to God.

April 14.—ST. BENEZET, or Little Bennet.

S T. Benezet kept his mother's sheep in the country, and as a mere child was devoted to practices of piety. As many persons were drowned in crossing the Rhone, Benezet was inspired by God to build a bridge over that rapid river at Avignon. He obtained the approbation of the bishop, proved his mission by miracles, and began the work in 1177, which he directed during seven years. He died when the difficulty of the undertaking was over, in 1184. This is attested by public monuments drawn up at that time and still preserved at Avignon, where the story is in everybody's mouth. His body was buried upon the bridge itself, which was not completely finished till four years after his decease, the structure whereof was attended with miracles from the first laying of the foundations till it was completed in 1188. Other miracles wrought after this at his tomb induced the city to build a chapel upon the

bridge, in which his body lay nearly five hundred years.
But in 1669 a greater part of the bridge falling down
through the impetuosity of the waters, the coffin was taken
up, and being opened in 1670 in presence of the grand
vicar, during the vacancy of the archiepiscopal see, the
body was found entire, without the least sign of corruption; even the bowels were perfectly sound, and the color
of the eyes lively and sprightly, though, through the damp-
ness of the situation, the iron bars about the coffin were
much damaged with rust.   The body was found in the
same condition by the Archbishop of Avignon in 1674,
when, accompanied by the Bishop of Orange and a great
concourse of nobility, he performed the translation of it,
with great pomp, into the Church of the Celestines, this
Order having obtained of Louis XIV. the honor of being
intrusted with the custody of his relics till such time as
the bridge and chapel should be rebuilt.

Reflection.—Let us pray for perseverance in good works.
St. Augustine says, " When the Saints pray in the words
which Christ taught, they ask for little else than the gift
of perseverance."

April 15.—ST. PATERNUS, Bishop.

T. PATERNUS was born at Poitiers, about the year 482.
His father, Patranus, with the consent of his wife,
went into Ireland, where he ended his days in holy solitude.
Paternus, fired by his example, embraced a monastic life in
the abbey of Marnes.   After some time, burning with a
desire of attaining to the perfection of Christian virtue, he
passed over to Wales, and in Cardiganshire founded a monastery called Llan-patern-vaur, or the church of the great
Paternus.   He made a visit to his father in Ireland, but
being called back to his monastery of Marnes, he soon after
retired with St. Scubilion, a monk of that house, and embraced an austere anchoretical life in the forests of Scicy,
in the diocese of Coutances, near the sea, having first obtained leave of the bishop and of the lord of the place.
This desert, which was then of great extent, but which has
been since gradually gained upon by the sea, was anciently

in great request among the Druids. St. Paternus converted to the faith the idolaters of that and many neighboring parts, as far as Bayeux, and prevailed upon them to
demolish a pagan temple in this desert, which was held in
great veneration by the ancient Gauls. In his old age he
was consecrated Bishop of Avranches by Germanus, Bishop
of Rouen.

Some false brethren having created a division of opinion
among the bishops of the province with respect to St. Paternus, he preferred retiring rather than to afford any
ground for dissension, and, after governing his diocese for
thirteen years, he withdrew to a solitude in France, and
there ended his days about the year 550.

Reflection.—The greatest sacrifices imposed by the love
of peace will appear as naught if we call to mind the example of Our Saviour, and remember His words, " Blessed are
the peacemakers, for they shall be called the children of
God."

April 16.—EIGHTEEN MARTYRS OF SARA-GOSSA, and ST. ENCRATIS, or ENGRATIA, Virgin, Martyr.

ST. OPTATUS and seventeen other holy men received the
crown of martyrdom on the same day, at Saragossa,
under the cruel Governor Dacian, in the persecution of
Diocletian, in 304. Two others, Caius and Crementius,
died of their torments after a second conflict.

The Church also celebrates on this day the triumph of
St. Encratis, or Engratia, Virgin. She was a native of
Portugal. Her father had promised her in marriage to a
man of quality in Rousillon; but fearing the dangers and
despising the vanities of the world, and resolving to preserve her virginity, in order to appear more agreeable to
her heavenly Spouse and serve Him without hindrance, she
stole from her father's house and fled privately to Saragossa, where the persecution was hottest, under the eyes of
Dacian. She even reproached him with his barbarities,
upon which he ordered her to be long tormented in the

most inhuman manner: her sides were torn with iron hooks, and one of her breasts was cut off, so that the inner parts of her chest were exposed to view, and part of her liver was pulled out. In this condition she was sent back to prison, being still alive, and died by the mortifying of her wounds, in 304. The relics of all these martyrs were found at Saragossa in 1389.

Reflection.—Men do not pursue temporal goods at haphazard, or by fits and starts. Let us be as punctual and orderly in the service of God, not casting about for new paths, but perfecting our ordinary devotions. If we persevere in these, Paradise is ours.

April 17.—ST. ANICETUS, Pope, Martyr.

ST. ANICETUS succeeded St. Pius, and sat about eight years, from 165 to 173. If he did not shed his blood for the Faith, he at least purchased the title of martyr by great sufferings and dangers. He received a visit from St. Polycarp, and tolerated the custom of the Asiatics in celebrating Easter on the 14th day of the first moon after the vernal equinox, with the Jews. His vigilance protected his flock from the wiles of the heretics Valentine and Marcion, who sought to corrupt the faith in the capital of the world.

The first thirty-six bishops at Rome, down to Liberius, and, this one excepted, all the popes to Symmachus, the fifty-second, in 498, are honored among the Saints; and out of two hundred and forty-eight popes, from St. Peter to Clement XIII. seventy-eight are named in the Roman Martyrology. In the primitive ages, the spirit of fervor and perfect sanctity, which is nowadays so rarely to be found, was conspicuous in most of the faithful, and especially in their pastors. The whole tenor of their lives breathed it in such a manner as to render them the miracles of the world, angels on earth, living copies of their divine Redeemer, the odor of whose virtues and holy law and religion they spread on every side.

Reflection.—If, after making the most solemn protestations of inviolable friendship and affection for a fellow-creature, we should the next moment revile and contemn him, without having received any provocation or affront, and this habitually, would not the whole world justly call our protestations hypocrisy, and our pretended friendship a mockery? Let us by this rule judge if our love of God be sovereign, so long as our inconstancy betrays the insincerity of our hearts.

April 18.—ST. APOLLONIUS, Martyr.

MARCUS AURELIUS had persecuted the Christians, but his son Commodus, who in 180 succeeded him, showed himself favorable to them out of regard to his Empress Marcia, who was an admirer of the Faith. During this calm the number of the faithful was exceedingly increased, and many persons of the first rank, among them Apollonius, a Roman senator, enlisted themselves under the banner of the cross. He was a person very well versed both in philosophy and the Holy Scripture. In the midst of the peace which the Church enjoyed, he was publicly accused of Christianity by one of his own slaves. The slave was immediately condemned to have his legs broken, and to be put to death, in consequence of an edict of Marcus Aurelius, who, without repealing the former laws against convicted Christians, ordered by it that their accusers should be put to death. The slave being executed, the same judge sent an order to St. Apollonius to renounce his religion as he valued his life and fortune. The Saint courageously rejected such ignominious terms of safety, wherefore Perennis referred him to the judgment of the Roman senate, to give an account of his faith to that body. Persisting in his refusal to comply with the condition, the Saint was condemned by a decree of the Senate, and beheaded about the year 186.

Reflection.—It is the prerogative of the Christian religion to inspire men with such resolution, and form them to such heroism, that they rejoice to sacrifice their life to truth. This is not the bare force and exertion of nature, but the undoubted power of the Almighty, Whose strength is thus made perfect in weakness. Every Christian ought, by his manner, to bear witness to the sanctity of his faith. Such would be the force of universal good example, that no libertine or infidel could withstand it.

April 19.—ST. ELPHEGE, Archbishop.

ST. ELPHEGE was born in the year 954, of a noble Saxon family. He first became a monk in the monastery of Deerhurst, near Tewkesbury, England, and afterwards lived as a hermit near Bath, where he founded a community under the rule of St. Benedict, and became its first abbot. At thirty years of age he was chosen Bishop of Winchester, and twenty-two years later he became Archbishop of Canterbury. In 1011, when the Danes landed in Kent and took the city of Canterbury, putting all to fire and sword, St. Elphege was captured and carried off in the expectation of a large ransom. He was unwilling that his ruined church and people should be put to such expense, and was kept in a loathsome prison at Greenwich for seven months. While so confined some friends came and urged him to lay a tax upon his tenants to raise the sum demanded for his ransom. "What reward can I hope for," said he, " if I spend upon myself what belongs to the poor? Better give up to the poor what is ours, than take from them the little which is their own." As he still refused to give ransom, the enraged Danes fell upon him in a fury, beat him with the blunt sides of their weapons, and bruised him with stones until one, whom the Saint had baptized shortly before, put an end to his sufferings by the blow of an axe. He died on Easter Saturday, April 19, 1012, his last words being a prayer for his murderers. His body was first buried in St. Paul's, London, but was afterwards translated to Canterbury by King Canute. A church dedicated to St. Elphege still stands upon the place of his martyrdom at Greenwich.

Reflection.—Those who are in high positions should consider themselves as stewards rather than masters of the wealth or power intrusted to them for the benefit of the poor and weak. St. Elphege died rather than extort his ransom from the poor tenants of the Church lands.

April 20.—ST. MARCELLINUS, Bishop.

Ｓ T. MARCELLINUS was born in Africa, of a noble family; accompanied by Vincent and Domninus, he went over into Gaul, and there preached the Gospel, with great success, in the neighborhood of the Alps. He afterwards settled at Embrun, where he built a chapel in which he passed his nights in prayer, after laboring all the day in the exercise of his sacred calling. By his pious example as well as by his earnest words, he converted many of the heathens among whom he lived. He was afterwards made bishop of the people whom he had won over to Christ, but the date of his consecration is not positively known. Burning with zeal for the glory of God, he sent Vincent and Domninus to preach the faith in those parts which he could not visit in person. He died at Embrun about the year 374, and was there interred. St. Gregory of Tours, who speaks of Marcellinus in terms of highest praise, mentions many miracles as happening at his tomb.

Reflection.—Though you may not be called upon to preach, at least endeavor to set a good example, remembering that deeds often speak louder than words.

April 21.—ST. ANSELM, Archbishop.

Ａ NSELM was a native of Piedmont. When a boy of fifteen, being forbidden to enter religion, he for a while lost his fervor, left his home, and went to various schools in France. At length his vocation revived, and he became a monk at Bec in Normandy. The fame of his sanctity in this cloister led William Rufus, when dangerously ill, to take him for his confessor, and to name him to the vacant see of Canterbury. Now began the strife of Anselm's life. With new health the king relapsed into his former sins, plundered the Church lands, scorned the archbishop's rebukes, and forbade him to go to Rome for the pallium. Anselm went, and returned only to enter into a more bitter strife with William's successor, Henry I. This sovereign claimed the right of investing prelates with the ring and crozier, symbols of the spiritual jurisdiction which belongs to the Church alone. The worldly prelates did not scruple to call St. Anselm a traitor for his defence of the Pope's supremacy; on which the Saint rose, and with calm dignity exclaimed, " If any man pretends that I violate my faith to my king because I will not reject the authority of the Holy See of Rome, let him stand forth, and in the name of God I will answer him as I ought." No one took up the challenge; and to the disappointment of the king, the barons sided with the Saint, for they respected his courage, and saw that his cause was their own. Sooner than yield, the archbishop went again into exile, till at last the king was obliged to submit to the feeble but inflexible old man. In the midst of his harassing cares, St. Anselm found time for writings which have made him celebrated as the father of scholastic theology; while in metaphysics and in science he had few equals. He is yet more famous for his devotion to our blessed Lady, whose Feast of the Immaculate Conception he was the first to establish in the West. He died in 1109.

Reflection.—Whoever, like St. Anselm, contends for the Church's rights, is fighting on the side of God against the tyranny of Satan.

April 22.—ST. SOTER, Pope, Martyr.

ST. SOTER was raised to the papacy upon the death of St. Anicetus, in 173. By the sweetness of his discourses he comforted all persons with the tenderness of a father, and assisted the indigent with liberal alms, especially those who suffered for the faith. He liberally extended his charities, according to the custom of his predecessors, to remote churches, particularly to that of Corinth, to which he addressed an excellent letter, as St. Dionysius of Corinth testifies in his letter of thanks, who adds that his letter was found worthy to be read for their edification on Sundays at their assemblies to celebrate the divine mysteries, together with the letter of St. Clement, pope. St. Soter vigorously opposed the heresy of Montanus, and governed the Church to the year 177.

ST. LEONIDES, Martyr.

THE Emperor Severus, in the year 202, which was the
tenth of his reign, raised a bloody persecution, which
filled the whole empire with martyrs, but especially Egypt.
The most illustrious of those who by their triumphs en-
nobled and edified the city of Alexandria was Leonides,
father of the great Origen. He was a Christian philosopher, and excellently versed both in the profane and
sacred sciences. He had seven sons, the eldest of whom
was Origen, whom he brought up with abundance of care,
returning God thanks for having blessed him with a son of
such an excellent disposition for learning, and a very great
zeal for piety. These qualifications endeared him greatly
to his father, who, after his son was baptized, would come
to his bedside while he was asleep, and, opening his bosom,
kiss it respectfully, as being the temple of the Holy Ghost.
When the persecution raged at Alexandria, under Lætus,
governor of Egypt, in the tenth year of Severus, Leonides
was cast into prison. Origen, who was then only seventeen years of age, burned with an incredible desire of
martyrdom, and sought every opportunity of meeting with
it. But his mother conjured him not to forsake her, and
his ardor being redoubled at the sight of his father's chains,
she was forced to lock up all his clothes to oblige him to
stay at home. So, not being able to do any more, he wrote
a letter to his father in very moving terms, strongly exhorting him to look on the crown that was offered him
with courage and joy, adding this clause, "Take heed, sir,
that for our sakes you do not change your mind." Leonides was accordingly beheaded for the faith in 202. His
estates and goods being all confiscated, and seized for the
emperor's use, his widow was left with seven children to
maintain in the poorest condition imaginable; but Divine
Providence was both her comfort and support.

April 23.—ST. GEORGE, Martyr.

S T. GEORGE was born in Cappadocia, at the close of the third century, of Christian parents. In early youth he chose a soldier's life, and soon obtained the favor of Diocletian, who advanced him to the grade of tribune. When, however, the emperor began to persecute the Christians, George rebuked him at once sternly and openly for his cruelty, and threw up his commission. He was in consequence subjected to a lengthened series of torments, and finally beheaded. There was something so inspiriting in the defiant cheerfulness of the young soldier, that every Christian felt a personal share in this triumph of Christian fortitude; and as years rolled on St. George became a type of successful combat against evil, the slayer of the dragon, the darling theme of camp song and story, until " so thick a shade his very glory round him made " that his real lineaments became hard to trace. Even beyond the circle of Christendom he was held in honor, and invading Saracens taught themselves to except from desecration the image of him they hailed as the " White-horsed Knight." The devotion to St. George is one of the most ancient and widely spread in the Church. In the East, a church of St. George is ascribed to Constantine, and his name is invoked in the most ancient liturgies; whilst in the West, Malta, Barcelona, Valencia, Arragon, Genoa, and England have chosen him as their patron.

Reflection.—" What shall I say of fortitude, without which neither wisdom nor justice is of any worth? Fortitude is not of the body, but is a constancy of soul; wherewith we are conquerors in righteousness, patiently bear all adversities, and in prosperity are not puffed up. This fortitude he lacks who is overcome by pride, anger, greed, drunkenness, and the like. Neither have they fortitude who when in adversity make shift to escape at their souls' expense; wherefore the Lord saith, ' Fear not those who kill the body, but cannot kill the soul.' In like manner those who are puffed up in prosperity and abandon themselves to excessive joviality cannot be called strong. For how can they be called strong who cannot hide and repress the heart's emotion? Fortitude is never conquered, or if conquered, is not fortitude."— *St. Bruno.*

April 24.—ST. FIDELIS OF SIGMARINGEN.

FIDELIS was born at Sigmaringen in 1577, of noble parents. In his youth he frequently approached the sacraments, visited the sick and the poor, and spent moreover many hours before the altar. For a time he followed the legal profession, and was remarkable for his advocacy of the poor and his respectful language towards his opponents. Finding it difficult to become both a rich lawyer and a good Christian, Fidelis entered the Capuchin Order, and embraced a life of austerity and prayer. Hair shirts, iron-pointed girdles, and disciplines were penances too light for his fervor; and being filled with a desire of martyrdom, he rejoiced at being sent to Switzerland by the newly-founded Congregation of Propaganda, and braved every peril to rescue souls from the diabolical heresy of Calvin. When preaching at Sevis he was fired at by a Calvinist, but the fear of death could not deter him from proclaiming divine truth. After his sermon he was waylaid by a body of Protestants headed by a minister, who attacked him and tried to force him to embrace their so-called reform. But he said, " I came to refute your errors, not to embrace them; I will never renounce Catholic doctrine, which is the truth of all ages, and I fear not death." On this they fell upon him with their poignards, and the first martyr of Propaganda went to receive his palm.

Reflection.—We delight in decorating the altars of God with flowers, lights, and jewels, and it is right to do so; but if we wish to offer to God gifts of higher value, let us, in imitation of St. Fidelis, save the souls who but for us would be lost; for so we shall offer Him, as it were, the jewels of paradise.

April 25.—ST. MARK, Evangelist.

ST. MARK was converted to the Faith by the Prince of the Apostles, whom he afterwards accompanied to Rome, acting there as his secretary or interpreter. When St. Peter was writing his first epistle to the churches of Asia, he affectionately joins with his own salutation that of his faithful companion, whom he calls " my son Mark." The Roman people entreated St. Mark to put in writing for them the substance of St. Peter's frequent discourses on Our Lord's life. This the Evangelist did under the eye and with the express sanction of the apostle, and every page of his brief but graphic gospel so bore the impress of St. Peter's character, that the Fathers used to name it " Peter's Gospel." St. Mark was now sent to Egypt to found the Church of Alexandria. Here his disciples became the wonder of the world for their piety and asceticism, so that St. Jerome speaks of St. Mark as the father of the anchorites, who at a later time thronged the Egyptian deserts. Here, too, he set up the first Christian school, the fruitful mother of many illustrious doctors and bishops. After governing his see for many years, St. Mark was one day seized by the heathen, dragged by ropes over stones, and thrown into prison. On the morrow the torture was repeated, and having been consoled by a vision of angels and the voice of Jesus, St. Mark went to his reward.

It is to St. Mark that we owe the many slight touches which often give such vivid coloring to the Gospel scenes, and help us to picture to ourselves the very gestures and looks of our blessed Lord. It is he alone who notes that in the temptation Jesus was " with the beasts; " that He slept in the boat " on a pillow; " that He " embraced " the little children. He alone preserves for us the commanding words " Peace, be still ! " by which the storm was quelled; or even the very sounds of His voice, the " Ephpheta " and " Talitha cumi," by which the dumb were made to speak and the dead to rise. So, too, the " looking round about with anger," and the " sighing deeply," long treasured in the memory of the penitent apostle, who was himself converted by his Saviour's look, are here recorded by his faithful interpreter.

Reflection.—Learn from St. Mark to keep the image of the Son of man ever before your mind, and to ponder every syllable which fell from His lips.

April 26.—STS. CLETUS and MARCELLINUS, Popes, Martyrs.

ST. CLETUS was the third Bishop of Rome, and succeeded St. Linus, which circumstance alone shows his eminent virtue among the first disciples of St. Peter in the West. He sat twelve years, from 76 to 89. The canon of the Roman Mass, Bede, and other martyrologists, style him a martyr. He was buried near St. Linus, in the Vatican, and his relics still remain in that church.

St. Marcellinus succeeded St. Caius in the bishopric of Rome in 296, about the time that Diocletian set himself up for a deity, and impiously claimed divine honors. In those stormy times of persecution Marcellinus acquired great glory. He sat in St. Peter's chair eight years, three months, and twenty-five days, dying in 304, a year after the cruel persecution broke out, in which he gained much honor. He has been styled a martyr, though his blood was not shed in the cause of religion.

Reflection.—It is a fundamental maxim of the Christian morality, and a truth which Christ has established in the clearest terms and in innumerable passages of the Gospel, that the cross or sufferings and mortification are the road to eternal bliss. They, therefore, who lead not here a crucified and mortified life are unworthy ever to possess the unspeakable joys of His kingdom. Our Lord Himself, our model and our head, walked in this path, and His great Apostle puts us in mind that He entered into bliss only by His blood and by the cross.

April 27.—ST. ZITA, Virgin.

ZITA lived for forty-eight years in the service of Fatinelli, a citizen of Lucca. During this time she rose each morning, while the household were asleep, to hear Mass, and then toiled incessantly till night came, doing the work of others as well as her own. Once Zita, absorbed in prayer, remained in church past the usual hour of her bread-making. She hastened home, reproaching herself with neglect of duty, and found the bread made and ready for the oven. She never doubted that her mistress or one of her servants had kneaded it, and going to them, thanked them; but they were astonished. No human being had made the bread. A delicious perfume rose from it, for angels had made it during her prayer. For years her master and mistress treated her as a mere drudge, while her fellow-servants, resenting her diligence as a reproach to themselves, insulted and struck her. Zita united these sufferings with those of Christ her Lord, never changing the sweet tone of her voice, nor forgetting her gentle and quiet ways. At length Fatinelli, seeing the success which attended her undertakings, gave her charge of his children and of the household. She dreaded this dignity more than the worst humiliation, but scrupulously fulfilled her trust. By her holy economy her master's goods were multiplied, while the poor were fed at his door. Gradually her unfailing patience conquered the jealousy of her fellow-servants, and she became their advocate with their hot-tempered master, who dared not give way to his anger before Zita. In the end her prayer and toil sanctified the whole house, and drew down upon it the benediction of Heaven. She died in 1272, and in the moment of her death a bright star appearing above her attic showed that she had gained eternal rest.

Reflection.—" What must I do to be saved? " said a certain one in fear of damnation. " Work and pray, pray and work," a voice replied, " and thou shalt be saved." The whole life of St. Zita teaches us this truth.

April 28.—ST. PAUL OF THE CROSS.

THE eighty-one years of this Saint's life were modelled on the Passion of Jesus Christ. In his childhood, when praying in church, a heavy bench fell on his foot, but the boy took no notice of the bleeding wound, and spoke of it as " a rose sent from God." A few years later, the vision of a scourge with " love " written on its lashes assured him that his thirst for penance would be satisfied. In the hope of dying for the faith, he enlisted in a crusade against the Turks; but a voice from the Tabernacle warned him that he was to serve Christ alone, and that he should found a congregation in His honor. At the command of his bishop he began while a layman to preach the Passion, and a series of crosses tried the reality of his vocation. All his first companions, save his brother, deserted him; the Sovereign Pontiff refused him an audience; and it was only after a delay of seventeen years that the Papal approbation was obtained, and the first house of the Passionists was opened on Monte Argentario, the spot which Our Lady had pointed out. St. Paul chose as the badge of his Order a heart with three nails, in memory of the sufferings of Jesus, but for himself he invented a more secret and durable sign. Moved by the same holy impulse as Blessed Henry Suso, St. Jane Frances, and other Saints, he branded on his side the Holy Name, and its characters were found there after death. His heart beat with a supernatural palpitation, which was especially vehement on Fridays, and the heat at times was so intense as to scorch his shirt in the region of his heart. Through fifty years of incessant bodily pain, and amidst all his trials, Paul read the love of Jesus everywhere, and would cry out to the flowers and grass, " Oh! be quiet, be quiet," as if they were reproaching him with ingratitude. He died whilst the Passion was being read to him, and so passed with Jesus from the cross to glory.

ST. VITALIS, Martyr.

ST. VITALIS was a citizen of Milan, and is said to have been the father of Sts. Gervasius and Protasius. The divine providence conducted him to Ravenna, where he saw a Christian named Ursicinus, who was condemned to lose his head for his faith, standing aghast at the sight of death, and seeming ready to yield. Vitalis was extremely moved at this spectacle. He knew his double obligation of preferring the glory of God and the eternal salvation of his neighbor to his own corporal life: he therefore boldly and successfully encouraged Ursicinus to triumph over death, and after his martyrdom carried off his body, and respectfully interred it. The judge, whose name was Paulinus, being informed of this, caused Vitalis to be apprehended, stretched on the rack, and, after other torments, to be buried alive in a place called the Palm-tree, in Ravenna. His wife, Valeria, returning from Ravenna to Milan, was beaten to death by peasants, because she refused to join them in an idolatrous festival and riot.

Reflection.—We are not all called to the sacrifice of martyrdom; but we are all bound to make our lives a continued sacrifice of ourselves to God, and to perform every action in this perfect spirit of sacrifice. Thus we shall both live and die to God, perfectly resigned to His holy will in all His appointments.

April 29.—ST. PETER, Martyr.

IN 1205 the glorious martyr Peter was born at Verona of heretical parents. He went to a Catholic school, and his Manichean uncle asked what he learnt. "The Creed," answered Peter; "I believe in God, Creator of heaven and earth." No persuasion could shake his faith, and at fifteen he received the habit from St. Dominic himself at Bologna. After ordination, he preached to the heretics of Lombardy, and converted multitudes. St. Peter was constantly obliged to dispute with heretics, and although he was able to confound them, still the devil took occasion thence to tempt him once against faith. Instantly he had recourse to prayer before an image of Our Lady, and heard a voice saying to him the words of Jesus Christ in the Gospel, "I have prayed for thee, Peter, that thy faith may not fail; and thou shalt confirm thy brethren in it." Once when exhorting a vast crowd under the burning sun, the heretics defied him to procure shade. He prayed, and a cloud overshadowed the audience. In spite of his sanctity, he was foully slandered and even punished for immorality. He submitted humbly, but complained in prayer to Jesus crucified. The crucifix spoke, "And I, Peter, what did I do?" Every day, as he elevated at Mass the precious blood, he prayed, "Grant, Lord, that I may die for Thee, Who for me didst die." His prayer was answered. The heretics, confounded by him, sought his life. Two of them attacked him as he was returning to Milan, and struck his head with an axe. St. Peter fell, commended himself to God, dipped his finger in his own blood, and wrote on the ground, "I believe in God, Creator of heaven and earth." They then stabbed him in the side, and he received his crown.

Reflection.—From a boy St. Peter boldly professed his faith among heretics. He spent his life in preaching the faith to heretics, and received the glorious and long-desired crown of martyrdom from heretics. We are surrounded by heretics. Are we courageous, firm, zealous, full of prayer for their conversion, unflinching in our profession of faith?

ST. HUGH, Abbot of Cluny.

ST. HUGH was a prince related to the sovereign house of the dukes of Burgundy, and had his education under the tuition of his pious mother, and under the care of Hugh, Bishop of Auxerre, his great-uncle. From his infancy he was exceedingly given to prayer and meditation, and his life was remarkably innocent and holy. One day, hearing an account of the wonderful sanctity of the monks of Cluny, under St. Odilo, he was so moved that he set out that moment, and going thither, humbly begged the monas-

tic habit.   After a rigid novitiate, he made his profession
in 1039, being sixteen years old.   His extraordinary virtue,
especially his admirable humility, obedience, charity, sweetness, prudence, and zeal, gained him the respect of the
whole community; and upon the death of St. Odilo, in
1049, though only twenty-five years old, he succeeded to
the government of that great abbey, which he held sixty-
two years.   He received to the religious profession Hugh,
Duke of Burgundy, and died on the twenty-ninth of April,
in 1109, aged eighty-five.   He was canonized twelve years
after his death by Pope Calixtus II.

April 30.—ST. CATHERINE OF SIENA.

CATHERINE, the daughter of a humble tradesman, was
raised up to be the guide and guardian of the Church
in one of the darkest periods of its history, the fourteenth
century.   As a child, prayer was her delight.   She would
say the "Hail Mary" on each step as she mounted the
stairs, and was granted in reward a vision of Christ in
glory.   When but seven years old, she made a vow of virginity, and afterwards endured bitter persecution for refusing to marry.   Our Lord gave her His Heart in
exchange for her own, communicated her with His own
hands, and stamped on her body the print of His wounds.
At the age of fifteen she entered the Third Order of St.
Dominic, but continued to reside in her father's shop,
where she united a life of active charity with the prayer
of a contemplative Saint.   From this obscure home the
seraphic virgin was summoned to defend the Church's
cause.   Armed with Papal authority, and accompanied by
three confessors, she travelled through Italy, reducing re-
bellious cities to the obedience of the Holy See, and winning hardened souls to God.   In the face well-nigh of the
whole world she sought out Gregory XI. at Avignon,
brought him back to Rome, and by her letters to the kings
and queens of Europe made good the Papal cause.   She
was the counsellor of Urban VI., and sternly rebuked the
disloyal cardinals who had part in electing an antipope.
Long had the holy virgin foretold the terrible schism which

began ere she died.   Day and night she wept and prayed
for unity and peace.   But the devil excited the Roman
people against the Pope, so that some sought the life of
Christ's Vicar.   With intense earnestness did St. Catherine
beg Our Lord to prevent this enormous crime.   In spirit
she saw the whole city full of demons tempting the people
to resist and even slay the Pope.   The seditious temper
was subdued by Catherine's prayers; but the devils vented
their malice by scourging the Saint herself, who gladly
endured all for God and His Church.   She died at Rome,
in 1380, at the age of thirty-three.

Reflection.—The seraphic St. Catherine willingly sacrificed the delights of contemplation to labor for the Church
and the Apostolic See.   How deeply do the troubles of the
Church and the consequent loss of souls afflict us?   How
often do we pray for the Church and the Pope?

May 1.—STS. PHILIP and JAMES, Apostles.

PHILIP was one of the first chosen disciples of Christ.
On the way from Judea to Galilee Our Lord found
Philip, and said, "Follow Me." Philip straightway
obeyed; and then in his zeal and charity sought to win
Nathaniel also, saying, "We have found Him of Whom
Moses and the prophets did write, Jesus of Nazareth;"
and when Nathaniel in wonder asked, "Can any good
come out of Nazareth?" Philip simply answered, "Come
and see," and brought him to Jesus.   Another characteristic saying of this apostle is preserved for us by St. John.
Christ in His last discourse had spoken of His Father; and
Philip exclaimed, in the fervor of his thirst for God,
"Lord, show us the Father, and it is enough."
    St. James the Less, the author of an inspired epistle,
was also one of the Twelve.   St. Paul tells us that he was
favored by a special apparition of Christ after the Resurrection.   On the dispersion of the apostles among the
nations, St. James was left as Bishop of Jerusalem; and
even the Jews held in such high veneration his purity,
mortification, and prayer, that they named him the Just.
The earliest of Church historians has handed down many

traditions of St. James's sanctity.   He was always a virgin,
says Hegesippus, and consecrated to God.   He drank no
wine, wore no sandals on his feet, and but a single garment on his body.   He prostrated himself so much in
prayer that the skin of his knees was hardened like a
camel's hoof.   The Jews, it is said, used out of respect to
touch the hem of his garment.   He was indeed a living
proof of his own words, " The wisdom that is from above
first indeed is chaste, then peaceable, modest, full of mercy
and good fruits."   He sat beside St. Peter and St. Paul at
the Council of Jerusalem ; and when St. Paul at a later
time escaped the fury of the Jews by appealing to Cæsar,
the people took vengeance on James, and crying, " The
just one hath erred," stoned him to death.

Reflection.— The Church commemorates on the same
day Sts. Philip and James, whose bodies lie side by side at
Rome.   They represent to us two aspects of Christian holiness.   The first preaches faith, the second works ; the one
holy aspirations, the other purity of heart.

May 2.—ST. ATHANASIUS, Bishop.

ATHANASIUS was born in Egypt towards the end of
the third century, and was from his youth pious,
learned, and deeply versed in the sacred writings, as be-
fitted one whom God had chosen to be the champion and
defender of His Church against the Arian heresy.   Though
only a deacon, he was chosen by his bishop to go with him
to the Council of Nicæa, in 325, and attracted the attention of all by the learning and ability with which he
defended the faith.   A few months later, he became Patriarch of Alexandria, and for forty-six years he bore, often
well-nigh alone, the whole brunt of the Arian assault.   On
the refusal of the Saint to restore Arius to Catholic communion, the emperor ordered the Patriarch of Constantinople to do so.   The wretched heresiarch took an oath
that he had always believed as the Church believes ; and
the patriarch, after vainly using every effort to move the
emperor, had recourse to fasting and prayer, that God
would avert from the Church the frightful sacrilege.   The

day came for the solemn entrance of Arius into the great church of Sancta Sophia. The heresiarch and his party set out glad and in triumph. But before he reached the church, death smote him swiftly and awfully, and the dreaded sacrilege was averted. St. Athanasius stood unmoved against four Roman emperors; was banished five times; was the butt of every insult, calumny, and wrong the Arians could devise, and lived in constant peril of death. Though firm as adamant in defence of the Faith, he was meek and humble, pleasant and winning in converse, beloved by his flock, unwearied in labors, in prayer, in mortifications, and in zeal for souls. In the year 373 his stormy life closed in peace, rather that his people would have it so than that his enemies were weary of persecuting him. He left to the Church the whole and ancient Faith, defended and explained in writings rich in thought and learning, clear, keen, and stately in expression. He is honored as one of the greatest of the Doctors of the Church.

Reflection.—The Catholic Faith, says St. Augustine, is more precious far than all the riches and treasures of earth; more glorious and greater than all its honors, all its possessions. This it is which saves sinners, gives light to the blind, restores penitents, perfects the just, and is the crown of martyrs.

May 3.—THE DISCOVERY OF THE HOLY CROSS.

GOD having restored peace to His Church, by exalting Constantine the Great to the imperial throne, that pious prince, who had triumphed over his enemies by the miraculous power of the cross, was very desirous of expressing his veneration for the holy places which had been honored and sanctified by the presence and sufferings of our blessed Redeemer on earth, and accordingly resolved to build a magnificent church in the city of Jerusalem. St. Helen, the emperor's mother, desiring to visit the holy places there, undertook a journey into Palestine in 326, though at that time near eighty years of age; and on her arrival at Jerusalem was inspired with a great desire to find the identical cross on which Christ had suffered for our sins. But there was no mark or tradition, even amongst the Christians, to show where it lay. The heathens, out of an aversion to Christianity, had done what they could to conceal the place where Our Saviour was buried, by heaping on it a great quantity of stones and rubbish, and building on it a temple to Venus. They had, moreover, erected a statue of Jupiter in the place where Our Saviour rose from the dead. Helen, to carry out her pious design, consulted every one at Jerusalem and near it whom she thought likely to assist her in finding out the cross; and was credibly informed that, if she could find out the sepulchre, she would likewise find the instruments of the punishment; it being the custom among the Jews to make a hole near the place where the body of a criminal was buried, and to throw into it whatever belonged to his execution. The pious empress, therefore, ordered the profane buildings to be pulled down, the statues to be broken in pieces, and the rubbish to be removed; and, upon digging to a great depth, the holy sepulchre, and near it three crosses, also the nails which had pierced Our Saviour's body, and the title which had been fixed to His cross, were found. By this discovery they knew that one of the three crosses was that which they were in quest of, and that the others belonged to the two malefactors between whom Our Saviour had been crucified. But, as the title was found separate from the cross, it was difficult to distinguish which of the three crosses was that on which our divine Redeemer consummated His sacrifice for the salvation of the world. In this perplexity the holy Bishop Macarius, knowing that one of the principal ladies of the city lay extremely ill, suggested to the empress to cause the three crosses to be carried to the sick person, not doubting but God would discover which was the cross they sought for. This being done, St. Macarius prayed that God would have regard to their faith, and, after his prayer, applied the crosses singly to the patient, who was immediately and perfectly recovered by the touch of one of the three crosses, the other two having been tried without effect. St. Helen, full of joy at having found the treasure which she had so earnestly sought and so highly esteemed, built a church on the spot, and lodged the cross there with great veneration, having provided an extraordinarily rich case for it.   She afterwards carried part of it to the Emperor Constantine, then at Constantinople, who received it with great veneration; another part she sent or rather carried to Rome, to be placed in the church which she had built there, called Of the Holy Cross of Jerusalem, where it remains to this day.   The title was sent by St. Helen to the same church, and placed on the top of an arch, where it was found in a case of lead in 1492. The inscription in Hebrew, Greek, and Latin is in red letters, and the wood was whitened.   Thus it was in 1492; but these colors are since faded.   Also the words *Jesus* and *Judæorum* are eaten away.   The board is nine, but must have been twelve, inches long.   The main part of the cross St. Helen inclosed in a silver shrine, and committed it to the care of St. Macarius, that it might be delivered down to posterity, as an object of veneration.   It was accordingly kept with singular care and respect in the magnificent church which she and her son built in Jerusalem.   St. Paulinus relates that, though chips were almost daily cut off from it and given to devout persons, yet the sacred wood suffered thereby no diminution.   It is affirmed by St. Cyril of Jerusalem, twenty-five years after the discovery, that pieces of the cross were spread all over the earth; he compares this wonder to the miraculous feeding of five thousand men, as recorded in the Gospel.   The discovery of the cross must have happened about the month of May, or early in the spring; for St. Helen went the same year to Constantinople, and from thence to Rome, where she died in the arms of her son on the 18th of August, 326.

Reflection.—In every pious undertaking the beginning merely does not suffice.   " Whoso shall persevere unto the end, he shall be saved."

May 4.—ST. MONICA.

ⅯONICA, the mother of St. Augustine, was born in 332. After a girlhood of singular innocence and piety, she was given in marriage to Patritius, a pagan.   She at once devoted herself to his conversion, praying for him always, and winning his reverence and love by the holiness of her life and her affectionate forbearance. She was rewarded by seeing him baptized a year before his death. When her son Augustine went astray in faith and manners her prayers and tears were incessant. She was once very urgent with a learned bishop that he would talk to her son in order to bring him to a better mind, but he declined, despairing of success with one at once so able and so headstrong. However, on witnessing her prayers and tears, he bade her be of good courage; for it might not be that the child of those tears should perish. By going to Italy, Augustine could for a time free himself from his mother's importunities; but he could not escape from her prayers, which encompassed him like the providence of God. She followed him to Italy, and there by his marvellous conversion her sorrow was turned into joy. At Ostia, on their homeward journey, as Augustine and his mother sat at a window conversing of the life of the blessed, she turned to him and said, " Son, there is nothing now I care for in this life. What I shall now do or why I am here, I know not. The one reason I had for wishing to linger in this life a little longer was that I might see you a Catholic Christian before I died. This has God granted me superabundantly in seeing you reject earthly happiness to become His servant. What do I here? " A few days afterwards she had an attack of fever, and died in the year 387.

Reflection.—It is impossible to set any bounds to what persevering prayer may do. It gives man a share in the Divine Omnipotence. St. Augustine's soul lay bound in the chains of heresy and impurity, both of which had by long habit grown inveterate. They were broken by his mother's prayers.

May 5.—ST. PIUS V.

A DOMINICAN friar from his fifteenth year, Michael Ghislieri, as a simple religious, as inquisitor, as bishop, and as cardinal, was famous for his intrepid defence of the Church's faith and discipline, and for the spotless purity of his own life. His first care as Pope was to reform the Roman court and capital by the strict example of his household and the severe punishment of all offenders. He next endeavored to obtain from the Catholic powers the recognition of the Tridentine decrees, two of which he urgently enforced — the residence of bishops, and the establishment of diocesan seminaries. He revised the Missal and Breviary, and reformed the ecclesiastical music. Nor was he less active in protecting the Church without. We see him at the same time supporting the Catholic King of France against the Huguenot rebels, encouraging Mary Queen of Scots, in the bitterness of her captivity, and excommunicating her rival the usurper Elizabeth, when the best blood of England had flowed upon the scaffold, and the measure of her crimes was full. But it was at Lepanto that the Saint's power was most manifest; there, in October, 1571, by the holy league which he had formed, but still more by his prayers to the great Mother of God, the aged Pontiff crushed the Ottoman forces, and saved Christendom from the Turk. Six months later, St. Pius died, having reigned but six years. St. Pius was accustomed to kiss the feet of his crucifix on leaving or entering his room. One day the feet moved away from his lips. Sorrow filled his heart, and he made acts of contrition, fearing that he must have committed some secret offence, but still he could not kiss the feet. It was afterwards found that they had been poisoned by an enemy.

Reflection.—"Thy cross, O Lord, is the source of all blessings, the cause of all graces: by it the faithful find strength in weakness, glory in shame, life in death."— *St. Leo.*

May 6.—ST. JOHN BEFORE THE LATIN GATE.

IN the year 95, St. John, who was the only surviving apostle, and governed all the churches of Asia, was apprehended at Ephesus, and sent prisoner to Rome. The Emperor Domitian did not relent at the sight of the venerable old man, but condemned him to be cast into a caldron of boiling oil. The martyr doubtless heard, with great joy, this barbarous sentence; the most cruel torments seemed to him light and most agreeable, because they would, he hoped, unite him forever to his divine Master and Saviour. But God accepted his will and crowned his desire; He conferred on him the honor and merit of martyrdom, but sus,ended the operation of the fire, as He had formerly preserved the three children from hurt in the Babylonian furnace. The seething oil was changed in his regard into an invigorating bath, and the Saint came out more refreshed than when he had entered the caldron. Domitian saw this miracle without drawing from it the least advantage, but remained hardened in his iniquity. However, he contented himself after this with banishing the holy apostle into the little island of Patmos. St. John returned to Ephesus, in the reign of Nerva, who by mildness, during his short reign of one year and four months, labored to restore the faded lustre of the Roman Empire. This glorious triumph of St. John happened without the gate of Rome called Latina. A church which since has always borne this title was consecrated in the same place in memory of this miracle, under the first Christian emperors.

Reflection.—St. John suffered above the other Saints a martyrdom of love, being a martyr, and more than a martyr, at the foot of the cross of his divine Master. All his sufferings were by love and compassion imprinted in his soul, and thus shared by him. O singular happiness, to have stood under the cross of Christ! O extraordinary privilege, to have suffered martyrdom in the person of Jesus, and been eye-witness of all He did or endured! If nature revolt within us against suffering, let us call to mind those words of the divine Master: "Thou knowest not now wherefore; but thou shalt know hereafter."

May 7.—ST. STANISLAS, Bishop, Martyr.

STANISLAS was born in answer to prayer when his parents were advanced in age. Out of gratitude they educated him for the Church, and from a holy priest he became in time Bishop of Cracow. Boleslas II. was then King of Poland — a prince of good disposition, but spoilt by a long course of victory and success. After many acts of lust and cruelty, he outraged the whole kingdom by carrying off the wife of one of his nobles. Against this public scandal the chaste and gentle bishop alone raised his voice. Having commended the matter to God, he went down to the palace and openly rebuked the king for his crime against God and his subjects, and threatened to excommunicate him if he persisted in his sin. To slander the Saint's character, Boleslas suborned the nephews of one Paul, lately dead, to swear that their uncle had never been paid for land bought by the bishop for the Church. The Saint stood fearlessly before the king's tribunal, though all his witnesses forsook him, and guaranteed to bring the dead man to witness for him within three days. On the third day, after many prayers and tears, he raised Paul to life, and led him in his grave-clothes before the king. Boleslas made a show for a while of a better life. Soon, however, he relapsed into the most scandalous excesses, and the bishop, finding all remonstrance useless, pronounced the sentence of excommunication. In defiance of the censure, on May 8, 1079, the king went down to a chapel where the bishop himself was saying Mass, and sent in three companies of soldiers to dispatch him at the altar. Each in turn came out, saying they had been scared by a light from heaven. Then the king rushed in and slew the Saint at the altar with his own hand.

Reflection.—The safest correction of vice is a blameless life. Yet there are times when silence would make us answerable for the sins of others. At such times let us, in the name of God, rebuke the offender without fear.

May 8.—THE APPARITION OF ST. MICHAEL THE ARCHANGEL.

IT is manifest, from the Holy Scriptures, that God is pleased to make frequent use of the ministry of the heavenly spirits in the dispensations of His providence in this world, and especially towards man. Hence the name of Angel (which is not properly a denomination of nature, but office) has been appropriated to them. The angels are all pure spirits; they are, by a property of their nature, immortal, as every spirit is. They have the power of moving or conveying themselves from place to place, and such is their activity that it is not easy for us to conceive it. Among the holy archangels, there are particularly distinguished in Holy Writ Sts. Michael, Gabriel, and Raphael. St. Michael, whom the Church honors this day, was the prince of the faithful angels who opposed Lucifer and his associates in their revolt against God. As the devil is the sworn enemy of God's holy Church, St. Michael is its special protector against his assaults and stratagems. This holy archangel has ever been honored in the Christian Church as her guardian under God, and as the protector of the faithful; for God is pleased to employ the zeal and charity of the good angels and their leader against the malice of the devil. To thank His adorable goodness for this benefit of His merciful providence is this festival instituted by the Church in honor of the good angels, in which devotion she has been encouraged by several apparitions of this glorious archangel. Among others, it is recorded that St. Michael, in a vision, admonished the Bishop of Siponto to build a church in his honor on Mount Gargano, near Manfredonia, in the kingdom of Naples. When the Emperor Otho III. had, contrary to his word, put to death, for rebellion, Crescentius, a Roman senator, being touched with remorse he cast himself at the feet of St. Romuald, who, in satisfaction for his crime, enjoined him to walk barefoot, on a penitential pilgrimage, to St. Michael's on Mount Gargano, which penance he performed in 1002. It is mentioned in particular of this special guardian and protector of the Church that, in the persecution of Antichrist, he will powerfully stand up in her defence: "At that time shall Michael rise up, the great prince, who standeth for the children of thy people."

Reflection.—St. Michael is not only the protector of the Church, but of every faithful soul. He defeated the devil by humility: we are enlisted in the same warfare. His arms were humility and ardent love of God: the same must be our weapons. We ought to regard this archangel as our leader under God; and, courageously resisting the

devil in all his assaults, to cry out, Who can be compared
to God?

May 9.—ST. GREGORY NAZIANZEN.

GREGORY was born of saintly parents, and was the
chosen friend of St. Basil. They studied together at
Athens, turned at the same time from the fairest worldly
prospects, and for some years lived together in seclusion,
self-discipline, and toil. Gregory was raised, almost by
force, to the priesthood; and was in time made Bishop of
Nazianzum by St. Basil, who had become Archbishop of
Cæsarea. When he was fifty years old, he was chosen, for
his rare gifts and his conciliatory disposition, to be Patriarch of Constantinople, then distracted and laid waste by
Arian and other heretics. In that city he labored with
wonderful success. The Arians were so irritated at the
decay of their heresy that they pursued the Saint with outrage, calumny, and violence, and at length resolved to take
away his life. For this purpose they chose a resolute young
man, who readily undertook the sacrilegious commission.
But God did not allow him to carry it out. He was
touched with remorse, and cast himself at the Saint's feet,
avowing his sinful intent. St. Gregory at once forgave
him, treated him with all kindness, and received him
amongst his friends, to the wonder and edification of the
whole city, and to the confusion of the heretics, whose
crime had served only as a foil to the virtue of the Saint.
St. Jerome boasts that he had sat at his feet, and calls him
his master and his catechist in Holy Scripture. But his
lowliness, his austerities, the insignificance of his person,
and above all his very success, drew down on him the
hatred of the enemies of the Faith. He was persecuted by
the magistrates, stoned by the rabble, and thwarted and
deserted even by his brother bishops. During the second
General Council he resigned his see, hoping thus to restore
peace to the tormented city, and retired to his native town,
where he died in 390. He was a graceful poet, a preacher
at once eloquent and solid; and as a champion of the Faith
so well equipped, so strenuous, and so exact, that he is
called St. Gregory the Theologian.

Reflection.—" We must overcome our enemies," said St. Gregory, " by gentleness; win them over by forbearance. Let them be punished by their own conscience, not by our wrath.   Let us not at once wither the fig-tree, from which a more skilful gardener may yet entice fruit."

May 10.—ST. ANTONINUS, Bishop.

NTONINUS, or Little Antony, as he was called from his small stature, was born at Florence in 1389.   After a childhood of singular holiness, he begged to be admitted into the Dominican house at Fiesole; but the Superior, to test his sincerity and perseverance, told him he must first learn by heart the book of the Decretals, containing several hundred pages.   This apparently impossible task was accomplished within twelve months; and Antoninus received the coveted habit in his sixteenth year.   While still very young, he filled several important posts of his Order, and was consulted on questions of difficulty by the most learned men of his day; being known, for his wonderful prudence, as " the Counsellor."   He wrote several works on theology and history, and sat as Papal Theologian at the Council of Florence.   In 1446 he was compelled to accept the archbishopric of that city; and in this dignity earned for himself the title of " the Father of the Poor," for all he had was at their disposal.   St. Antoninus never refused an alms which was asked in the name of God.   When he had no money, he gave his clothes, shoes, or furniture.   One day, being sent by the Florentines to the Pope, as he approached Rome a beggar came up to him almost naked, and asked him for an alms for Christ's sake.   Outdoing St. Martin, Antoninus gave him his whole cloak.   When he entered the city, another was given him; by whom he knew not.   His household consisted of only six persons; his palace contained no plate or costly furniture, and was often nearly destitute of the necessaries of life.   His one mule was frequently sold for the relief of the poor, when it would be bought back for him by some wealthy citizen.   He died embracing the crucifix, May 2d, 1459, often repeating the words, " To serve God is to reign."

Reflection.—" Alms-deeds," says St. Augustine, " comprise every kind of service rendered to our neighbor who needs such assistance. He who supports a lame man bestows an alms on him with his feet; he who guides a blind man does him a charity with his eyes; he who carries an invalid or an old man upon his shoulders imparts to him an alms of his strength. Hence none are so poor but they may bestow an alms on the wealthiest man in the world."

May 11.—ST. MAMMERTUS, Archbishop.

S T. MAMMERTUS, Archbishop of Vienne in Dauphiné, was a prelate renowned for his sanctity, learning, and miracles. He instituted in his diocese the fasts and supplications called the Rogations, on the following occasions. Almighty God, to punish the sins of the people, visited them with wars and other public calamities, and awaked them from their spiritual lethargy by the terrors of earthquakes, fires, and ravenous wild beasts, which last were sometimes seen in the very market-place of cities. These evils the impious ascribed to blind chance; but religious and prudent persons considered them as tokens of the divine anger, which threatened their entire destruction. Amidst these scourges, St. Mammertus received a token of the divine mercy. A terrible fire happened in the city of Vienne, which baffled the efforts of men; but by the prayers of the good bishop the fire on a sudden went out. This miracle strongly affected the minds of the people. The holy prelate took this opportunity to make them sensible of the necessity and efficacy of devout prayer, and formed a pious design of instituting an annual fast and supplication of three days, in which all the faithful should join, with sincere compunction of heart, to appease the divine indignation by fasting, prayer, tears, and the confession of sins. The Church of Auvergne, of which St. Sidonius was bishop, adopted this pious institution before the year 475, and it became in a very short time a universal practice. St. Mammertus died about the year 477.

Reflection.—" Know ye that the Lord will hear your prayers, if you continue with perseverance in fastings and prayers in the sight of the Lord " (Judith iv. 11).

May 12.—ST. EPIPHANIUS, Archbishop.

S T. EPIPHANIUS was born about the year 310, in Palestine. In his youth he began the study of the Holy Scriptures, embraced a monastic life, and went into Egypt to perfect himself in the exercises of that state, in the deserts of that country. He returned to Palestine about the year 333, and built a monastery near the place of his birth. His labors in the exercise of virtue seemed to some to surpass his strength; but his apology always was: " God gives not the kingdom of heaven but on condition that we labor; and all we can do bears no proportion to such a crown." To his corporal austerities he added an indefatigable application to prayer and study. Most books then in vogue passed through his hands; and he improved himself very much in learning by his travels into many parts.

Although the skilful director of many others, St. Epiphanius took the great St. Hilarion as his master in a spiritual life, and enjoyed the happiness of his direction and intimate acquaintance from the year 333 to 356. The reputation of his virtue made St. Epiphanius known to distant countries, and about the year 367 he was chosen Bishop of Salamis in Cyprus. But he still wore the monastic habit, and continued to govern his monastery in Palestine, which he visited from time to time. He sometimes relaxed his austerities in favor of hospitality, preferring charity to abstinence. No one surpassed him in tenderness and charity to the poor. The veneration which all men had for his sanctity exempted him from the persecution of the Arian Emperor Valens. In 376 he undertook a journey to Antioch in the hope of converting Vitalis, the Apollinarist bishop; and in 382 he accompanied St. Paulinus from that city to Rome, where they lodged at the house of St. Paula; our Saint in return entertained her afterward ten days in Cyprus in 385. The very name of an error in faith, or the shadow of danger of evil, affrighted him, and the Saint fell into some mistakes on certain occasions, which proceeded from zeal and simplicity. He was on his way back to Salamis, after a short absence, when he died in 403, having been bishop thirty-six years.

Reflection.—" In this is charity: not as though we had loved God, but because He hath first loved us."

May 13.—ST. JOHN THE SILENT.

JOHN was born of a noble family at Nicopolis, in Armenia, in the year 454; but he derived from the virtue of his parents a much more illustrious nobility than that of their pedigree. After their death, he built at Nicopolis a church in honor of the Blessed Virgin, as also a monastery, in which, with ten fervent companions, he shut himself up when only eighteen years of age, with a view of making the salvation and most perfect sanctification of his soul his only and earnest pursuit. Not only to shun the danger of sin by the tongue, but also out of sincere humility and contempt of himself, and the love of interior recollection and prayer, he very seldom spoke; and when obliged to, it was always in a very few words, and with great discretion. To his extreme affliction, when he was only twenty-eight years old, the Archbishop of Sebaste obliged him to quit his retreat, and ordained him Bishop of Colonian in Armenia, in 482. In this dignity John preserved always the same spirit, and, as much as was compatible with the duties of his charge, continued his monastic austerities and exercises. Whilst he was watching one night in prayer, he saw before him a bright cross formed in the air, and heard a voice which said to him, " If thou desirest to be saved, follow this light." It seemed to move before him, and at length point out to the monastery of St. Sabas. Being satisfied what the sacrifice was which God required at his hands, he found means to abdicate the episcopal charge, and retired to the neighboring monastery of St. Sabas, which at that time contained one hundred and fifty fervent monks. St. John was then thirty-eight years old. After living there unknown for some years, fetching water, carrying stones, and doing other menial work, St. Sabas, judging him worthy to be promoted to the priesthood, presented him to the Patriarch Elias.   St. John took the patriarch aside, and, having obtained from him a promise of secrecy, said, " Father, I have been ordained bishop; but on account of the multitude of my sins have fled, and am come into this desert to wait the visit of the Lord." The patriarch was startled, but God revealed to St. Sabas the state of the affair, whereupon, calling for John, he complained to him of his unkindness in concealing the matter from him.   Finding himself discovered, John wished to quit the monastery, nor could St. Sabas prevail on him to stay, but on a promise never to divulge the secret.   In the year 503, St. John withdrew into a neighboring wilderness, but in 510 went back to the monastery, and confined himself for forty years to his cell.   St. John, by his example and counsels, conducted many fervent souls to God, and continued to emulate, as much as this mortal state will allow, the glorious employment of the heavenly spirits in an uninterrupted exercise of love and praise, till he passed to their blessed company, soon after the year 558; having lived seventy-six years in the desert, which had only been interrupted by the nine years of his episcopal dignity.

Reflection.—A love of Christian silence is a proof that a soul makes it her chiefest delight to be occupied on God, and finds no comfort like that of conversing with Him. This is the paradise of all devout souls.

May 14.—ST. PACHOMIUS, Abbot.

IN the beginning of the fourth century great levies of troops were made throughout Egypt for the service of the Roman emperor.   Among the recruits was Pachomius, a young heathen, then in his twenty-first year.   On his way down the Nile he passed a village, whose inhabitants gave him food and money.   Marvelling at this kindness, Pachomius was told they were Christians, and hoped for a reward in the life to come.   He then prayed God to show him the truth, and promised to devote his life to His service. On being discharged, he returned to a Christian village in Egypt, where he was instructed and baptized. Instead of going home, he sought Palemon, an aged solitary, to learn from him a perfect life, and with great joy embraced the most severe austerities. Their food was bread and water, once a day in summer, and once in two days in winter; sometimes they added herbs, but mixed ashes with them. They only slept one hour each night, and this short repose Pachomius took sitting upright without support. Three times God revealed to him that he was to found a religious order at Tabenna; and an angel gave him a rule of life. Trusting in God, he built a monastery, although he had no disciples; but vast multitudes soon flocked to him, and he trained them in perfect detachment from creatures and from self. One day a monk, by dint of great exertions, contrived to make two mats instead of the one which was the usual daily task, and set them both out in front of his cell, that Pachomius might see how diligent he had been. But the Saint, perceiving the vainglory which had prompted the act, said, " This brother has taken a great deal of pains from morning till night to give his work to the devil." Then, to cure him of his delusion, Pachomius imposed on him as a penance to keep his cell for five months and to taste no food but bread and water. His visions and miracles were innumerable, and he read all hearts. His holy death occurred in 348.

Reflection.—" To live in great simplicity," said St. Pachomius, " and in a wise ignorance, is exceeding wise."

May 15.—STS. PETER and DIONYSIA.

IN the Decian persecution the blood of the Christians flowed at Lampsacus, a city of Asia Minor. St. Peter was the first who was led before the proconsul and condemned to die for the name of Christ. Young though he was, he went joyfully to his torments. He was bound to a wheel by iron chains, and his bones were broken, but he raised his eyes to heaven with a smiling countenance and said, " I give Thee thanks, O Lord Jesus Christ, because Thou hast given me patience, and made me victorious over the tyrant." The proconsul saw how little suffering availed, and ordered the martyr to be beheaded. But a little later, in the same city, the virgin Dionysia showed a like eagerness to suffer. St. Dionysia gained the crown which an apostate lost, and his history may teach us that those who lose Christ rather than suffer with Him lose all. With the strength that was left he cried out, " I never was a Christian. I sacrifice to the gods." Therefore he was taken down, and he offered sacrifice. But he was possessed by the devil, whom he had chosen for his master. He fell to the earth in a fit, bit out his tongue, and so expired. He escaped a little pain, and instead he went to the endless torments of hell, and forfeited eternal rest. " O wretched man ! " Dionysia cried, " why have you feared a little suffering and chosen eternal pain instead ? " She was seized and led away to horrible outrage, but her angel guardian appeared by her side and protected the spouse of Christ. Escaping from prison, she still burned with the desire to be dissolved and to be with Christ. She threw herself upon the bodies of the martyrs, saying, " I would fain die with you on earth, that I may live with you in heaven." And Christ, Who is the crown of virgins and the strength of martyrs, gave her the desire of her heart.

Reflection.—The martyrs were even like us, with natures which shrank from suffering. They were patient under it because they looked to the eternal recompense, and endured as seeing Him Who is invisible.

May 16.—ST. JOHN NEPOMUCEN.

ST. JOHN was born, in answer to prayer, 1330, of poor parents, at Nepomuc in Bohemia. In gratitude they consecrated him to God; and his holy life as a priest led to his appointment as chaplain to the court of the Emperor Wenceslas, where he converted numbers by his preaching and example. Amongst those who sought his advice was the empress, who suffered much from her husband's unfounded jealousy. St. John taught her to bear her cross with joy; but her piety only incensed the emperor, and he tried to extort her confessions from the

Saint. He threw St. John into a dungeon, but gained
nothing; then, inviting him to his palace, he promised him
riches if he would yield, and threatened death if he refused. The Saint was silent. He was racked and burnt
with torches; but no words, save Jesus and Mary, fell from
his lips. At last set free, he spent his time in preaching,
and preparing for the death he knew to be at hand. On
Ascension Eve, May 16, Wenceslas, after a final and fruit-
less attempt to move his constancy, ordered him to be cast
into the river, and that night the martyr's hands and feet
were bound, and he was thrown from the bridge of Prague.
As he died, a heavenly light shining on the water discovered
the body, which was buried with the honors due to a Saint.
A few years later, Wenceslas was deposed by his own subjects, and died an impenitent and miserable death. In
1618 the Calvinist and Hussite soldiers of the Protestant
Elector Frederick tried repeatedly to demolish the shrine
of St. John at Prague. Each attempt was miraculously
frustrated; and once the persons engaged in the sacrilege,
among whom was an Englishman, were killed on the spot.
In 1620 the imperial troops recovered the town by a victory
which was ascribed to the Saint's intercession, as he was
seen on the eve of the battle, radiant with glory, guarding
the cathedral. When his shrine was opened, three hundred
and thirty years after his decease, the flesh had disappeared,
and one member alone remained incorrupt, the tongue;
thus still, in silence, giving glory to God.

Reflection.—St. John, who by his invincible sacramental
silence won his crown, teaches us to prefer torture and
death to offending the Creator with our tongue. How
many times each day do we forfeit grace and strength by
sins of speech!

May 17.—ST. PASCHAL BAYLON.

FROM a child Paschal seems to have been marked out
for the service of God; and amidst his daily labors
he found time to instruct and evangelize the rude herds-
men who kept their flocks on the hills of Arragon. At the
age of twenty-four he entered the Franciscan Order, in

which, however, he remained, from humility, a simple lay-brother, and occupied himself, by preference, with the roughest and most servile tasks. He was distinguished by an ardent love and devotion to the Blessed Sacrament. He would spend hours on his knees before the tabernacle — often he was raised from the ground in the fervor of his prayer — and there, from the very and eternal Truth, he drew such stores of wisdom that, unlettered as he was, he was counted by all a master in theology and spiritual science. Shortly after his profession he was called to Paris on business connected with his Order. The journey was full of peril, owing to the hostility of the Huguenots, who were numerous at the time in the south of France; and on four separate occasions Paschal was in imminent danger of death at the hands of the heretics. But it was not God's will that His servant should obtain the crown of martyrdom which, though judging himself all unworthy of it, he so earnestly desired, and he returned in safety to his convent, where he died in the odor of sanctity, May 15, 1592.

As Paschal was watching his sheep on the mountain-side, he heard the consecration bell ring out from a church in the valley below, where the villagers were assembled for Mass. The Saint fell on his knees, when suddenly there stood before him an angel of God, bearing in his hands the Sacred Host, and offering it for his adoration. Learn from this how pleasing to Jesus Christ are those who honor Him in this great mystery of His love; and how to them especially this promise is fulfilled: "I will not leave you orphans: I will come unto you" (John xiv. 18).

Reflection.—St. Paschal teaches us never to suffer a day to pass without visiting Jesus in the narrow chamber where He, Whom the heaven itself cannot contain, abides day and night for our sake.

May 18.—ST. VENANTIUS, Martyr.

ST. VENANTIUS was born at Camerino in Italy, and at the age of fifteen was seized as a Christian and carried before a judge. As it was found impossible to shake his constancy either by threats or promises, he was

condemned to be scourged, but was miraculously saved by
an angel. He was then burnt with torches and hung over
a low fire that he might be suffocated by the smoke. The
judge's secretary, admiring the steadfastness of the Saint,
and seeing an angel robed in white, who trampled out the
fire and again set free the youthful martyr, proclaimed
his faith in Christ, was baptized with his whole family, and
shortly after won the martyr's crown himself. Venantius
was then carried before the governor, who, unable to make
him renounce his faith, cast him into prison with an apostate, who vainly strove to tempt him. The governor then
ordered his teeth and jaws to be broken, and had him
thrown into a furnace, from which the angel once more
delivered him. The Saint was again led before the judge,
who at sight of him fell headlong from his seat and expired, crying, " The God of Venantius is the true God; let
us destroy our idols." This circumstance being told to the
governor, he ordered Venantius to be thrown to the lions;
but these brutes, forgetting their natural ferocity, crouched
at the feet of the Saint. Then, by order of the tyrant, the
young martyr was dragged through a heap of brambles and
thorns, but again God manifested the glory of His servant;
the soldiers suffering from thirst, the Saint knelt on a rock
and signed it with a cross, when immediately a jet of clear,
cool water spurted up from the spot. This miracle converted many of those who beheld it, whereupon the governor
had Venantius and his converts beheaded together in the
year 250. The bodies of these martyrs are kept in the
church at Camerino which bears the Saint's name.

Reflection.—Love of suffering marks the most perfect
degree in the love of God. Our Lord Himself was consumed with the desire to suffer, because He burnt with the
love of God. We must begin with patience and detachment.
At last we shall learn to love the sufferings which conform
us to the Passion of our Redeemer.

May 19.—ST. PETER CELESTINE.

As a child, Peter had visions of our blessed Lady, and of the angels and saints. They encouraged him in his prayer, and chided him when he fell into any fault. His mother, though only a poor widow, put him to school, feeling sure that he would one day be a Saint. At the age of twenty, he left his home in Apulia to live in a mountain solitude. Here he passed three years, assaulted by the evil spirits and beset with temptations of the flesh, but consoled by angels' visits. After this his seclusion was invaded by disciples, who refused to be sent away; and the rule of life which he gave them formed the foundation of the Celestine Order. Angels assisted in the church which Peter built; unseen bells rang peals of surpassing sweetness, and heavenly music filled the sanctuary when he offered the Holy Sacrifice. Suddenly he found himself torn from his loved solitude by his election to the Papal throne. Resistance was of no avail. He took the name of Celestine, to remind him of the heaven he was leaving and for which he sighed, and was consecrated at Aquila. After a reign of four months, Peter summoned the cardinals to his presence, and solemnly resigned his trust. St. Peter built himself a boarded cell in his palace, and there continued his hermit's life; and when, lest his simplicity might be taken advantage of to distract the peace of the Church, he was put under guard, he said, " I desired nothing but a cell, and a cell they have given me." There he enjoyed his former loving intimacy with the saints and angels, and sang the Divine praises almost continually. At length, on Whit-Sunday, he told his guards he should die within the week, and immediately fell ill. He received the last sacraments; and the following Saturday, as he finished the concluding verse of Lauds, " Let every spirit bless the Lord! " he closed his eyes to this world and opened them to the vision of God.

Reflection.—" Whoso," says the *Imitation of Christ,* " withdraweth himself from acquaintances and friends, to him will God draw near with His holy angels."

May 20.—ST. BERNARDINE OF SIENA.

IN 1408 St. Vincent Ferrer once suddenly interrupted his sermon to declare that there was among his hearers a young Franciscan who would be one day a greater preacher than himself, and would be set before him in honor by the Church. This unknown friar was Bernardine. Of noble birth, he had spent his youth in works of mercy, and had then entered religion. Owing to a defective utterance, his success as a preacher at first seemed doubtful, but, by the prayers of Our Lady, this obstacle was miraculously removed, and Bernardine began an apostolate which lasted thirty-eight years. By his burning words and by the power of the Holy Name of Jesus, which he displayed on a tablet at the end of his sermons, he obtained miraculous conversions, and reformed the greater part of Italy. But this success had to be exalted by the cross. The Saint was denounced as a heretic and his devotion as idolatrous. After many trials he lived to see his innocence proved, and a lasting memorial of his work established in a church. The Feast of the Holy Name commemorates at once his sufferings and his triumph. He died on Ascension Eve, 1444, while his brethren were chanting the antiphon, " Father, I have manifested Thy Name to men." St. Bernardine, when a youth, undertook the charge of a holy old woman, a relation of his, who had been left destitute. She was blind and bedridden, and during her long illness could only utter the Holy Name. The Saint watched over her till she died, and thus learned the devotion of his life.

Reflection.—Let us learn from the life of St. Bernardine the power of the Holy Name in life and death.

May 21.—ST. HOSPITIUS, Recluse.

ST. HOSPITIUS shut himself up in the ruins of an old tower near Villafranca, one league from Nice in Provence. He girded himself with a heavy iron chain and lived on bread and dates only. During Lent he redoubled his austerities, and, in order to conform his life more closely to that of the anchorites of Egypt, ate nothing but roots. For his great virtues Heaven honored him with the gifts of prophecy and of miracles. He foretold the ravages which the Lombards would make in Gaul. These barbarians, having come to the tower in which Hospitius lived, and seeing the chain with which he was bound, mistook him for some criminal who was there imprisoned. On questioning the Saint, he acknowledged that he was a great sinner and unworthy to live. Whereupon one of the soldiers lifted his sword to strike him; but God did not desert His faithful servant: the soldier's arm stiffened and became numb, and it was not until Hospitius made the sign of the cross over it that the man recovered the use of it. The soldier embraced Christianity, renounced the world, and passed the rest of his days in serving God. When our Saint felt that his last hour was nearing, he took off his chain and knelt in prayer for a long time. Then, stretching himself on a little bank of earth, he calmly gave up his soul to God, on the 21st of May, 681.

Reflection.—If we do not love penitence for its own sake, let us love it on account of our sins; for we should " work out our salvation in fear and trembling."

May 22.—ST. YVO, Confessor.

ST. YVO HELORI, descended from a noble and virtuous family near Treguier, in Brittany, was born in 1253. At fourteen years of age he went to Paris, and afterwards to Orleans, to pursue his studies. His mother was wont frequently to say to him that he ought so to live as became a Saint, to which his answer always was, that he hoped to be one. This resolution took deep root in his soul, and was a continual spur to virtue, and a check against the least shadow of any dangerous course. His time was chiefly divided between study and prayer; for his recreation he visited the hospitals, where he attended the sick with great charity, and comforted them under the severe trials of their suffering condition. He made a private vow of perpetual chastity; but this not being known, many honorable matches were proposed to him, which he modestly

rejected as incompatible with his studious life. He long
deliberated whether to embrace a religious or a clerical
state; but the desire of serving his neighbor determined
him at length in favor of the latter. He wished, out of
humility, to remain in the lesser orders; but his bishop
compelled him to receive the priesthood,— a step which
cost him many tears, though he had qualified himself for
that sacred dignity by the most perfect purity of mind and
body, and by a long and fervent preparation. He was appointed ecclesiastical judge for the diocese of Rennes. St.
Yvo protected the orphans and widows, defended the poor,
and administered justice to all with an impartiality, application, and tenderness which gained him the good-will even
of those who lost their causes. He was surnamed the advocate and lawyer of the poor. He built a house near his
own for a hospital of the poor and sick; he washed their
feet, cleansed their ulcers, served them at table, and ate
himself only the scraps which they had left. He distributed his corn, or the price for which he sold it, among
the poor immediately after the harvest. When a certain
person endeavored to persuade him to keep it some months,
that he might sell it at a better price, he answered, " I know
not whether I shall be then alive to give it." Another time
the same person said to him, " I have gained a fifth by
keeping my corn." " But I," replied the Saint, " a hun-
dredfold by giving it immediately away." During the
Lent of 1303 he felt his strength failing him; yet, far from
abating anything in his austerities, he thought himself
obliged to redouble his fervor in proportion as he advanced
nearer to eternity. On the eve of the Ascension he
preached to his people, said Mass, being upheld by two
persons, and gave advice to all who addressed themselves
to him. After this he lay down on his bed, which was a
hurdle of twigs plaited together, and received the last sacraments. From that moment he entertained himself with
God alone, till his soul went to possess Him in His glory.
His death happened on the 19th of May, 1303, in the
fiftieth year of his age.

Reflection.—St. Yvo was a Saint amidst the dangers of
the world; but he preserved his virtue untainted only by

arming himself carefully against them, by conversing assiduously with God in prayer and holy meditation, and by most watchfully shunning the snares of bad company. Without this precaution all the instructions of parents and all other means of virtue are ineffectual; and the soul is sure to split against this rock which does not steer wide of it.

May 23.—ST. JULIA, Virgin, Martyr.

ST. JULIA was a noble virgin of Carthage, who, when the city was taken by Genseric in 439, was sold for a slave to a pagan merchant of Syria named Eusebius. Under the most mortifying employments of her station, by cheerfulness and patience she found a happiness and comfort which the world could not have afforded. All the time she was not employed in her master's business was devoted to prayer and reading books of piety. Her master, who was charmed with her fidelity and other virtues, thought proper to carry her with him on one of his voyages to Gaul. Having reached the northern part of Corsica, he cast anchor, and went on shore to join the pagans of the place in an idolatrous festival. Julia was left at some distance, because she would not be defiled by the superstitious ceremonies which she openly reviled. Felix, the governor of the island, who was a bigoted pagan, asked who this woman was who dared to insult the gods. Eusebius informed him that she was a Christian, and that all his authority over her was too weak to prevail with her to renounce her religion, but that he found her so diligent and faithful he could not part with her. The governor offered him four of his best female slaves in exchange for her. But the merchant replied, " No; all you are worth will not purchase her; for I would freely lose the most valuable thing I have in the world rather than be deprived of her." However, the governor, while Eusebius was drunk and asleep, took upon him to compel her to sacrifice to his gods. He offered to procure her liberty if she would comply. The Saint made answer that she was as free as she desired to be as long as she was allowed to serve Jesus Christ.

Felix, thinking himself derided by her undaunted and resolute air, in a transport of rage caused her to be struck
on the face, and the hair of her head to be torn off, and,
lastly, ordered her to be hanged on a cross till she expired.
Certain monks of the isle of Gorgon carried off her body;
but in 763 Desiderius, King of Lombardy, removed her
relics to Brescia, where her memory is celebrated with great
devotion.

Reflection.—St. Julia, whether free or a slave, whether
in prosperity or in adversity, was equally fervent and devout. She adored all the sweet designs of Providence; and
far from complaining, she never ceased to praise and thank
God under all His holy appointments, making them always
the means of her virtue and sanctification. God, by an
admirable chain of events, raised her by her fidelity to the
honor of the saints, and to the dignity of a virgin and
martyr.

May 24.—STS. DONATIAN and ROGATIAN, Martyrs.

THERE lived at Nantes an illustrious young nobleman
named Donatian, who, having received the holy Sacrament of Regeneration, led a most edifying life, and strove
with much zeal to convert others to faith in Christ. His
elder brother, Rogatian, was not able to resist the moving
example of his piety and the force of his discourses, and
desired to be baptized. But the bishop having withdrawn
and concealed himself for fear of the persecution, he was
not able to receive that sacrament, but was shortly after
baptized in his blood; for he declared himself a Christian
at a time when to embrace that sacred profession was to
become a candidate for martyrdom. Donatian was impeached for professing himself a Christian, and for having
withdrawn others, particularly his brother, from the worship of the gods. Donatian was therefore apprehended,
and having boldly confessed Christ before the governor,
was cast into prison and loaded with irons. Rogatian was
also brought before the prefect, who endeavored first to
gain him by flattering speeches, but finding him inflexible,

sent him to prison with his brother. Rogatian grieved that he had not been able to receive the Sacrament of Baptism, and prayed that the kiss of peace which his brother gave him might supply it. Donatian also prayed for him that his faith might procure for him the effect of Baptism, and the effusion of his blood that of the Sacrament of Confirmation. They passed that night together in fervent prayer. They were the next day called for again by the prefect, to whom they declared that they were ready to suffer for the name of Christ whatever torments were prepared for them. By the order of the inhuman judge they were first stretched on the rack, afterwards their hands were pierced with lances, and lastly cut off, about the year 287.

Reflection.—Three things are pleasing unto God and man : concord among brethren, the love of parents, and the union of man and wife.

May 25.—ST. GREGORY VII.

GREGORY VII., by name Hildebrand, was born in Tuscany, about the year 1013. He was educated in Rome. From thence he went to France, and became a monk at Cluny. Afterwards he returned to Rome, and for many years filled high trusts of the Holy See. Three great evils then afflicted the Church : simony, concubinage, and the custom of receiving investiture from lay hands. Against these three corruptions Gregory never ceased to contend. As legate of Victor II. he held a Council at Lyons, where simony was condemned. He was elected Pope in 1073, and at once called upon the pastors of the Catholic world to lay down their lives rather than betray the laws of God to the will of princes. Rome was in rebellion through the ambition of the Cenci. Gregory excommunicated them. They laid hands on him at Christmas during the midnight Mass, wounded him, and cast him into prison. The following day he was rescued by the people. Next arose his conflict with Henry IV., Emperor of Germany. This monarch, after openly relapsing into simony, pretended to depose the Pope. Gregory excommunicated the emperor. His subjects turned against him, and at last he sought absolution of Gregory at Canossa. But he did not persevere. He set up an antipope, and besieged Gregory in the castle of St. Angelo. The aged pontiff was obliged to flee, and on May 25, 1085, about the seventy-second year of his life and the twelfth year of his pontificate, Gregory entered into his rest. His last words were full of a divine wisdom and patience. As he was dying, he said, " I have loved justice and hated iniquity, therefore I die in exile." His faithful attendant answered, " Vicar of Christ, an exile thou canst never be, for to thee God has given the Gentiles for an inheritance, and the uttermost ends of the earth for thy possession."

Reflection.—Eight hundred years are passed since St. Gregory died, and we see the same conflict renewed before our eyes. Let us learn from him to suffer any persecution from the world or the state, rather than betray the rights of the Holy See.

May 26.—ST. PHILIP NERI.

PHILIP was one of the noble line of Saints raised up by God in the sixteenth century to console and bless His Church. After a childhood of angelic beauty the Holy Spirit drew him away from Florence, the place of his birth, showed him the world, that he might freely renounce it, led him to Rome, modelled him in mind and heart and will, and then, as by a second Pentecost, came down in visible form and filled his soul with light and peace and joy. He would have gone to India, but God reserved him for Rome. There he went on simply from day to day, drawing souls to Jesus, exercising them in mortification and charity, and binding them together by cheerful devotions; thus, unconsciously to himself, under the hands of Mary, as he said, the Oratory grew up, and all Rome was pervaded and transformed by its spirit. His life was a continuous miracle, his habitual state an ecstasy. He read the hearts of men, foretold their future, knew their eternal destiny. His touch gave health of body; his very look calmed souls in trouble and drove away temptations. He was gay, genial, and irresistibly winning; neither insult nor wrong could dim the brightness of his joy.

Philip lived in an atmosphere of sunshine and gladness which brightened all who came near him. "When I met him in the street," says one, "he would pat my cheek and say, 'Well, how is Don Pellegrino?' and leave me so full of joy that I could not tell which way I was going." Others said that when he playfully pulled their hair or their ears, their hearts would bound with joy. Marcio Altieri felt such overflowing gladness in his presence that he said Philip's room was a paradise on earth. Fabrizio de Massimi would go in sadness or perplexity and stand at Philip's door; he said it was enough to see him, to be near him. And long after his death it was enough for many, when troubled, to go into his room to find their hearts lightened and gladdened. He inspired a boundless confidence and love, and was the common refuge and consoler of all. A gentle jest would convey his rebukes and veil his miracles. The highest honors sought him out, but he put them from him. He died in his eightieth year, in 1595, and bears the grand title of Apostle of Rome.

Reflection.—Philip wished his children to serve God, like the first Christians, in gladness of heart. He said this was the true filial spirit; this expands the soul, giving it liberty and perfection in action, power over temptations, and fuller aid to perseverance.

ST. AUGUSTINE, Apostle of England.

AUGUSTINE was prior of the monastery of St. Andrew on the Cœlian, and was appointed by St. Gregory the great chief of the missionaries whom he sent to England.

St. Augustine and his companions, having heard on their journey many reports of the barbarism and ferocity of the pagan English, were afraid, and wished to turn back. But St. Gregory replied, "Go on, in God's name! The greater your hardships, the greater your crown. May the grace of Almighty God protect you, and give me to see the fruit of your labor in the heavenly country! If I cannot share your toil, I shall yet share the harvest, for God knows that it is not good-will which is wanting." The band of missionaries went on in obedience.

Landing at Ebbsfleet, between Sandwich and Ramsgate, they met King Ethelbert and his thanes under a great oak-tree at Minster, and announced to him the Gospel of Jesus Christ. Instant and complete success attended their preaching. On Whit-Sunday, 596, King Ethelbert was baptized, and his example was followed by the greater number of his nobles and people. By degrees the Faith spread far and wide, and Augustine, as Papal Legate, set out on a visitation of Britain. He failed in his attempt to enlist the Britons of the west in the work of his apostolate, through their obstinate jealousy and pride; but his success was triumphant from south to north. St. Augustine died after eight years of evangelical labors. The Anglo-Saxon Church, which he founded, is still famous for its learning, zeal, and devotion to the Holy See, while its calendar commemorates no less than 300 Saints, half of whom were of royal birth.

Reflection.—The work of an apostle is the work of the right hand of God. He often chooses weak instruments for His mightiest purposes. The most sure augury of lasting success in missionary labor is obedience to superiors and diffidence in self.

May 27.—ST. MARY MAGDALEN OF PAZZI.

ST. MARY MAGDALEN OF PAZZI, of an illustrious house in Florence, was born in the year 1566, and baptized by the name of Catherine. She received her first Communion at ten years of age, and made a vow of virginity at twelve. She took great pleasure in carefully teaching the Christian doctrine to the ignorant. Her father, not knowing her vow, wished to give her in marriage, but she persuaded him to allow her to become a religious. It was more difficult to obtain her mother's consent; but at last she gained it, and she was professed, being then eighteen years of age, in the Carmelite monastery of Santa Maria degli Angeli in Florence, May 17, 1584. She changed her name Catherine into that of Mary Magdalen on becoming a

nun, and took as her motto, " To suffer or die ; " and her
life henceforth was a life of penance for sins not her own,
and of love of Our Lord, Who tried her in ways fearful and
strange.   She was obedient, observant of the rule, humble
and mortified, and had a great reverence for the religious
life.   She loved poverty and suffering, and hungered after
Communion.   The day of Communion she called the day
of love.   The charity that burned in her heart led her in
her youth to choose the house of the Carmelites, because
the religious therein communicated every day.   She rejoiced to see others communicate, even when she was not
allowed to do so herself ; and her love for her sisters grew
when she saw them receive Our Lord.

God raised her to high states of prayer, and gave her rare
gifts, enabling her to read the thoughts of her novices, and
filling her with wisdom to direct them aright.   She was
twice chosen mistress of novices, and then made superioress,
when God took her to Himself, May 25, 1607.   Her body
is incorrupt.

Reflection.—St. Mary Magdalen of Pazzi was so filled
with the love of God that her sisters in the monastery
observed it in her love of themselves, and called her " the
Mother of Charity " and " the Charity of the Monastery."

VENERABLE BEDE.

VENERABLE BEDE, the illustrious ornament of the Anglo-
Saxon Church and the first English historian, was
consecrated to God at the age of seven, and intrusted to the
care of St. Benedict Biscop at Wearmouth.   He became a
monk in the sister-house of Jarrow, and there trained no
less than six hundred scholars, whom his piety, learning,
and sweet disposition had gathered round him.   To the
toils of teaching and the exact observance of his rule he
added long hours of private prayer, and the study of every
branch of science and literature then known.   He was
familiar with Latin, Greek, and Hebrew.   In the treatise
which he compiled for his scholars, still extant, he threw
together all that the world had then stored in history,
chronology, physics, music, philosophy, poetry, arithmetic,

and medicine. In his Ecclesiastical History he has left us beautiful lives of Anglo-Saxon Saints and holy Fathers, while his commentaries on the Holy Scriptures are still in use by the Church. It was to the study of the Divine Word that he devoted the whole energy of his soul, and at times his compunction was so overpowering that his voice would break with weeping, while the tears of his scholars mingled with his own. He had little aid from others, and during his later years suffered from constant illness; yet he worked and prayed up to his last hour.

The Saint was employed in translating the Gospel of St. John from the Greek up to the hour of his death, which took place on Ascension Day, 735. " He spent that day joyfully," writes one of his scholars. And in the evening the boy who attended him said, " Dear master, there is yet one sentence unwritten." He answered, " Write it quickly." Presently the youth said, " Now it is written." He replied, " Good! thou hast said the truth — *consummatum est;* take my head into thy hands, for it is very pleasant to me to sit facing my old praying-place, and there to call upon my Father." And so on the floor of his cell he sang, " Glory be to the Father, Son, and Holy Ghost; " and just as he said " Holy Ghost," he breathed his last, and went to the realms above.

Reflection.—" The more," says the *Imitation of Christ,* " a man is united within himself and interiorly simple, so much the more and deeper things doth he understand without labor; for he receiveth the light of understanding from on high."

May 28.—ST. GERMANUS, Bishop.

S T. GERMANUS, the glory of the Church of France in the sixth century, was born in the territory of Autun, about the year 469. In his youth he was conspicuous for his fervor. Being ordained priest, he was made abbot of St. Symphorian's; he was favored at that time with the gifts of miracles and prophecy. It was his custom to watch the great part of the night in the church in prayer, whilst his monks slept. One night, in a dream, he thought

a venerable old man presented him with the keys of the
city of Paris, and said to him that God committed to his
care the inhabitants of that city, that he should save them
from perishing.   Four years after this divine admonition,
in 554, happening to be at Paris when that see became
vacant on the demise of the Bishop Eusebius, he was exalted to the episcopal chair, though he endeavored by many
tears to decline the charge.   His promotion made no alteration in his mode of life.   The same simplicity and
frugality appeared in his dress, table, and furniture.   His
house was perpetually crowded with the poor and the afflicted, and he had always many beggars at his own table.
God gave to his sermons a wonderful influence over the
minds of all ranks of people; so that the face of the whole
city was in a very short time quite changed.   King Childebert, who till then had been an ambitious, worldly prince,
was entirely converted by the sweetness and the powerful
discourses of the Saint, and founded many religious institutions, and sent large sums of money to the good bishop,
to be distributed among the indigent.   In his old age St.
Germanus lost nothing of that zeal and activity with
which he had filled the great duties of his station in the
vigor of his life; nor did the weakness to which his corporal austerities had reduced him make him abate anything
in the mortifications of his penitential life, in which he
redoubled his fervor as he approached nearer to the end
of his course.   By his zeal the remains of idolatry were
extirpated in France.   The Saint continued his labors for
the conversion of sinners till he was called to receive the
reward of them, on the 28th of May, 576, being eighty
years old.

Reflection.—" In the churches bless ye God the Lord.
From Thy temple kings shall offer presents to Thee."

May 29.—ST. CYRIL, Martyr.

S̩T. CYRIL suffered while still a boy at Cæsarea in Cappadocia, during the persecutions of the third century.
He used to repeat the name of Christ at all times, and
confessed that the mere utterance of this name moved him

strangely. He was beaten and reviled by his heathen father. But he bore all this with joy, increasing in the strength of Christ, Who dwelt within him, and drawing many of his own age to the imitation of his heavenly life. When his father in his fury turned him out of doors, he said he had lost little, and would receive a great recompense instead.

Soon after, he was brought before the magistrate on account of his faith. No threats could make him show a sign of fear, and the judge, pitying perhaps his tender years, offered him his freedom, assured him of his father's forgiveness, and besought him to return to his home and inheritance. But the blessed youth replied, " I left my home gladly; for I have a greater and a better which is waiting for me." He was filled with the same heavenly desires to the end. He was taken to the fires as if for execution, and was then brought back and re-examined, but he only protested against the cruel delay. Led out to die, he hurried on the executioners, gazed unmoved at the flames which were kindled for him, and expired, hastening, as he said, to his home.

Reflection.—Ask Our Lord to make all earthly joy insipid, and to fill you with the constant desire of heaven. This desire will make labor easy and suffering light. It will make you fervent and detached, and bring you even here a foretaste of that eternal joy and peace to which you are hastening.

May 30.—ST. FELIX I., Pope and Martyr.

ST. FELIX was a Roman by birth, and succeeded St. Dionysius in the government of the Church in 269. Paul of Samosata, the proud Bishop of Antioch, to the guilt of many enormous crimes added that of heresy, teaching that Christ was no more than a mere man, in whom the Divine Word dwelt by its operation and as in its temple, with many other gross errors concerning the capital mysteries of the Trinity and Incarnation. Three councils were held at Antioch to examine his cause, and in the third, assembled in 269, being clearly convicted of heresy,

pride, and many scandalous crimes, he was excommunicated and deposed, and Domnus was substituted in his
place.   As Paul still kept possession of the episcopal house,
our Saint had recourse to the Emperor Aurelian, who,
though a pagan, gave an order that the house should be-
long to him to whom the bishops of Rome and Italy ad-
judged it.   The persecution of Aurelian breaking out, St.
Felix, fearless of danger, strengthened the weak, encouraged all, baptized the catechumens, and continued to exert
himself in converting infidels to the Faith.   He himself obtained the glory of martyrdom.   He governed
the Church five years, and passed to a glorious eternity
in 274.

Reflection.—The example of Our Saviour and of all His
saints ought to encourage us under all trials to suffer with
patience and even with joy.   We shall soon begin to feel
that it is sweet to tread in the steps of a God-man, and
shall find that if we courageously take up our crosses, He
will make them light by sharing the burden with us.

May 31.—ST. PETRONILLA, Virgin.

AMONG the disciples of the apostles in the primitive
age of saints this holy virgin shone as a bright star
in the Church.   She lived when Christians were more
solicitous to live well than to write much: they knew how
to die for Christ, but did not compile long books in which
vanity has often a greater share than charity.   Hence no
particular account of her actions has been handed down to
us.   But how eminent her sanctity was we may judge from
the lustre by which it was distinguished among apostles,
prophets, and martyrs.   She is said to have been a daughter of the apostle St. Peter; that St. Peter was married
before his vocation to the apostleship we learn from the
Gospel.   St. Clement of Alexandria assures us that his
wife attained to the glory of martyrdom, at which Peter
himself encouraged her, bidding her to remember Our
Lord.   But it seems not certain whether St. Petronilla
was more than the spiritual daughter of that apostle.   She
flourished at Rome, and was buried on the way to Ardea,

where in ancient times a cemetery and a church bore her name.

Reflection.—With the saints the great end for which they lived was always present to their minds, and they thought every moment lost in which they did not make some advances toward eternal bliss. How will their example condemn at the last day the trifling fooleries and the greatest part of the conversation and employments of the world, which aim at nothing but present amusements, and forget the only important affair — the business of eternity.

June 1.—ST. JUSTIN, Martyr.

ST. JUSTIN was born of heathen parents at Neapolis in Samaria, about the year 103. He was well educated, and gave himself to the study of philosophy, but always with one object, that he might learn the knowledge of God. He sought this knowledge among the contending schools of philosophy, but always in vain, till at last God himself appeased the thirst which He had created. One day, while Justin was walking by the seashore, meditating on the thought of God, an old man met him and questioned him on the subject of his doubts; and when he had made Justin confess that the philosophers taught nothing certain about God, he told him of the writings of the inspired prophets and of Jesus Christ Whom they announced, and bade him seek light and understanding through prayer. The Scriptures and the constancy of the Christian martyrs led Justin from the darkness of human reason to the light of faith. In his zeal for the Faith he travelled to Greece, Egypt, and Italy, gaining many to Christ. At Rome he sealed his testimony with his blood, surrounded by his disciples. "Do you think," the prefect said to Justin, "that by dying you will enter heaven, and be rewarded by God?" "I do not think," was the Saint's answer; "I know." Then, as now, there were many religious opinions, but only one certain — the certainty of the Catholic faith. This certainty should be the measure of our confidence and our zeal.

Reflection.—We have received the gift of faith with little labor of our own. Let us learn how to value it from those who reached it after long search, and lived in the misery of a world which did not know God. Let us fear, as St. Justin did, the account we shall have to render for the gift of God.

ST. PAMPHILUS, Martyr.

ST. PAMPHILUS was of a rich and honorable family, and a native of Berytus, in which city, at that time famous for its schools, he in his youth ran through the whole circle of the sciences, and was afterward honored with the first employments of the magistracy. After he began to know Christ, he could relish no other study but that of salvation, and renounced everything else that he might apply himself wholly to the exercise of virtue and the studies of the Holy Scriptures. This accomplished master in profane sciences, and this renowned magistrate, was not ashamed to become the humble scholar of Pierius, the successor of Origen, in the great catechetical school of Alexandria. He afterward made Cæsarea, in Palestine, his residence, where, at his private expense, he collected a great library, which he bestowed on the church of that city. The Saint established there also a public school of sacred literature, and to his labors the Church was indebted for a most correct edition of the Holy Bible, which, with infinite care, he transcribed himself. But nothing was more remarkable in this Saint than his extraordinary humility. His paternal estate he at length distributed among the poor; towards his slaves and domestics his behavior was always that of a brother or a tender father. He led a most austere life, sequestered from the world and its company, and was indefatigable in labor. Such a virtue was his apprenticeship to the grace of martyrdom. In the year 307, Urbanus, the cruel governor of Palestine, caused him to be apprehended, and commanded him to be most inhumanly tormented. But the iron hooks which tore the martyr's sides served only to cover the judge with confusion. After this, the Saint remained almost two years in prison. Urbanus, the governor, was himself beheaded by an order of the Emperor Maximinus, but was succeeded by Firmilian, a man not less barbarous than bigoted and superstitious. After several butcheries, he caused St. Pamphilus to be brought before him, and passed sentence of death upon him. His flesh was torn off to the very bones, and his bowels exposed to view, and the torments were continued a long time without intermission, but he never once opened his mouth so much as to groan. He finished his martyrdom by a slow fire, and died invoking Jesus, the Son of God.

Reflection.—A cloud of witnesses, a noble army of martyrs, teach us by their constancy to suffer wrong with patience, and strenuously to resist evil. The daily trials we meet with from others or from ourselves are always sent us by God, Who sometimes throws difficulties in our way on purpose to reward our conquest; and sometimes, like a wise physician, restores us to our health by bitter potions.

June 2.—STS. POTHINUS, Bishop, SANCTUS, ATTALUS, BLANDINA, and the other Martyrs of Lyons.

AFTER the miraculous victory obtained by the prayers of the Christians under Marcus Aurelius, in 174, the Church enjoyed a kind of peace, though it was often disturbed in particular places by popular commotions, or by the superstitious fury of certain governors. This appears from the violent persecution which was raised three years after the aforesaid victory, at Vienne and Lyons, in 177, whilst St. Pothinus was Bishop of Lyons, and St. Irenæus, who had been sent thither by St. Polycarp out of Asia, was a priest of that city. Many of the principal Christians were brought before the Roman governor. Among them was a slave, Blandina: and her mistress, also a Christian, feared that Blandina lacked strength to brave the torture. She was tormented a whole day through, but she bore it all with joy till the executioners gave up, confessing themselves outdone. Red-hot plates were held to the sides of Sanctus, a deacon of Vienne, till his body became one great sore, and he looked no longer like a man; but in the midst of his tortures he was "bedewed and strengthened by the stream of heavenly water which flows from the side of Christ." Meantime, many confessors were kept in prison and with them were some who had been terrified into apostasy. Even the heathens marked the joy of martyrdom in the Christians who were decked for their eternal espousals, and the misery of the apostates. But the faithful confessors brought back those who had fallen, and the Church, "that Virgin Mother," rejoiced when she saw her children live again in Christ. Some died in prison, the rest were martyred one by one, St. Blandina last of all, after seeing her younger brother put to a cruel death, and encouraging him to victory.

Reflection.—In early times the Christians were called the children of joy. Let us seek the joy of the Holy Spirit to sweeten suffering, to temper earthly delight, till we enter into the joy of Our Lord.

June 3.—ST. CLOTILDA, Queen.

ST. CLOTILDA was daughter of Chilperic, younger brother to Gondebald, the tyrannical King of Burgundy, who put him and his wife, and his other brothers, except one, to death, in order to usurp their dominions. Clotilda was brought up in her uncle's court, and, by a singular providence, was instructed in the Catholic religion, though she was educated in the midst of Arians. Her wit, beauty, meekness, modesty, and piety made her the adoration of all the neighboring kingdoms, and Clovis I., surnamed the Great, the victorious king of the Franks, demanded and obtained her in marriage. She honored her royal husband, studied to sweeten his warlike temper by Christian meekness, conformed herself to his humor in things that were indifferent, and, the better to gain his affections, made those things the subject of her discourse and praises in which she knew him to take the greatest delight. When she saw herself mistress of his heart she did not defer the great work of endeavoring to win him to God, but the fear of giving offence to his people made him delay his conversion.   His miraculous victory over the Alemanni, and his entire conversion in 496, were at length the fruit of our Saint's prayers.   Clotilda, having gained to God this great monarch, never ceased to excite him to glorious actions for the divine honor; among other religious foundations, he built in Paris, at her request, about the year 511, the great church of Sts. Peter and Paul, now called St. Genevieve's.   This great prince died on the 27th of November, in the year 511, at the age of forty-five, having reigned thirty years.   His eldest son, Theodoric, reigned at Rheims over the eastern parts of France, Clodomir reigned at Orleans, Childebert at Paris, and Clotaire I. at Soissons.   This division produced wars and mutual jealousies, till in 560 the whole monarchy was reunited under Clotaire, the youngest of these brothers.   The dissension in her family contributed more perfectly to wean Clotilda's heart from the world.   She spent the remaining part of her life in exercises of prayer, almsdeeds, watching, fasting, and penance, seeming totally to forget that she had been queen or that her sons sat on the throne.   Eternity filled her heart and employed all her thoughts.   She foretold her death thirty days before it happened.   On the thirtieth day of her illness, she received the sacraments, made a public confession of her faith, and departed to the Lord on the 3d of June, in 545.

Reflection.—St. Peter defines the mission of the Christian woman; to win the heart of those who believe not the word.

June 4.—ST. FRANCIS CARACCIOLO.

FRANCIS was born in the kingdom of Naples, of the princely family of Caracciolo.   In childhood he shunned all amusements, recited the Rosary regularly, and loved to visit the Blessed Sacrament and to distribute his food to the poor.   An attack of leprosy taught him the vileness of the human body and the vanity of the world.

Almost miraculously cured, he renounced his home to study for the priesthood at Naples, where he spent his leisure hours in the prisons or visiting the Blessed Sacrament in unfrequented churches. God called him, when only twenty-five, to found an Order of Clerks Regular, whose rule was that each day one father fasted on bread and water, another took the discipline, a third wore a hairshirt, while they always watched by turns in perpetual adoration before the Blessed Sacrament. They took the usual vows, adding a fourth — not to desire dignities. To establish his Order, Francis undertook many journeys through Italy and Spain, on foot and without money, content with the shelter and crusts given him in charity. Being elected general, he redoubled his austerities, and devoted seven hours daily to meditation on the Passion, besides passing most of the night praying before the Blessed Sacrament. Francis was commonly called the Preacher of Divine Love. But it was before the Blessed Sacrament that his ardent devotion was most clearly perceptible. In presence of his divine Lord his face usually emitted brilliant rays of light; and he often bathed the ground with his tears when he prayed, according to his custom, prostrate on his face before the tabernacle, and constantly repeating, as one devoured by internal fire, " The zeal of Thy house hath eaten me up." He died of fever, aged forty-four, on the eve of Corpus Christi, 1608, saying, " Let us go, let us go to heaven ! " When his body was opened after death, his heart was found as it were burnt up, and these words imprinted around it: Zelus domus Tuæ comedit me "—" The zeal of Thy house hath eaten me up."

Reflection.—It is for men, and not for angels, that our blessed Lord resides upon the altar. Yet angels throng our churches to worship Him while men desert Him. Learn from St. Francis to avoid such ingratitude, and to spend, as he did, every possible moment before the Most Holy Sacrament.

June 5.—ST. BONIFACE, Bishop, Martyr.

ST. BONIFACE was born at Crediton in Devonshire, England, in the year 680. Some missionaries staying at his father's house spoke to him of heavenly things, and inspired him with a wish to devote himself, as they did, to God. He entered the monastery of Exminster, and was there trained for his apostolic work. His first attempt to convert the pagans in Holland having failed, he went to Rome to obtain the Pope's blessing on his mission, and returned with authority to preach to the German tribes. It was a slow and dangerous task; his own life was in constant peril, while his flock was often reduced to abject poverty by the wandering robber bands. Yet his courage never flagged. He began with Bavaria and Thuringia, next visited Friesland, then passed on to Hesse and Saxony, everywhere destroying the idol temples and raising churches on their site. He endeavored, as far as possible, to make every object of idolatry contribute in some way to the glory of God; on one occasion, having cut down on immense oak which was consecrated to Jupiter, he used the tree in building a church, which he dedicated to the Prince of the Apostles. He was now recalled to Rome, consecrated Bishop by the Pope, and returned to extend and organize the rising German Church. With diligent care he reformed abuses among the existing clergy, and established religious houses throughout the land. At length, feeling his infirmities increase, and fearful of losing his martyr's crown, Boniface appointed a successor to his monastery, and set out to convert a fresh pagan tribe. While St. Boniface was waiting to administer Confirmation to some newly-baptized Christians, a troop of pagans arrived, armed with swords and spears. His attendants would have opposed them, but the Saint said to his followers: " My children, cease your resistance; the long-expected day is come at last. Scripture forbids us to resist evil. Let us put our hope in God: He will save our souls." Scarcely had he ceased speaking, when the barbarians fell upon him and slew him with all his attendants, to the number of fifty-two.

Reflection.—St. Boniface teaches us how the love of Christ changes all things. It was for Christ's sake that he toiled for souls, preferring poverty to riches, labor to rest, suffering to pleasure, death to life, that by dying he might live with Christ.

June 6.—ST. NORBERT, Bishop.

OF noble rank and rare talents, Norbert passed a most pious youth, and entered the ecclesiastical state. By a strange contradiction, his conduct now became a scandal to his sacred calling, and at the court of the Emperor Henry IV. he led, like many clerics of that age, a life of dissipation and luxury. One day, when he was thirty years of age, he was thrown half dead from his horse, and on recovering his senses, resolved upon a new life. After a severe and searching preparation, he was ordained priest, and began to expose the abuses of his Order. Silenced at first by a local council, he obtained the Pope's sanction and preached penance to listening crowds in France and the Netherlands. In the wild vale of Prémontré he gave to some trained disciples the rule of St. Austin, and a white habit to denote the angelic purity proper to the priesthood. The Canons Regular, or *Premonstratensians,* as they were called, were to unite the active work of the country clergy with the obligations of the monastic life. Their fervor renewed the spirit of the priesthood, quickened the faith of the people, and drove out heresy. A vile heretic, named Tankelin, appeared at Antwerp, in the time of St. Norbert, and denied the reality of the priesthood, and especially blasphemed the Blessed Eucharist. The Saint was sent for to drive out the pest. By his burning words he exposed the impostor and rekindled the faith in the Blessed Sacrament. Many of the apostates had proved their contempt for the Blessed Sacrament by burying it in filthy places. Norbert bade them search for the Sacred Hosts. They found them entire and uninjured, and the Saint bore them back in triumph to the tabernacle. Hence he is generally painted with the monstrance in his hand. In 1126 Norbert found himself appointed Bishop of Magdeburg; and there, at the risk of his life, he zealously carried on his work of reform, and died, worn out with toil, at the age of fifty-three.

Reflection.—Reparation for the injuries offered to the Blessed Sacrament was the aim of St. Norbert's great work of reform — in himself, in the clergy, and in the faithful. How much does our present worship repair for our own past irreverences, and for the outrages offered by others to the Blessed Eucharist.

June 7.—ST. ROBERT OF NEWMINSTER.

IN 1132 Robert was a monk at Whitby, England, when news arrived that thirteen religious had been violently expelled from the Abbey of St. Mary, in York, for having proposed to restore the strict Benedictine rule. He at once set out to join them, and found them on the banks of the Skeld, near Ripon, living in the midst of winter in a hut made of hurdles and roofed with turf. In the spring they affiliated themselves to St. Bernard's reform at Clairvaux, and for two years struggled on in extreme poverty. At length the fame of their sanctity brought another novice, Hugh, Dean of York, who endowed the community with all his wealth, and thus laid the foundation of Fountains Abbey. In 1137 Raynulph, Baron of Morpeth, was so edified by the example of the monks at Fountains that he built them a monastery in Northumberland, called Newminster, of which St. Robert became abbot. The holiness of his life, even more than his words, guided his brethren to perfection, and within the next ten years three new communities went forth from this one house to become centres of holiness in other parts. The abstinence of St. Robert in refectory alone sufficed to maintain the mortified spirit of the community. One Easter Day, his stomach, weakened by the fast of Lent, could take no food, and he at last consented to try to eat some bread sweetened with honey. Before it was brought, he felt this relaxation would be a dangerous example for his subjects, and sent the food untouched to the poor at the gate. The plate was received by a young man of shining countenance, who straightway disappeared. At the next meal the plate descended empty, and by itself, to the abbot's place in the refectory, proving that what the Saint sacrificed for his brethren had been accepted by Christ. At the moment of Robert's death, in 1159, St. Godric, the hermit of Finchale, saw his soul, like a globe of fire, borne up by the angels in a pathway of light; and as the gates of heaven opened before them, a voice repeated twice, " Enter now, my friends."

Reflection.—Reason and authority prove that virtue ought to be practised. But facts alone prove that it is practised; and this is why examples have more power to move our souls, and why our individual actions are of such fearful importance for others as well as for ourselves.

ST. CLAUDE, Archbishop.

THE province of Eastern Burgundy received great lustre from this glorious Saint. He was born at Salins, about the year 603, and was both the model and the oracle of the clergy of Besançon, when, upon the death of Archbishop Gervaise, about the year 683, he was chosen to be his successor. Fearing the obligations of that charge, he fled and hid himself, but was discovered and compelled to take it upon him. During seven years he acquitted himself of the pastoral functions with the zeal and vigilance of an apostle; but finding then an opportunity of resigning his see, which, out of humility and love of solitude, he had always sought, he retired to the great monastery of St. Oyend, and there took the monastic habit, in 690. Violence was used to oblige him soon after to accept the abbatial dignity. Such was the sanctity of his life, and his zeal in conducting his monks in the paths of evangelical perfection, that he deserved to be compared to the Antonines and Pachomiuses, and his monastery to those of ancient Egypt. Manual labor, silence, prayer, reading of pious books, especially the Holy Bible, fasting, watching, humility, obedience, poverty, mortification, and the close union of their hearts with God, made up the whole occupation of these fervent servants of God, and were the rich patrimony which St. Claude left to his disciples. He died in 703.

June 8.—ST. MEDARD, Bishop.

ST. MEDARD, one of the most illustrious prelates of the Church of France in the sixth century, was born of a pious and noble family, at Salency, about the year 457. From his childhood he evinced the most tender compassion for the poor. On one occasion he gave his coat to a destitute blind man, and when asked why he had done so, he answered that the misery of a fellow-member in Christ so affected him that he could not help giving him part of his own clothes. Being promoted to the priesthood in the thirty-third year of his age, he became a bright ornament of that sacred order. He preached the word of God with an unction which touched the hearts of the most hardened; and the influence of his example, by which he enforced the precepts which he delivered from the pulpit, seemed irresistible. In 530, Alomer, the thirteenth bishop of that country, dying, St. Medard was unanimously chosen to fill the see, and was consecrated by St. Remigius, who had baptized King Clovis in 496, and was then exceeding old. Our Saint's new dignity did not make him abate anything of his austerities, and, though at that time seventy-two years old, he thought himself obliged to redouble his labors. Though his diocese was very wide, it seemed not to suffice for his zeal, which could not be confined; wherever he saw the opportunity of advancing the honor of God, and of abolishing the remains of idolatry, he overcame all obstacles, and by his zealous labors and miracles the rays of the Gospel dispelled the mists of idolatry throughout the whole extent of his diocese. What rendered this task more difficult and perilous was the savage and fierce disposition of the ancient inhabitants of Flanders, who were the most barbarous of all the nations of the Gauls and Franks. Our Saint, having completed this great work in Flanders, returned to Noyon, where he shortly after fell sick, and soon rested from his labors at an advanced age, in 545. The whole kingdom lamented his death as the loss of their common father and protector. His body was buried in his own cathedral, but the many miracles wrought at his tomb so moved King Clotaire that he translated the precious remains to Soissons.

Reflection.—The Church takes delight in styling her founder " THE AMIABLE JESUS," and He likewise says of Himself, " I am meek and humble of heart."

June 9.—STS. PRIMUS and FELICIANUS, Martyrs.

THESE two martyrs were brothers, and lived in Rome, toward the latter part of the third century, for many years, mutually encouraging each other in the practice of all good works. They seemed to possess nothing but for the poor, and often spent both nights and days with the confessors in their dungeons, or at the places of their torments and execution. Some they encouraged to perseverance, others, who had fallen, they raised again, and they made themselves the servants of all in Christ, that all might attain to salvation through Him. Though their zeal was most remarkable, they had escaped the dangers of many bloody persecutions, and were grown old in the heroic exercises of virtue, when it pleased God to crown their labors with a glorious martyrdom. The pagans raised so great an outcry against them that they were both apprehended and put in chains. They were inhumanly scourged, and then sent to a town twelve miles from Rome to be farther chastised, as avowed enemies to the gods. There they were cruelly tortured, first both together, afterward separately. But the grace of God strengthened them, and they were at length both beheaded on the 9th of June.

Reflection.—A soul which truly loves God regards all the things of this world as nothing. The loss of goods, the disgrace of the world, torments, sickness, and other afflictions are bitter to the senses, but appear light to him that loves. If we cannot bear our trials with patience and silence, it is because we love God only in words. " One who is slothful and lukewarm complains of everything, and calls the lightest precepts hard," says Thomas à Kempis.

ST. COLUMBA, or COLUMKILLE, Abbot.

ST. COLUMBA, the apostle of the Picts, was born of a noble family, at Gartan, in the county of Tyrconnel, Ireland, in 521. From early childhood he gave himself to God. In all his labors — and they were many — his chief thought was heaven and how he should secure the way thither. The result was that he lay on the bare floor, with a stone for his pillow, and fasted all the year round; yet the sweetness of his countenance told of the holy soul's interior serenity. Though austere, he was not morose; and, often as he longed to die, he was untiring in good works, throughout his life. After he had been made abbot, his zeal offended King Dermot; and in 565 the Saint departed for Scotland, where he founded a hundred religious houses and converted the Picts, who in gratitude gave him the island of Iona. There St. Columba founded his celebrated monastery, the school of apostolic missionaries and martyrs, and for centuries the last resting-place of Saints and kings. Four years before his death, our Saint had a vision of angels, who told him that the day of his death had been deferred four years, in answer to the prayers of his children; whereat the Saint wept bitterly, and cried out, " Woe is me that my sojourning is prolonged! " for he desired above all things to reach his true home. How different is the conduct of most men, who dread death above everything, instead of wishing " to be dissolved, and to be with Christ "! On the day of his peaceful death, in the seventy-seventh year of his age, surrounded in choir by his spiritual children, the 9th of June, 597, he said to his disciple Diermit, "This day is called the Sabbath, that is, the day of rest, and such will it truly be to me; for it will put an end to my labors." Then, kneeling before the altar, he received the Viaticum, and sweetly slept in the Lord. His relics were carried to Down, and laid in the same shrine with the bodies of St. Patrick and St. Brigid.

Reflection.—The thought of the world to come will always make us happy, and yet strict with ourselves in all our duties. The more perfect we become, the sooner shall we behold that for which St. Columba sighed.

June 10.—ST. MARGARET OF SCOTLAND.

ST. MARGARET's name signifies "pearl;" "a fitting name," says Theodoric, her confessor and her first biographer, "for one such as she." Her soul was like a precious pearl. A life spent amidst the luxury of a royal court never dimmed its lustre, or stole it away from Him who had bought it with His blood. She was the grand-daughter of an English king; and in 1070 she became the bride of Malcolm, and reigned Queen of Scotland till her death in 1093. How did she become a Saint in a position where sanctity is so difficult? First, she burned with zeal for the house of God. She built churches and monasteries; she busied herself in making vestments; she could not rest till she saw the laws of God and His Church observed throughout her realm. Next, amidst a thousand cares, she found time to converse with God — ordering her piety with such sweetness and discretion that she won her husband to sanctity like her own. He used to rise with her at night for prayer; he loved to kiss the holy books she used, and sometimes he would steal them away, and bring them back to his wife covered with jewels. Lastly, with virtues so great, she wept constantly over her sins, and begged her confessor to correct her faults. St. Margaret did not neglect her duties in the world because she was not of it. Never was a better mother. She spared no pains in the education of her eight children, and their sanctity was the fruit of her prudence and her zeal. Never was a better queen. She was the most trusted counsellor of her husband, and she labored for the material improvement of the country. But, in the midst of the world's pleasures, she sighed for the better country, and accepted death as a release. On her death-bed she received the news that her husband and her eldest son were slain in battle. She thanked God, Who had sent this last

affliction as a penance for her sins.   After receiving Holy
Viaticum, she was repeating the prayer from the Missal,
" O Lord Jesus Christ, Who by Thy death didst give life
to the world, deliver me."   At the words " deliver me,"
says her biographer, she took her departure to Christ, the
Author of true liberty.

Reflection.—All perfection consists in keeping a guard
upon the heart.   Wherever we are, we can make a solitude
in our hearts, detach ourselves from the world, and converse familiarly with God.   Let us take St. Margaret for
our example and encouragement.

June 11.—ST. BARNABAS, Apostle.

WE read that in the first days of the Church, " the
multitude of believers had but one heart and one
soul; neither did any one say that aught of the things
which he possessed was his own."   Of this fervent company, one only is singled out by name, Joseph, a rich
Levite, from Cyprus.   " He having land sold it, and
brought the price and laid it at the feet of the apostles."
They now gave him a new name, Barnabas, the son of
consolation.   " He was a good man, full of the Holy Ghost
and of faith, and was soon chosen for an important mission
to the rapidly-growing Church of Antioch.   Here he perceived the great work which was to be done among the
Greeks, so he hastened to fetch St. Paul from his retirement at Tarsus.   It was at Antioch that the two Saints
were called to the apostolate of the Gentiles, and hence
they set out together to Cyprus and the cities of Asia
Minor.   Their preaching struck men with amazement, and
some cried out, " The gods are come down to us in the
likeness of men," calling Paul *Mercury,* and Barnabas
Jupiter.   The Saints travelled together to the Council
of Jerusalem, but shortly after this they parted.   When
Agabus prophesied a great famine, Barnabas, no longer
rich, was chosen by the faithful at Antioch as most fit to
bear, with St. Paul, their generous offerings to the Church
of Jerusalem.   The gentle Barnabas, keeping with him
John, surnamed Mark, whom St. Paul distrusted, betook

himself to Cyprus, where the sacred history leaves him; and here, at a later period, he won his martyr's crown.

Reflection.—St. Barnabas's life is full of suggestions to us who live in days when once more the abundant alms of the faithful are sorely needed by the whole Church, from the Sovereign Pontiff to the poor children in our streets.

June 12.—ST. JOHN OF ST. FAGONDEZ.

ST. JOHN was born at St. Fagondez, in Spain. At an early age he held several benefices in the diocese of Burgos, till the reproaches of his conscience forced him to resign them all except one chapel, where he said Mass daily, preached, and catechised. After this he studied theology at Salamanca, and then labored for some time as a most devoted missionary priest. Ultimately he became a hermit of the Augustinian Order, in the same city. There his life was marked by a singular devotion to the Holy Mass. Each night after Matins he remained in prayer till the hour of celebration, when he offered the Adorable Sacrifice with the most tender piety, often enjoying the sight of Jesus in glory, and holding sweet colloquies with Him. The power of his personal holiness was seen in his preaching, which produced a complete reformation in Salamanca. He had a special gift of reconciling differences, and was enabled to put an end to the quarrels and feuds among noblemen, at that period very common and fatal. The boldness shown by St. John in reproving vice endangered his life. A powerful noble, having been corrected by the Saint for oppressing his vassals, sent two assassins to slay him. The holiness of the Saint's aspect, however, caused by that peace which continually reigned in his soul, struck such awe into their minds that they could not execute their purpose, but humbly besought his forgiveness. And the nobleman himself, falling sick, was brought to repentance, and recovered his health by the prayers of the Saint whom he had endeavored to murder. He was also most zealous in denouncing those hideous vices which are a fruitful source of strife, and it was in defence of holy purity that he met his death. A lady of noble birth but evil life, whose companion in sin St. John had converted, contrived to administer a fatal poison to the Saint. After several months of terrible suffering, borne with unvarying patience, St. John went to his reward on June 11, 1479.

Reflection.—All men desire peace, but those alone enjoy it who, like St. John, are completely dead to themselves, and love to bear all things for Christ.

June 13.—ST. ANTONY OF PADUA.

IN 1221 St. Francis held a general chapter at Assisi; when the others dispersed, there lingered behind, unknown and neglected, a poor Portuguese friar, resolved to ask for and to refuse nothing. Nine months later, Fra Antonio rose under obedience to preach to the religious assembled at Forli, when, as the discourse proceeded, " the Hammer of Heretics," " the Ark of the Testament," " the eldest son of St. Francis," stood revealed in all his sanctity, learning, and eloquence before his rapt and astonished brethren. Devoted from earliest youth to prayer and study among the Canons Regular, Ferdinand de Bulloens, as his name was in the world, had been stirred, by the spirit and example of the first five Franciscan martyrs, to put on their habit and preach the Faith to the Moors in Africa. Denied a martyr's palm, and enfeebled by sickness, at the age of twenty-seven he was taking silent but merciless revenge upon himself in the humblest offices of his community. From this obscurity he was now called forth, and for nine years France, Italy, and Sicily heard his voice, saw his miracles, and men's hearts turned to God. One night, when St. Antony was staying with a friend in the city of Padua, his host saw brilliant rays streaming under the door of the Saint's room, and on looking through the keyhole he beheld a little Child of marvellous beauty standing upon a book which lay open upon the table, and clinging with both arms round Antony's neck. With an ineffable sweetness he watched the tender caresses of the Saint and his wondrous Visitor. At last the Child vanished, and Fra Antonio, opening the door, charged his friend, by the love of Him Whom he had seen, to " tell the vision to no

.man " as long as he was alive. Suddenly, in 1231, our Saint's brief apostolate was closed, and the voices of children were heard crying along the streets of Padua, " Our father, St. Antony, is dead." The following year, the church-bells of Lisbon rang without ringers, while at Rome one of its sons was inscribed among the Saints of God.

Reflection.—Let us love to pray and labor unseen, and cherish in the secret of our hearts the graces of God and the growth of our immortal souls. Like St. Antony, let us attend to this, and leave the rest to God.

June 14.—ST. BASIL THE GREAT.

ST. BASIL was born in Asia Minor. Two of his brothers became bishops, and, together with his mother and sister, are honored as Saints. He studied with great success at Athens, where he formed with St. Gregory Nazianzen the most tender friendship. He then taught oratory; but dreading the honors of the world, he gave up all, and became the father of the monastic life in the East. The Arian heretics, supported by the court, were then persecuting the Church; and Basil was summoned from his retirement by his bishop to give aid against them. His energy and zeal soon mitigated the disorders of the Church, and his solid and eloquent words silenced the heretics. On the death of Eusebius, he was chosen Bishop of Cæsarea. His commanding character, his firmness and energy, his learning and eloquence, and not less his humility and the exceeding austerity of his life, made him a model for bishops. When St. Basil was required to admit the Arians to Communion, the prefect, finding that soft words had no effect, said to him, " Are you mad, that you resist the will before which the whole world bows? Do you not dread the wrath of the emperor, nor exile, nor death?" "No," said Basil calmly; "he who has nothing to lose need not dread loss of goods; you cannot exile me, for the whole earth is my home; as for death, it would be the greatest kindness you could bestow upon me; torments cannot harm me: one blow would end my frail life and my sufferings together." "Never," said the prefect, "has any one dared to address me thus." "Perhaps," suggested Basil, "you never before measured your strength with a Christian bishop." The emperor desisted from his commands. St. Basil's whole life was one of suffering. He lived amid jealousies and misunderstandings and seeming disappointments. But he sowed the seed which bore goodly fruit in the next generation, and was God's instrument in beating back the Arian and other heretics in the East, and restoring the spirit of discipline and fervor in the Church. He died in 379, and is venerated as a Doctor of the Church.

Reflection.—"Fear God," says the *Imitation of Christ,* " and thou shalt have no need of being afraid of any man."

June 15.—STS. VITUS, CRESCENTIA, and MODESTUS, Martyrs.

VITUS was a child nobly born, who had the happiness to be instructed in the Faith, and inspired with the most perfect sentiments of his religion, by his Christian nurse, named Crescentia, and her faithful husband, Modestus. His father, Hylas, was extremely incensed when he discovered the child's invincible aversion to idolatry; and finding him not to be overcome by stripes and such like chastisements, he delivered him up to Valerian, the governor, who in vain tried all his arts to work him into compliance with his father's will and the emperor's edicts. He escaped out of their hands, and, together with Crescentia and Modestus, fled into Italy. They there met with the crown of martyrdom in Lucania, in the persecution of Diocletian. The heroic spirit of martyrdom which we admire in St. Vitus was owing to the early impressions of piety which he received from the lessons and example of a virtuous nurse. Of such infinite importance is the choice of virtuous preceptors, nurses, and servants about children.

Reflection.—What happiness for an infant to be formed naturally to all virtue, and for the spirit of simplicity, meekness, goodness, and piety to be moulded in its tender frame! Such a foundation being well laid, further graces

are abundantly communicated, and a soul improves daily
these seeds, and rises to the height of Christian virtue often
without experiencing severe conflicts of the passions.

June 16.—ST. JOHN FRANCIS REGIS.

ST. JOHN FRANCIS REGIS was born in Languedoc, in
1597. From his tenderest years he showed evi-
dences of uncommon sanctity by his innocence of life,
modesty, and love of prayer. At the age of eighteen he
entered the Society of Jesus. As soon as his studies were
over, he gave himself entirely to the salvation of souls.
The winter he spent in country missions, principally in
mountainous districts; and in spite of the rigor of the
weather and the ignorance and roughness of the inhabitants, he labored with such success that he gained innumerable souls to God both from heresy and from a bad
life. The summer he gave to the towns. There his time
was taken up in visiting hospitals and prisons, in preaching and instructing, and in assisting all who in any way
stood in need of his services. In his works of mercy God
often helped him by miracles. In November, 1637, the
Saint set out for his second mission at Marthes. His road
lay across valleys filled with snow and over mountains
frozen and precipitous. In climbing one of the highest,
a bush to which he was clinging gave way, and he broke
his leg in the fall. By the help of his companion he
accomplished the remaining six miles, and then, instead
of seeing a surgeon, insisted on being taken straight to
the confessional. There, after several hours, the curate
of the parish found him still seated, and when his leg was
examined the fracture was found to be miraculously healed.
He was so inflamed with the love of God that he seemed to
breathe, think, speak of that alone, and he offered up the
Holy Sacrifice with such attention and fervor that those
who assisted at it could not but feel something of the fire
with which he burned. After twelve years of unceasing
labor, he rendered his pure and innocent soul to his
Creator, at the age of forty-four.

Reflection.—When St. John Francis was struck in the face by a sinner whom he was reproving, he replied, " If you only knew me, you would give me much more than that." His meekness converted the man, and it is in this spirit that he teaches us to win souls to God. How much might we do if we could forget our own wants in remembering those of others, and put our trust in God!

June 17.—ST. AVITUS, Abbot.

ST. AVITUS was a native of Orleans, and, retiring into Auvergne, took the monastic habit, together with St. Calais, in the abbey of Menat, at that time very small, though afterward enriched by Queen Brunehault, and by St. Boner, Bishop of Clermont. The two Saints soon after returned to Miscy, a famous abbey situated a league and a half below Orleans. It was founded toward the end of the reign of Clovis I. by St. Euspicius, a holy priest, honored on the 14th of June, and his nephew St. Maximin or Mesnim, whose name this monastery, which is now of the Cistercian Order, bears. Many call St. Maximin the first abbot, others St. Euspicius the first, St. Maximin the second, and St. Avitus the third. But our Saint and St. Calais made not a long stay at Miscy, though St. Maximin gave them a gracious reception. In quest of a closer retirement, St. Avitus, who had succeeded St. Maximin, soon after resigned the abbacy, and with St. Calais lived a recluse in the territory now called Dunois, on the frontiers of La Perche. Others joining them, St. Calais retired into a forest in Maine, and King Clotaire built a church and monastery for St. Avitus and his companions. This is at present a Benedictine nunnery, called St. Avy of Chateaudun, and is situated on the Loire, at the foot of the hill on which the town of Chateaudun is built, in the diocese of Chartres. Three famous monks, Leobin, afterwards Bishop of Chartres, Euphronius, and Rusticus, attended our Saint to his happy death, which happened about the year 530. His body was carried to Orleans, and buried with great pomp in that city.

June 18.—STS. MARCUS and MARCELLIANUS, Martyrs.

MARCUS AND MARCELLIANUS were twin brothers of an illustrious family in Rome, who had been converted to the Faith in their youth and were honorably married. Diocletian ascending the imperial throne in 284, the heathens raised persecutions. These martyrs were thrown into prison, and condemned to be beheaded. Their friends obtained a respite of the execution for thirty days, that they might prevail on them to worship the false gods. Tranquillinus and Martia, their afflicted heathen parents, in company with their sons' own wives and their little babes, endeavored to move them by the most tender entreaties and tears. St. Sebastian, an officer of the emperor's household, coming to Rome soon after their commitment, daily visited and encouraged them. The issue of the conferences was the happy conversion of the father, mother, and wives, also of Nicostratus, the public register, and soon after of Chromatius, the judge, who set the Saints at liberty, and, abdicating the magistracy, retired into the country. Marcus and Marcellianus were hid by a Christian officer of the household in his apartments in the palace; but they were betrayed by an apostate, and retaken. Fabian, who had succeeded Chromatius, condemned them to be bound to two pillars, with their feet nailed to the same. In this posture they remained a day and a night, and on the following day were stabbed with lances.

Reflection.—We know not what we are till we have been tried. It costs nothing to say we love God above all things, and to show the courage of martyrs at a distance from the danger; but that love is sincere which has stood the proof. "Persecution shows who is a hireling, and who a true pastor," says St. Bernard.

June 19.—ST. JULIANA FALCONIERI.

JULIANA FALCONIERI was born in answer to prayer, in 1270. Her father built the splendid church of the Annunziata in Florence, while her uncle, Blessed Alexius, became one of the founders of the Servite Order. Under his care Juliana grew up, as he said, more like an angel than a human being. Such was her modesty that she never used a mirror or gazed upon the face of a man during her whole life. The mere mention of sin made her shudder and tremble, and once hearing a scandal related she fell into a dead swoon. Her devotion to the sorrows of Our Lady drew her to the Servants of Mary; and, at the age of fourteen, she refused an offer of marriage, and received the habit from St. Philip Benizi himself. Her sanctity attracted many novices, for whose direction she was bidden to draw up a rule, and thus with reluctance she became foundress of the " Mantellate." She was with her children as their servant rather than their mistress, while outside her convent she led a life of apostolic charity, converting sinners, reconciling enemies, and healing the sick by sucking with her own lips their ulcerous sores. She was sometimes rapt for whole days in ecstasy, and her prayers saved the Servite Order when it was in danger of being suppressed. She was visited in her last hour by angels in the form of white doves, and Jesus Himself, as a beautiful child, crowned her with a garland of flowers. She wasted away through a disease of the stomach, which prevented her taking food. She bore her silent agony with constant cheerfulness, grieving only for the privation of Holy Communion. At last, when, in her seventieth year, she had sunk to the point of death, she begged to be allowed once more to see and adore the Blessed Sacrament. It was brought to her cell, and reverently laid on a corporal, which was placed over her heart. At this moment she expired, and the Sacred Host disappeared. After her death the form of the Host was found stamped upon her heart in the exact spot over which the Blessed Sacrament had been placed. Juliana died A. D. 1340.

Reflection.—" Meditate often," says St. Paul of the Cross, " on the sorrows of the holy Mother, sorrows inseparable from those of her beloved Son. If you seek the Cross, there you will find the Mother; and where the Mother is, there also is the Son."

June 20.—ST. SILVERIUS, Pope and Martyr.

SILVERIUS was son of Pope Hermisdas, who had been married before he entered the ministry. Upon the death of St. Agapetas, after a vacancy of forty-seven days, Silverius, then subdeacon, was chosen Pope, and ordained on the 8th of June, 536.

Theodora, the empress of Justinian, resolved to promote the sect of the Acephali. She endeavored to win Silverius over to her interest, and wrote to him, ordering that he should acknowledge Anthimus lawful bishop, or repair in person to Constantinople and reëxamine his cause on the spot. Without the least hesitation or delay, Silverius returned her a short answer, by which he peremptorily gave her to understand that he neither could nor would obey her unjust demands and betray the cause of the Catholic faith. The empress, finding that she could expect nothing from him, resolved to have him deposed. Vigilius, archdeacon of the Roman Church, a man of address, was then at Constantinople. To him the empress made her application, and finding him taken by the bait of ambition, promised to make him Pope, and to bestow on him seven hundred pieces of gold, provided he would engage himself to condemn the Council of Chalcedon and receive to Communion the three deposed Eutychian patriarchs, Anthimus of Constantinople, Severus of Antioch, and Theodosius of Alexandria. The unhappy Vigilius having assented to these conditions, the empress sent him to Rome, charged with a letter to the general Belisarius, commanding him to drive out Silverius and to contrive the election of Vigilius to the pontificate. Vigilius urged the general to execute the project. The more easily to carry out this project the Pope was accused of corresponding with the enemy and a letter was produced which was pretended to have been written by him to the king of the Goths, inviting him into the city, and promising to open the gates to him. Silverius was banished to Patara in Lycia. The bishop of that city received the illustrious exile with all possible marks of honor and respect; and thinking himself bound to undertake his defence, repaired to Constantinople, and spoke boldly to the emperor, terrifying him with the threats of the divine judgments for the expulsion of a bishop of so great a see, telling him, " There are many kings in the world, but there is only one Pope over the Church of the whole world." It must be observed that these were the words of an Oriental bishop, and a clear confession of the supremacy of the Roman See. Justinian appeared startled at the atrocity of the proceedings, and gave orders that Silverius should be sent back to Rome, but the enemies of the Pope contrived to prevent it, and he was intercepted on his road toward Rome and carried to a desert island, where he died on the 20th of June, 538.

June 21.—ST. ALOYSIUS GONZAGA.

ALOYSIUS, the eldest son of Ferdinand Gonzaga, Marquis of Castiglione, was born on the 9th of March, 1568. The first words he pronounced were the holy names of Jesus and Mary. When he was nine years of age he made a vow of perpetual virginity, and by a special grace was ever exempted from temptations against purity. He received his first Communion at the hands of St. Charles Borromeo. At an early age he resolved to leave the world, and in a vision was directed by our blessed Lady to join the Society of Jesus. The Saint's mother rejoiced on learning his determination to become a religious, but his father for three years refused his consent. At length St. Aloysius obtained permission to enter the novitiate on the 25th of November, 1585. He took his vows after two years, and went through the ordinary course of philosophy and theology. He was wont to say he doubted whether without penance grace would continue to make head against nature, which, when not afflicted and chastised, tends gradually to relapse into its old state, losing the habit of suffer-

ing acquired by the labor of years. " I am a crooked piece
of iron," he said, " and am come into religion to be made
straight by the hammer of mortification and penance."
During his last year of theology a malignant fever broke
out in Rome; the Saint offered himself for the service of
the sick, and he was accepted for the dangerous duty.
Several of the brothers caught the fever, and Aloysius was
of the number. He was brought to the point of death, but
recovered, only to fall, however, into slow fever, which
carried him off after three months. He died, repeating the
Holy Name, a little after midnight between the 20th and
21st of June, on the octave-day of Corpus Christi, being
rather more than twenty-three years of age.

Reflection.—Cardinal Bellarmine, the Saint's confessor,
testified that he had never mortally offended God. Yet he
chastised his body rigorously, rose at night to pray, and
shed many tears for his sins. Pray that, not having followed his innocence, you may yet imitate his penance.

June 22.—ST. PAULINUS OF NOLA.

PAULINUS was of a family which boasted of a long line
of senators, prefects, and consuls. He was educated
with great care, and his genius and eloquence, in prose
and verse, were the admiration of St. Jerome and St. Augustine. He had more than doubled his wealth by marriage, and was one of the foremost men of his time.
Though he was the chosen friend of Saints, and had a great
devotion to St. Felix of Nola, he was still only a catechumen, trying to serve two masters. But God drew him to
Himself along the way of sorrows and trials. He received
baptism, withdrew into Spain to be alone, and then, in
consort with his holy wife, sold all their vast estates in
various parts of the empire, distributing their proceeds
so prudently that St. Jerome says East and West were filled
with his alms. He was then ordained priest, and retired to
Nola in Campania. There he rebuilt the Church of St.
Felix with great magnificence, and served it night and day,
living a life of extreme abstinence and toil. In 409 he was
chosen bishop, and for more than thirty years so ruled as to

be conspicuous in an age blessed with many great and wise bishops. St. Gregory the Great tells us that when the Vandals of Africa had made a descent on Campania, Paulinus spent all he had in relieving the distress of his people and redeeming them from slavery. At last there came a poor widow; her only son had been carried off by the son-in-law of the Vandal king. " Such as I have I give thee," said the Saint to her; " we will go to Africa, and I .will give myself for your son." Having overborne her resistance, they went, and Paulinus was accepted in place of the widow's son, and employed as gardener. After a time the king found out, by divine interposition, that his son-in-law's slave was the great Bishop of Nola. He at once set him free, granting him also the freedom of all the townsmen of Nola who were in slavery. One who knew him well says he was meek as Moses, priestlike as Aaron, innocent as Samuel, tender as David, wise as Solomon, apostolic as Peter, loving as John, cautious as Thomas, keen-sighted as Stephen, fervent as Apollos. He died in 431.

Reflection.—" Go to Campania," writes St. Augustine; " there study Paulinus, that choice servant of God. With what generosity, with what still greater humility, he has flung from him the burden of this world's grandeurs to take on him the yoke of Christ, and in His service how serene and unobtrusive his life! "

June 23.—ST. ETHELDREDA, Abbess.

BORN and brought up in the fear of God — her mother and three sisters are numbered among the Saints — Etheldreda had but one aim in life, to devote herself to His service in the religious state. Her parents, however, had other views for her, and, in spite of her tears and prayers, she was compelled to become the wife of Tonbercht, a tributary of the Mercian king. She lived with him as a virgin for three years, and at his death retired to the isle of Ely, that she might apply herself wholly to heavenly things. This happiness was but short-lived; for Egfrid, the powerful King of Northumbria, pressed his suit upon her with such eagerness that she was forced into a second marriage.

Her life at his court was that of an ascetic rather than a queen: she lived with him not as a wife, but as a sister, and, observing a scrupulous regularity of discipline, devoted her time to works of mercy and love.   After twelve years, she retired with her husband's consent to Coldingham Abbey, which was then under the rule of St. Ebba, and received the veil from the hands of St. Wilfrid.   As soon as Etheldreda had left the court of her husband, he repented of having consented to her departure, and followed her, meaning to bring her back by force.   She took refuge on a headland on the coast near Coldingham; and here a miracle took place, for the waters forced themselves a passage round the hill, barring the further advance of Egfrid. The Saint remained on this island refuge for seven days, till the king, recognizing the divine will, agreed to leave her in peace.   God, Who by a miracle confirmed the Saint's vocation, will not fail us if, with a single heart, we elect for Him.   In 672 she returned to Ely, and founded there a double monastery.   The nunnery she governed herself, and was by her example a living rule of perfection to her sisters. Some time after her death, in 679, her body was found incorrupt, and St. Bede records many miracles worked by her relics.

Reflection.—The soul cannot truly serve God while it is involved in the distractions and pleasures of the world. Etheldreda knew this, and chose rather to be a servant of Christ her Lord than the mistress of an earthly court. Resolve, in whatever state you are, to live absolutely detached from the world, and to separate yourself as much as possible from it.

June 24.—ST. JOHN THE BAPTIST.

THE birth of St. John was foretold by an angel of the Lord to his father, Zachary, who was offering incense in the Temple.   It was the office of St. John to prepare the way for Christ, and before he was born into the world he began to live for the Incarnate God.   Even in the womb he knew the presence of Jesus and of Mary, and he leaped with joy at the glad coming of the Son of man.   In

his youth he remained hidden, because He for Whom he
waited was hidden also. But before Christ's public life
began, a divine impulse led St. John into the desert; there,
with locusts for his food and haircloth on his skin, in silence and in prayer, he chastened his own soul. Then, as
crowds broke in upon his solitude, he warned them to flee
from the wrath to come, and gave them the baptism of
penance, while they confessed their sins. At last there
stood in the crowd One Whom St. John did not know, till a
voice within told him that it was his Lord. With the baptism of St. John, Christ began His penance for the sins of
His people, and St. John saw the Holy Ghost descend in
bodily form upon Him. Then the Saint's work was done.
He had but to point his own disciples to the Lamb, he had
but to decrease as Christ increased. He saw all men leave
him and go after Christ. " I told you," he said, " that I
am not the Christ. The friend of the Bridegroom rejoiceth
because of the Bridegroom's voice. This my joy therefore
is fulfilled." St. John had been cast into the fortress of
Machærus by a worthless tyrant whose crimes he had rebuked, and he was to remain there till he was beheaded, at
the will of a girl who danced before this wretched king.
In this time of despair, if St. John could have known despair, some of his old disciples visited him. St. John did
not speak to them of himself, but he sent them to Christ,
that they might see the proofs of His mission. Then the
Eternal Truth pronounced the panegyric of the Saint who
had lived and breathed for Him alone: " Verily I say
unto you, Among them that are born of women there hath
not risen a greater than John the Baptist."

Reflection.—St. John was great before God because he
forgot himself and lived for Jesus Christ, Who is the source
of all greatness. Remember that you are nothing; your
own will and your own desires can only lead to misery and
sin. Therefore sacrifice every day some one of your natural
inclinations to the Sacred Heart of Our Lord, and learn
little by little to lose yourself in Him.

June 25.—ST. PROSPER OF AQUITAINE.—ST. WILLIAM OF MONTE-VERGINE.

ST. PROSPER was born at Aquitaine, in the year 403. His works show that in his youth he had happily applied himself to all the branches both of polite and sacred learning. On account of the purity and sanctity of his manners, he is called by those of his age a holy and venerable man. Our Saint does not appear to have been any more than a layman; but being of great virtue, and of extraordinary talents and learning, he wrote several works in which he ably refuted the errors of heresy. St. Leo the Great, being chosen Pope in 440, invited St. Prosper to Rome, made him his secretary, and employed him in the most important affairs of the Church. Our Saint crushed the Pelagian heresy, which began again to raise its head in that capital, and its final overthrow is said to be due to his zeal, learning, and unwearied endeavors. The date of his death is uncertain, but he was still living in 463.

St. WILLIAM, having lost his father and mother in his infancy, was brought up by his friends in great sentiments of piety; and at fifteen years of age, out of an earnest desire to lead a penitential life, he left Piedmont, his native country, made an austere pilgrimage to St. James's in Galicia, and afterward retired into the kingdom of Naples, where he chose for his abode a desert mountain, and lived in perpetual contemplation and the exercises of most rigorous penitential austerities. Finding himself discovered and his contemplation interrupted, he changed his habitation and settled in a place called Monte-Vergine, situated between Nola and Benevento, in the same kingdom; but his reputation followed him, and he was obliged by two neighboring priests to permit certain fervent persons to live with him and to imitate his ascetic practices. Thus, in 1119, was laid the foundation of the religious congregation called *de Monte-Vergine*. The Saint died on the 25th of June, 1142.

June 26.—STS. JOHN AND PAUL, Martyrs.

THESE two Saints were both officers in the army under Julian the Apostate, and received the crown of martyrdom, probably in 362. They glorified God by a double victory; they despised the honors of the world, and triumphed over its threats and torments. They saw many wicked men prosper in their impiety, but were not dazzled by their example. They considered that worldly prosperity which attends impunity in sin is the most dreadful of all judgments; and how false and short-lived was this glittering prosperity of Julian, who in a moment fell into the pit which he himself had dug! But the martyrs, by the momentary labor of their conflict, purchased an immense weight of never-fading glory; their torments were, by their heroic patience and invincible virtue and fidelity, a spectacle worthy of God, Who looked down upon them from the throne of His glory, and held His arm stretched out to strengthen them, and to put on their heads immortal crowns in the happy moment of their victory.

Reflection.—The Saints always accounted that they had done nothing for Christ so long as they had not resisted to blood, and by pouring forth the last drop completed their sacrifice. Every action of our lives ought to spring from this fervent motive, and we should consecrate ourselves to the divine service with our whole strength; we must always bear in mind that we owe to God all that we are, and, after all we can do, are unprofitable servants, and do only what we are bound to do.

June 27.—ST. LADISLAS, King.

LADISLAS the First, son of Bela, King of Hungary, was born in 1041. By the pertinacious importunity of the people he was compelled, much against his own inclination, to ascend the throne, in 1080. He restored the good laws and discipline which St. Stephen had established, and which seem to have been obliterated by the confusion of the times. Chastity, meekness, gravity, charity, and piety were from his infancy the distinguishing parts of his character; avarice and ambition were his sovereign aversion, so perfectly had the maxims of the Gospel extinguished in him all propensity to those base passions. His life in the palace was most austere; he was frugal and abstemious, but most liberal to the Church and the poor. Vanity, pleasure, or idle amusements had no share in his actions or time, because all his moments were consecrated to the exercises of religion and the duties of his station, in which he had only the divine will in view, and sought only God's greater honor. He watched over a strict and impartial administration of justice, was generous and merciful to his enemies, and vigorous in the defence of his country and the Church. He drove the Huns out of his territories, and vanquished the Poles, Russians, and Tartars. He was preparing to command, as general-in-chief, the great expedition of the Christians against the Saracens for the recovery of the Holy Land, when God called him to Himself, on the 30th of July, 1095.

Reflection.—The Saints filled all their moments with good works and great actions; and, whilst they labored for an immortal crown, the greatest share of worldly happiness of which this life is capable fell in their way without being even looked for by them. In their afflictions themselves virtue afforded them the most solid comfort, pointed out the remedy, and converted their tribulations into the greatest advantages.

June 28.—ST. IRENÆUS, Bishop, Martyr.

THIS Saint was born about the year 120. He was a Grecian, probably a native of Lesser Asia. His parents, who were Christians, placed him under the care of the great St. Polycarp, Bishop of Smyrna. It was in so holy a school that he learned that sacred science which rendered him afterward a great ornament of the Church and the terror of her enemies. St. Polycarp cultivated his rising genius, and formed his mind to piety by precepts and example; and the zealous scholar was careful to reap all the advantages which were offered him by the happi-

ness of such a master. Such was his veneration for his
tutor's sanctity that he observed every action and whatever
he saw in that holy man, the better to copy his example
and learn his spirit. He listened to his instructions with
an insatiable ardor, and so deeply did he engrave them on
his heart that the impressions remained most lively even to
his old age. In order to confute the heresies of his age,
this father made himself acquainted with the most absurd
conceits of their philosophers, by which means he was
qualified to trace up every error to its sources and set it in
its full light. St. Polycarp sent St. Irenæus into Gaul, in
company with some priest; he was himself ordained priest
of the Church of Lyons by St. Pothinus. St. Pothinus
having glorified God by his happy death, in the year 177,
our Saint was chosen the second Bishop of Lyons. By his
preaching, he in a short time converted almost that whole
country to the Faith. He wrote several works against
heresy, and at last, with many others, suffered martyrdom
about the year 202, under the Emperor Severus, at Lyons.

Reflection.—Fathers and mothers, and heads of families, spiritual and temporal, should bear in mind that inferiors " will not be corrected by words " alone, but that
example is likewise needful.

June 29.—ST. PETER, Apostle.

PETER was of Bethsaida in Galilee, and as he was fish-
ing on the lake was called by Our Lord to be one of
His apostles. He was poor and unlearned, but candid,
eager, and loving. In his heart, first of all, grew up the
conviction, and from his lips came the confession, " Thou
art the Christ, the Son of the living God; " and so Our
Lord chose him, and fitted him to be the Rock of His
Church, His Vicar on earth, the head and prince of His
apostles, the centre and very principle of the Church's one-
ness, the source of all spiritual powers, and the unerring
teacher of His truth. All Scripture is alive with him; but
after Pentecost he stands out in the full grandeur of his
office. He fills the vacant apostolic throne; admits the
Jews by thousands into the fold; opens it to the Gentiles

in the person of Cornelius; founds, and for a time rules, the Church at Antioch, and sends Mark to found that of Alexandria.   Ten years after the Ascension he went to Rome, the centre of the majestic Roman Empire, where were gathered the glories and the wealth of the earth and all the powers of evil.   There he established his Chair, and for twenty-five years labored with St. Paul in building up the great Roman Church.   He was crucified by order of Nero, and buried on the Vatican Hill.   He wrote two Epistles, and suggested and approved the Gospel of St. Mark.   Two hundred and sixty years after St. Peter's martyrdom came the open triumph of the Church.   Pope St. Sylvester, with bishops and clergy and the whole body of the faithful, went through Rome in procession to the Vatican Hill, singing the praises of God till the seven hills rang again.   The first Christian emperor, laying aside his diadem and his robes of state, began to dig the foundations of St. Peter's Church.   And now on the site of that old church stands the noblest temple ever raised by man; beneath a towering canopy lie the great apostles, in death, as in life, undivided; and there is the Chair of St. Peter.   All around rest the martyrs of Christ — Popes, Saints, Doctors, from east and west — and high over all, the words, " Thou art Peter, and on this Rock I will build My Church."   It is the threshold of the apostles and the centre of the world.

Reflection.—Peter still lives on in his successors, and rules and feeds the flock committed to him.   The reality of our devotion to him is the surest test of the purity of our faith.

June 30.—ST. PAUL.

ST. PAUL was born at Tarsus, of Jewish parents, and studied at Jerusalem, at the feet of Gamaliel. While still a young man, he held the clothes of those who stoned the proto-martyr Stephen; and in his restless zeal he pressed on to Damascus, " breathing out threatenings and slaughter against the disciples of Christ."   But near Damascus a light from heaven struck him to the earth.   He heard a voice which said, " Why persecutest thou Me? " He saw the form of Him Who had been crucified for his sins, and then for three days he saw nothing more. He awoke from his trance another man — a new creature in Jesus Christ. He left Damascus for a long retreat in Arabia, and then, at the call of God, he carried the Gospel to the uttermost limits of the world, and for years he lived and labored with no thought but the thought of Christ crucified, no desire but to spend and be spent for Him. He became the apostle of the Gentiles, whom he had been taught to hate, and wished himself anathema for his own countrymen, who sought his life. Perils by land and sea could not damp his courage, nor toil and suffering and age dull the tenderness of his heart. At last he gave blood for blood. In his youth he had imbibed the false zeal of the Pharisees at Jerusalem, the holy city of the former dispensation. With St. Peter he consecrated Rome, our holy city, by his martyrdom, and poured into its Church all his doctrine with all his blood. He left fourteen Epistles, which have been a fountain-head of the Church's doctrine, the consolation and delight of her greatest Saints. His interior life, so far as words can tell it, lies open before us in these divine writings, the life of one who has died forever to himself and risen again in Jesus Christ. " In what," says St. Chrysostom, " in what did this blessed one gain an advantage over the other apostles? How comes it that he lives in all men's mouths throughout the world? Is it not through the virtue of his Epistles? " Nor will his work cease while the race of man continues. Even now, like a most chivalrous knight, he stands in our midst, and takes captive every thought to the obedience of Christ.

Reflection.—St. Paul complains that all seek the things which are their own, and not the things which are Christ's. See if these words apply to you, and resolve to give yourself without reserve to God.

July 1.—ST. GAL, Bishop.

ST. GAL was born at Clermont in Auvergne, about the year 489. His father was of the first houses of that province, and his mother was descended from the family of Vettius Apagatus, the celebrated Roman who suffered at

Lyons for the faith of Christ. They both took special care
of the education of their son, and, when he arrived at a
proper age, proposed to have him married to the daughter
of a respectable senator. The Saint, who had taken a resolution to consecrate himself to God, withdrew privately
from his father's house to the monastery of Cournon, near
the city of Auvergne, and earnestly prayed to be admitted
there amongst the monks; and having soon after obtained
the consent of his parents, he with joy renounced all
worldly vanities to embrace religious poverty. Here his
eminent virtues distinguished him in a particular manner,
and recommended him to Quintianus, Bishop of Auvergne,
who promoted him to holy orders. The bishop dying in
527, St. Gal was appointed to succeed him, and in this new
character his humility, charity, and zeal were conspicuous;
above all, his patience in bearing injuries. Being once
struck on the head by a brutal man, he discovered not the
least emotion of anger or resentment, and by this meekness
disarmed the savage of his rage. At another time, Evodius, who from a senator became a priest, having so far
forgotten himself as to treat him in the most insulting
manner, the Saint, without making the least reply, arose
meekly from his seat and went to visit the churches of the
city. Evodius was so touched by this conduct that he cast
himself at the Saint's feet, in the middle of the street, and
asked his pardon. From this time they both lived on
terms of the most cordial friendship. St. Gal was favored
with the gift of miracles, and died about the year 553.

July 2.—THE VISITATION OF THE BLESSED VIRGIN.

THE angel Gabriel, in the mystery of the Annunciation,
informed the Mother of God that her cousin Elizabeth had miraculously conceived, and was then pregnant
with a son who was to be the precursor of the Messias.
The Blessed Virgin out of humility concealed the wonderful
dignity to which she was raised by the incarnation of the
Son of God in her womb, but, in the transport of her holy
joy and gratitude, determined she would go to congratulate

the mother of the Baptist. " Mary therefore arose," saith
St. Luke, " and with haste went into the hilly country into
a city of Judea, and entering into the house of Zachary,
saluted Elizabeth." What a blessing did the presence of
the God-man bring to this house, the first which He honored in His humanity with His visit! But Mary is the
instrument and means by which He imparts to it His divine
benediction, to show us that she is a channel through which
He delights to communicate to us His graces, and to encourage us to ask them of Him through her intercession.
At the voice of the Mother of God, but by the power and
grace of her divine Son in her womb, Elizabeth was filled
with the Holy Ghost, and the Infant in her womb conceived
so great a joy as to leap and exult. At the same time
Elizabeth was filled with the Holy Ghost, and by His in-
fused light she understood the great mystery of the Incarnation which God had wrought in Mary, whom humility
prevented from disclosing it even to a Saint, and an intimate friend. In raptures of astonishment Elizabeth pronounced her blessed above all other women, and cried out,
" Whence is this to me that the mother of my Lord should
come to me?" Mary, hearing her own praise, sunk the
lower in the abyss of her nothingness, and in the transport
of her humility, and melting in an ecstasy of love and
gratitude, burst into that admirable canticle, the *Mag-
nificat*. Mary stayed with her cousin almost three months,
after which she returned to Nazareth.

Reflection.—Whilst with the Church we praise God for
the mercies and wonders which He wrought in this mystery,
we ought to apply ourselves to the imitation of the virtues
of which Mary sets us a perfect example. From her we
ought particularly to learn the lessons by which we shall
sanctify our visits and conversation, actions which are to
so many Christians the sources of innumerable dangers and
sins.

July 3.—ST. HELIODORUS, Bishop.

THIS Saint was born at Dalmatia, St. Jerome's native country, and soon sought out that great Doctor, in order not only to follow his advice in matters relating to Christian perfection, but also to profit by his deep learning. The life of a recluse possessed peculiar attractions for him, but to enter a monastery it would be necessary to leave his spiritual master and director, and such a sacrifice he was not prepared to make. He remained in the world, though not of it, and, following the example of the holy anchorites, passed his time in prayer and devout reading. He accompanied St. Jerome to the East, but the desire to revisit his native land, and to see his parents once more, drew him back to Dalmatia, although St. Jerome tried to persuade him to remain. He promised to return as soon as he had fulfilled the duty he owed his parents. In the meantime, finding his absence protracted, and fearing that the love of family and attachment to worldly things might lure him from his vocation, St. Jerome wrote him an earnest letter, exhorting him to break entirely with the world and to consecrate himself to the service of God. But the Lord, Who disposes all things, had another mission for His servant. After the death of his mother, Heliodorus went to Italy, where he soon became noted for his eminent piety. He was made Bishop of Altino, and became one of the most distinguished prelates of an age fruitful in great men. He died about the year 290.

July 4.—ST. BERTHA, Widow, Abbess.

BERTHA was the daughter of Count Rigobert and Ursana, related to one of the kings of Kent in England. In the twentieth year of her age she was married to Sigefroi, by whom she had five daughters, two of whom, Gertrude and Deotila, are Saints. After her husband's death she put on the veil in the nunnery which she had built at Blangy in Artois, a little distance from Hesdin. Her daughters Gertrude and Deotila followed her example. She was persecuted by Roger, or Rotgar, who endeavored to asperse her with King Thierri III., to revenge his being refused Gertrude in marriage. But this prince, convinced of the innocence of Bertha, then abbess over her nunnery, gave her a kind reception and took her under his protection. On her return to Blangy, Bertha finished her nunnery and caused three churches to be built, one in honor of St. Omer, another she called after St. Vaast, and the third in honor of St. Martin of Tours. And then, after establishing a regular observance in her community, she left St. Deotila abbess in her stead, and shut herself in a cell, to pass the remainder of her days in prayer. She died about the year 725. A great part of her relics are kept at Blangy.

July 5.—ST. PETER OF LUXEMBURG.

PETER OF LUXEMBURG, descended both by his father and mother from the noblest families in Europe, was born in Lorraine, in the year 1369. When but a schoolboy, twelve years of age, he went to London as a hostage for his brother, the Count of St. Pol, who had been taken prisoner. The English were so won by Peter's holy example that they released him at the end of the year, taking his word for the ransom. Richard II. now invited him to remain at the English court; but Peter returned to Paris, determined to have no master but Christ. At the early age of fifteen he was appointed, on account of his prudence and sanctity, Bishop of Metz, and made his public entry into his see barefoot and riding an ass. He governed his diocese with all the zeal and prudence of maturity, and divided his revenues in three parts — for the Church, the poor, and his household. His charities often left him personally destitute, and he had but twenty pence left when he died. Created Cardinal of St. George, his austerities in the midst of a court were so severe that he was ordered to moderate them. Peter replied, " I shall always be an unprofitable servant, but I can at least obey." Ten months after his promotion he fell sick of a fever, and lingered for some time in a sinking condition, his holiness increasing as he drew near his end. St. Peter, it was believed, never

stained his soul by mortal sin; yet as he grew in grace
his holy hatred of self became more and more intense.   At
length, when he had received the last sacraments, he forced
his attendants each in turn to scourge him for his faults,
and then lay silent till he died.   But God was pleased to
glorify His servant.   Among other miracles is the following: On July 5, 1432, a child about twelve years old was
killed by falling from a high tower, in the palace of Avignon, upon a sharp rock.   The father, distracted with
grief, picked up the scattered pieces of the skull and
brains, and carried them in a sack, with the mutilated body
of his son, to St. Peter's shrine, and with many tears besought the Saint's intercession.   After a while the child
returned to life, and was placed upon the altar for all to
witness.   In honor of this miracle the city of Avignon
chose St. Peter as its patron Saint.   He died in 1387, aged
eighteen years.

Reflection.—St. Peter teaches us how, by self-denial,
rank, riches, the highest dignities, and all this world can
give, may serve to make a Saint.

July 6.—ST. GOAR, Priest.

S T. GOAR was born of an illustrious family, at Aquitaine.   From his youth he was noted for his earnest
piety, and, having been raised to sacred orders, he converted many sinners by the fervor of his preaching and the
force of his example.   Wishing to serve God entirely unknown to the world, he went over into Germany, and
settling in the neighborhood of Trier, he shut himself up
in his cell, and arrived at such an eminent degree of sanctity as to be esteemed the oracle and miracle of the whole
country.   Sigebert, King of Austrasia, learning of the
sanctity of Goar, wished to have him made Bishop of Metz,
and for that purpose summoned him to court.   The Saint,
fearing the responsibilities of the office, prayed that he
might be excused.   He was seized with a fever, and died
in 575.

ST. PALLADIUS, Bishop, Apostle of the Scots.

THE name of Palladius shows this Saint to have been a Roman, and most authors agree that he was deacon of the Church of Rome. At least St. Prosper, in his chronicle, informs us that when Agricola, a noted Pelagian, had corrupted the churches of Britain by introducing that pestilential heresy, Pope Celestine, at the instance of Palladius the deacon, in 429, sent thither St. Germanus, Bishop of Auxerre, in quality of his legate, who, having ejected the heretics, brought back the Britons to the Catholic faith. In 431 Pope Celestine sent Palladius, the first bishop, to the Scots then believing in Christ. The Irish writers of the lives of St. Patrick say that St. Palladius had preached in Ireland a little before St. Patrick, but that he was soon banished by the King of Leinster, and returned to North Britain, where he had first opened his mission. There seems to be no doubt that he was sent to the whole nation of the Scots, several colonies of whom had passed from Ireland into North Britain, and possessed themselves of part of the country since called Scotland. After St. Palladius had left Ireland, he arrived among the Scots in North Britain, according to St. Prosper, in the consulate of Bassus and Antochius, in the year of Christ 431. He preached there with great zeal, and formed a considerable Church. The Scottish historians tell us that the Faith was planted in North Britain about the year 200, in the time of King Donald, when Victor was Pope of Rome. But they all acknowledge that Palladius was the first bishop in that country, and style him their first apostle. The Saint died at Fordun, fifteen miles from Aberdeen, about the year 450.

Reflection.—St. Palladius surmounted every obstacle which a fierce nation had opposed to the establishment of the kingdom of Jesus Christ. Ought not our hearts to be impressed with the most lively sentiments of love and gratitude to our merciful God for having raised up such great and zealous men, by whose ministry the light of true faith has been conveyed to us?

July 7.—ST. PANTÆNUS, Father of the Church.

THIS learned father and apostolic man flourished in the second century. He was by birth a Sicilian, by profession a Stoic philosopher. His esteem for virtue led him into an acquaintance with the Christians, and being charmed with the innocence and sanctity of their conversation, he opened his eyes to the truth. He studied the Holy Scriptures under the disciples of the apostles, and his thirst after sacred learning brought him to Alexandria, in Egypt, where the disciples of St. Mark had instituted a celebrated school of the Christian doctrine. Pantænus sought not to display his talents in that great mart of literature and commerce; but this great progress in sacred learning was after some time discovered, and he was drawn out of that obscurity in which his humility sought to bury itself. Being placed at the head of the Christian school some time before the year 179, by his learning and excellent manner of teaching he raised its reputation above all the schools of the philosophers, and the lessons which he read, and which were gathered from the flowers of the prophets and apostles, conveyed light and knowledge into the minds of all his hearers. The Indians who traded at Alexandria entreated him to pay their country a visit, whereupon he forsook his school and went to preach the Gospel to the Eastern nations. St. Pantænus found some seeds of the faith already sown in the Indies, and a book of the Gospel of St. Matthew in Hebrew, which St. Bartholomew had carried thither. He brought it back with him to Alexandria, whither he returned after he had zealously employed some years in instructing the Indians in the faith. St. Pantænus continued to teach in private till about the year 216, when he closed a noble and excellent life by a happy death.

Reflection.—"Have a care that none lead you astray by a false philosophy," says St. Paul, for philosophy without religion is a vain thing.

July 8.—ST. ELIZABETH OF PORTUGAL.

ELIZABETH was born in 1271. She was daughter of Pedro III. of Arragon, being named after her aunt, St. Elizabeth of Hungary. At twelve years of age she was given in marriage to Denis, King of Portugal, and from a holy child became a saintly wife. She heard Mass and recited the Divine Office daily, but her devotions were arranged with such prudence that they interfered with no duty of her state. She prepared for her frequent communions by severe austerities, fasting thrice a week, and by heroic works of charity. She was several times called on to make peace between her husband and her son Alphonso, who had taken up arms against him. Her husband tried her much, both by his unfounded jealousy and by his infidelity to herself. A slander affecting Elizabeth and one of her pages made the king determine to slay the youth, and he told a lime-burner to cast into his kiln the first page who should arrive with a royal message. On the day fixed the page was sent; but the boy, who was in the habit of hearing Mass daily, stopped on his way to do so. The king, in suspense, sent a second page, the very originator of the calumny, who, coming first to the kiln, was at once cast into the furnace and burned. Shortly after, the first page arrived from the church, and took back to the king the lime-burner's reply that his orders had been fulfilled. Thus hearing Mass saved the page's life and proved the queen's innocence. Her patience, and the wonderful sweetness with which she even cherished the children of her rivals, completely won the king from his evil ways, and he became a devoted husband and a truly Christian king. She built many charitable institutions and religious houses, among others a convent of Poor Clares. After her husband's death, she wished to enter their Order; but being dissuaded by her people, who could not do without her, she took the habit of the Third Order of St. Francis, and spent the rest of her life in redoubled austerities and almsgiving. She died at the age of sixty-five, while in the act of making peace between her children.

Reflection.—In the Holy Sacrifice of the Altar St. Elizabeth daily found strength to bear with sweetness suspicion and cruelty; and by that same Holy Sacrifice her innocence was proved. What succor do we forfeit by neglect of daily Mass!

July 9.—ST. EPHREM, Deacon.

ST. EPHREM is the light and glory of the Syriac Church. A mere youth, he entered on the religious life at Nisibis, his native place. Long years of retirement taught him the science of the Saints, and then God called him to Edessa, there to teach what he had learned so well. He defended the Faith against heresies, in books which have made him known as the Prophet of the Syrians. Crowds hung upon his words. Tears used to stop his voice when he preached. He trembled and made his hearers tremble at the thought of God's judgments; but he found in compunction and humility the way to peace, and he rested with unshaken confidence in the mercy of our blessed Lord. " I am setting out," he says, speaking of his own death, " I am setting out on a journey hard and dangerous. Thee, O Son of God, I have taken for my Viaticum. When I am hungry, I will feed on Thee. The infernal fire will not venture near me, for it cannot bear the fragrance of Thy Body and Thy Blood." His hymns won the hearts of the people, drove out the hymns of the Gnostic heretics, and gained for him the title which he bears in the Syriac Liturgy to this day—" the Harp of the Holy Ghost." Passionate as he was by nature, from the time he entered religion no one ever saw him angry. Abounding in labors till the last, he toiled for the suffering poor at Edessa in the famine of 378, and there lay down to die in extreme old age. What was the secret of success so various and so complete? Humility, which made him distrust himself and trust God. Till his death, he wept for the slight sins committed in the thoughtlessness of boyhood. He refused the dignity of the priesthood. " I," he told St. Basil, whom he went to see at the bidding of the Holy Spirit, " I am that Ephrem who has wandered from the path of heaven." Then bursting into tears, he cried out, " O my father, have pity on a sinful wretch, and lead me on the narrow way."

Reflection.—Humility is the path which leads to abiding peace and brings us near to the consolations of God.

July 10.—THE SEVEN BROTHERS, Martyrs, and ST. FELICITAS, their Mother.

THE illustrious martyrdom of these Saints happened at Rome, under the Emperor Antoninus. The seven brothers were the sons of St. Felicitas, a noble, pious, Christian widow in Rome, who, after the death of her husband, served God in a state of continency and employed herself wholly in prayer, fasting, and works of charity. By the public and edifying example of this lady and her whole family many idolaters were moved to renounce the worship of their false gods, and to embrace the Faith of Christ. This excited the anger of the heathen priests, who complained to the emperor that the boldness with which Felicitas publicly practised the Christian religion drew many from the worship of the immortal gods, who were the guardians and protectors of the empire, and that, in order to appease these false gods, it was necessary to compel this lady and her children to sacrifice to them. Publius, the prefect of Rome, caused the mother and her sons to be apprehended and brought before him, and, addressing her, said, " Take pity on your children, Felicitas; they are in the bloom of youth, and may aspire to the greatest honors and preferments." The holy mother answered, " Your pity is really impiety, and the compassion to which you exhort me would make me the most cruel of mothers." Then turning herself towards her children, she said to them, " My sons, look up to heaven, where Jesus Christ with His Saints expects you. Be faithful in His love, and fight courageously for your souls." Publius, being exasperated at this behavior, commanded her to be cruelly buffeted; he then called the children to him one after another, and used many artful speeches, mingling promises with threats to induce them to adore the gods. His arguments and threats were equally in vain, and the brothers were condemned to be scourged. After being whipped, they were remanded to prison, and the prefect, despairing to overcome their resolution, laid the whole process before the emperor. Antoninus gave an order that they should be sent to different judges, and be condemned to different deaths. Januarius was scourged to death with whips loaded with plummets of lead. The two next, Felix and Philip, were beaten with clubs till they expired. Sylvanus, the fourth, was thrown headlong down a steep precipice. The three youngest, Alexander, Vitalis, and Martialis, were beheaded, and the same sentence was executed upon the mother four months after.

Reflection.—What afflictions do parents daily meet with from the disorders into which their children fall through their own bad example or neglect! Let them imitate the earnestness of St. Felicitas in forming to perfect virtue the tender souls which God hath committed to their charge, and with this Saint they will have the greatest of all comforts in them, and will by His grace count as many Saints in their family as they are blessed with children.

July 11.—ST. JAMES, Bishop.

THIS eminent Saint and glorious Doctor of the Syriac Church was a native of Nisibis, in Mesopotamia. In his youth, entering the world, he trembled at the sight of its vices and the slippery path of its pleasures, and he thought it the safer part to strengthen himself in retirement, that he might afterward be the better able to stand his ground in the field. He accordingly chose the highest mountain for his abode, sheltering himself in a cave in the winter, and the rest of the year living in the woods, continually exposed to the open air. Notwithstanding his desire to live unknown to men, he was discovered, and many were not afraid to climb the rugged rocks that they might recommend themselves to his prayers and receive the comfort of his spiritual advice. He was favored with the gifts of prophecy and miracles in an uncommon measure. One day, as he was travelling, he was accosted by a gang of

beggars, with the view of extorting money from him under
pretence of burying their companion, who lay stretched
on the ground as if he were dead. The holy man gave
them what they asked, and "offering up supplications to
God as for a soul departed, he prayed that his Divine
Majesty would pardon him the sins he had committed
whilst he lived, and that he would admit him into the company of the Saints." As soon as the Saint was gone by,
the beggars, calling upon their companion to rise and take
his share of the booty, were surprised to find him really
dead. Seized with sudden fear and grief, they shrieked in
the utmost consternation, and immediately ran after the
man of God, cast themselves at his feet, confessed the cheat,
begged forgiveness, and besought him by his prayers to
restore their unhappy companion to life, which the Saint
did. The most famous miracle of our Saint was that by
which he protected his native city from the barbarians.
Sapor II., the haughty King of Persia, besieged Nisibis
with the whole strength of his empire, whilst our Saint was
Bishop. The Bishop would not pray for the destruction
of any one, but he implored the Divine Mercy that the city
might be delivered from the calamities of so long a siege.
Afterward, going to the top of a high tower, and turning
his face towards the enemy, and seeing the prodigious multitude of men and beasts which covered the whole country,
he said, "Lord, Thou art able by the weakest means to
humble the pride of Thy enemies; defeat these multitudes
by an army of gnats." God heard the humble prayer of
His servant. Scarce had the Saint spoken those words,
when whole clouds of gnats and flies came pouring down
upon the Persians, got into the elephants' trunks and the
horses' ears and nostrils, which made them chafe and foam,
throw their riders, and put the whole army into confusion
and disorder. A famine and pestilence, which followed,
carried off a great part of the army; and Sapor, after lying
above three months before the place, set fire to all his own
engines of war, and was forced to abandon the siege and
return home with the loss of twenty thousand men. Sapor
received a third foil under the walls of Nisibis, in 359,
upon which he turned his arms against Amidus, took that
strong city, and put the garrison and the greatest part of

the inhabitants to the sword. The citizens of Nisibis attributed their preservation to the intercession of their glorious patron, St. James, although he had already gone to his reward. He died in 350.

July 12.—ST. JOHN GUALBERT.

ST. JOHN GUALBERT was born at Florence, A. D. 999. Following the profession of arms at that troubled period, he became involved in a blood-feud with a near relative. One Good Friday, as he was riding into Florence accompanied by armed men, he encountered his enemy in a place where neither could avoid the other. John would have slain him; but his adversary, who was totally unprepared to fight, fell upon his knees with his arms stretched out in the form of a cross, and implored him, for the sake of Our Lord's holy Passion, to spare his life. St. John said to his enemy, " I cannot refuse what you ask in Christ's name. I grant you your life, and I give you my friendship. Pray that God may forgive me my sin." Grace triumphed. A humble and changed man, he entered the Church of St. Miniato, which was near; and whilst he prayed, the figure of our crucified Lord, before which he was kneeling, bowed its head toward him as if to ratify his pardon. Abandoning the world, he gave himself up to prayer and penance in the Benedictine Order. Later he was led to found the congregation called of Vallombrosa, from the shady valley a few miles from Florence, where he established his first monastery. Once the enemies of the Saint came to his convent of St. Salvi, plundered it, and set fire to it, and having treated the monks with ignominy, beat them and wounded them. St. John rejoiced. " Now," he said, " you are true monks. Would that I myself had had the honor of being with you when the soldiers came, that I might have had a share in the glory of your crowns! " He fought manfully against simony, and in many ways promoted the interest of the Faith in Italy. After a life of great austerity, he died whilst the angels were singing round his bed, July 11, 1073.

Reflection.—The heroic act which merited for St. John Gualbert his conversion was the forgiveness of his enemy. Let us imitate him in this virtue, resolving never to revenge ourselves in deed, in word, or in thought.

July 13.—ST. EUGENIUS, Bishop.

THE episcopal see of Carthage had remained vacant twenty-four years, when, in 481, Huneric permitted the Catholics on certain conditions to choose one who should fill it. The people, impatient to enjoy the comfort of a pastor, pitched upon Eugenius, a citizen of Carthage, eminent for his learning, zeal, piety, and prudence. His charities to the distressed were excessive, and he refused himself everything that he might give all to the poor. His virtue gained him the respect and esteem even of the Arians; but at length envy and blind zeal got the ascendant in their breasts, and the king sent him an order never to sit on the episcopal throne, preach to the people, or admit into his chapel any Vandals, among whom several were Catholics. The Saint boldly answered that the laws of God commanded him not to shut the door of His church to any that desired to serve Him in it. Huneric, enraged at this answer, persecuted the Catholics in various ways. Many nuns were so cruelly tortured that they died on the rack. Great numbers of bishops, priests, deacons, and eminent Catholic laymen were banished to a desert filled with scorpions and venomous serpents. The people followed their bishops and priests with lighted tapers in their hands, and mothers carried their little babes in their arms and laid them at the feet of the confessors, all crying out with tears, " Going yourselves to your crowns, to whom do you leave us? Who will baptize our children? Who will impart to us the benefit of penance, and discharge us from the bonds of sin by the favor of reconciliation and pardon? Who will bury us with solemn supplications at our death? By whom will the Divine Sacrifice be made?" The Bishop Eugenius was spared in the first storm, but afterwards was carried into the uninhabited desert country in the province of Tripolis, and committed to the guard of

Antony, an inhuman Arian bishop, who treated him with the utmost barbarity. Gontamund, who succeeded Huneric, recalled our Saint to Carthage, opened the Catholic churches, and allowed all the exiled priests to return. After reigning twelve years, Gontamund died, and his brother Thrasimund was called to the crown. Under this prince St. Eugenius was again banished, and died in exile, on the 13th of July, 505, in a monastery which he built and governed, near Albi.

Reflection.—" Alms shall be a great confidence before the Most High God to them that give it. Water quencheth a flaming fire, and alms resisteth sin."

July 14.—ST. BONAVENTURE.

ANCTITY and learning raised Bonaventure to the Church's highest honors, and from a child he was the companion of Saints. Yet at heart he was ever the poor Franciscan friar, and practised and taught humility and mortification. St. Francis gave him his name; for, having miraculously cured him of a mortal sickness, he prophetically exclaimed of the child, " O bona ventura ! "—good luck. He is known also as the " Seraphic Doctor," from the fervor of divine love which breathes in his writings. He was the friend of St. Thomas Aquinas, who asked him one day whence he drew his great learning. He replied by pointing to his crucifix. At another time St. Thomas found him in ecstasy while writing the life of St. Francis, and exclaimed, " Let us leave a Saint to write of a Saint." They received the Doctor's cap together. He was the guest and adviser of St. Louis, and the director of St. Isabella, the king's sister. At the age of thirty-five he was made general of his Order; and only escaped another dignity, the Archbishopric of York, by dint of tears and entreaties. Gregory X. appointed him Cardinal Bishop of Albano. When the Saint heard of the Pope's resolve to create him a Cardinal, he quietly made his escape from Italy. But Gregory sent him a summons to return to Rome. On his way, he stopped to rest himself at a convent of his Order near Florence; and there two Papal messengers, sent to meet him with the Cardinal's hat, found him washing the dishes. The Saint desired them to hang the hat on a bush that was near, and take a walk in the garden until he had finished what he was about. Then taking up the hat with unfeigned sorrow, he joined the messengers, and paid them the respect due to their character. He sat at the Pontiff's right hand, and spoke first at the Council of Lyons. His piety and eloquence won over the Greeks to Catholic union, and then his strength failed. He died while the Council was sitting, and was buried by the assembled bishops, A. D. 1274.

Reflection.—" The fear of God," says St. Bonaventure, " forbids a man to give his heart to transitory things, which are the true seeds of sin."

July 15.—ST. HENRY, Emperor.

HENRY, Duke of Bavaria, saw in a vision his guardian, St. Wolfgang, pointing to the words " after six." This moved him to prepare for death, and for six years he continued to watch and pray, when, at the end of the sixth year, he found the warning verified in his election as emperor. Thus trained in the fear of God, he ascended the throne with but one thought — to reign for His greater glory. The pagan Slavs were then despoiling the empire. Henry attacked them with a small force; but angels and Saints were seen leading his troops, and the heathen fled in despair. Poland and Bohemia, Moravia and Burgundy, were in turn annexed to his kingdom, Pannonia and Hungary won to the Church. With the Faith secured in Germany, Henry passed into Italy, drove out the Antipope Gregory, brought Benedict VIII. back to Rome, and was crowned in St. Peter's by that Pontiff, in 1014. It was Henry's custom, on arriving in any town, to spend his first night in watching in some church dedicated to our blessed Lady. As he was thus praying in St. Mary Major's, the first night of his arrival in Rome, he " saw the Sovereign and Eternal Priest Christ Jesus " enter to say Mass. Sts. Laurence and Vincent assisted as deacon and sub-deacon. Saints innumerable filled the church, and angels sang in

the choir. After the Gospel, an angel was sent by Our
Lady to give Henry the book to kiss. Touching him
lightly on the thigh, as the angel did to Jacob, he said,
" Accept this sign of God's love for your chastity and justice ; " and from that time the emperor always was lame.
Like holy David, Henry employed the fruits of his con-
quests in the service of the temple. The forests and mines
of the empire, the best that his treasury could produce,
were consecrated to the sanctuary. Stately cathedrals,
noble monasteries, churches innumerable, enlightened and
sanctified the once heathen lands. In 1022 Henry lay on
his bed of death. He gave back to her parents his wife,
St. Cunegunda, " a virgin still, as a virgin he had received
her from Christ," and surrendered his own pure soul to
·God.

Reflection.—St. Henry deprived himself of many things
to enrich the house of God. We clothe ourselves in purple
and fine linen, and leave Jesus in poverty and neglect.

July 16.—ST. SIMON STOCK.

SIMON was born in the county of Kent, England, and
left his home when he was but twelve years of age, to
live as a hermit in the hollow trunk of a tree, whence he
was known as Simon of the Stock. Here he passed twenty
years in penance and prayer, and learned from Our Lady
that he was to join an Order not then known in England.
He waited in patience till the White Friars came, and then
entered the Order of Our Lady of Mount Carmel. His
great holiness moved his brethren in the general chapter
held at Aylesford, near Rochester, in 1245, to choose him
prior-general of the Order. In the many persecutions
raised against the new religious, Simon went with filial
confidence to the Blessed Mother of God. As he knelt in
prayer in the White Friars' convent at Cambridge, on July
16, 1251, she appeared before him and presented him with
the scapular, in assurance of her protection. The devotion to the blessed habit spread quickly throughout the
Christian world. Pope after Pope enriched it with indulgences, and miracles innumerable put their seal upon its

efficacy. The first of them was worked at Winchester on a man dying in despair, who at once asked for the Sacraments, when the scapular was laid upon him by St. Simon Stock. In the year 1636, M. de Guge, a cornet in a cavalry regiment, was mortally wounded at the engagement of Tehin, a bullet having lodged near his heart. He was then in a state of grievous sin, but had time left him to make his confession, and with his own hands wrote his last testament. When this was done, the surgeon probed his wound, and the bullet was found to have driven his scapular into his heart. On its being withdrawn, he presently expired, making profound acts of gratitude to the Blessed Virgin, who had prolonged his life miraculously, and thus preserved him from eternal death. St. Simon Stock died at Bordeaux in 1265.

Reflection.—To enjoy the privileges of the scapular, it is sufficient that it be received lawfully and worn devoutly. How, then, can any one fail to profit by a devotion so easy, so simple, and so wonderfully blessed? "He that shall overcome, shall thus be clothed in white garments, and I will not blot out his name out of the book of life, and I will confess his name before My Father and before His angels" (Apoc. iii. 5).

July 17.—ST. ALEXIUS.

ST. ALEXIUS was the only son of parents pre-eminent among the Roman nobles for virtue, birth, and wealth. On his wedding-night, by God's special inspiration, he secretly quitted Rome, and journeying to Edessa, in the far East, gave away all that he had brought with him, content thenceforth to live on alms at the gate of Our Lady's church in that city. It came to pass that the servants of St. Alexius, whom his father sent in search of him, arrived at Edessa, and seeing him among the poor at the gate of Our Lady's church, gave him an alms, not recognizing him. Whereupon the man of God, rejoicing, said, "I thank thee, O Lord, Who hast called me and granted that I should receive for Thy name's sake an alms from my own slaves. Deign to fulfil in me the work Thou

hast begun." After seventeen years, when his sanctity
was miraculously manifested by the Blessed Virgin's
image, he once more sought obscurity by flight.   On his
way to Tarsus contrary winds drove his ship to Rome.
There no one recognized in the wan and tattered mendi-
cant the heir of Rome's noblest house; not even his sor-
rowing parents, who had vainly sent throughout the world
in search of him.   From his father's charity he begged a
mean corner of his palace as a shelter, and the leavings
of his table as food.   Thus he spent seventeen years, bearing patiently the mockery and ill-usage of his own slaves,
and witnessing daily the inconsolable grief of his spouse
and parents.   At last, when death had ended this cruel
martyrdom, they learned too late, from a writing in his
own hand, who it was that they had unknowingly sheltered.   God bore testimony to His servant's sanctity by
many miracles.   He died early in the fifth century.

Reflection.—We must always be ready to sacrifice our
dearest and best natural affections in obedience to the call
of our heavenly Father.   " Call none your father upon
earth, for one is your Father in heaven " (Matt. xxiii. 9).
Our Lord has taught us this not by words only, but by His
own example and by that of His Saints.

July 18.—ST. CAMILLUS OF LELLIS.

THE early years of Camillus gave no sign of sanctity.
At the age of nineteen he took service with his
father, an Italian noble, against the Turks, and after four
years' hard campaigning found himself, through his violent temper, reckless habits, and inveterate passion for
gambling, a discharged soldier, and in such straitened circumstances that he was obliged to work as a laborer on a
Capuchin convent which was then building.   A few words
from a Capuchin friar brought about his conversion, and
he resolved to become a religious.   Thrice he entered the
Capuchin novitiate, but each time an obstinate wound in
his leg forced him to leave.   He repaired to Rome for
medical treatment, and there took St. Philip as his con-

fessor, and entered the hospital of St. Giacomo, of which he became in time the superintendent. The carelessness of the paid chaplains and nurses towards the suffering patients now inspired him with the thought of founding a congregation to minister to their wants. With this end he was ordained priest, and in 1586 his community of the Servants of the Sick was confirmed by the Pope. Its usefulness was soon felt, not only in hospitals, but in private houses. Summoned at every hour of the day and night, the devotion of Camillus never grew cold. With a woman's tenderness he attended to the needs of his patients. He wept with them, consoled them, and prayed with them. He knew miraculously the state of their souls; and St. Philip saw angels whispering to two Servants of the Sick who were consoling a dying person. One day a sick man said to the Saint, " Father, may I beg you to make up my bed? it is very hard." Camillus replied, " God forgive you, brother! You beg me! Don't you know yet that you are to command me, for I am your servant and slave." " Would to God," he would cry, " that in the hour of my death one sigh or one blessing of these poor creatures might fall upon me! " His prayer was heard. He was granted the same consolations in his last hour which he had so often procured for others. In the year 1614 he died with the full use of his faculties, after two weeks' saintly preparation, as the priest was reciting the words of the ritual, " May Jesus Christ appear to thee with a mild and joyful countenance! "

Reflection.—St. Camillus venerated the sick as living images of Christ, and by ministering to them in this spirit did penance for the sins of his youth, led a life precious in merit, and from a violent and quarrelsome soldier became a gentle and tender Saint.

July 19.—ST. VINCENT OF PAUL.

ST. VINCENT was born in 1576. In after-years, when adviser of the queen and oracle of the Church in France, he loved to recount how, in his youth, he had guarded his father's pigs. Soon after his ordination he was captured by corsairs, and carried into Barbary. He converted his renegade master, and escaped with him to France. Appointed chaplain-general of the galleys of France, his tender charity brought hope into those prisons where hitherto despair had reigned. A mother mourned her imprisoned son. Vincent put on his chains and took his place at the oar, and gave him to his mother. His charity embraced the poor, young and old, provinces desolated by civil war, Christians enslaved by the infidel. The poor man, ignorant and degraded, was to him the image of Him Who became as " a leper and no man." " Turn the medal," he said, " and you then will see Jesus Christ." He went through the streets of Paris at night, seeking the children who were left there to die. Once robbers rushed upon him, thinking he carried a treasure, but when he opened his cloak, they recognized him and his burden, and fell at his feet. Not only was St. Vincent the saviour of the poor, but also of the rich, for he taught them to do works of mercy. When the work for the foundlings was in danger of failing from want of funds, he assembled the ladies of the Association of Charity. He bade his most fervent daughters be present to give the spur to the others. Then he said, " Compassion and charity have made you adopt these little creatures as your children. You have been their mothers according to grace, when their own mothers abandoned them. Cease to be their mothers, that you may become their judges; their life and death are in your hands. I shall now take your votes: it is time to pronounce sentence." The tears of the assembly were his only answer, and the work was continued. The Society of St. Vincent, the Priests of the Mission, and 25,000 Sisters of Charity still comfort the afflicted with the charity of St. Vincent of Paul. He died in 1660.

Reflection.—Most people who profess piety ask advice of directors about their prayers and spiritual exercises. Few inquire whether they are not in danger of damnation from neglect of works of charity.

July 20.—ST. MARGARET, Virgin and Martyr.

CCORDING to the ancient Martyrologies, St. Margaret suffered at Antioch in Pisidia, in the last general persecution. She is said to have been instructed in the Faith by a Christian nurse, to have been persecuted by her own father, a pagan priest, and, after many torments, to have gloriously finished her martyrdom by the sword. From the East, her veneration was exceedingly propagated in England, France, and Germany, in the eleventh century, during the holy wars. Her body is now kept at Monte-Fiascone in Tuscany.

ST. JEROME EMILIANI.

T. JEROME EMILIANI was a member of one of the patrician families of Venice, and, like many other Saints, in early life a soldier. He was appointed governor of a fortress among the mountains of Treviso, and whilst bravely defending his post, was made prisoner by the enemy. In the misery of his dungeon he invoked the great Mother of God, and promised, if she would set him free, to lead a new and a better life. Our Lady appeared, broke his fetters, and led him forth through the midst of his enemies. At Treviso he hung up his chains at her altar, dedicated himself to her service, and on reaching his home at Venice devoted himself to a life of active charity. His special love was for the deserted orphan children whom, in the times of the plague and famine, he found wandering in the streets. He took them home, clothed and fed them, and taught them the Christian truths. From Venice he passed to Padua and Verona, and in a few years had founded orphanages through Northern Italy. Some pious clerics and laymen, who had been his fellow-workers, fixed their abode in one of these establishments, and devoted themselves to the cause of education. The Saint drew up for them a rule of life and thus was founded the Congregation, which still exists, of the Clerks Regular of Somascha. St. Jerome died February 8, 1537, of an illness which he had caught in visiting the sick.

Reflection.—Let us learn from St. Jerome to exert ourselves in behalf of the many hundred children whose souls are perishing around us for want of some one to show them the way to heaven.

July 21.—ST. VICTOR, Martyr.

THE Emperor Maximian, reeking with the blood of the Thebæan legion and many other martyrs, arrived at Marseilles, where the Church then flourished. The tyrant breathed here nothing but slaughter and fury, and his coming filled the Christians with fear and alarm. In this general consternation, Victor, a Christian officer in the troops, went about in the night-time from house to house, visiting the faithful and inspiring them with contempt of a temporal death and the love of eternal life. He was surprised in this, and brought before the prefects Asterius and Eutychius, who exhorted him not to lose the fruit of all his services and the favor of his prince for the worship of a dead man, as they called Jesus Christ. He answered that he renounced those recompenses if he could not enjoy them without being unfaithful to Jesus Christ, the eternal Son of God, Who vouchsafed to become man for our salvation, but Who raised Himself from the dead, and reigns with the Father, being God equally with Him. The whole court heard him with shouts of rage. Victor was bound hand and foot and dragged through the streets of the city, exposed to the blows and insults of the populace. He was brought back bruised and bloody to the tribunal of the prefects, who, thinking his resolution must have been weakened by his sufferings, pressed him again to adore their gods. But the martyr, filled with the Holy Ghost, expressed his respect for the emperor and his contempt for their gods. He was then hoisted on the rack and tortured a long time, until, the tormentors being at last weary, the prefect ordered him to be taken down and thrown into a dark dungeon. At midnight, God visited him by His angels; the prison was filled with a light brighter than that of the sun, and the martyr sung with the angels the praises of God. Three soldiers who guarded the prison, seeing this light, cast themselves at the martyr's feet, asked his pardon, and desired Baptism. Victor instructed them as well as time would permit, sent for priests the same night, and, going with them to the seaside, had them baptized, and returned with them again to his prison. The next morning Maximian was informed of the conversion of the guards, and in a transport of rage sent officers to bring them all four before him. The three soldiers persevered in the confession of Jesus Christ, and by the emperor's orders were forthwith beheaded. Victor, after having been exposed to the insults of the whole city and beaten with clubs and scourged with leather thongs, was carried back to prison, where he continued three days, recommending to God his martyrdom with many tears. After that term the emperor called him again before his tribunal, and commanded the martyr to offer incense to a statue of Jupiter. Victor went up to the profane altar, and by a kick of his foot threw it down. The emperor ordered the foot to be forthwith chopped off, which the Saint suffered with great joy, offering to God these first-fruits of his body. A few moments after, the emperor condemned him to be put under the grindstone of a hand-mill and crushed to death. The executioners turned the wheel, and when part of his body was bruised and crushed the mill broke down. The Saint still breathed a little, but his head was immediately ordered to be cut off. His and the other three bodies were thrown into the sea, but, being cast ashore, were buried by the Christians in a grotto hewn out of a rock.

July 22.—ST. MARY MAGDALEN.

OF the earlier life of Mary Magdalen we know only that she was " a woman who was a sinner." From the depth of her degradation she raised her eyes to Jesus with sorrow, hope, and love. All covered with shame, she came in where Jesus was at meat, and knelt behind him. She said not a word, but bathed His feet with her tears, wiped them with the hair of her head, kissed them in humility, and at their touch her sins and her stain were gone. Then she poured on them the costly unguent prepared for far

other uses; and His own divine lips rolled away her reproach, spoke her absolution, and bade her go in peace.
Thenceforward she ministered to Jesus, sat at His feet,
and heard His words. She was one of the family "whom
Jesus so loved" that He raised her brother Lazarus from
the dead. Once again, on the eve of His Passion, she
brought the precious ointment, and, now purified and beloved, poured it on His head, and the whole house of God
is still filled with the fragrance of her anointing. She
stood with Our Lady and St. John at the foot of the cross,
the representative of the many who have had much forgiven. To her first, after His blessed Mother, and through
her to His apostles, Our Lord gave the certainty of His resurrection; and to her first He made Himself known, calling
her by her name, because she was His. When the faithful
were scattered by persecution the family of Bethany found
refuge in Provence. The cave in which St. Mary lived for
thirty years is still seen, and the chapel on the mountain-
top, in which she was caught up daily, like St. Paul, to
"visions and revelations of the Lord." When her end
drew near she was borne to a spot still marked by a "sacred pillar," where the holy Bishop Maximin awaited her;
and when she had received her Lord, she peacefully fell
asleep in death.

Reflection.—" Compunction of heart," says St. Bernard,
" is a treasure infinitely to be desired, and an unspeakable
gladness to the heart. It is healing to the soul; it is remission of sins; it brings back again the Holy Spirit into
the humble and loving heart."

July 23.—ST. APOLLINARIS, Bishop and Martyr.

ST. APOLLINARIS was the first Bishop of Ravenna; he sat
twenty years, and was crowned with martyrdom in
the reign of Vespasian. He was a disciple of St. Peter,
and made by him Bishop of Ravenna. St. Peter Chrysolo-
gus, the most illustrious among his successors, has left us a
sermon in honor of our Saint, in which he often styles him
a martyr; but adds, that though he frequently suffered for
the Faith, and ardently desired to lay down his life for

Christ, yet God preserved him a long time to His Church, and did not allow the persecutors to take away his life. So he seems to have been a martyr only by the torments he endured for Christ, which he survived at least some days. His body lay first at Classis, four miles from Ravenna, still a kind of suburb to that city, and its seaport till it was choked up by the sands. In the year 549 his relics were removed into a more secret vault in the same church. St. Fortunatus exhorted his friends to make pilgrimages to the tomb, and St. Gregory the Great ordered parties in doubtful suits at law to be sworn before it. Pope Honorius built a church under the name of Apollinaris in Rome, about the year 630. It occurs in all martyrologies, and the high veneration which the Church paid early to his memory is a sufficient testimony of his eminent sanctity and apostolic spirit.

Reflection.—The virtue of the Saints was true and heroic, because humble and proof against all trials. Persevere in your good resolutions: it is not enough to begin well; you must so continue to the end.

July 24.—ST. CHRISTINA, Virgin and Martyr.

ST. CHRISTINA was the daughter of a rich and powerful magistrate named Urbain. Her father, who was deep in the practices of heathenism, had a number of golden idols, which our Saint destroyed, and distributed the pieces among the poor. Infuriated by this act, Urbain became the persecutor of his daughter; he had her whipped with rods and then thrown into a dungeon. Christina remained unshaken in her faith. Her tormentor then had her body torn by iron hooks, and fastened her to a rack beneath which a fire was kindled. But God watched over His servant and turned the flames upon the lookers-on. Christina was next seized, a heavy stone tied about her neck, and she was thrown into the lake of Bolsena, but she was saved by an angel, and outlived her father, who died of spite. Later, this martyr suffered the most inhuman torments under the judge who succeeded her father, and finally was thrown into a burning furnace, where she remained, unhurt, for five days. By the power of Christ she overcame the serpents among which she was thrown; then her tongue was cut out, and afterwards, being pierced with arrows, she gained the martyr's crown at Tyro, a city which formerly stood on an island in the lake of Bolsena in Italy, but was long since swallowed up by the waters. Her relics are now at Palermo in Sicily.

July 25.—ST. JAMES, Apostle.

AMONG the twelve, three were chosen as the familiar companions of our blessed Lord, and of these James was one. He alone, with Peter and John, was admitted to the house of Jairus when the dead maiden was raised to life. They alone were taken up to the high mountain apart, and saw the face of Jesus shining as the sun, and His garments white as snow; and these three alone witnessed the fearful agony in Gethsemane. What was it that won James a place among the favorite three? Faith, burning, impetuous, and outspoken, but which needed purifying before the "Son of Thunder" could proclaim the gospel of peace. It was James who demanded fire from heaven to consume the inhospitable Samaritans, and who sought the place of honor by Christ in His Kingdom. Yet Our Lord, in rebuking his presumption, prophesied his faithfulness to death. When St. James was brought before King Herod Agrippa, his fearless confession of Jesus crucified so moved the public prosecutor that he declared himself a Christian on the spot. Accused and accuser were hurried off together to execution, and on the road the latter begged pardon of the Saint. The apostle had long since forgiven him, but hesitated for a moment whether publicly to accept as a brother one still unbaptized. God quickly recalled to him the Church's faith, that the blood of martyrdom supplies for every sacrament, and, falling on his companion's neck, he embraced him, with the words, "Peace be with thee!" Together then they knelt for the sword, and together received the crown.

Reflection.—We must all desire a place in the kingdom of our Father; but can we drink the chalice which He holds out to each? *Possumus,* we must say with St. James — " We can " — but only in the strength of Him Who has drunk it first for us.

July 26.—ST. ANNE.

ST. ANNE was the spouse of St. Joachim, and was chosen by God to be the mother of Mary, His own blessed Mother on earth. They were both of the royal house of David, and their lives were wholly occupied in prayer and good works. One thing only was wanting to their union — they were childless, and this was held as a bitter misfortune among the Jews. At length, when Anne was an aged woman, Mary was born, the fruit rather of grace than of nature, and the child more of God than of man. With the birth of Mary the aged Anne began a new life: she watched her every movement with reverent tenderness, and felt herself hourly sanctified by the presence of her immaculate child. But she had vowed her daughter to God, to God Mary had consecrated herself again, and to Him Anne gave her back. Mary was three years old when Anne and Joachim led her up the Temple steps, saw her pass by herself into the inner sanctuary, and then saw her no more. Thus was Anne left childless in her lone old age, and deprived of her purest earthly joy just when she needed it most. She humbly adored the Divine Will, and began again to watch and pray, till God called her to unending rest with the Father and the Spouse of Mary in the home of Mary's Child.

Reflection.—St. Anne is glorious among the Saints, not only as the mother of Mary, but because she gave Mary to God. Learn from her to reverence a divine vocation as the highest privilege, and to sacrifice every natural tie, however holy, at the call of God.

July 27.—ST. PANTALEON, Martyr.

ST. PANTALEON was physician to the Emperor Galerius Maximianus, and a Christian, but, deceived by often hearing the false maxims of the world applauded, was unhappily seduced into an apostasy. But a zealous

Christian called Hermolaus awakened his conscience to a sense of his guilt, and brought him again into the fold of the Church. The penitent ardently wished to expiate his crime by martyrdom; and to prepare himself for the conflict, when Diocletian's bloody persecution broke out at Nicomedia, in 303, he distributed all his possessions among the poor. Not long after this action he was taken up, and in his house were also apprehended Hermolaus, Hermippus, and Hermocrates. After suffering many torments, they were all condemned to lose their heads. St. Pantaleon suffered the day after the rest. His relics were translated to Constantinople, and there kept with great honor. The greatest part of them are now shown in the abbey of St. Denys near Paris, but his head is at Lyons.

Reflection.—" With the elect thou shalt be elect, and with the perverse wilt be perverted."

July 28.—STS. NAZARIUS and CELSUS, Martyrs.

S T. NAZARIUS's father was a heathen, and held a considerable post in the Roman army. His mother, Perpetua, was a zealous Christian, and was instructed by St. Peter, or his disciples, in the most perfect maxims of our holy faith. Nazarius embraced it with so much ardor that he copied in his life all the great virtues he saw in his teachers; and out of zeal for the salvation of others, he left Rome, his native city, and preached the Faith in many places with a fervor and disinterestedness becoming a disciple of the apostles. Arriving at Milan, he was there beheaded for the Faith, together with Celsus, a youth whom he carried with him to assist him in his travels. These martyrs suffered soon after Nero had raised the first persecution. Their bodies were buried separately in a garden without the city, where they were discovered and taken up by St. Ambrose, in 395. In the tomb of St. Nazarius, a vial of the Saint's blood was found as fresh and red as if it had been spilt that day. The faithful stained handkerchiefs with some drops, and also formed a certain paste with it, a portion of which St. Ambrose sent to St. Gaudentius, Bishop of Brescia. St. Ambrose conveyed the bodies of the two martyrs into the new church of the apostles, which he had just built. A woman was delivered of an evil spirit in their presence. St. Ambrose sent some of these relics to St. Paulinus of Nola, who received them with great respect, as a most valuable present, as he testifies.

Reflection.—The martyrs died as the outcasts of the world, but are crowned by God with immortal honor. The glory of the world is false and transitory, and an empty bubble or shadow, but that of virtue is true, solid, and permanent, even in the eyes of men.

July 29.—ST. MARTHA, Virgin.

ST. JOHN tells us that "Jesus loved Martha and Mary and Lazarus," and yet but few glimpses are vouchsafed us of them. First, the sisters are set before us with a word. Martha received Jesus into her house, and was busy in outward, loving, lavish service, while Mary sat in silence at the feet she had bathed with her tears. Then, their brother is ill, and they send to Jesus, "Lord, he whom Thou lovest is sick." And in His own time the Lord came, and they go out to meet Him; and then follows that scene of unutterable tenderness and of sublimity unsurpassed: the silent waiting of Mary; Martha strong in faith, but realizing so vividly, with her practical turn of mind, the fact of death, and hesitating: "Canst Thou show Thy wonders in the grave?" And then once again, on the eve of His Passion, we see Jesus at Bethany. Martha, true to her character, is serving; Mary, as at first, pours the precious ointment, in adoration and love, on His divine head. And then we find the tomb of St. Martha, at Tarascon, in Provence. When the storm of persecution came, the family of Bethany, with a few companions, were put into a boat, without oars or sail, and borne to the coast of France. St. Mary's tomb is at St. Baume; St. Lazarus is venerated as the founder of the Church of Marseilles; and the memory of the virtues and labors of St. Martha is still fragrant at Avignon and Tarascon.

Reflection.—When Martha received Jesus into her house, she was naturally busy in preparations for such a Guest. Mary sat at His feet, intent alone on listening to His gracious words. Her sister thought that the time required other service than this, and asked our Lord to bid Mary help in serving. Once again Jesus spoke in defence of Mary. "Martha, Martha," He said, "thou art lovingly anxious about many things; be not over-eager; do thy chosen work with recollectedness. Judge not Mary. Hers is the good part, the one only thing really necessary. Thine will be taken away, that something better be given thee." The life of action ceases when the body is laid down; but the life of contemplation endures and is perfected in heaven.

July 30.—ST. GERMANUS, Bishop.

IN his youth Germanus gave little sign of sanctity. He was of noble birth, and at first practised the law at Rome. After a time the emperor placed him high in the army. But his one passion was the chase. He was so carried away as even to retain in his sports the superstitions of the pagan huntsmen. Yet it was revealed to the Bishop of Auxerre that Germanus would be his successor, and he gave him the tonsure almost by main force. Forthwith Germanus became another man, and, making over his lands to the Church, adopted a life of humble penance. At that time the Pelagian heresy was laying waste England, and Germanus was chosen by the reigning Pontiff to rescue the Britons from the snare of Satan. With St. Lupus he preached in the fields and highways throughout the land. At last, near Verulam, he met the heretics face to face, and overcame them utterly with the Catholic and Roman faith. He ascribed this triumph to the intercession of St. Alban, and offered public thanks at his shrine. Towards the end of his stay, his old skill in arms won over the Picts and Scots the complete but bloodless "Alleluia" victory, so called because the newly-baptized Britons, led by the Saint, routed the enemy with the Paschal cry. Germanus visited England a second

time with St. Severus. He died in 448, while interceding with the emperor for the people of Brittany.

Reflection.—"Hold the form of sound words, which
thou hast heard of me in faith, and in the love which is in
Christ Jesus" (II. Tim. i. 13).

July 31.—ST. IGNATIUS OF LOYOLA.

ST. IGNATIUS was born at Loyola in Spain, in the year
1491. He served his king as a courtier and a soldier till his thirtieth year. At that age, being laid low by
a wound, he received the call of divine grace to leave the
world. He embraced poverty and humiliation, that he
might become more like to Christ, and won others to join
him in the service of God. Prompted by their love for
Jesus Christ, Ignatius and his companions made a vow to
go to the Holy Land, but war broke out, and prevented the
execution of their project. Then they turned to the Vicar
of Jesus Christ, and placed themselves under his obedience. This was the beginning of the Society of Jesus.
Our Lord promised St. Ignatius that the precious heritage
of His Passion should never fail his Society, a heritage of
contradictions and persecutions. St. Ignatius was cast
into prison at Salamanca, on a suspicion of heresy. To a
friend who expressed sympathy with him on account of
his imprisonment, he replied, "It is a sign that you have
but little love of Christ in your heart, or you would not
deem it so hard a fate to be in chains for His sake. I
declare to you that all Salamanca does not contain as
many fetters, manacles, and chains as I long to wear for
the love of Jesus Christ." St. Ignatius went to his crown
on the 31st July, 1556.

Reflection.—Ask St. Ignatius to obtain for you the
grace to desire ardently the greater glory of God, even
though it may cost you much suffering and humiliation.

August 1.—ST. PETER'S CHAINS.

EROD AGRIPPA, King of the Jews, having put to death St. James the Great in the year 44, in order to gain the affection and applause of his people, caused St. Peter, the prince of the sacred college, to be cast into prison. It was his intention to put him publicly to death after Easter. The whole Church at Jerusalem put up its prayers to God for the deliverance of the chief pastor of His whole flock, and God favorably heard them. The king took all precautions possible to prevent the escape of his prisoner. St. Peter lay fast asleep, on the very night before the day intended for his execution, when it pleased God to deliver him out of the hands of his enemies. He was guarded by sixteen soldiers, four of whom always kept sentry in their turns: two in the same dungeon with him, and two at the gate. He was fastened to the ground by two chains, and slept between the two soldiers. In the middle of the night, a bright light shone in the prison, and an angel appeared near him, and, striking him on the side, awaked him out of his sleep, and bade him instantly arise, gird his coat about him, put on his sandals and his cloak, and follow him. The apostle did so, for the chains had dropped off from his hands. Following his guide, he passed after him through the first and second wards of watches, and through the iron gate which led into the city, which opened to them of its own accord. The angel conducted him through one street, then, suddenly disappearing, left him to seek some asylum. The apostle went directly to the house of Mary the mother of John, surnamed Mark, where several disciples were met together, and were sending up their prayers to heaven for his deliverance. As he stood knocking without, a young woman, knowing Peter's voice, ran in and informed the company that he was at the door; they concluded it must be his guardian angel, sent by God upon some extraordinary account, until, being let in, he related to them the whole manner of his miraculous escape; and having enjoined them to give notice thereof to St. James and the rest of the brethren, he withdrew to a place of more retirement and security, carrying, wherever he went, the heavenly blessing and life.

Reflection.—This miracle affords a confirmation of the divine promise, " If two of you shall consent upon earth concerning anything whatsoever they shall ask, it shall be done to them by My Father Who is in heaven."

August 2.—ST. STEPHEN, Pope and Martyr.

T. STEPHEN was by birth a Roman, and, being promoted to holy orders, was made archdeacon under the holy Popes St. Cornelius and St. Lucius. The latter having suffered martyrdom, St. Stephen was chosen to succeed him, and was elected Pope on the 3d of May, 253. The controversy concerning the rebaptization of heretics gave St. Stephen much trouble. It is the teaching of the Catholic Church, that Baptism given in the name of the three persons of the Blessed Trinity is valid, though it be conferred by a heretic. St. Stephen suffered himself patiently to be traduced as a favorer of heresy in approving heretical baptism, not doubting but those great men who by mistaken zeal were led astray would, when the heat of the dispute had subsided, calmly open their eyes to the truth. Thus by his zeal he preserved the integrity of faith, and by his toleration and forbearance saved many souls. The persecutions becoming violent, he assembled the faithful together in the underground tombs of the martyrs, to celebrate Mass and to exhort them to remain true to Christ. On the 2d of August, 257, while seated in his pontifical chair, he was beheaded by the satellites of the emperor; and the chair is still shown, stained with his blood.

ST. ALPHONSUS LIGUORI.

T. ALPHONSUS was born of noble parents, near Naples, in 1696. His spiritual training was intrusted to the Fathers of the Oratory in that city, and from his boyhood Alphonsus was known as a most devout Brother of the Little Oratory. At the early age of sixteen he was made doctor in law, and he threw himself into this career with ardor and success. A mistake, by which he lost an important cause, showed him the vanity of human fame, and determined him to labor only for the glory of God. He entered the priesthood, devoting himself to the most neglected souls; and to carry on this work he founded later the missionary Congregation of the Most Holy Redeemer. At the age of sixty-six he became Bishop of St. Agatha, and undertook the reform of his diocese with the zeal of a Saint. He made a vow never to lose time, and, though his life was spent, in prayer and work, he composed a vast number of books, filled with such science, unction, and wisdom that he has been declared one of the Doctors of the Church. St. Alphonsus wrote his first book at the age of forty-nine, and in his eighty-third year had published about sixty volumes, when his director forbade him to write more. Very many of these books were written in the half-hours snatched from his labors as missionary, religious superior, and Bishop, or in the midst of continual bodily and mental sufferings. With his left hand he would hold a piece of marble against his aching head while his right hand wrote. Yet he counted no time wasted which was spent in charity. He did not refuse to hold a long correspondence with a simple soldier who asked his advice, or to play the harpsichord while he taught his novices to sing spiritual canticles. He lived in evil times, and met with many persecutions and disappointments. For his last seven years he was prevented by constant sickness from offering the Adorable Sacrifice; but he received Holy Communion daily, and his love for Jesus Christ and his trust in Mary's prayers sustained him to the end. He died in 1787, in his ninety-first year.

Reflection.—Let us do with all our heart the duty of each day, leaving the result to God, as well as the care of the future.

August 3.—THE FINDING OF ST. STEPHEN'S RELICS.

THIS second festival in honor of the holy protomartyr St. Stephen was instituted by the Church on the occasion of the discovery of his precious remains. His body lay long concealed, under the ruins of an old tomb, in a place twenty miles from Jerusalem, called Caphargamala, where stood a church which was served by a venerable priest named Lucian. In the year 415, on Friday, the 3d of December, about nine o'clock at night, Lucian was sleeping in his bed in the baptistery, where he commonly lay in order to guard the sacred vessels of the church. Being half awake, he saw a tall, comely old man of a venerable aspect, who approached him, and, calling him thrice by his name, bid him go to Jerusalem and tell Bishop John to come and open the tombs in which his remains and those of certain other servants of Christ lay, that through their means God might open to many the gates of His clemency. This vision was repeated twice. After the second time, Lucian went to Jerusalem and laid the whole affair before Bishop John, who bade him go and search for the relics, which, the Bishop concluded, would be found under a heap of small stones which lay in a field near his church. In digging up the earth here, three coffins or chests were found. Lucian sent immediately to acquaint Bishop John with this. He was then at the Council of Diospolis, and, taking along with him Eutonius, Bishop of Sebaste, and Eleutherius, Bishop of Jericho, came to the place. Upon the opening of St. Stephen's coffin the earth shook, and there came out of the coffin such an agreeable odor that no one remembered to have ever smelled anything like it. There was a vast multitude of people assembled in that place, among whom were many persons afflicted with divers distempers, of whom seventy-three recovered their health upon the spot. They kissed the holy relics, and then shut them up. The Bishop consented to leave a small portion of them at Caphargamala; the rest were carried in the coffin, with singing of psalms and hymns, to the Church of Sion at Jerusalem. The translation was performed on the 26th of December, on which day the Church hath ever since honored the memory of St. Stephen, commemorating the discovery of his relics on the 3d of August probably on account of the dedication of some church in his honor.

Reflection.—St. Austin, speaking of the miracles of St. Stephen, addresses himself to his flock as follows: " Let us so desire to obtain temporal blessings by his intercession that we may merit, in imitating him, those which are eternal."

August 4.—ST. DOMINIC.

ST. Dominic was born in Spain, in 1170. As a student, he sold his books to feed the poor in a famine, and offered himself in ransom for a slave. At the age of twenty-five he became superior of the Canons Regular of Osma, and accompanied his Bishop to France. There his heart was well-nigh broken by the ravages of the Albigensian heresy, and his life was henceforth devoted to the conversion of heretics and the defence of the Faith. For this end he established his threefold religious Order. The convent for nuns was founded first, to rescue young girls from heresy and crime. Then a company of apostolic men gathered around him, and became the Order of Friar Preachers. Lastly came the Tertiaries, persons of both sexes living in the world. God blessed the new Order, and France, Italy, Spain, and England welcomed the Preaching Friars. Our Lady took them under her special protection, and whispered to St. Dominic as he preached. It was in 1208, while St. Dominic knelt in the little chapel of Notre Dame de la Prouille, and implored the great Mother of God to save the Church, that Our Lady appeared to him, gave him the Rosary, and bade him go forth and preach. Beads in hand, he revived the courage of the Catholic troops, led them to victory against overwhelming numbers, and finally crushed the heresy. His nights were spent in prayer; and, though pure as a virgin, thrice before morning broke he scourged himself to blood. His words rescued countless souls, and three times raised the dead to life. At length, on August 6, 1221, at the age of fifty-one, he gave up his soul to God.

Reflection.—" God has never," said St. Dominic, " refused me what I have asked; " and he has left us the Rosary, that we may learn, with Mary's help, to pray easily and simply in the same holy trust.

August 5.—THE DEDICATION OF ST. MARY AD NIVES.

THERE are in Rome three patriarchal churches, in which the Pope officiates on different festivals. These are the Basilics of St. John Lateran, St. Peter's on the Vatican Hill, and St. Mary Major. This last is so called because it is, both in antiquity and dignity, the first church in Rome among those that are dedicated to God in honor of the Virgin Mary. The name of the Liberian Basilic was given it because it was founded in the time of Pope Liberius, in the fourth century; it was consecrated, under the title of the Virgin Mary, by Sixtus III., about the year 435. It is also called St. Mary ad Nives, or *at the snow,* from a popular tradition that the Mother of God chose this place for a church under her invocation by a miraculous snow that fell upon this spot in summer, and by a vision in which she appeared to a patrician named John, who munificently founded and endowed this church in the pontificate of Liberius. The same Basilic has sometimes been known by the name of St. Mary *ad Præsepe,* from the holy crib or manger of Bethlehem, in which Christ was laid at His birth. It resembles an ordinary manger, is kept in a case of massive silver, and in it lies an image of a little child, also of silver. On Christmas Day the holy manger is taken out of the case, and exposed. It is kept in a sumptuous subterraneous chapel in this church.

Reflection.—To render our supplications the more efficacious, we ought to unite them in spirit to those of all fervent penitents and devout souls, in invoking this advocate for sinners.

August 6.—THE TRANSFIGURATION OF OUR LORD.

OUR divine Redeemer, being in Galilee about a year before His sacred Passion, took with Him St. Peter and the two sons of Zebedee, Sts. James and John, and led them to a retired mountain. Tradition assures us that this was Mount Thabor, which is exceedingly high and beautiful, and was anciently covered with green trees and shrubs, and was very fruitful. It rises something like a sugar-loaf, in a vast plain in the middle of Galilee. This was the place in which the Man-God appeared in His glory. Whilst Jesus prayed, He suffered that glory which was always due to His sacred humility, and of which, for our sake, He deprived it, to diffuse a ray over His whole body. His face was altered and shone as the sun, and His garments became white as snow. Moses and Elias were seen by the three apostles in His company on this occasion, and were heard discoursing with Him of the death which He was to suffer in Jerusalem. The three apostles were wonderfully delighted with this glorious vision, and St. Peter cried out to Christ, " Lord, it is good for us to be here. Let us make three tents: one for Thee, one for Moses, and one for Elias." Whilst St. Peter was speaking, there came, on a sudden, a bright shining cloud from heaven, an emblem of the presence of God's majesty, and from out of this cloud was heard a voice which said, " This is My beloved Son, in Whom I am well pleased; hear ye Him." The apostles that were present, upon hearing this voice, were seized with a sudden fear, and fell upon the ground; but Jesus, going to them, touched them, and bade them to rise. They immediately did so, and saw no one but Jesus standing in his ordinary state. This vision happened in the night. As they went down the mountain early the next morning, Jesus bade them not to tell any one what they had seen till He should be risen from the dead.

Reflection.—From the contemplation of this glorious mystery we ought to conceive a true idea of future happiness; if this once possess our souls, we will think nothing of any difficulties or labors we can meet with here, but regard with great indifference all the goods and evils of this life, provided we can but secure our portion in the kingdom of God's glory.

August 7.—ST. CAJETAN.

CAJETAN was born at Vicenza, in 1480, of pious and noble parents, who dedicated him to our blessed Lady. From childhood he was known as the Saint, and in later years as "the hunter of souls." A distinguished student, he left his native town to seek obscurity in Rome, but was there forced to accept office at the court of Julius II. On the death of that Pontiff he returned to Vicenza, and disgusted his relatives by joining the Confraternity of St. Jerome, whose members were drawn from the lowest classes; while he spent his fortune in building hospitals, and devoted himself to nursing the plague-stricken. To renew the lives of the clergy, he instituted the first community of Regular Clerks, known as Theatines. They devoted themselves to preaching, the administration of the sacraments, and the careful performance of the Church's rites and ceremonies. St. Cajetan was the first to introduce the Forty Hours' Adoration of the Blessed Sacrament, as an antidote to the heresy of Calvin. He had a most tender love for our blessed Lady, and his piety was rewarded, for one Christmas eve she placed the Infant Jesus in his arms. When the Germans, under the Constable Bourbon, sacked Rome, St. Cajetan was barbarously scourged, to extort from him riches which he had long before securely stored in heaven. When St. Cajetan was on his death-bed, resigned to the will of God, eager for pain to satisfy his love, and for death to attain to life, he beheld the Mother of God, radiant with splendor and surrounded by ministering seraphim. In profound veneration, he said, " Lady, bless me! " Mary replied, " Cajetan, receive the blessing of my Son, and know that I am here as a reward for the sincerity of your love, and to lead you to paradise." She then exhorted him to patience in fighting an evil spirit who troubled him, and gave orders to the choirs of angels to escort his soul in triumph to heaven. Then, turning her countenance full of majesty and sweetness upon him, she said, "Cajetan, my Son calls thee. Let us go in peace." Worn out with toil and sickness, he went to his reward in 1547.

Reflection.—Imitate St. Cajetan's devotion to our blessed Lady, by invoking her aid before every work.

August 8.—ST. CYRIACUS and His Companions, Martyrs.

ST. CYRIACUS was a holy deacon at Rome, under the Popes Marcellinus and Marcellus. In the persecution of Diocletian, in 303, he was crowned with a glorious martyrdom in that city. With him suffered also Largus and Smaragdus, and twenty others. Their bodies were first buried near the place of their execution, on the Salarian Way, but were soon after removed to a farm of the devout Lady Lucina, on the Ostian Road, on the eighth day of August.

Reflection.—To honor the martyrs and duly celebrate their festivals, we must learn their spirit and study to imitate them according to the circumstances of our state. We must, like them, resist evil, must subdue our passions, suffer afflictions with patience, and bear with others without murmuring or complaining. The cross is the ladder by which we must ascend to heaven.

BLESSED PETER FAVRE.

BORN in 1506 of poor Savoyard shepherds, Peter, at his earnest request, was sent to school, and in after years to the University of Paris. His college friends were St. Ignatius of Loyola and St. Francis Xavier. Ignatius found the young man's heart ready for his thoughts of apostolic zeal; Peter became his first companion, and in the year of England's revolt was ordained the first priest of the new Society of Jesus. From that day to the close of his life he was ever in the van of the Church's strug-

gles with falsehood and sin. Boldly facing heresy in
Germany, he labored not less diligently to rouse up the
dormant faith and charity of Catholic courts and Catholic
lands. The odor of Blessed Peter's virtues drew after him
into religion the Duke of Gandia, Francis Borgia, and a
young student of Nimeguen, Peter Canisius, both to become Saints like their master. The Pope, Paul III., had
chosen Blessed Favre to be his theologian at the Council of
Trent, and King John III., of Portugal, wished to send
him as patriarch and apostle into Abyssinia. Sick and
worn with labor, but obedient unto death, the father hastened back to Rome, where his last illness came upon him.
He died, in his fortieth year, as one would wish to die, in
the very arms of his best friend and spiritual father, St.
Ignatius.

Reflection.—As the body sinks under fatigue unless
supported by food, so external works, however holy, wear
out the soul which is not regularly nourished by prayer.
In the most crowded day we can make time briefly and
secretly to lift our soul to God and draw new strength
from Him.

August 9.—ST. ROMANUS, Martyr.

S T. ROMANUS was a soldier in Rome at the time of the
martyrdom of St. Laurence. Seeing the joy and
constancy with which that holy martyr suffered his torments, he was moved to embrace the Faith, and addressing
himself to St. Laurence, was instructed and baptized by
him in prison. Confessing aloud what he had done, he
was arraigned, condemned, and beheaded the day before
the martyrdom of St. Laurence. Thus he arrived at his
crown before his guide and master. The body of St.
Romanus was first buried on the road to Tibur, but his
remains were translated to Lucca, where they are kept
under the high altar of a beautiful church which bears his
name.

Reflection.—We are bound to glorify God by our lives,
and Christ commands that our good works shine before

men. It was the usual saying of the apostle St. Matthias, " The faithful sins if his neighbor sins." Such ought to be the zeal of every one to instruct and edify his neighbor by word and example.

August 10.—ST. LAURENCE, Martyr.

ST. LAURENCE was the chief among the seven deacons of the Roman Church. In the year 258 Pope Sixtus was led out to die, and St. Laurence stood by, weeping that he could not share his fate. " I was your minister," he said, " when you consecrated the blood of Our Lord; why do you leave me behind now that you are about to shed your own? " The holy Pope comforted him with the words, " Do not weep, my son; in three days you will follow me." This prophecy came true. The prefect of the city knew the rich offerings which the Christians put into the hands of the clergy, and he demanded the treasures of the Roman Church from Laurence, their guardian. The Saint promised, at the end of three days, to show him riches exceeding all the wealth of the empire, and set about collecting the poor, the infirm, and the religious who lived by the alms of the faithful. He then bade the prefect " see the treasures of the Church." Christ, whom Laurence had served in his poor, gave him strength in the conflict which ensued. Roasted over a slow fire, he made sport of his pains. " I am done enough," he said, " eat, if you will." At length Christ, the Father of the poor, received him into eternal habitations. God showed by the glory which shone around St. Laurence the value He set upon his love for the poor. Prayers innumerable were granted at his tomb; and he continued from his throne in heaven his charity to those in need, granting them, as St. Augustine says, " the smaller graces which they sought, and leading them to the desire of better gifts."

Reflection.—Our Lord appears before us in the persons of the poor. Charity to them is a great sign of predestination. It is almost impossible, the holy Fathers assure us, for any one who is charitable to the poor for Christ's sake to perish.

August 11.—STS. TIBURTIUS and SUSANNA, Martyrs.

AGRESTIUS CHROMATIUS was vicar to the prefect of Rome, and had condemned several martyrs in the reign of Carinus; and in the first years of Diocletian, St. Tranquillinus, being brought before him, assured him that, having been afflicted with the gout, he had recovered a perfect state of health by being baptized. Chromatius was troubled with the same distemper, and being convinced by this miracle of the truth of the Gospel, sent for a priest, and, receiving the Sacrament of Baptism, was freed from that corporal infirmity. Chromatius's son, Tiburtius, was ordained subdeacon, and was soon after betrayed to the persecutors, condemned to many torments, and at length beheaded on the Lavican Road, three miles from Rome, where a church was afterward built. His father, Chromatius, retiring into the country, lived there concealed, in the fervent practice of all Christian virtues.

ST. SUSANNA was nobly born in Rome, and is said to have been niece to Pope Caius. Having made a vow of virginity, she refused to marry, on which account she was impeached as a Christian, and suffered with heroic constancy a cruel martyrdom. St. Susanna suffered towards the beginning of Diocletian's reign, about the year 295.

Reflection.—Sufferings were to the martyrs the most distinguishing mercy, extraordinary graces, and sources of the greatest crowns and glory. All afflictions which God sends are in like manner the greatest mercies and blessings; they are the most precious talents to be improved by us to the increasing of our love and affection to God, and the exercise of the most heroic virtues of self-denial, patience, humility, resignation, and penance.

August 12.—ST. CLARE, Abbess.

ON Palm Sunday, March 17, 1212, the Bishop of Assisi left the altar to present a palm to a noble maiden, eighteen years of age, whom bashfulness had detained in her place. This maiden was St. Clare. Already she had

learnt from St. Francis to hate the world, and was secretly
resolved to live for God alone. The same night she escaped, with one companion, to the Church of the Portiuncula, where she was met by St. Francis and his
brethren. At the altar of Our Lady, St. Francis cut off
her hair, clothed her in his habit of penance, a piece of
sack-cloth, with his cord as a girdle. Thus she was espoused to Christ. In a miserable house outside Assisi she
founded her Order, and was joined by her sister, fourteen
years of age, and afterwards by her mother and other
noble ladies. They went barefoot, observed perpetual
abstinence, constant silence, and perfect poverty. While
the Saracen army of Frederick II. was ravaging the valley
of Spoleto, a body of infidels advanced to assault St.
Clare's convent, which stood outside Assisi. The Saint
caused the Blessed Sacrament to be placed in a monstrance,
above the gate of the monastery facing the enemy, and
kneeling before it, prayed, " Deliver not to beasts, O Lord,
the souls of those who confess to Thee." A voice from the
Host replied, " My protection will never fail you." A
sudden panic seized the infidel host, which took to flight,
and the Saint's convent was spared. During her illness
of twenty-eight years the Holy Eucharist was her only
support and spinning linen for the altar the one work of
her hands. She died in 1253, as the Passion was being
read, and Our Lady and the angels conducted her to glory.

Reflection.—In a luxurious and effeminate age, the
daughters of St. Clare still bear the noble title of poor,
and preach by their daily lives the poverty of Jesus Christ.

August 13.—ST. RADEGUNDES, Queen.

S T. RADEGUNDES was the daughter of a king of Thuringia who was assassinated by his brother; a war en-
suing, our Saint, at the age of twelve, was made prisoner
and carried captive by Clotaire, King of Soissons, who had
her instructed in the Christian religion and baptized. The
great mysteries of our Faith made such an impression on
her tender soul that she gave herself to God with her whole
heart, and desired to consecrate to him her virginity; she

was obliged at last, however, to yield to the king's wish that she should become his wife. As a great queen, she continued no less an enemy to sloth and vanity than she was before, and divided her time chiefly between her oratory, the Church, and the care of the poor. She also kept long fasts, and during Lent wore a hair-cloth under her rich garments. Clotaire was at first pleased with her devotions, and allowed her full liberty in them, but afterward used frequently to reproach her for her pious exercises, saying he had married a nun rather than a queen, who converted his court into a monastery. Seeing that Clotaire was inflamed by bad passions, our Saint asked and obtained his leave to retire from court. She went to Noyon, and was consecrated deaconess by St. Medard. Radegundes first withdrew to Sais, and some time after she went to Poitiers, and there built a great monastery. She had a holy virgin, named Agnes, made the first abbess, and paid to her an implicit obedience in all things, not reserving to herself the disposal of the least thing. King Clotaire, repenting of his evil conduct, wished her to return to court, but, through the intercession of St. Germanus of Paris, she was allowed to remain in her retirement, where she died on the 13th of August, 587.

August 14.—ST. EUSEBIUS, Priest.

THE Church celebrates this day the memory of St. Eusebius, who opposed the Arians, at Rome, with so much zeal. He was imprisoned in his room by order of the Emperor Constantius, and sanctified his captivity by constant prayer. Another Saint of the same name, a priest and martyr, is commemorated on this day. In the reign of Diocletian and Maximian, before they had published any new edicts against the Christians, Eusebius, a holy priest, a man eminently endowed with the spirit of prayer and all apostolical virtues, suffered death for the Faith, probably in Palestine. The Emperor Maximian happening to be in that country, complaint was made to Maxentius, president of the province, that Eusebius distinguished himself by his zeal in invoking and preaching

Christ, and the holy man was seized. Maximian was by birth a barbarian, and one of the roughest and most brutal and savage of all men. Yet the undaunted and modest virtue of this stranger, set off by a heavenly grace, struck him with awe. He desired to save the servant of Christ, but, like Pilate, would not give himself any trouble or hazard incurring the displeasure of those whom on all other occasions he despised. Maxentius commanded Eusebius to sacrifice to the gods, and on the Saint refusing, the president condemned him to be beheaded. Eusebius, hearing the sentence pronounced, said aloud, " I thank Your goodness and praise Your power, O Lord Jesus Christ, that, by calling me to the trial of my fidelity, You have treated me as one of Yours." He at that instant heard a voice from heaven saying to him, " If you had not been found worthy to suffer, you could not be admitted into the court of Christ or to the seats of the just." Being come to the place of execution, he knelt down, and his head was struck off.

Reflection.—Let us learn, from the example of the Saints, courage in the service of God. He calls upon us to endure suffering of body and of mind, if it is necessary, to prove our fidelity to Him ; and He promises to support us by His strength, His light, and His heavenly consolation.

August 15.—THE ASSUMPTION OF THE BLESSED VIRGIN MARY.

O N this festival the Church commemorates the happy departure from life of the Blessed Virgin Mary, and her translation into the kingdom of her Son, in which she received from Him a crown of immortal glory, and a throne above all the other Saints and heavenly spirits. After Christ, as the triumphant Conqueror of death and hell, ascended into heaven, His blessed Mother remained at Jerusalem, persevering in prayer with the disciples, till, with them, she had received the Holy Ghost. She lived to a very advanced age, but finally paid the common debt of nature, none among the children of Adam being exempt from that rigorous law. But the death of the Saints is rather to be called a sweet sleep than death; much more that of the Queen of Saints, who had been exempt from all sin. It is a traditionary pious belief, that the body of the Blessed Virgin was raised by God soon after her death, and taken up to glory, by a singular privilege, before the general resurrection of the dead. The Assumption of the Blessed Virgin Mary is the greatest of all the festivals which the Church celebrates in her honor. It is the consummation of all the other great mysteries by which her life was rendered most wonderful; it is the birthday of her true greatness and glory, and the crowning of all the virtues of her whole life, which we admire single in her other festivals.

Reflection.—Whilst we contemplate, in profound sentiments of veneration, astonishment, and praise, the glory to which Mary is raised by her triumph on this day, we ought, for our own advantage, to consider by what means she arrived at this sublime degree of honor and happiness, that we may walk in her steps. No other way is open to us. The same path which conducted her to glory will also lead us thither; we shall be partners in her reward if we copy her virtues.

August 16.—ST. HYACINTH.

HYACINTH, the glorious apostle of Poland and Russia, was born of noble parents in Poland, about the year 1185. In 1218, being already Canon of Cracow, he accompanied his uncle, the bishop of that place, to Rome. There he met St. Dominic, and received the habit of the Friar Preachers from the patriarch himself, of whom he became a living copy. So wonderful was his progress in virtue that within a year Dominic sent him to preach and plant the Order in Poland, where he founded two houses. His apostolic journeys extended over numerous regions. Austria, Bohemia, Livonia, the shores of the Black Sea, Tartary, and Northern China on the east, and Sweden and Norway to the west, were evangelized by him, and he is said to have visited Scotland. Everywhere multitudes were converted, churches and convents were built; one

hundred and twenty thousand pagans and infidels were
baptized by his hands. He worked numerous miracles,
and at Cracow raised a dead youth to life. He had inherited from St. Dominic a most filial confidence in the
Mother of God; to her he ascribed his success, and to her
aid he looked for his salvation. When St. Hyacinth was
at Kiev the Tartars sacked the town, but it was only as he
finished Mass that the Saint heard of the danger. Without waiting to unvest, he took the ciborium in his hands,
and was leaving the church. As he passed by an image of
Mary a voice said: " Hyacinth, my son, why dost thou
leave me behind? Take me with thee, and leave me not to
mine enemies." The statue was of heavy alabaster, but
when Hyacinth took it in his arms it was light as a reed.
With the Blessed Sacrament and the image he came to the
river Dnieper, and walked dry-shod over the surface of the
waters. On the eve of the Assumption he was warned of
his coming death. In spite of a wasting fever, he celebrated Mass on the feast, and communicated as a dying
man. He was anointed at the foot of the altar, and died
the same day, 1257.

Reflection.—St. Hyacinth teaches us to employ every
effort in the service of God, and to rely for success not on
our own industry, but on the prayer of His Immaculate
Mother.

August 17.—ST. LIBERATUS, Abbot, and Six Monks, Martyrs.

HUNERIC, the Arian Vandal king in Africa, in the
seventh year of his reign, published fresh edicts
against the Catholics, and ordered their monasteries to be
everywhere demolished. Seven monks, named Liberatus,
Boniface, Servus, Rusticus, Rogatus, Septimus, and Maximus, who lived in a monastery near Capsa, in the province
of Byzacena, were at that time summoned to Carthage.
They were first tempted with great promises, but as they
remained constant in the belief of the Trinity, and of one
Baptism, they were loaded with irons and thrown into a
dark dungeon. The faithful, having bribed the guards,

visited the Saints day and night, to be instructed by them and mutually to encourage one another to suffer for the faith of Christ. The king, learning this, commanded them to be more closely confined, loaded with heavier irons, and tortured with a cruelty never heard of till that time. Soon after, he condemned them to be put into an old ship and burnt at sea. The martyrs walked cheerfully to the shore, contemning the insults of the Arians as they passed along. Particular endeavors were used by the persecutors to gain Maximus, who was very young; but God, Who makes the tongues of children eloquent to praise His name, gave him strength to withstand all their efforts, and he boldly told them that they should never be able to separate him from his holy abbot and brethren, with whom he had borne the labors of a penitential life for the sake of everlasting glory. An old vessel was filled with dry sticks, and the seven martyrs were put on board and bound on the wood; and fire was put to it several times, but it went out immediately, and all endeavors to kindle it were in vain. The tyrant, in rage and confusion, gave orders that the martyrs' brains should be dashed out with oars, which was done, and their bodies cast into the sea, which threw them all on the shore. The Catholics interred them honorably in the monastery of Bigua, near the Church of St. Celerinus. They suffered in the year 483.

Reflection.—" Let none of you suffer as a murderer, or a thief, or a railer, or a coveter of other men's things; but if as a Christian, let him not be ashamed, but let him glorify God in that name."

August 18.—ST. HELENA, Empress; ST. AGAPE-TUS, Martyr.

IT was the pious boast of the city of Colchester, England, for many ages, that St. Helena was born within its walls; and though this honor has been disputed, it is certain that she was a British princess. She embraced Christianity late in life; but her incomparable faith and piety greatly influenced her son Constantine, the first Christian emperor, and served to kindle a holy zeal in the hearts of the Roman people. Forgetful of her high dignity, she delighted to assist at the Divine Office amid the poor ; and by her alms-deeds showed herself a mother to the indigent and distressed. In her eightieth year she made a pilgrimage to Jerusalem, with the ardent desire of discovering the cross on which our blessed Redeemer suffered. After many labors, three crosses were found on Mount Calvary, together with the nails and the inscription recorded by the Evangelists. It still remained to identify the true cross of Our Lord. By the advice of the bishop, Macarius, the three were applied successively to a woman afflicted with an incurable disease, and no sooner had the third touched her than she arose, perfectly healed. The pious empress, transported with joy, built a most glorious church on Mount Calvary to receive the precious relic, sending portions of it to Rome and Constantinople, where they were solemnly exposed to the adoration of the faithful. In the year 312 Constantine found himself attacked by Maxentius with vastly superior forces, and the very existence of his empire threatened. In this crisis he bethought him of the crucified Christian God Whom his mother Helena worshipped, and kneeling down, prayed God to reveal Himself and give him the victory. Suddenly, at noonday, a cross of fire was seen by his army in the calm and cloudless sky, and beneath it the words, *In hoc signo vinces* —" Through this sign thou shalt conquer." By divine command, Constantine made a standard like the cross he had seen, which was borne at the head of his troops ; and under this Christian ensign they marched against the enemy, and obtained a complete victory. Shortly after, Helena herself returned to Rome, where she expired, 328.

ST. AGAPETUS suffered in his youth a cruel martyrdom at Præneste, now called Palestrina, twenty-four miles from Rome, under Aurelian, about the year 275. His name is famous in the ancient calendars of the Church of Rome. Two churches in Palestrina and others in other places are dedicated to God under his name.

Reflection.—St. Helena thought it the glory of her life to find the cross of Christ, and to raise a temple in its

honor. How many Christians in these days are ashamed
to make this life-giving sign, and to confess themselves the
followers of the Crucified!

August 19.—ST. LOUIS, Bishop.

THIS Saint was little nephew to St. Louis, King of
France, and nephew, by his mother, to St. Elizabeth
of Hungary. He was born at Brignoles, in Provence, in
1274. He was a Saint from the cradle, and from his childhood made it his earnest study to do nothing which was
not directed to the divine service, and with a view only to
eternity. Even his recreations he referred to this end,
and chose only such as were serious and seemed barely
necessary for the exercise of the body and preserving the
vigor of the mind. His walks usually led him to some
church or religious house. It was his chief delight to hear
the servants of God discourse of mortification or the most
perfect practices of piety. His modesty and recollection
in the church inspired with devotion all who saw him.
When he was only seven years old his mother found him
often lying in the night on a mat which was spread on the
floor near his bed, which he did out of an early spirit of
penance. In 1284 our Saint's father, Charles II., then
Prince of Salerno, was taken prisoner in a sea-fight by the
King of Arragon, and was only released on condition that
he sent into Arragon, as hostages, fifty gentlemen and
three of his sons, one of whom was our Saint. Louis was
set at liberty in 1294, by a treaty concluded between the
King of Naples, his father, and James II., King of Arragon, one condition of which was the marriage of his sister
Blanche with the King of Arragon. Both courts had at
the same time extremely at heart the project of a double
marriage, and that the princess of Majorca, sister to King
James of Arragon, should be married to Louis, but the
Saint's resolution of dedicating himself to God was inflexible, and he resigned his right to the crown of Naples,
which he begged his father to confer on his next brother,
Robert. The opposition of his family obliged the superiors of the Friar Minors to refuse for some time to admit

him into their body, wherefore he took holy orders at
Naples. The pious Pope St. Celestine had nominated him
Archbishop of Lyons in 1294; but, as he had not then
taken the tonsure, he found means to defeat that project.
Boniface VIII. gave him a dispensation to receive priestly
orders in the twenty-third year of his age, and afterward
sent him a like dispensation for the episcopal character,
together with his nomination to the archbishopric of Toulouse, and a severe injunction, in virtue of holy obedience,
to accept the same.   However, he first made his religious
profession among the Friar Minors on Christmas eve, 1296,
and received the episcopal consecration in the beginning of
the February following. He travelled to his bishopric as
a poor religious, but was received at Toulouse with the
veneration due to a Saint and the magnificence that became a prince. His modesty, mildness, and devotion inspired a love of piety in all who beheld him. It was his
first care to provide for the relief of the indigent, and his
first visits were made to the hospitals and the poor.   In
his apostolical labors, he abated nothing of his austerities,
said Mass every day, and preached frequently. Being
obliged to go into Provence for certain very urgent ecclesiastical affairs, he fell sick at the castle of Brignoles.
Finding his end draw near, he received the Viaticum on
his knees, melting in tears, and in his last moments ceased
not to repeat the Hail Mary. He died on the 19th of
August, 1297, being only twenty-three years and six months
old.

August 20.—ST. BERNARD.

BERNARD was born at the castle of Fontaines, in Burgundy. The grace of his person and the vigor of his
intellect filled his parents with the highest hopes, and the
world lay bright and smiling before him when he renounced it forever and joined the monks at Citeaux. All
h:s brothers followed Bernard to Citeaux except Nivard,
the youngest, who was left to be the stay of his father in
his old age. " You will now be heir of everything," said
they to him, as they departed. " Yes," said the boy; " you
leave me earth, and keep heaven for yourselves; do you

call that fair?" And he too left the world. At length
their aged father came to exchange wealth and honor for
the poverty of a monk of Clairvaux. One only sister
remained behind; she was married, and loved the world
and its pleasures. Magnificently dressed, she visited Bernard; he refused to see her, and only at last consented
to do so, not as her brother, but as the minister of Christ.
The words he then spoke moved her so much that, two
years later, she retired to a convent with her husband's
consent, and died in the reputation of sanctity. Bernard's
holy example attracted so many novices that other monasteries were erected, and our Saint was appointed abbot of
that of Clairvaux. Unsparing with himself, he at first
expected too much of his brethren, who were disheartened
at his severity; but soon perceiving his error, he led them
forward, by the sweetness of his correction and the mildness of his rule, to wonderful perfection. In spite of his
desire to lie hid, the fame of his sanctity spread far and
wide, and many churches asked for him as their Bishop.
Through the help of Pope Eugenius III., his former subject, he escaped this dignity; yet his retirement was continually invaded: the poor and the weak sought his protection; bishops, kings, and popes applied to him for
advice; and at length Eugenius himself charged him to
preach the crusade. By his fervor, eloquence, and miracles Bernard kindled the enthusiasm of Christendom, and
two splendid armies were despatched against the infidel.
Their defeat was only due, said the Saint, to their own
sins. Bernard died in 1153. His most precious writings have earned for him the titles of the last of the
Fathers and a Doctor of Holy Church.

Reflection.—St. Bernard used to say to those who applied for admission to the monastery, "If you desire to
enter here, leave at the threshold the body you have brought
with you from the world; here there is room only for your
soul." Let us constantly ask ourselves St. Bernard's daily
question, "To what end didst thou come hither?"

August 21.—ST. JANE FRANCES DE CHANTAL.

A T the age of sixteen, Jane Frances de Frémyot, already a motherless child, was placed under the care of a worldly-minded governess. In this crisis she offered herself to the Mother of God, and secured Mary's protection for life. When a Protestant sought her hand, she steadily refused to marry " an enemy of God and His Church," and shortly afterwards, as the loving and beloved wife of the Baron de Chantal, made her house the pattern of a Christian home. But God had marked her for something higher than domestic sanctity. Two children and a dearly beloved sister died, and, in the full tide of prosperity, her husband's life was taken by the innocent hand of a friend. For seven years the sorrows of her widowhood were increased by ill-usage from servants and inferiors, and the cruel importunities of friends, who urged her to marry again. Harassed almost to despair by their entreaties, she branded on her heart the name of Jesus, and in the end left her beloved home and children to live for God alone. It was on the 19th of March, 1609, that Madame de Chantal bade farewell to her family and relations. Pale, and with tears in her eyes, she passed round the large room, sweetly and humbly taking leave of each. Her son, a boy of fifteen, used every entreaty, every endearment, to induce his mother not to leave them, and at last passionately flung himself across the door of the room. In an agony of distress, she passed on over the body of her son to the embrace of her aged and disconsolate father. The anguish of that parting reached its height when, kneeling at the feet of the venerable old man, she sought and obtained his last blessing, promising to repay in her new home his sacrifice by her prayers. Well might St. Francis call her " the valiant woman." She was to found with St. Francis de Sales a great Order. Sickness, opposition, want, beset her, and the death of children, friends, and of St. Francis himself followed, while eighty-seven houses of the Visitation rose under her hand. Nine long years of interior desolation completed the work of God's grace; and in her seventieth year St. Vincent of Paul saw, at the moment of her death, her soul ascend, as a ball of fire, to heaven.

Reflection.—Profit by the successive trials of life to gain the strength and courage of St. Jane Frances, and they will become stepping-stones from earth to heaven.

August 22.—ST. SYMPHORIAN, Martyr.

ABOUT the year 180 there was a great procession of the heathen goddess Ceres, at Autun, in France. Amongst the crowd was one who refused to pay the ordinary marks of worship. He was therefore dragged before the magistrate and accused of sacrilege and sedition. When asked his name and condition, he replied, " My name is Symphorian; I am a Christian." He came of a noble and Christian family. He was still young, and so innocent that he was said to converse with the holy angels. The Christians of Autun were few and little known, and the judge could not believe that the youth was serious in his purpose. He caused the laws enforcing heathen worship to be read, and looked for a speedy compliance. Symphorian replied that he must obey the laws of the King of kings. " Give me a hammer," he said, " and I will break your idol in pieces." He was scourged and thrown into a dungeon. Some days later this son of light came forth from the darkness of his prison, haggard and worn, but full of joy. He despised the riches and honors offered to him as he had despised torments. He died by the sword, and went to the court of the heavenly King. The mother of St. Symphorian stood on the city walls and saw her son led out to die. She knew the honors he had refused and the dishonor of his death, but she esteemed the reproach of Christ better than all the riches of Egypt, and she cried out to him, " My son, my son, keep the living God in your heart; look up to Him Who reigns in heaven." Thus she shared in the glory of his passion, and her name lives with his in the records of the Church. Little more than a century later the Roman Empire bowed before the faith of Christ. Many miracles spread the glory of St. Symphorian, and of Christ the King of Saints.

Reflection.—The Catholic religion teaches us to be subject to every rightful authority. But no earthly authority has any right against Christ and His Church. If we are accused of sedition or disobedience because we are faithful to our religion, then we must choose as St. Symphorian chose, and obey God rather than man.

August 23.—ST. PHILIP BENIZI.

S T. PHILIP BENIZI was born in Florence, on the Feast of the Assumption, 1233. That same day the Order of Servites was founded by the Mother of God. As an infant at the breast, Philip broke out into speech at the sight of these new religious, and begged his mother to give them alms. Amidst all the temptations of his youth, he longed to become himself a servant of Mary, and it was only the fear of his own unworthiness which made him yield to his father's wish and begin to practise medicine. After long and weary waiting, his doubts were solved by Our Lady herself, who in a vision bade him enter her Order. Still Philip dared only offer himself as a lay brother, and in this humble state he strove to do penance for his sins. In spite of his reluctance, he was promoted to the post of master of novices; and as his rare abilities were daily discovered, he was bidden to prepare for the priesthood. Thenceforth honors were heaped upon him; he became general of the Order, and only escaped by flight elevation to the Papal throne. His preaching restored peace to Italy, which was wasted by civil wars; and at the Council of Lyons, he spoke to the assembled prelates with the gift of tongues. Amid all these favors Philip lived in extreme penitence, constantly examining his soul before the judgment-seat of God, and condemning himself as only fit for hell. St. Philip, though he was free from the stain of mortal sin, was never weary of beseeching God's mercy. From the time he was ten years old he said daily the Penitential Psalms. On his death-bed he kept reciting the verses of the *Miserere,* with his cheeks streaming with tears; and during his agony he went through a terrible contest to overcome the fear of damnation. But a few minutes before he died, all his doubts disappeared and were succeeded by a holy trust. He uttered the responses in a low but audible voice; and when at last the Mother of God appeared before him, he lifted up his arms with joy and breathed a gentle sigh, as if placing his soul in her hand. He died on the Octave of the Assumption, 1285.

Reflection.—Endeavor so to act as you would wish to have acted when you stand before your Judge. This is the rule of the Saints, and the only safe rule for all.

August 24.—ST. BARTHOLOMEW, Apostle.

ST. BARTHOLOMEW was one of the twelve who were called to the apostolate by our blessed Lord Himself. Several learned interpreters of the Holy Scripture take this apostle to have been the same as Nathaniel, a native of Cana, in Galilee, a doctor in the Jewish law, and one of the seventy-two disciples of Christ, to whom he was conducted by St. Philip, and whose innocence and simplicity of heart deserved to be celebrated with the highest eulogium by the divine mouth of Our Redeemer. He is mentioned among the disciples who were met together in prayer after Christ's ascension, and he received the Holy Ghost with the rest. Being eminently qualified by the divine grace to discharge the functions of an apostle, he carried the Gospel through the most barbarous countries of the East, penetrating into the remoter Indies. He then returned again into the northwest part of Asia, and met St. Philip, at Hierapolis, in Phrygia. Hence he travelled into Lycaonia, where he instructed the people in the Christian Faith; but we know not even the names of many of the countries in which he preached. St. Bartholomew's last removal was into Great Armenia, where, preaching in a place obstinately addicted to the worship of idols, he was crowned with a glorious martyrdom. The modern Greek historians say that he was condemned by the governor of Albanopolis to be crucified. Others affirm that he was flayed alive, which might well enough consist with his crucifixion, this double punishment being in use not only in Egypt, but also among the Persians.

Reflection.—The characteristic virtue of the apostles was zeal for the divine glory, the first property of the love of God. A soldier is always ready to defend the honor of his prince, and a son that of his father; and can a Christian say he loves God who is indifferent to His honor?

August 25.—ST. LOUIS, King.

THE mother of Louis told him she would rather see him die than commit a mortal sin, and he never forgot her words. King of France at the age of twelve, he made the defence of God's honor the aim of his life. Before two years, he had crushed the Albigensian heretics, and forced them by stringent penalties to respect the Catholic faith. Amidst the cares of government, he daily recited the Divine Office and heard two Masses, and the most glorious churches in France are still monuments of his piety. When his courtiers remonstrated with Louis for his law that blasphemers should be branded on the lips, he replied, " I would willingly have my own lips branded to root out blasphemy from my kingdom." The fearless protector of the weak and the oppressed, he was chosen to arbitrate in all the great feuds of his age, between the Pope and the Emperor, between Henry III. and the English barons. In 1248, to rescue the land which Christ had trod, he gathered round him the chivalry of France, and embarked for the East. There, before the infidel, in victory or defeat, on the bed of sickness or a captive in chains, Louis showed himself ever the same,— the first, the best, and the bravest of Christian knights. When a captive at Damietta, an Emir rushed into his tent brandishing a dagger red with the blood of the Sultan, and threatened to stab him also unless he would make him a knight, as the Emperor Frederick had Facardin. Louis calmly replied that no unbeliever could perform the duties of a Christian knight. In the same captivity he was offered his liberty on terms lawful in themselves, but enforced by an oath which implied a blasphemy, and though the infidels held their swords' points at his throat, and threatened a massacre of the Christians, Louis inflexibly refused. The death of his mother recalled him to France; but when order was re-established he again set forth on a second crusade. In August, 1270, his army landed at Tunis, and, though victorious over the enemy, succumbed to a malignant fever. Louis was one of the victims. He received the Viaticum kneeling by his camp-bed, and gave up his life with the same joy that he had given all else for the honor of God.

Reflection.—If we cannot imitate St. Louis in dying for the honor of God, we can at least resemble him in resenting the blasphemies offered against God by the infidel, the heretic, and the scoffer.

August 26.—ST. ZEPHYRINUS, Pope and Martyr.

ST. ZEPHYRINUS, a native of Rome, succeeded Victor in the pontificate, in the year 202, in which Severus raised the fifth most bloody persecution against the Church, which continued not for two years only, but until the death of that emperor in 211. Under this furious storm this holy pastor was the support and comfort of the distressed flock of Christ, and he suffered by charity and compassion what every confessor underwent. The triumphs of the martyrs were indeed his joy, but his heart received many deep wounds from the fall of apostates and heretics. Neither did this latter affliction cease when peace was restored to the Church. Our Saint had also the affliction to see the fall of Tertullian, which seems to have been owing partly to his pride. Eusebius tells us that this holy Pope exerted his zeal so strenuously against the blasphemies of the heretics that they treated him in the most contumelious manner; but it was his glory that they called him the principal defender of Christ's divinity. St. Zephyrinus filled the pontifical chair seventeen years, dying in 219. He was buried in his own cemetery, on the 26th of August. He is, in some Martyrologies, styled a martyr, which title he might deserve by what he suffered in the persecution, though he perhaps did not die by the executioner.

Reflection.—God has always raised up holy pastors zealous to maintain the faith of His Church inviolable, and to watch over the purity of its morals and the sanctity of its discipline. We enjoy the greatest advantages of the divine grace through their labors, and we owe to God a tribute of perpetual thanksgiving and immortal praise for all those mercies which He has afforded His Church on earth.

August 27.—ST. JOSEPH CALASANCTIUS.

ST. JOSEPH CALASANCTIUS was born in Arragon, in 1556. When only five years old, he led a troop of children through the streets to find the devil and kill him. He became a priest, and was engaged in various reforms, when he heard a voice saying, "Go to Rome," and had a vision of many children who were being taught by him and by a company of angels. When he reached the Holy City, his heart was moved by the vice and ignorance of the children of the poor. Their need mastered his humility, and he founded the Order of Clerks Regular of the Pious Schools. He himself provided all that was necessary for the education of the children, receiving nothing from them in payment, and there were soon about a thousand scholars of every rank under his care. Each lesson began with prayer. Every half-hour devotion was renewed by acts of faith, hope, and charity, and towards the end of school-time the children were instructed in the Christian doctrine. They were then escorted home by the masters, so as to escape all harm by the way. But enemies arose against Joseph from among his own subjects. They accused him to the Holy Office, and at the age of eighty-six he was led through the streets to prison. At last the Order was reduced to a simple congregation. It was not restored to its former privileges till after the Saint's death. Yet he died full of hope. "My work," he said, "was done solely for the love of God."

Reflection.—" My children," said the Curé of Ars, " I often think that most of the Christians who are lost are lost for want of instruction; they do not know their religion well."

August 28.—ST. AUGUSTINE OF HIPPO.

ST. AUGUSTINE was born in 354, at Tagaste in Africa.
He was brought up in the Christian faith, but without receiving baptism. An ambitious school-boy of brilliant talents and violent passions, he early lost both his
faith and his innocence. He persisted in his irregular life
until he was thirty-two. Being then at Milan professing
rhetoric, he tells us that the faith of his childhood had
regained possession of his intellect, but that he could not
as yet resolve to break the chains of evil habit. One day,
however, stung to the heart by the account of some sudden
conversions, he cried out, " The unlearned rise and storm
heaven, and we, with all our learning, for lack of heart
lie wallowing here." He then withdrew into a garden,
when a long and terrible conflict ensued. Suddenly a
young fresh voice (he knows not whose) breaks in upon his
strife with the words, " Take and read ; " and he lights
upon the passage beginning, " Walk honestly as in the
day." The battle was won. He received baptism, returned home, and gave all to the poor. At Hippo, where
he settled, he was consecrated bishop in 395. For thirty-
five years he was the centre of ecclesiastical life in Africa,
and the Church's mightiest champion against heresy ; whilst
his writings have been everywhere accepted as one of the
principal sources of devotional thought and theological
speculation. He died in 430.

Reflection.—Read the lives of the Saints, and you will
find that you are gradually creating a society about you to
which in some measure you will be forced to raise the
standard of your daily life.

August 29.—THE BEHEADING OF ST. JOHN THE BAPTIST.

ST. JOHN THE BAPTIST was called by God to be the
forerunner of His divine Son. In order to preserve
his innocence spotless, and to improve the extraordinary
graces which he had received, he was directed by the Holy
Ghost to lead an austere and contemplative life in the

wilderness, in the continual exercises of devout prayer and penance, from his infancy till he was thirty years of age. At this age the faithful minister began to discharge his mission. Clothed with the weeds of penance, he announced to all men the obligation they lay under of washing away their iniquities with the tears of sincere compunction; and proclaimed the Messias, Who was then coming to make His appearance among them. He was received by the people as the true herald of the Most High God, and his voice was, as it were, a trumpet sounding from heaven to summon all men to avert the divine judgments, and to prepare themselves to reap the benefit of the mercy that was offered them. The tetrarch Herod Antipas having, in defiance of all laws divine and human, married Herodias, the wife of his brother Philip, who was yet living, St. John the Baptist boldly reprehended the tetrarch and his accomplice for so scandalous an incest and adultery, and Herod, urged on by lust and anger, cast the Saint into prison. About a year after St. John had been made a prisoner, Herod gave a splendid entertainment to the nobility of Galilee. Salome, a daughter of Herodias by her lawful husband, pleased Herod by her dancing, insomuch that he promised her to grant whatever she asked. On this, Salome consulted with her mother what to ask. Herodias instructed her daughter to demand the death of John the Baptist, and persuaded the young damsel to make it part of her petition that the head of the prisoner should be forthwith brought to her in a dish. This strange request startled the tyrant himself; he assented, however, and sent a soldier of his guard to behead the Saint in prison, with an order to bring his head in a charger and present it to Salome, who delivered it to her mother. St. Jerome relates that the furious Herodias made it her inhuman pastime to prick the sacred tongue with a bodkin. Thus died the great forerunner of our blessed Saviour, about two years and three months after his entrance upon his public ministry, about a year before the death of our blessed Redeemer.

Reflection.—All the high graces with which St. John as favored sprang from his humility; in this all his other virtues were founded.   If we desire to form ourselves upon so great a model, we must, above all things, labor to lay the same deep foundation.

August 30.—ST. ROSE OF LIMA.

THIS lovely flower of sanctity, the first canonized Saint of the New World, was born at Lima in 1586.   She was christened Isabel, but the beauty of her infant face earned for her the title of Rose, which she ever after bore. As a child, while still in the cradle, her silence under a painful surgical operation proved the thirst for suffering already consuming her heart.   At an early age she took service to support her impoverished parents, and worked for them day and night.   In spite of hardships and austerities her beauty ripened with increasing age, and she was much and openly admired.   From fear of vanity she cut off her hair, blistered her face with pepper and her hands with lime.   For further security she enrolled herself in the Third Order of St. Dominic, took St. Catherine of Siena as her model, and redoubled her penance.   Her cell was a garden hut, her couch a box of broken tiles. Under her habit Rose wore a hair-shirt studded with iron nails, while, concealed by her veil, a silver crown armed with ninety points encircled her head.   More than once, when she shuddered at the prospect of a night of torture, a voice said, " My cross was yet more painful."   The Blessed Sacrament seemed almost her only food.   Her love for it was intense.   When the Dutch fleet prepared to attack the town, Rose took her place before the tabernacle, and wept that she was not worthy to die in its defence. All her sufferings were offered for the conversion of sinners, and the thought of the multitudes in hell was ever before her soul.   She died in 1617, at the age of thirty-one.

Reflection.—Rose, pure as driven snow, was filled with deepest contrition and humility, and did constant and terrible penance.   Our sins are continual, our repentance passing, our contrition slight, our penance nothing.   How will it fare with us?

ST. FIAKER, Anchorite.

ST. FIAKER was nobly born in Ireland, and had his education under the care of a bishop of eminent sanctity who was, according to some, Conan, Bishop of Soder or the Western Islands. Looking upon all worldly advantages as dross, he left his country and friends in the flower of his age, and with certain pious companions sailed over to France, in quest of some solitude in which he might devote himself to God, unknown to the rest of the world. Divine Providence conducted him to St. Faro, who was the Bishop of Meaux, and eminent for sanctity. When St. Fiaker addressed himself to him, the prelate, charmed with the marks of extraordinary virtue and abilities which he discovered in this stranger, gave him a solitary dwelling in a forest called Breuil which was his own patrimony, two leagues from Meaux. In this place the holy anchorite cleared the ground of trees and briers, made himself a cell, with a small garden, and built an oratory in honor of the Blessed Virgin, in which he spent a great part of the days and nights in devout prayer. He tilled his garden and labored with his own hands for his subsistence. The life he led was most austere, and only necessity or charity ever interrupted his exercises of prayer and heavenly contemplation. Many resorted to him for advice, and the poor for relief. But, following an inviolable rule among the Irish monks, he never suffered any woman to enter the enclosure of his hermitage. St. Chillen, or Kilian, an Irishman of high birth, on his return from Rome, visited St. Fiaker, who was his kinsman, and having passed some time under his discipline, was directed by his advice, with the authority of the bishops, to preach in that and the neighboring dioceses. This commission he executed with admirable sanctity and fruit. St. Fiaker died about the year 670, on the 30th of August.

Reflection.—Ye who love indolence, ponder well these words of St. Paul: "If any man will not work, neither let him eat."

August 31.—ST. RAYMUND NONNATUS.

ST. RAYMUND NONNATUS was born in Catalonia, in the year 1204, and was descended of a gentleman's family of a small fortune. In his childhood he seemed to find pleasure only in his devotions and serious duties. His father, perceiving in him an inclination to a religious state, took him from school, and sent him to take care of a farm which he had in the country. Raymund readily obeyed, and, in order to enjoy the opportunity of holy solitude, kept the sheep himself, and spent his time in the mountains and forests in holy meditation and prayer. Some time after, he joined the new Order of Our Lady of Mercy for the redemption of captives, and was admitted to his profession at Barcelona by the holy founder, St. Peter Nolasco. Within two or three years after his profession, he was sent into Barbary with a considerable sum of money, where he purchased, at Algiers, the liberty of a great number of slaves. When all this treasure was exhausted, he gave himself up as a hostage for the ransom of certain others. This magnanimous sacrifice served only to exasperate the Mohammedans, who treated him with uncommon barbarity, till, fearing lest if he died in their hands they should lose the ransom which was to be paid for the slaves for whom he remained a hostage, they gave orders that he should be treated with more humanity. Hereupon he was permitted to go abroad about the streets, which liberty he made use of to comfort and encourage the Christians in their chains, and he converted and baptized some Mohammedans. For this the governor condemned him to be put to death by thrusting a stake into the body, but his punishment was commuted, and he underwent a cruel bastinado. This torment did not daunt his courage. So long as he saw souls in danger of perishing eternally, he thought he had yet done nothing. St. Raymund had no more money to employ in releasing poor captives, and to speak to a Mohammedan upon the subject of religion was death. He could, however, still exert his endeavors, with hopes of some success, or of dying a martyr of charity. He therefore resumed his former method of instructing and exhorting both the Christians and the infidels. The governor, who was enraged, ordered our Saint to be barbarously tortured and imprisoned till his ransom was brought by some religious men of his Order, who were sent with it by St. Peter. Upon his return to Spain, he was nominated cardinal by Pope Gregory IX., and the Pope, being desirous to have so holy a man about his person, called him to Rome. The Saint obeyed, but went no further than Cardona, when he was seized with a violent fever, which proved mortal. He died on the 31st of August, in the year 1240, the thirty-seventh of his age.

Reflection.—This Saint gave not only his substance but his liberty, and even exposed himself to the most cruel torments and death, for the redemption of captives and the salvation of souls. But alas! do not we, merely to gratify our prodigality, vanity, or avarice, refuse to give the superfluous part of our possessions to the poor, who for want of it are perishing with cold and hunger? Let us remember that " He that giveth to the poor shall not want."

September 1.—ST. GILES, Abbot.

S T. GILES, whose name has been held in great veneration for several ages in France and England, is said to have been an Athenian by birth, and of noble extraction. His extraordinary piety and learning drew the admiration of the world upon him in such a manner that it was impossible for him to enjoy in his own country that obscurity and retirement which was the chief object of his desires on earth. He therefore sailed to France, and chose a hermitage first in the open deserts near the mouth of the Rhone, afterward near the river Gard, and lastly in a forest in the diocese of Nismes. He passed many years in this close solitude, living on wild herbs or roots and water, and conversing only with God. We read in his life that he was for some time nourished with the milk of a hind in the forest, which, being pursued by hunters, fled for refuge to the Saint, who was thus discovered. The reputation of the sanctity of this holy hermit was much increased by many miracles which he wrought, and which rendered his name famous throughout all France. St. Giles was highly esteemed by the French king, but could not be prevailed upon to forsake his solitude. He, however, admitted several disciples, and settled excellent discipline in the monastery of which he was the founder, and which, in succeeding ages, became a flourishing abbey of the Benedictine Order.

Reflection.—He who accompanies the exercises of contemplation and arduous penance with zealous and undaunted endeavors to conduct others to the same glorious term with himself, shall be truly great in the kingdom of heaven.

September 2.—ST. STEPHEN, King.

GEYSA, fourth Duke of Hungary, was, with his wife, converted to the Faith, and saw in a vision the martyr St. Stephen, who told him that he should have a son who would perfect the work he had begun. This son was born in 977, and received the name of Stephen. He was most carefully educated, and succeeded his father at an early age. He began to root out idolatry, suppressed a rebellion of his pagan subjects, and founded monasteries and churches all over the land. He sent to Pope Sylvester, begging him to appoint bishops to the eleven sees he had endowed, and to bestow on him, for the greater success of his work, the title of king. The Pope granted his requests, and sent him a cross to be borne before him, saying that he regarded him as the true apostle of his people. His devotion was fervent. He placed his realms under the protection of our blessed Lady, and kept the feast of her Assumption with peculiar affection. He gave good laws, and saw to their execution. Throughout his life, we are told, he had Christ on his lips, Christ in his heart, and Christ in all he did. His only wars were wars of defence, and he was always successful. God sent him many and sore trials. One by one his children died, but he bore all with perfect submission to the will of God. When St. Stephen was about to die, he summoned the bishops and nobles, and gave them charge concerning the choice of a successor. Then he urged them to nurture and cherish the

Catholic Church, which was still as a tender plant in Hungary, to follow justice, humility, and charity, to be obedient to the laws, and to show ever a reverent submission to the Holy See. Then, raising his eyes towards heaven, he said, " O Queen of Heaven, august restorer of a prostrate world, to thy care I commend the Holy Church, my people, and my realm, and my own departing soul." And then, on his favorite feast of the Assumption, in 1038, he died in peace.

Reflection.—" Our duty," says Father Newman, " is to follow the Vicar of Christ whither he goeth, and never to desert him, however we may be tried; but to defend him at all hazards and against all comers, as a son would a father, and as a wife a husband, knowing that his cause is the cause of God."

September 3.—ST. SERAPHIA, Virgin and Martyr.

ST. SERAPHIA was born at Antioch, of Christian parents, who, flying from the persecutions of Adrian, went to Italy and settled there. Her parents dying, Seraphia was sought in marriage by many, but having resolved to consecrate herself to God alone, she sold all her possessions and distributed the proceeds to the poor; finally she sold herself into a voluntary slavery, and entered the services of a Roman lady named Sabina. The piety of Seraphia, her love of work, and her charity soon gained the heart of her mistress, who was not long in becoming a Christian. Having been denounced as a follower of Christ, Seraphia was condemned to death. She was at first placed on a burning pile, but remained uninjured by the flames. Almost despairing of being able to inflict death upon her, the prefect Berillus ordered her to be beheaded, and she thus received the crown which she so richly merited. Her mistress gathered her remains, and interred them with every mark of respect. Sabina, meeting with a martyr's death, a year after, was laid in the same tomb with her faithful servant. As early as the fifth century there was a church at Rome placed under their invocation.

Reflection.—Christian courage bears relation to our faith. "If we continue in the faith, grounded, and settled, and immovable," all things will be found possible to us.

September 4.—ST. ROSALIA, Virgin.

ST. ROSALIA was daughter of a noble family descended from Charlemagne. She was born at Palermo in Sicily, and despising in her youth worldly vanities, made herself an abode in a cave on Mount Pelegrino, three miles from Palermo, where she completed the sacrifice of her heart to God by austere penance and manual labor, sanctified by assiduous prayer and the constant union of her soul with God. She died in 1160. Her body was found buried in a grot under the mountain, in the year of the jubilee, 1625, under Pope Urban VIII., and was translated into the metropolitan church of Palermo, of which she was chosen a patroness. To her patronage that island ascribes the ceasing of a grievous pestilence at the same time.

ST. ROSE OF VITERBO, who is honored on this same day, was born in the spring of 1240, a time when Frederick II. was oppressing the Church and many were faithless to the Holy See. The infant at once seemed filled with grace; with tottering steps she sought Jesus in His tabernacle, she knelt before sacred images, she listened to pious talk, retaining all she heard, and this when she was scarcely three years old. One coarse habit covered her flesh; fasts and disciplines were her delight. To defend the Church's rights was her burning wish, and for this she received her mission from the Mother of God, who gave her the Franciscan habit, with the command to go forth and preach. When hardly ten years old, Rose went down to the public square at Viterbo, called upon the inhabitants to be faithful to the Sovereign Pontiff, and vehemently denounced all his opponents. So great was the power of her word, and of the miracles which accompanied it, that the Imperial party, in fear and anger, drove her from the city, but she continued to preach till Innocent IV. was brought back in triumph to Rome and the cause of God was won. Then she retired to a little cell at Viterbo, and prepared in solitude for her end. She died in her eighteenth year. Not long after, she appeared in glory to Alexander IV., and bade him translate her body. He found it as the vision had said, but fragrant and beautiful, as if still in life.

Reflection.—Rose lived but seventeen years, saved the Church's cause, and died a Saint. We have lived, perhaps, much longer, and yet with what result? Every minute something can be done for God. Let us be up and doing.

September 5.—ST. LAURENCE JUSTINIAN.

LAURENCE from a child longed to be a Saint; and when he was nineteen years of age there was granted to him a vision of the Eternal Wisdom. All earthly things paled in his eyes before the ineffable beauty of this sight, and as it faded away a void was left in his heart which none but God could fill. Refusing the offer of a brilliant marriage, he fled secretly from his home at Venice, and joined the Canons Regular of St. George. One by one he crushed every natural instinct which could bar his union with his Love. When Laurence first entered religion, a nobleman went to dissuade him from the folly of thus sacrificing every earthly prospect. The young monk listened patiently in turn to his friend's affectionate appeal, scorn, and violent abuse. Calmly and kindly he then replied. He pointed out the shortness of life, the uncertainty of earthly happiness, and the incomparable superiority of the prize he sought to any his friend had named. The nobleman could make no answer; he felt in truth that Laurence was wise, himself the fool. He left the world, became a fellow-novice with the Saint, and his holy death bore every mark that he too had secured the treasures which never fail. As superior and as general, Laurence enlarged and strengthened his Order, and as bishop of his diocese, in spite of slander and insult, thoroughly reformed his see. His zeal led to his being appointed the first patriarch of Venice, but he remained ever in heart and soul an humble priest, thirsting for the sight of heaven. At length the eternal vision began to dawn. " Are you laying a bed of feathers for me? " he said. " Not so; my Lord was stretched on a hard and painful tree." Laid upon the straw, he exclaimed in rapture, " Good Jesus, behold I come." He died in 1435, aged seventy-four.

Reflection.—Ask St. Laurence to vouchsafe you such a sense of the sufficiency of God that you too may fly to Him and be at rest.

September 6.—ST. ELEUTHERIUS, Abbot.

A WONDERFUL simplicity and spirit of compunction were the distinguishing virtues of this holy man. He was chosen abbot of St. Mark's near Spoleto, and favored by God with the gift of miracles. A child who was possessed by the devil, being delivered by being educated in his monastery, the abbot said one day: " Since the child is among the servants of God, the devil dares not approach him." These words seemed to savor of vanity, and thereupon the devil again entered and tormented the child. The abbot humbly confessed his fault, and fasted and prayed with his whole community till the child was again freed from the tyranny of the fiend. St. Gregory the Great not being able to fast on Easter-eve on account of extreme weakness, engaged this Saint to go with him to the church of St. Andrew's and put up his prayers to God for his health, that he might join the faithful in that solemn practice of penance. Eleutherius prayed with many tears, and the Pope, coming out of the church, found his breast suddenly strengthened, so that he was enabled to perform the fast as he desired. St. Eleutherius raised a dead man to life. Resigning his abbacy, he died in St. Andrew's monastery in Rome, about the year 585.

Reflection.—" Appear not to men to fast, but to thy Father Who is in heaven, and thy Father, Who seeth in secret, He will repay thee."

September 7.—ST. CLOUD, Confessor.

ST. CLOUD is the first and most illustrious Saint among the princes of the royal family of the first race in France. He was son of Chlodomir, King of Orleans, the eldest son of St. Clotilda, and was born in 522. He was scarce three years old when his father was killed in Burgundy; but his grandmother Clotilda brought up him and his two brothers at Paris, and loved them extremely. Their ambitious uncles divided the kingdom of Orleans between them, and stabbed with their own hands two of their nephews. Cloud, by a special providence, was saved from the massacre, and, renouncing the world, devoted himself to the service of God in a monastic state. After a time he put himself under the discipline of St. Severinus, a holy recluse who lived near Paris, from whose hands he received the monastic habit. Wishing to live unknown to the world, he withdrew secretly into Provence, but his hermitage being made public, he returned to Paris, and was received with the greatest joy imaginable. At the earnest request of the people, he was ordained priest by Eusebius, Bishop of Paris, in 551, and served that Church some time in the functions of the sacred ministry. He afterward retired to St. Cloud, two leagues below Paris, where he built a monastery. Here he assembled many pious men, who fled out of the world for fear of losing their souls in it. St. Cloud was regarded by them as their superior, and he animated them to all virtue both by word and example. He was indefatigable in instructing and exhorting the people of the neighboring country, and piously ended his days about the year 560.

Reflection.—Let us remember that " the just shall live for evermore; they shall receive a kingdom of glory, and a crown of beauty at the hand of the Lord."

September 8.—THE NATIVITY OF THE BLESSED VIRGIN.

THE birth of the Blessed Virgin Mary announced joy and the near approach of salvation to the lost world. Mary was brought forth in the world not like other children of Adam, infected with the loathsome contagion of sin, but pure, holy, beautiful, and glorious, adorned with all the most precious graces which became her who was chosen to be the Mother of God. She appeared indeed in the weak state of our mortality; but in the eyes of Heaven she already transcended the highest seraph in purity, brightness, and the richest ornaments of grace. If we celebrate the birthdays of the great ones of this earth, how ought we to rejoice in that of the Virgin Mary, presenting to God the best homage of our praises and thanksgiving for the great mercies He has shown in her, and imploring her mediation with her Son in our behalf! Christ will not reject the supplications of His mother, whom He was pleased to obey whilst on earth. Her love, care, and tenderness for Him, the title and qualities which she bears, the charity and graces with which she is adorned, and the crown of glory with which she is honored, must incline Him readily to receive her recommendations and petitions.

THE FESTIVAL, ON THE SUNDAY WITHIN THE OCTAVE OF HER NATIVITY, OF THE HOLY NAME OF MARY.

THIS festival was appointed by Pope Innocent XI., that on it the faithful may be called upon in a particular manner to recommend to God, through the intercession of the Blessed Virgin, the necessities of His Church, and to return Him thanks for His gracious protection and numberless mercies. What gave occasion to the institution of this feast was a solemn thanksgiving for the relief of Vienna when it was besieged by the Turks in 1683. If we desire to deprecate the divine anger, justly provoked by our sins, with our prayers, we must join the tears of sincere compunction with a perfect conversion of our manners. The first grace we should always beg of God is that He will bring us to the disposition of condign penance. Our supplications for the divine mercies, and our thanksgivings for benefits received, will only thus be rendered acceptable. By no other means can we deserve the blessing of God, or be recommended to it by the patronage of His holy mother. To the invocation of Jesus it is a pious and wholesome practice to join our application to the Blessed Virgin, that, through her intercession, we may more easily and more abundantly obtain the effects of our petitions. In this sense devout souls pronounce, with great affection and confidence, the holy names of Jesus and Mary.

September 9.—ST. OMER, Bishop.

ST. OMER was born toward the close of the sixth century, in the territory of Constance. His parents, who were noble and wealthy, gave great attention to his education, but, above all, strove to inspire him with a love for virtue. Upon the death of his mother he entered the monastery of Luxen, whither he persuaded his father to follow him, after having sold his worldly goods and distributed the proceeds among the poor. The father and son made their religious profession together. The humility, obedience, mildness, and devotion, together with the admirable purity of manners, which shone forth in every action of St. Omer, distinguished him among his saintly brethren, and he was soon called from his solitude to take charge of the government of the Church in Terouenne. The greater part of those living in his diocese were still pagans, and even the few Christians were, through a scarcity of priests, fallen into a sad corruption of manners. The great and difficult work of their conversion was reserved for St. Omer. The holy bishop applied himself to his task with such zeal that in a short time his diocese became one of the most flourishing in France. In his old age St. Omer became blind, but that affliction did not lessen his pastoral concern for his flock. He died in the odor of sanctity, while on a pastoral visit to Wavre, in 670.

BLESSED PETER CLAVER.

PETER CLAVER was a Spanish Jesuit. In Majorca he fell in with the holy lay-brother Alphonsus Rodriguez, who, having already learned by revelation the saintly career of Peter, became his spiritual guide, foretold to him the labors he would undergo in the Indies, and the throne he would gain in heaven. Ordained priest in New Granada, Peter was sent to Cartagena, the great slave-mart of the West Indies, and there he consecrated himself by vow to the salvation of those ignorant and miserable creatures. For more than forty years he labored in this work. He called himself " the slave of the slaves." He was their apostle, father, physician, and friend. He fed them, nursed them with the utmost tenderness in their loathsome diseases, often applying his own lips to their hideous sores. His cloak, which was the constant covering of the naked, though soiled with their filthy ulcers, sent forth a miraculous perfume. His rest after his great labors was in nights of penance and prayer. However tired he might be, when news arrived of a fresh slave-ship, Blessed Peter immediately revived, his eyes brightened, and he was at once on board amongst his dear slaves, bringing them comfort for body and soul. A false charge of reiterating Baptism for a while stopped his work. He submitted without a murmur till the calumny was refuted, and then God so blessed his toil that 40,000 negroes were baptized before he went to his reward, in 1654.

Reflection.—When you see any one standing in need of your assistance, either for body or soul, do not ask yourself why some one else did not help him, but think to yourself that you have found a treasure.

September 10.—ST. NICHOLAS OF TOLEN- TINO.

BORN in answer to the prayer of a holy mother, and vowed before his birth to the service of God, Nicholas never lost his baptismal innocence. His austerities were conspicuous even in the austere Order — the Hermits of

St. Augustine — to which he belonged, and to the remonstrances which were made by his superiors he only replied, " How can I be said to fast, while every morning at the altar I receive my God? " He conceived an ardent charity for the Holy Souls, so near and yet so far from their Saviour; and often after his Mass it was revealed to him that the souls for whom he had offered the Holy Sacrifice had been admitted to the presence of God. Amidst his loving labors for God and man, he was haunted by fear of his own sinfulness. " The heavens," said he, " are not pure in the sight of Him Whom I serve; how then shall I, a sinful man, stand before Him? " As he pondered on these things, Mary, the Queen of all Saints, appeared before him. " Fear not, Nicholas," she said, " all is well with you: my Son bears you in His Heart, and I am your protection." Then his soul was at rest; and he heard, we are told, the songs which the angels sing in the presence of their Lord. He died September 10, 1310.

Reflection.—Would you die the death of the just? there is only one way to secure the fulfilment of your wish. Live the life of the just. For it is impossible that one who has been faithful to God in life should make a bad or an unhappy end.

September 11.—ST. PAPHNUTIUS, Bishop.

THE holy confessor Paphnutius was an Egyptian, and after having spent several years in the desert, under the direction of the great St. Antony, was made bishop in Upper Thebais. He was one of those confessors who, under the tyrant Maximin Daia, lost their right eye, and were afterward sent to work in the mines. Peace being restored to the Church, Paphnutius returned to his flock. The Arian heresy being broached in Egypt, he was one of the most zealous in defending the Catholic faith, and for his eminent sanctity and the glorious title of confessor (or one who had confessed the Faith before the persecutors and under torments) was highly considered in the great Council of Nice. Constantine the Great, during the celebration of that synod, sometimes conferred privately with him in his

palace, and never dismissed him without kissing respectfully the place which had once held the eye he had lost for
the Faith. St. Paphnutius remained always in a close
union with St. Athanasius, and accompanied him to the
Council of Tyre, in 335, where they found much the greater
part of that assembly to be professed Arians. Seeing
Maximus, Bishop of Jerusalem, among them, Paphnutius
took him by the hand, led him out, and told him he could
not see that any who bore the same marks as he in defence
of the Faith should be seduced and imposed upon by persons who were resolved to oppress the most strenuous as-
sertor of its fundamental article. We have no particular
account of the death of St. Paphnutius, but his name stands
in the Roman Martyrology on the 11th of September.

Reflection.—If to fight for our country be glorious, " it
is likewise great glory to follow the Lord," saith the Wise
Man.

September 12.—ST. GUY OF ANDERLECHT.

As a child Guy had two loves, the Church and the poor.
The love of prayer growing more and more, he left
his poor home at Brussels to seek greater poverty and closer
union with God. He arrived at Laeken, near Brussels, and
there showed such devotion before Our Lady's shrine that
the priest besought him to stay and serve the Church.
Thenceforth his great joy was to be always in the church,
sweeping the floor and ceiling, polishing the altars, and
cleansing the sacred vessels. By day he still found time
and means to befriend the poor, so that his almsgiving became famous in all those parts. A merchant of Brussels,
hearing of the generosity of this poor sacristan, came to
Laeken, and offered him a share in his business. Guy
could not bear to leave the church; but the offer seemed
providential, and he at last closed with it. Their ship,
however, was lost on the first voyage, and on returning to
Laeken Guy found his place filled. The rest of his life
was one long penance for his inconstancy. About the
year 1033, finding his end at hand, he returned to Ander-

lecht, in his own country. As he died, a light shone round him, and a voice was heard proclaiming his eternal reward.

Reflection.—Jesus was only nine months in the womb of Mary, three hours on the cross, three days in the sepulchre, but He is always in the tabernacle. Does our reverence before Him bear witness to this most blessed truth?

September 13.—ST. EULOGIUS, Patriarch of Alexandria.

ST. EULOGIUS was a Syrian by birth, and while young embraced the monastic state in that country. The Eutychian heresy had thrown the Churches of Syria and Egypt into much confusion, and a great part of the monks of Syria were at that time become remarkable for their loose morals and errors against faith. Eulogius learned from the fall of others to stand more watchfully and firmly upon his guard, and was not less distinguished by the innocence and sanctity of his manners than by the purity of his doctrine. Having, by an enlarged pursuit of learning, attained to a great variety of useful knowledge in the different branches of literature, he set himself to the study of divinity in the sacred sources of that science, which are the Holy Scriptures, the tradition of the Church as explained in its councils, and the approved writings of its eminent pastors. In the great dangers and necessities of the Church he was drawn out of his solitude, and made priest of Antioch by the patriarch St. Anastasius. Upon the death of John, the Patriarch of Alexandria, St. Eulogius was raised to that patriarchal dignity toward the close of the year 583. About two years after his promotion our Saint was obliged to make a journey to Constantinople, in order to concert measures concerning certain affairs of his Church. He met at court St. Gregory the Great, and contracted with him a holy friendship, so that from that time they seemed to be one heart and one soul. Among the letters of St. Gregory we have several extant which he wrote to our Saint. St. Eulogius composed many excellent works against different heresies, and died in the year 606.

Reflection.—We admire the great actions and the glorious triumph of the Saints; yet it is not so much in these that their sanctity consisted, as in the constant, habitual heroic disposition of their souls. There is no one who does not sometimes do good actions; but he can never be called virtuous who does well only by humor, or by fits and starts, not by steady habits.

September 14.—THE EXALTATION OF THE HOLY CROSS OF OUR LORD JESUS CHRIST.

CONSTANTINE was still wavering between Christianity and idolatry when a luminous cross appeared to him in the heavens, bearing the inscription, " In this sign shalt thou conquer." He became a Christian, and triumphed over his enemies, who were at the same time the enemies of the Faith. A few years later, his saintly mother having found the cross on which Our Saviour suffered, the feast of the " Exaltation " was established in the Church; but it was only at a later period still, namely, after the Emperor Heraclius had achieved three great and wondrous victories over Chosroes, King of Persia, who had possessed himself of the holy and precious relic, that this festival took a more general extension, and was invested with a higher character of solemnity. The feast of the " Finding " was thereupon instituted, in memory of the discovery made by St. Helena; and that of the " Exaltation " was reserved to celebrate the triumphs of Heraclius. The greatest power of the Catholic world was at that time centred in the Empire of the East, and was verging toward its ruin, when God put forth His hand to save it: the re-establishment of the great cross at Jerusalem was the sure pledge thereof. This great event occurred in 629.

Reflection.—Herein is found the accomplishment of the Saviour's word: " If I be lifted up from the earth, I will draw all things to Myself."

September 15.—ST. CATHERINE OF GENOA.

NOBLE in birth, rich, and exceedingly beautiful, Catherine had as a child rejected the solicitations of the world, and begged her divine Master for some share in His sufferings. At sixteen years of age she found herself promised in marriage to a young nobleman of dissolute habits, who treated her with such harshness that, after five years, wearied out by his cruelty, she somewhat relaxed the strictness of her life and entered into the worldly society of Genoa. At length, enlightened by divine grace as to the danger of her state, she resolutely broke with the world and gave herself up to a life of rigorous penance and prayer. The charity with which she devoted herself to the service of the hospitals, undertaking the vilest of offices with joy, induced her husband to amend his evil ways and he died penitent. Her heroic fortitude was sustained by the constant thought of the Holy Souls, whose sufferings were revealed to her, and whose state she has described in a treatise full of heavenly wisdom. A long and grievous malady during the last years of her life only served to perfect her union with God, till, worn out in body and purified in soul, she breathed her last on September 14, 1510.

Reflection.—The constant thought of purgatory will help us not only to escape its dreadful pains, but also to avoid the least imperfection which hinders our approach to God.

September 16.—ST. CYPRIAN, Bishop, Martyr.

CYPRIAN was an African of noble birth, but of evil life, a pagan, and a teacher of rhetoric. In middle life he was converted to Christianity, and shortly after his baptism was ordained priest, and made Bishop of Carthage, notwithstanding his resistance. When the persecution of Decius broke out, he fled from his episcopal city, that he might be the better able to minister to the wants of his flock, but returned on occasion of a pestilence. Later on he was banished, and saw in a vision his future martyrdom. Being recalled from exile, sentence of death was pronounced against him, which he received with the words " Thanks be to God." His great desire was to die whilst in the act of preaching the faith of Christ, and he had the consolation of being surrounded at his martyrdom by crowds of his faithful children. He was beheaded on the 14th of September, 258, and was buried with great solemnity. Even the pagans respected his memory.

Reflection.—The duty of almsgiving is declared both by nature and revelation: by nature, because it flows from the principle imprinted within us of doing to others as we would they should do to us; by revelation, in many special commands of Scripture, and in the precept of divine charity which binds us to love God for His own sake, and our neighbor for the sake of God.

September 17.—ST. LAMBERT, Bishop, Martyr.

ST. LAMBERT was a native of Maestricht. His father intrusted his education to the holy Bishop St. Theodard, and on that good man being assassinated, Lambert was chosen his successor. A revolution breaking out which overturned the kingdom of Austrasia, our Saint was banished from his see on account of his devotion to his sovereign. He retired to the monastery of Stavelo, and there obeyed the rule as strictly as the youngest novice could have done. One instance will suffice to show with how perfect a sacrifice of himself he devoted his heart to serve God. As he was rising one night in winter to his private devotions, he happened to let fall his wooden sandal or slipper. The abbot, without asking who had caused the noise, gave orders that the offender should go and pray before the cross, which stood before the church door. Lambert, without making any answer, went out as he was, barefoot, and covered only with his hair shirt; and in this condition he prayed, kneeling before the cross, where he was found some hours after. At the sight of the holy bishop the abbot and the monks fell on the ground and asked his pardon. " God forgive you," said he, " for thinking you stand in need of pardon for this action. As for myself, is it not in cold and nakedness that, according to St. Paul, I am to tame my flesh and to serve God?" While St. Lambert enjoyed the quiet of holy retirement, he wept to see the greatest part of the churches of France laid waste. In the mean time the political clouds began to break away, and Lambert was restored to his see, but his zeal in suppressing the many and notorious disorders which existed in his diocese led to his assassination on the 17th of September, 709.

Reflection.—How noble and heroic is this virtue of fortitude! how necessary for every Christian, especially for a pastor of souls, that neither worldly views nor fears may ever in the least warp his integrity or blind his judgment!

September 18.—ST. THOMAS OF VILLANOVA.

ST. THOMAS, the glory of the Spanish Church in the sixteenth century, was born in 1488. A thirst for the science of the Saints led him to enter the house of the Austin Friars at Salamanca. Charles V. listened to him as an oracle, and appointed him Archbishop of Valencia. On being led to his throne in church, he pushed the silken cushions aside, and with tears kissed the ground. His first visit was to the prison; the sum with which the chapter presented him for his palace was devoted to the public hospital. As a child he had given his meal to the poor, and two thirds of his episcopal revenues were now annually spent in alms. He daily fed five hundred needy persons, brought up himself the orphans of the city, and sheltered the neglected foundlings with a mother's care. During his eleven years' episcopate not one poor maiden was married without an alms from the Saint. Spurred by his example, the rich and the selfish became liberal and generous; and when, on the Nativity of Our Lady, 1555, St. Thomas came to die, he was well-nigh the only poor man in his see.

Reflection.—"Answer me, O sinner!" St. Thomas would say, "what can you purchase with your money better or more necessary than the redemption of your sins?"

September 19.—ST. JANUARIUS, Martyr.

MANY centuries ago, St. Januarius died for the Faith in the persecution of Diocletian, and to this day God confirms the faith of His Church, and works a continual miracle, through the blood which Januarius shed for Him. The Saint was Bishop of Beneventum, and on one occasion he travelled to Misenum in order to visit a deacon named Sosius. During this visit Januarius saw the head of Sosius, who was singing the gospel in the church, girt with flames, and took this for a sign that ere long Sosius would wear the crown of martyrdom. So it proved. Shortly after Sosius was arrested, and thrown into prison. There St. Januarius visited and encouraged him, till the bishop also was arrested in turn. Soon the number of the confessors was swollen by some of the neighboring clergy. They were exposed to the wild beasts in the amphitheatre. The beasts, however, did them no harm; and at last the Governor of Campania ordered the Saints to be beheaded. Little did the heathen governor think that he was the instrument in God's hand of ushering in the long succession of miracles which attest the faith of Januarius. The relics of St. Januarius rest in the cathedral of Naples, and it is there that the liquefaction of his blood occurs. The blood is congealed in two glass vials, but when it is brought near the martyr's head it melts and flows like the blood of a living man.

Reflection.—Thank God Who has given you superabundant motives for your faith; and pray for the spirit of the first Christians, the spirit which exults and rejoices in belief.

September 20.—STS. EUSTACHIUS and Companions, Martyrs.

EUSTACHIUS, called Placidus before his conversion, was a distinguished officer of the Roman army under the Emperor Trajan. One day, whilst hunting a deer, he suddenly perceived between the horns of the animal the image of our crucified Saviour. Responsive to what he considered a voice from heaven, he lost not a moment in becoming a Christian. In a short time he lost all his possessions and his position, and his wife and children were taken from him. Reduced to the most abject poverty, he took service with a rich land-owner to tend his fields. In the mean time the empire suffered greatly from the ravages of barbarians. Trajan sought out our Saint, and placed him in command of the troops sent against the enemy. During this campaign he found his wife and children, whom he despaired of ever seeing again. Returning home victorious, he was received in triumph and loaded with honors; but the emperor having commanded him to sacrifice to the false gods, he refused. Infuriated at this, Trajan ordered Eustachius with his wife and children to be exposed to two starved lions; but instead of harming these faithful servants of God, the beasts merely frisked and frolicked about them. The emperor, grown more furious at this, caused the martyrs to be shut up inside a brazen bull, under which a fire was kindled, and in this horrible manner they were roasted to death.

Reflection.—It is not enough to encounter dangers with resolution; we must with equal courage and constancy vanquish pleasure and the softer passions, or we possess not the virtue of true fortitude.

September 21.—ST. MATTHEW, Apostle.

ONE day, as Our Lord was walking by the Sea of Galilee, He saw, sitting at the receipt of custom, Matthew the publican, whose business it was to collect the taxes from the people for their Roman masters. Jesus said to him, " Follow Me; " and leaving all, Matthew arose and followed Him. Now the publicans were abhorred by the Jews as enemies of their country, outcasts, and notorious sinners, who enriched themselves by extortion and fraud. No Pharisee would sit with one at table. Our Saviour alone had compassion for them. So St. Matthew made a great feast, to which he invited Jesus and His disciples, with a number of these publicans, who henceforth began eagerly to listen to Him. It was then, in answer to the murmurs of the Pharisees, that He said, " They that are in health need not the physician. I have not come to call the just, but sinners to penance." After the Ascension, St. Matthew remained some years in Judæa, and there wrote his gospel, to teach his countrymen that Jesus was their true Lord and King, foretold by the prophets. St. Matthew afterward preached the Faith far and wide, and is said to have finished his course in Parthia.

Reflection.—Obey all inspirations of Our Lord as promptly as St. Matthew, who, at a single word, " laid down," says St. Bridget, " the heavy burden of the world to put on the light and sweet yoke of Christ."

September 22.—THE THEBAN LEGION.

THE Theban legion numbered more than six thousand men. They marched from the East into Gaul, and proved their loyalty at once to their Emperor and to their God. They were encamped near the Lake of Geneva, under the Emperor Maximian, when they got orders to turn their swords against the Christian population, and refused to obey. In his fury Maximian ordered them to be decimated. The order was executed once and again, but they endured this without a murmur or an effort to defend themselves. St. Maurice, the chief captain in this legion of martyrs, encouraged the rest to persevere and follow their comrades to heaven. " Know, O Emperor," he said, " that we are your soldiers, but we are servants also of the true God. In all things lawful we will most readily obey, but we cannot stain our hands in this innocent blood. We have seen our comrades slain, and we rejoice at their honor. We have arms, but we resist not, for we had rather die without shame than live by sin." As the massacre began, these generous soldiers flung down their arms, offered their necks to the sword, and suffered themselves to be butchered in silence.

Reflection.—Thank God for every slight and injury you have to bear. An injury borne in meekness and silence is a true victory. It is the proof that we are good soldiers of Jesus Christ, disciples of that heavenly wisdom which is first pure, then peaceable.

September 23.—ST. THECLA, Virgin, Martyr.

ST. THECLA is one of the most ancient, as she is one of the most illustrious, Saints in the calendar of the Church. It was at Iconium that St. Paul met St. Thecla, and kindled the love of virginity in her heart. She had been promised in marriage to a young man who was rich and generous. But at the Apostle's words she died to the thought of earthly espousals; she forgot her beauty; she was deaf to her parents' threats, and at the first opportunity she fled from a luxurious home and followed St. Paul. The rage of her parents and of her intended spouse followed hard upon her; and the Roman power did its worst against the virgin whom Christ had chosen for His own. She was stripped and placed in the public theatre; but her innocence shrouded her like a garment. Then the lions were let loose against her; they fell crouching at her feet, and licked them as if in veneration. Even fire could not harm her. Torment after torment was inflicted upon her without effect, till at last her Spouse spoke the word and called her to Himself, with the double crown of virginity and martyrdom on her head.

Reflection.—It is purity in soul and body which will make you strong in pain, in temptation, and in the hour of death. Imitate the purity of this glorious virgin, and take her for your special patroness in your last agony.

September 24.—THE BLESSED VIRGIN MARY OF MERCY.

ST. PETER, of the noble family of Nolasco, was born in Languedoc, about 1189. At the age of twenty-five he took a vow of chastity, and made over his vast estates to the Church. Some time after, he conceived the idea of establishing an order for the redemption of captives. The

divine will was soon manifested.   The Blessed Virgin appeared on the same night to Peter, to Raymund of Penna-
fort, his confessor, and to James, King of Arragon, his
ward, and bade them prosecute without fear their holy
designs.   After great opposition, the Order was solemnly
established, and approved by Gregory IX., under the name
of *Our Lady of Mercy*.   By the grace of God, and under
the protection of His Virgin Mother, the Order spread rapidly, its growth being increased by the charity and piety of
its members, who devoted themselves not only to collecting
alms for the ransom of the Christians, but even gave themselves up to voluntary slavery to aid the good work.   It is
to return thanks to God and the Blessed Virgin that a feast
was instituted which was observed in the Order of Mercy,
then in Spain and France, and at last extended to the
whole Church by Innocent XII., and the 24th September
named as the day on which it is to be observed.

Reflection.—St. Peter Nolasco and his knights were laymen, not priests, and yet they considered the salvation of
their neighbor intrusted to them.   We can each of us by
counsel, by prayer, but above all by holy example, assist
the salvation of our brethren, and thus secure our own.

September 25.—ST. FIRMIN, Bishop, Martyr.—ST. FINBARR, Bishop.

S͟T. Firmin was a native of Pampelone in Navarre,
initiated in the Christian faith by Honestus, a disciple of St. Saturninus of Toulouse, and consecrated bishop
by St. Honoratus, successor to St. Saturninus, in order to
preach the Gospel in the remoter parts of Gaul.   He
preached the Faith in the countries of Agen, Anjou, and
Beauvais, and being arrived at Amiens, there chose his
residence, and founded there a numerous church of faithful disciples.   He received the crown of martyrdom in that
city, whether under the prefect Rictius Varus, or in some
other persecution from Decius, in 250, to Diocletian, in
303, is uncertain.

St. Finbarr, who lived in the sixth century, was a native of Connaught, and instituted a monastery or school at

Lough Eire, to which such numbers of disciples flocked, as changed, as it were, a desert into a large city. This was the origin of the city of Cork, which was built chiefly upon stakes, in marshy little islands formed by the river Lea. The right name of our Saint, under which he was baptized, was Lochan; the surname Finbarr, or Barr the White, was afterward given him. He was Bishop of Cork seventeen years, and died in the midst of his friends at Cloyne, fifteen miles from Cork. His body was buried in his own cathedral at Cork, and his relics, some years after, were put in a silver shrine, and kept there, this great church bearing his name to this day. St. Finbarr's cave or hermitage was shown in a monastery which seems to have been begun by our Saint, and stood to the west of Cork.

September 26.—STS. CYPRIAN and JUSTINA, Martyrs.

THE detestable superstition of St. Cyprian's idolatrous parents devoted him from his infancy to the devil, and he was brought up in all the impious mysteries of idolatry, astrology, and the black art. When Cyprian had learned all the extravagances of these schools of error and delusion, he hesitated at no crimes, blasphemed Christ, and committed secret murders. There lived at Antioch a young Christian lady called Justina, of high birth and great beauty. A pagan nobleman fell deeply in love with her, and finding her modesty inaccessible, and her resolution invincible, he applied to Cyprian for assistance. Cyprian, no less smitten with the lady, tried every secret with which he was acquainted to conquer her resolution. Justina, perceiving herself vigorously attacked, studied to arm herself by prayer, watchfulness, and mortification against all his artifices and the power of his spells. Cyprian finding himself worsted by a superior power, began to consider the weakness of the infernal spirits, and resolved to quit their service and become a Christian. Agladius, who had been the first suitor to the holy virgin, was likewise converted and baptized. The persecution of Diocletian breaking out, Cyprian and Justina were seized, and presented to the same judge. She was inhumanly scourged, and Cyprian was torn with iron hooks. After this they were both sent in chains to Diocletian, who commanded their heads to be struck off, which sentence was executed.

Reflection.—If the errors and disorders of St. Cyprian show the degeneracy of human nature corrupted by sin and enslaved to vice, his conversion displays the power of grace and virtue to repair it. Let us beg of God to send us grace to resist temptation, and to do His holy will in all things.

September 27.—STS. COSMAS and DAMIAN, Martyrs.

STS. Cosmas and Damian were brothers, and born in Arabia, but studied the sciences in Syria, and became eminent for their skill in physic. Being Christians, and full of that holy temper of charity in which the spirit of our divine religion consists, they practised their profession with great application and wonderful success, but never took any fee. They were loved and respected by the people on account of the good offices received from their charity, and for their zeal for the Christian faith, which they took every opportunity to propagate. When the persecution of Diocletian began to rage, it was impossible for persons of so distinguished a character to lie concealed. They were therefore apprehended by the order of Lysias, Governor of Cilicia, and after various torments were bound hand and foot and thrown into the sea.

Reflection.—We may sanctify our labor or industry, if actuated by the motive of charity toward others, even whilst we fulfil the obligation we owe to ourselves and our families of procuring an honest and necessary subsistence, which of itself is no less noble a virtue, if founded in motives equally pure and perfect.

September 28.—ST. WENCESLAS, Martyr.

WENCESLAS was the son of a Christian Duke of Bohemia, but his mother was a hard and cruel pagan. Through the care of his holy grandmother, Ludmilla, herself a martyr, Wenceslas was educated in the true faith, and imbibed a special devotion to the Blessed Sacrament. On the death of his father, his mother, Drahomira, usurped the government and passed a series of persecuting laws. In the interests of the Faith Wenceslas claimed and obtained, through the support of the people, a large portion of the country as his own kingdom. His mother secured the apostasy and alliance of her second son, Boleslas, who became henceforth her ally against the Christians. Wenceslas meanwhile ruled as a brave and pious king, provided for all the needs of his people, and when his kingdom was attacked, overcame in single combat, by the sign of the cross, the leader of an invading army. In the service of God he was most constant, and planted with his own hands the wheat and grapes for the Holy Mass, at which he never failed daily to assist. His piety was the occasion of his death. Once, after a banquet at his brother's palace, to which he had been treacherously invited, he went, as was his wont at night, to pray before the tabernacle. There, at midnight on the feast of the Angels, 938, he received his crown of martyrdom, his brother dealing him the death-blow.

Reflection.—St. Wenceslas teaches us that the safest place to meet the trials of life, or to prepare for the stroke of death, is before Jesus in the Blessed Sacrament.

September 29.—ST. MICHAEL, Archangel.

"MI-CA-EL," or "Who is like to God?" Such was the cry of the great Archangel when he smote the rebel Lucifer in the conflict of the heavenly hosts, and from that hour he has been known as "Michael," the captain of the armies of God, the type of divine fortitude, the champion of every faithful soul in strife with the powers of evil.

Thus he appears in Holy Scripture as the guardian of the children of Israel, their comfort and protector in times of sorrow or conflict. He it is who prepares for their return from the Persian captivity, who leads the valiant Maccabees to victory, and who rescues the body of Moses from the envious grasp of the Evil One. And since Christ's coming the Church has ever venerated St. Michael as her special patron and protector. She invokes him by name in her confession of sin, summons him to the side of her children in the agony of death, and chooses him as their escort from the chastening flames of purgatory to the realms of holy light. Lastly, when Antichrist shall have set up his kingdom on earth, it is Michael who will unfurl once more the standard of the Cross, sound the last trumpet, and binding together the false prophet and the beast, hurl them for all eternity into the burning pool.

Reflection.—" Whenever," says St. Bernard, " any grievous temptation or vehement sorrow oppresses thee, invoke thy guardian, thy leader; cry out to him, and say, ' Lord, save us, lest we perish ! ' "

September 30.—ST. JEROME, Doctor.

ST. JEROME, born in Dalmatia, in 329, was sent to school at Rome. His boyhood was not free from fault. His thirst for knowledge was excessive, and his love of books a passion. He had studied under the best masters, visited foreign cities, and devoted himself to the pursuit of science. But Christ had need of his strong will and active intellect for the service of His Church. St. Jerome felt and obeyed the call, made a vow of celibacy, fled from Rome to the wild Syrian desert, and there for four years learnt in solitude, penance, and prayer a new lesson of divine wisdom. This was his novitiate. The Pope soon summoned him to Rome, and there put upon the now famous Hebrew scholar the task of revising the Latin Bible, which was to be his noblest work. Retiring thence to his beloved Bethlehem, the eloquent hermit poured forth from his solitary cell for thirty years a stream of luminous writings upon the Christian world.

Reflection.—" To know," says St. Basil, " how to submit thyself with thy whole soul, is to know how to imitate Christ."

October 1.—ST. REMIGIUS, Bishop.

REMIGIUS, or Remi, was born of noble and pious parents. At the age of twenty-two, in spite of the canons and of his own reluctance, he was acclaimed Archbishop of Rheims. He was unusually tall, his face impressed with blended majesty and serenity, his bearing gentle, humble, and retiring. He was learned and eloquent, and had the gift of miracles. His pity and charity were boundless, and in toil he knew no weariness. His body was the outward expression of a noble and holy soul, breathing the spirit of meekness and compunction. For so choice a workman God had fitting work. The South of France was in the hands of Arians, and the pagan Franks were wresting the North from the Romans. St. Remigius confronted Clovis, their king, and converted and baptized him at Christmas, in 496. With him he gained the whole Frank nation. He threw down the idol altars, built churches, and appointed bishops. He withstood and silenced the Arians, and converted so many that he left France a Catholic kingdom, its king the oldest and at the time the only crowned son of the Church. He died in 533, after an episcopate of seventy-four years, the longest on record.

Reflection.—Few men have had such natural advantages and such gifts of grace as St. Remi, and few have done so great a work. Learn from him to bear the world's praise as well as its scorn with a lowly and chastened heart.

October 2.—THE HOLY GUARDIAN ANGELS.

GOD does not abandon to mere chance any of His handiworks; by His providence He is everywhere present; not a hair falls from the head or a sparrow to the ground without His knowledge. Not content, however, with yielding such familiar help in all things, not content with affording that existence which He communicates and perpetuates through every living being, He has charged His angels with the ministry of watching and safeguarding every one of His creatures that behold not His face. Kingdoms have their angels assigned to them, and men have their angels; these latter it is whom religion designates as the Holy Guardian Angels. Our Lord says in the Gospel, " Beware lest ye scandalize any of these little ones, for their angels in heaven see the face of My Father." The existence of Guardian Angels is, hence, a dogma of the Christian faith: this being so, what ought not our respect be for that sure and holy intelligence that is ever present at our side; and how great should our solicitude be, lest, by any act of ours, we offend those eyes which are ever bent upon us in all our ways!

Reflection.—Ah! let us not give occasion, in the language of Holy Scripture, to the angels of peace to weep bitterly.

October 3.—ST. GERARD, Abbot.

ST. GERARD was of a noble family of the county of Namur, France. An engaging sweetness of temper, and a strong inclination to piety and devotion, gained him from the cradle the esteem and affection of every one. Having been sent on an important mission to the Court of France, he was greatly edified at the fervor of the monks of St. Denis, at Paris, and earnestly desired to consecrate himself to God with them. Returning home he settled his temporal affairs, and went back with great joy to St. Denis'. He had lived ten years with great fervor in this monastery, when in 931 he was sent by his abbot to found an abbey upon his estate at Brogne, three leagues from Namur. He settled this new abbey, and then built himself a little cell near the church, and lived in it a recluse until God called him to undertake the reformation of many monasteries, which he did successfully. When he had spent almost twenty years in these zealous labors, he shut himself up in his cell, to prepare his soul to receive the recompense of his labors, to which he was called on the 3d of October in 959.

Reflection.—Though we are in the world, let us strive to separate ourselves from it and consecrate ourselves to God, remembering that " the world passeth away, but he that doth the will of God abideth forever."

October 4.—ST. FRANCIS OF ASSISI.

T. FRANCIS, the son of a merchant of Assisi, was born in that city in 1182. Chosen by God to be a living manifestation to the world of Christ's poor and suffering life on earth, he was early inspired with a high esteem and burning love of poverty and humiliation. The thought of the Man of Sorrows, Who had not where to lay His head, filled him with holy envy of the poor, and constrained him to renounce the wealth and worldly station which he abhorred. The scorn and hard usage which he met with from his father and townsmen when he appeared among them in the garb of poverty were delightful to him. " Now," he exclaimed, " I can say truly, ' Our Father Who art in heaven.' " But divine love burned in him too mightily not to kindle like desires in other hearts. Many joined themselves to him, and were constituted by Pope Innocent III. into a religious Order, which spread rapidly throughout Christendom. St. Francis, after visiting the East in the vain quest of martyrdom, spent his life like his Divine Master — now in preaching to the multitudes, now amid desert solitudes in fasting and contemplation. During one of these retreats he received on his hands, feet, and side the print of the five bleeding wounds of Jesus. With the cry, " Welcome, sister Death," he passed to the glory of his God October 4, 1226.

Reflection.—" My God and my all," St. Francis' constant prayer, explains both his poverty and his wealth.

October 5.—ST. PLACID, Martyr.

ST. PLACID was born in Rome, in the year 515, of a patrician family, and at seven years of age was taken by his father to the monastery of Subiaco. At thirteen years of age he followed St. Benedict to the new foundation at Monte Casino, where he grew up in the practice of a wonderful austerity and innocence of life. He had scarcely completed his twenty-first year when he was selected to establish a monastery in Sicily upon some estates which had been given by his father to St. Benedict. He spent four years in building his monastery, and the fifth had not elapsed before an inroad of barbarians burned everything to the ground, and put to a lingering death not only St. Placid and thirty monks who had joined him, but also his two brothers, Eutychius and Victorinus, and his holy sister Flavia, who had come to visit him. The monastery was rebuilt, and still stands under his invocation.

Reflection.—Adversity is the touchstone of the soul, because it discovers the character of the virtue which it possesses. One act of thanksgiving when matters go wrong with us is worth a thousand thanks when things are agreeable to our inclinations.

October 6.—ST. BRUNO.

BRUNO was born at Cologne, about 1030, of an illustrious family. He was endowed with rare natural gifts, which he cultivated with care at Paris. He became canon of Cologne, and then of Rheims, where he had the direction of theological studies. On the death of the bishop the see fell for a time into evil hands, and Bruno retired with a few friends into the country. There he resolved to forsake the world, and to live a life of retirement and penance. With six companions he applied to Hugh, Bishop of Grenoble, who led them into a wild solitude called the Chartreuse. There they lived in poverty, self-denial, and silence, each apart in his own cell, meeting only for the worship of God, and employing themselves in copying books. From the name of the spot the Order of St. Bruno was called the Carthusian. Six years later, Urban II. called Bruno to Rome, that he might avail himself of his guidance. Bruno tried to live there as he had lived in the desert; but the echoes of the great city disturbed his solitude, and, after refusing high dignities, he wrung from the Pope permission to resume his monastic life in Calabria. There he lived, in humility and mortification and great peace, till his blessed death in 1101.

Reflection.—" O everlasting kingdom," said St. Augustine; " kingdom of endless ages, whereon rests the untroubled light and the peace of God which passeth all understanding, where the souls of the Saints are in rest, and everlasting joy is on their heads, and sorrow and sighing have fled away! When shall I come and appear before God?"

October 7.—ST. MARK, Pope.

ST. MARK was by birth a Roman, and served God with such fervor among the clergy of that Church, that, advancing continually in sincere humility and the knowledge and sense of his own weakness and imperfections, he strove every day to surpass himself in the fervor of his charity and zeal, and in the exercise of all virtues. The persecution ceased in the West, in the beginning of the year 305, but was revived a short time after by Maxentius. St. Mark abated nothing of his watchfulness, but endeavored rather to redouble his zeal during the peace of the Church; knowing that if men sometimes cease openly to persecute the faithful, the devil never allows them any truce, and his snares are generally most to be feared in the time of the calm. St. Mark succeeded St. Sylvester in the apostolic chair on the 18th of January, 336. He held that dignity only eight months and twenty days, dying on the 7th of October following. He was buried in a cemetery in the Ardeatine Way, which has since borne his name.

Reflection.—A Christian ought to be afraid of no enemy more than himself, whom he carries always about with him, and from whom he is not able to flee. He should therefore never cease to cry out to God, " Unless Thou, O Lord, art my light and support, I watch in vain."

October 8.—ST. BRIDGET OF SWEDEN.

BRIDGET was born of the Swedish royal family, in 1304. In obedience to her father, she was married to Prince Ulpho of Sweden, and became the mother of eight children, one of whom, Catherine, is honored as a Saint. After some years she and her husband separated by mutual consent. He entered the Cistercian Order, and Bridget founded the Order of St. Saviour, in the Abbey of Wastein, in Sweden. In 1344 she became a widow, and thenceforth received a series of the most sublime revelations, all of which she scrupulously submitted to the judgment of her confessor. By the command of Our Lord, Bridget went on a pilgrimage to the Holy Land, and amidst the very scenes of the Passion was further instructed in the sacred mysteries. She died in 1373.

Reflection.—" Is confession a matter of much time or expense? " asks St. John Chrysostom. " Is it a difficult and painful remedy? Without cost or hurt, the medicine is ever ready to restore you to perfect health."

October 9.—ST. DIONYSIUS and his Companions, Martyrs.—ST. LOUIS BERTRAND.

OF all the Roman missionaries sent into Gaul, St. Dionysius carried the Faith the furthest into the country, fixing his see at Paris, and by him and his disciples the sees of Chartres, Senlis, Meaux, and Cologne were erected in the fourth century. During the persecution of Valerian he was arrested and thrown into prison, and after remaining there for some time was beheaded, together with St. Rusticus, a priest, and Eleutherius, a deacon.

ST. LOUIS BERTRAND was born at Valencia, in Spain, in 1526, of the same family as St. Vincent Ferrer. In 1545, after severe trials, he was professed in the Dominican Order, and at the age of twenty-five was made master of novices, and trained up many great servants of God. When the plague broke out in Valencia he devoted himself to the sick and dying, and with his own hands buried the dead. In 1562 he obtained leave to embark for the American mission, and there converted vast multitudes to the Faith. He was favored with the gift of miracles, and while preaching in his native Spanish was understood in various languages. After seven years he returned to Spain, to plead the cause of the oppressed Indians, but he was not permitted to return and labor among them. He spent his remaining days toiling in his own country, till at length, in 1580, he was carried from the pulpit in the Cathedral at Valencia to the bed from whence he never rose. He died on the day he had foretold — October 9, 1581.

Reflection.—The Saints fasted, toiled, and wept, not only for love of God, but for fear of damnation. How shall we, with our self-indulgent lives and unexamined consciences, face the judgment-seat of Christ?

October 10.—ST. FRANCIS BORGIA.

FRANCIS BORGIA, Duke of Gandia and Captain-General of Catalonia, was one of the handsomest, richest, and most honored nobles in Spain, when, in 1539, there was laid upon him the sad duty of escorting the remains of his sovereign, Queen Isabella, to the royal burying-place at Granada. The coffin had to be opened for him that he might verify the body before it was placed in the tomb, and so foul a sight met his eyes that he vowed never again to serve a sovereign who could suffer so base a change. It was some years before he could follow the call of his Lord; at length he entered the Society of Jesus to cut himself off from any chance of dignity or preferment. But his Order chose him to be its head. The Turks were threatening Christendom, and St. Pius V. sent his nephew to gather Christian princes into a league for its defence. The holy Pope chose Francis to accompany him, and, worn out though he was, the Saint obeyed at once. The fatigues of the embassy exhausted what little life was left. St. Francis died on his return to Rome, October 10, 1572.

Reflection.—St. Francis Borgia learnt the worthlessness of earthly greatness at the funeral of Queen Isabella. Do the deaths of friends teach us aught about ourselves?

October 11.—ST. TARACHUS and his Companions.

IN the year 304, Tarachus, Probus, and Andronicus, differing in age and nationality, but united in the bonds of faith, being denounced as Christians to Numerian, Governor of Cilicia, were arrested at Pompeiopolis, and conducted to Tharsis. They underwent a first examination in that town, after which their limbs were torn with iron hooks, and they were taken back to prison covered with wounds. Being afterwards led to Mopsuestia, they were submitted to a second examination, ending in a manner equally cruel as the first. They underwent a third examination at Anazarbis, followed by greater torments still. The governor, unable to shake their constancy, had them kept imprisoned that he might torture them further at the approaching games. They were borne to the amphitheatre, but the most ferocious animals, on being let loose on them, came crouching to their feet and licked their wounds. The judge, reproaching the jailers with connivance, ordered the martyrs to be despatched by the gladiators.

Reflection.—Such is true Christian devotion. " Neither death nor life shall be able to separate us from the love that is in Christ Jesus."

October 12.—ST. WILFRID, Bishop.

"A QUICK walker, expert at all good works, with never a sour face "— such was the great St. Wilfrid, whose glory it was to secure the happy links which bound England to Rome.   He was born about the year 634, and was trained by the Celtic monks at Lindisfarne in the peculiar rites and usages of the British Church.   Yet even as a boy Wilfrid longed for perfect conformity in discipline, as in doctrine, with the Holy See, and at the first chance set off himself for Rome.   On his return he founded at Ripon a strictly Roman monastery, under the rule of St. Benedict.   In the year 664 he was elected Bishop of Lindisfarne, and five years later was transferred to the see of York.   He had to combat the passions of wicked kings, the cowardice of worldly prelates, the errors of holy men. He was twice exiled and once imprisoned; yet the battle which he fought was won.   He swept away the abuses of many years and a too national system, and substituted instead a vigorous Catholic discipline, modelled and dependent on Rome.   He died October 12, 709, and at his death was heard the sweet melody of the angels conducting his soul to Christ.

Reflection.—To look towards Rome is an instinct planted in us for the preservation of the Faith.   Trust in the Vicar of Christ necessarily results from the reign of His love in our hearts.

October 13.—ST. EDWARD THE CONFESSOR.

EDWARD was unexpectedly raised to the throne of England at the age of forty years, twenty-seven of which he had passed in exile.   On the throne, the virtues of his earlier years, simplicity, gentleness, lowliness, but above all his angelic purity, shone with new brightness. By a rare inspiration of God, though he married to content his nobles and people, he preserved perfect chastity in the wedded state.   So little did he set his heart on riches, that thrice when he saw a servant robbing his treasury he let

him escape, saying the poor fellow needed the gold more
than he. He loved to stand at his palace-gate, speaking
kindly to the poor beggars and lepers who crowded about
him, and many of whom he healed of their diseases. The
long wars had brought the kingdom to a sad state, but
Edward's zeal and sanctity soon wrought a great change.
His reign of twenty-four years was one of almost unbroken peace, the country grew prosperous, the ruined
churches rose under his hand, the weak lived secure, and
for ages afterwards men spoke with affection of the " laws
of good St. Edward." The holy king had a great devotion
to building and enriching churches. Westminster Abbey
was his latest and noblest work. He died January 5, 1066.

Reflection.—David longed to build a temple for God's
service. Solomon reckoned it his glory to accomplish the
work. But we, who have God made flesh dwelling in our
tabernacles, ought to think no time, no zeal, no treasures
too much to devote to the splendor and beauty of a Christian church.

October 14.—ST. CALLISTUS, Pope, Martyr.

EARLY in the third century, Callistus, then a deacon,
was intrusted by Pope St. Zephyrinus with the rule
of the clergy, and set by him over the cemeteries of the
Christians at Rome ; and, at the death of Zephyrinus, Callistus, according to the Roman usage, succeeded to the
Apostolic See. A decree is ascribed to him appointing the
four fasts of the Ember seasons, but his name is best
known in connection with the old cemetery on the Appian
Way, which was enlarged and adorned by him, and is
called to this day the Catacomb of St. Callistus. During
the persecution under the Emperor Severus, St. Callistus
was driven to take shelter in the poor and populous quar-
ters of the city; yet, in spite of these troubles, and of the
care of the Church, he made diligent search for the body
of Calipodius, one of his clergy who had suffered martyrdom shortly before, by being cast into the Tiber. When
he found it he was full of joy, and buried it, with hymns
of praise. Callistus was martyred October 14, 223.

Reflection.—In the body of a Christian we see that which has been the temple of the Holy Ghost, which even now is precious in the eyes of God, Who will watch over it, and one day raise it up in glory to shine forever in His kingdom. Let our actions bear witness to our belief in these truths.

October 15.—ST. TERESA.

WHEN a child of seven years, Teresa ran away from her home at Avila in Spain, in the hope of being martyred by the Moors. Being brought back and asked the reason of her flight, she replied, "I want to see God, and I must die before I can see Him." She then began with her brother to build a hermitage in the garden, and was often heard repeating "Forever, forever." Some years later she became a Carmelite nun. Frivolous conversations checked her progress towards perfection, but at last, in her thirty-first year, she gave herself wholly to God. A vision showed her the very place in hell to which her own light faults would have led her, and she lived ever after in the deepest distrust of self. She was called to reform her Order, favored with distinct commands from Our Lord, and her heart was pierced with divine love; but she dreaded nothing so much as delusion, and to the last acted only under obedience to her confessors, which both made her strong and kept her safe. She died on October 4, 1582.

Reflection.—" After all I die a child of the Church." These were the Saint's last words. They teach us the lesson of her life — to trust in humble, childlike obedience to our spiritual guides as the surest means of salvation.

October 16.—ST. GALL, Abbot.

ST. GALL was born in Ireland soon after the middle of the sixth century, of pious, noble, and rich parents. When St. Columban left Ireland, St. Gall accompanied him into England, and afterward into France, where they

arrived in 585. St. Columban founded the monastery of
Anegray, in a wild forest in the diocese of Besançon, and
two years afterward another in Luxeuil. Being driven
thence by King Theodoric, the Saints both withdrew into
the territories of Theodebert. St. Columban, however,
retired into Italy, but St. Gall was prevented from bearing
him company by a grievous fit of illness. St. Gall was a
priest before he left Ireland, and having learned the language of the country where he settled, near the Lake of
Constance, he converted to the faith a great number of
idolaters. The cells which this Saint built there for those
who desired to serve God with him, he gave to the monastery which bears his name. A synod of bishops, with the
clergy and people, earnestly desired to place the Saint in
the episcopal see of Constance; but his modesty refused
the dignity. He died in the year 646.

Reflection.—" If any one would be My disciple," says
Our Saviour, " let him deny himself." The denial of self
is, then, the royal road to perfection.

October 17.—ST. HEDWIGE.—BLESSED MARGARET MARY ALACOQUE.

ST. HEDWIGE, the wife of Henry, Duke of Silesia, and
the mother of his six children, led a humble, austere,
and most holy life amidst all the pomp of royal state.
Devotion to the Blessed Sacrament was the key-note of her
life. Her valued privilege was to supply the bread and
wine for the Sacred Mysteries, and she would attend each
morning as many Masses as were celebrated. After the
death of her husband she retired to the Cistercian convent
of Trebnitz, where she lived under obedience to her daughter Gertrude, who was abbess of the monastery, growing
day by day in holiness, till God called her to Himself, in
1242.

MARGARET MARY was born at Terreau in Burgundy, on
the 22d July, 1647. During her infancy she showed a
wonderfully sensitive horror of the very idea of sin. In
1671 she entered the Order of the Visitation, at Paray-le-
Monial, and was professed the following year. After

purifying her by many trials, Jesus appeared to her in numerous visions, displaying to her His Sacred Heart, sometimes burning as a furnace, and sometimes torn and bleeding on account of the coldness and sins of men. In 1675 the great revelation was made to her that she, in union with Father de la Colombière, of the Society of Jesus, was to be the chief instrument for instituting the feast of the Sacred Heart, and for spreading that devotion throughout the world. She died on the 17th October, 1690.

Reflection.—Love for the Sacred Heart especially honors the Incarnation, and makes the soul grow rapidly in humility, generosity, patience, and union with its Beloved.

October 18.—ST. LUKE.

ST. LUKE, a physician at Antioch, and a painter, became a convert of St. Paul, and afterwards his fellow-laborer. He is best known to us as the historian of the New Testament. Though not an eye-witness of Our Lord's life, the Evangelist diligently gathered information from the lips of the apostles, and wrote, as he tells us, all things in order. The acts of the Apostles were written by this Evangelist as a sequel to his Gospel, bringing the history of the Church down to the first imprisonment of St. Paul at Rome. The humble historian never names himself, but by his occasional use of " we " for " they " we are able to detect his presence in the scenes which he describes. We thus find that he sailed with St. Paul and Silas from Troas to Macedonia; stayed behind apparently for seven years at Philippi, and, lastly, shared the shipwreck and perils of the memorable voyage to Rome. Here his own narrative ends, but from St. Paul's Epistles we learn that St. Luke was his faithful companion to the end. He died a martyr's death some time afterwards in Achaia.

Reflection.—Christ has given all He had for thee; do thou give all thou hast for Him.

October 19.—ST. PETER OF ALCANTARA.

PETER, while still a youth, left his home at Alcantara in Spain, and entered a convent of Discalced Franciscans. He rose quickly to high posts in the Order, but his thirst for penance was still unappeased, and in 1539, being then forty years old, he founded the first convent of the " Strict Observance." The cells of the friars resembled graves rather than dwelling-places. That of St. Peter himself was four feet and a half in length, so that he could never lie down; he ate but once in three days; his sack-cloth habit and a cloak were his only garments, and he never covered his head or feet. In the bitter winter he would open the door and window of his cell that, by closing them again, he might experience some sensation of warmth. Amongst those whom he trained to perfection was St. Teresa. He read her soul, approved of her spirit of prayer, and strengthened her to carry out her reforms. St. Peter died, with great joy, kneeling in prayer, October 18, 1562, at the age of sixty-three.

Reflection.—If men do not go about barefoot now, nor undergo sharp penances, as St. Peter did, there are many ways of trampling on the world; and Our Lord teaches them when He finds the necessary courage.

October 20.—ST. JOHN CANTIUS.

ST. JOHN was born at Kenty in Poland in 1403, and studied at Cracow with great ability, industry, and success, while his modesty and virtue drew all hearts to him. He was for a short time in charge of a parish; but he shrank from the burden of responsibility, and returned to his life of professor at Cracow. There for many years he lived a life of unobtrusive virtue, self-denial, and charity. His love for the Holy See led him often in pilgrimage to Rome, on foot and alone, and his devotion to the Passion drew him once to Jerusalem, where he hoped to win a martyr's crown by preaching to the Turks. He died in 1473, at the age of seventy.

Reflection.—He who orders all his doings according to the will of God may often be spoken of by the world as simple and stupid; but in the end he wins the esteem and confidence of the world itself, and the approval and peace of God.

October 21.—ST. URSULA, Virgin and Martyr.

A NUMBER of Christian families had intrusted the education of their children to the care of the pious Ursula, and some persons of the world had in like manner placed themselves under her direction. England being then harassed by the Saxons, Ursula deemed that she ought, after the example of many of her compatriots, to seek an asylum in Gaul. She met with an abiding-place on the borders of the Rhine, not far from Cologne, where she hoped to find undisturbed repose; but a horde of Huns having invaded the country, she was exposed, together with all those who were under her guardianship, to the most shameful outrages. Without wavering, they preferred one and all to meet death rather than incur shame. Ursula herself gave the example, and was, together with her companions, cruelly massacred in the year 453. The name of St. Ursula has from remote ages been held in great honor throughout the Church; she has always been regarded as the patroness of young persons and the model of teachers.

Reflection.—In the estimation of the wise man, "the guarding of virtue" is the most important part of the education of youth.

October 22.—ST. MELLO, Bishop.—ST. HILARION, Abbot.

ST. MELLO is said to have been a native of Great Britain; his zeal for the Faith engaged him in the sacred ministry, and God having blessed his labors with wonderful success, he was consecrated first bishop of Rouen in Normandy, which see he is said to have held forty years.

He died in peace, about the beginning of the fourth century.

St. HILARION was born of heathen parents, near Gaza, and was converted while studying grammar in Alexandria. Shortly after, he visited St. Antony, and, still only in his fifteenth year, he became a solitary in the Arabian desert. A multitude of monks, attracted by his sanctity, peopled the desert where he lived. In consequence of this, he fled from one country to another, seeking to escape the praise of men; but everywhere his miracles of mercy betrayed his presence. Even his last retreat at Cyprus was broken by a paralytic, who was cured by St. Hilarion, and then spread the fame of the Saint. He died with the words, "Go forth, my soul; why dost thou doubt? Nigh seventy years hast thou served God, and dost thou fear death?"

October 23.—ST. THEODORET, Martyr.

ABOUT the year 361, Julian, uncle to the emperor of that name, and like his nephew an apostate, was made Count of the East. He closed the Christian churches at Antioch, and when St. Theodoret assembled the Christians in private, he was summoned before the tribunal of the Count and most inhumanly tortured. His arms and feet were fastened by ropes to pulleys, and stretched until his body appeared nearly eight feet long, and the blood streamed from his sides. "O most wretched man," he said to his judge, "you know well that at the day of judgment the crucified God Whom you blaspheme will send you and the tyrant whom you serve to hell." Julian trembled at this awful prophecy, but he had the Saint despatched quickly by the sword, and in a little while the judge himself was arraigned before the judgment-seat of God.

Reflection.—Those who do not go down to hell in spirit are very likely to go there in reality. Take care to meditate upon the four last things, and to live in holy fear. You will learn to love God better by thinking how He punishes those who do not love Him.

October 24.—ST. MAGLOIRE, Bishop.

ST. MAGLOIRE was born in Brittany towards the end of the fifth century. When he and his cousin St. Sampson came of an age to choose their way in life, Sampson retired into a monastery, and Magloire returned home, where he lived in the practice of virtue. Amon, Sampson's father, having been cured by prayer of a dangerous disease, left the world, and with his entire family consecrated himself to God. Magloire was so affected at this that, with his father, mother, and two brothers, he resolved to fly the world, and they gave all their goods to the poor and the Church. Magloire and his father attached themselves to Sampson, and obtained his permission to take the monastic habit in the house over which he presided. When Sampson was consecrated bishop, Magloire accompanied him in his apostolical labors in Armorica, or Brittany, and at his death he succeeded him in the Abbey of Dole and in the episcopal character. After three years he resigned his bishopric, being seventy years old, and retired into a desert on the continent, and some time after into the isle of Jersey, where he founded and governed a monastery of sixty monks. He died about the year 575.

Reflection.—" Be mindful of them that have rule over you, who have spoken to you the word of God, whose faith follow, considering the end."

October 25.—STS. CRISPIN and CRISPINIAN, Martyrs.

THESE two glorious martyrs came from Rome to preach the Faith in Gaul toward the middle of the third century. Fixing their residence at Soissons, they instructed many in the Faith of Christ, which they preached publicly in the day, and at night they worked at making shoes, though they are said to have been nobly born, and brothers. The infidels listened to their instructions, and were astonished at the example of their lives, especially of

their charity, disinterestedness, heavenly piety, and contempt of glory and all earthly things; and the effect was
the conversion of many to the Christian faith. The
brothers had continued their employment several years
when a complaint was lodged against them. The emperor, to gratify their accusers and give way to his savage
cruelty, gave orders that they should be convened before
Rictius Varus, the most implacable enemy of the Christians. The martyrs were patient and constant under the
most cruel torments, and finished their course by the
sword about the year 287.

Reflection.—Of how many may it be said that "they
labor in vain," since God is not the end and purpose that
inspires the labor?

October 26.—ST. EVARISTUS, Pope and Martyr.

S T. EVARISTUS succeeded St. Anacletus in the see of
Rome, in the reign of Trajan, governed the Church
nine years, and died in 112. The institution of cardinal
priests is by some ascribed to him, because he first divided
Rome into several titles or parishes, assigning a priest to
each; he also appointed seven deacons to attend the bishop.
He conferred holy orders thrice in the month of December,
when that ceremony was most usually performed, for holy
orders were always conferred in seasons appointed for
fasting and prayer. St. Evaristus was buried near St.
Peter's tomb on the Vatican.

Reflection.—The disciples of the apostles, by assiduous
meditation on heavenly things, were so swallowed up in
the life to come, that they seemed no longer inhabitants
of this world. If Christians esteem and set their hearts
on earthly goods, and lose sight of eternity in the course
of their actions, they are no longer animated by the spirit
of the primitive Saints, and are become children of this
world, slaves to its vanities, and to their own irregular
passions. If we do not correct this disorder of our hearts,
and conform our interior to the spirit of Christ, we cannot
be entitled to His promises.

October 27.—ST. FRUMENTIUS, Bishop.

ST. FRUMENTIUS was yet a child when his uncle, Meropius of Tyre, took him and his brother Edesius on a voyage to Ethiopia. In the course of their voyage the vessel touched at a certain port, and the barbarians of that country put the crew and all the passengers to the sword, except the two children. They were carried to the king, at Axuma, who, charmed with the wit and sprightliness of the two boys, took special care of their education; and, not long after made Edesius his cup-bearer, and Frumentius, who was the elder, his treasurer and secretary of state; on his death-bed he thanked them for their services, and in recompense gave them their liberty. After his death the queen begged them to remain at court, and assist her in the government of the state until the young king came of age. Edesius went back to Tyre, but St. Athanasius ordained Frumentius Bishop of the Ethiopians, and vested with this sacred character he gained great numbers to the Faith, and continued to feed and defend his flock until it pleased the Supreme Pastor to recompense his fidelity and labors.

Reflection.—"The soul that journeys in the light and the truths of the Faith is safe against all error."

October 28.—STS. SIMON and JUDE.

SIMON was a simple Galilean, called by Our Lord to be one of the pillars of His Church. Zelotes, "the zealot," was the surname which he bore among the disciples. Armed with this zeal he went forth to the combat against unbelief and sin, and made conquest of many souls for His divine Lord.

The apostle Jude, whom the Church commemorates on the same day, was a brother of St. James the Less. They were called "brethren of the Lord," on account of their relationship to His Blessed Mother. St. Jude preached first in Mesopotamia, as St. Simon did in Egypt; and finally they both met in Persia, where they won their crown together.

Reflection.—Zeal is an ardent love which makes a man fearless in defence of God's honor, and earnest at all costs to make known the truth. If we would be children of the Saints, we must be zealous for the Faith.

October 29.—ST. NARCISSUS, Bishop.

ST. NARCISSUS was consecrated Bishop of Jerusalem about the year 180. He was already an old man, and God attested his merits by many miracles, which were long held in memory by the Christians of Jerusalem. One Holy Saturday in the church the faithful were in great trouble, because no oil could be found for the lamps which were used in the Paschal feast. St. Narcissus bade them draw water from a neighboring well, and, praying over it, told them to put it in the lamps. It was changed into oil, and long after some of this oil was preserved at Jerusalem in memory of the miracle. But the very virtue of the Saint made him enemies, and three wretched men charged him with an atrocious crime. They confirmed their testimony by horrible imprecations: the first prayed that he might perish by fire, the second that he might be wasted by leprosy, the third that he might be struck blind, if they charged their bishop falsely. The holy bishop had long desired a life of solitude, and he withdrew secretly into the desert, leaving the Church in peace. But God spoke for His servant, and the bishop's accusers suffered the penalties they had invoked. Then Narcissus returned to Jerusalem and resumed his office. He died in extreme old age, bishop to the last.

Reflection.—God never fails those who trust in Him; He guides them through darkness and through trials secretly and surely to their end, and in the evening time there is light.

October 30.—ST. MARCELLUS, THE CEN-
TURION, Martyr.

THE birthday of the Emperor Maximian Herculeus, in the year 298, was celebrated with extraordinary feasting and solemnity. Marcellus, a Christian centurion or captain in the legion of Trajan, then posted in Spain, not to defile himself with taking part in those impious abominations, left his company, declaring aloud that he was a soldier of Jesus Christ, the eternal King. He was at once committed to prison. When the festival was over, Marcellus was brought before a judge, and, having declared his faith, was sent under a strong guard to Aurelian Agricolaus, vicar to the prefect of the prætorium, who passed sentence of death upon him. St. Marcellus was forthwith led to execution, and beheaded on the 30th of October. Cassian, the secretary or notary of the court, refused to write the sentence pronounced against the martyr, because it was unjust. He was immediately hurried to prison, and was beheaded, about a month after, on the 3d of December.

Reflection.—" We are ready to die rather than to transgress the laws of God! " exclaimed one of the Machabees. This sentiment should ever be that of a Christian in presence of temptation.

October 31.—ST. QUINTIN, Martyr.

ST. QUINTIN was a Roman, descended from a senatorial family. Full of zeal for the kingdom of Jesus Christ, he left his country, and, attended by St. Lucian of Beauvais, made his way to Gaul. They preached the Faith together in that country till they reached Amiens in Picardy, where they parted. Lucian went to Beauvais, and, having sown the seeds of divine faith in the hearts of many, received the crown of martyrdom in that city. St. Quintin stayed at Amiens, endeavoring by his prayers and labors to make that country a portion of Our Lord's inheritance. He was seized, thrown into prison, and loaded with chains. Finding the holy preacher proof against promises and threats, the magistrate condemned him to the most barbarous torture. His body was then pierced with two iron wires from the neck to the thighs, and iron nails were thrust under his nails, and in his flesh in many places, particularly into his skull; and, lastly, his head was cut off. His death happened on the 31st of October, 287.

Reflection.—Let us bear in mind that the ills of this life are not worthy to be compared to the glory " God has reserved for those who love Him."

November 1.—ALL-SAINTS.

THE Church pays, day by day, a special veneration to some one of the holy men and women who have helped to establish it by their blood, develop it by their labors, or edify it by their virtues. But, in addition to those whom the Church honors by special designation, or has inscribed in her calendar, how many martyrs are there whose names are not recorded! How many humble virgins and holy penitents! How many just and holy anchorites or young children snatched away in their innocence! How many Christians who have died in grace, whose merits are known only to God, and who are themselves known only in heaven! Now should we forget those who remember us in their intercessions? Besides, are they not our brethren, our ancestors, friends, and fellow-Christians, with whom we have lived in daily companionship — in other words, our own family? Yea, it is one family; and our place is marked out in this home of eternal light and eternal love.

Reflection.—Let us have a solicitude to render ourselves worthy of " that chaste generation, so beautiful amid the glory where it dwells."

November 2.—ALL-SOULS.

THE Church teaches us that the souls of the just who have left this world soiled with the stain of venial sin remain for a time in a place of expiation, where they suffer such punishment as may be due to their offences. It

is a matter of faith that these suffering souls are relieved
by the intercession of the Saints in heaven and by the
prayers of the faithful upon earth.   To pray for the dead
is, then, both an act of charity and of piety.   We read in
Holy Scripture: "It is a holy and wholesome thought to
pray for the dead, that they may be loosed from sins."
And when Our Lord inspired St. Odilo, Abbot of Cluny,
towards the close of the tenth century, to establish in his
Order a general commemoration of all the faithful departed, it was soon adopted by the whole Western Church,
and has been continued unceasingly to our day.   Let us,
then, ever bear in mind the dead and offer up our prayers
for them.   By showing this mercy to the suffering souls in
purgatory, we shall be particularly entitled to be treated
with mercy at our departure from this world, and to share
more abundantly in the general suffrages of the Church,
continually offered for all who have slept in Christ.

ST. MALACHI, Bishop.

DURING his childhood Malachi would often separate himself from his companions to converse in prayer with
God.   At the age of twenty-five he was ordained priest;
his devotion and zeal led to his being consecrated Bishop of
Connor, and shortly afterwards he was made Archbishop
of his native city, Armagh.   This see having by a long-
standing abuse been held as an heirloom in one family, it
required on the part of the Saint no little tact and firmness
to allay the dissensions caused by his election.   One day,
while St. Malachi was burying the dead, he was laughed at
by his sister.   When she died, he said many Masses for her.
Some time afterwards, in a vision, he saw her, dressed in
mourning, standing in a churchyard, and saying that she
had not tasted food for thirty days.   Remembering that it
was just thirty days since he last offered the Adorable Sacrifice for her, he began again to do so, and was rewarded
by other visions, in the last of which he saw her within the
church, clothed in white, near the altar, and surrounded by
bright spirits.   He twice made a pilgrimage to Rome, to
consult Christ's Vicar, the first time returning as Papal

Legate, amid the joy of his people, with the pall for
Armagh; but the second time bound for a happier home.
He was taken ill at Clairvaux.   He died, aged fifty-four,
where he fain would have lived, in St. Bernard's monastery,
on the 2d of November, 1148.

Reflection.—Our Lord said to St. Gertrude, " God accepts every soul you set free, as if you had redeemed him
from captivity, and will reward you in a fitting time for
the benefit you have conferred."

November 3.—ST. HUBERT, Bishop.

$\mathcal{S}$ T. HUBERT'S early life is so obscured by popular traditions that we have no authentic account of his actions.
He is said to have been passionately addicted to hunting,
and was entirely taken up in worldly pursuits.   One thing
is certain: that he is the patron saint of hunters.   Moved
by divine grace, he resolved to renounce the world.   His
extraordinary fervor, and the great progress which he
made in virtue and learning, strongly recommended him to
St. Lambert, Bishop of Maestricht, who ordained him
priest, and entrusted him with the principal share in the
administration of his diocese.   That holy prelate being
barbarously murdered in 681, St. Hubert was unanimously
chosen his successor.   With incredible zeal he penetrated
into the most remote and barbarous places of Ardenne, and
abolished the worship of idols; and, as he performed the
office of the apostles, God bestowed on him a like gift of
miracles.   He died on the 30th of May, in 727, reciting to
his last breath the Creed and the Lord's Prayer.

Reflection.—What the Wise Man has said of Wisdom
may be applied to Grace: " That it ordereth the means
with gentleness, and attaineth its end with power."

November 4.—ST. CHARLES BORROMEO.

$\mathcal{A}$ BOUT fifty years after the Protestant heresy had broken
out, Our Lord raised up a mere youth to renew the
face of His Church.   In 1560 Charles Borromeo, then
twenty-two years of age, was created cardinal, and by

the side of his uncle, Pius IV., administered the affairs of the Holy See. His first care was the direction of the Council of Trent. He urged forward its sessions, guided its deliberations by continual correspondence from Rome, and by his firmness carried it to its conclusion. Then he entered upon a still more arduous work — the execution of its decrees. As Archbishop of Milan he enforced their observance, and thoroughly restored the discipline of his see. He founded schools for the poor, seminaries for the clerics, and by his community of Oblates trained his priests to perfection. Inflexible in maintaining discipline, to his flock he was a most tender father. He would sit by the roadside to teach a poor man the *Pater* and *Ave,* and would enter hovels the stench of which drove his attendants from the door. During the great plague he refused to leave Milan, and was ever by the sick and dying, and sold even his bed for their support. So he lived and so he died, a faithful image of the Good Shepherd, up to his last hour giving his life for his sheep.

Reflection.—Daily resolutions to fulfil, at all cost, every duty demanded by God, is the lesson taught by St. Charles; and a lesson we must learn if we would overcome our corrupt nature and reform our lives.

November 5.—ST. BERTILLE, Abbess.

S︎T. BERTILLE was born of one of the most illustrious families in the territory of Soissons, in the reign of Dagobert I. As she grew up she learned perfectly to despise the world, and earnestly desired to renounce it. Not daring to tell this to her parents, she first consulted St. Ouen, by whom she was encouraged in her resolution. The Saint's parents were then made acquainted with her desire, which God inclined them not to oppose. They conducted her to Jouarre, a great monastery in Brie, four leagues from Meaux, where she was received with great joy and trained up in the strictest practice of monastic perfection. By her perfect submission to all her sisters she seemed every one's servant, and acquitted herself with such great charity and edification that she was chosen prioress to assist the abbess in her administration. About the year 646 she was appointed first abbess of the abbey of Chelles, which she governed for forty-six years with equal vigor and discretion, until she closed her penitential life in 692.

Reflection.—It is written that the Saints raise themselves heavenward, going from virtue to virtue, as by steps.

November 6.—ST. LEONARD.

LEONARD, one of the chief personages of the court of Clovis, and for whom this monarch had stood as sponsor in baptism, was so moved by the discourse and example of St. Remigius that he relinquished the world in order to lead a more perfect life. The Bishop of Rheims having trained Leonard to virtue, he became the apostle of such of the Franks as still remained pagans; but fearing that he might be summoned to the court by his reputation for sanctity, he withdrew secretly to the monastery of Micy, near Orleans, and afterwards to the solitude of Noblac near Limoges. His charity not allowing him to remain inactive while there was so much good to be done, he undertook the work of comforting prisoners, making them understand that the captivity of sin was more terrible than any mere bodily constraint. He won over a great many of these unfortunate persons, which gained for him many disciples, in whose behalf he founded a new monastery. St. Leonard died about the year 550.

Reflection.—" The wicked shall be taken with his own iniquities, and shall be held by the cords of his own sin."

November 7.—ST. WILLIBRORD.

WILLIBRORD was born in Northumberland in 657, and when twenty years old went to Ireland, to study under St. Egbert; twelve years later, he felt drawn to convert the great pagan tribes who were hanging as a cloud over the north of Europe. He went to Rome for the blessing of the Pope, and with eleven companions reached Utrecht. The pagans would not accept the religion of their enemies, the Franks; and St. Willibrord could only labor in the track of Pepin Heristal, converting the tribes whom Pepin subjugated. At Pepin's urgent request, he again went to Rome, and was consecrated Archbishop of Utrecht. He was stately and comely in person, frank and joyous, wise in counsel, pleasant in speech, in every work of God strenuous and unwearied. Multitudes were converted, and the Saint built churches and appointed priests all over the land. He wrought many miracles, and had the gift of prophecy. He labored unceasingly as bishop for more than fifty years, beloved alike of God and of man, and died full of days and good works.

Reflection.—True zeal has its root in the love of God. It can never be idle; it must labor, toil, be doing great things. It glows as fire; it is, like fire, insatiable. See if this spirit be in you!

November 8.—THE FEAST OF THE HOLY RELICS.

PROTESTANTISM pretends to regard the veneration which the Church pays to the relics of the Saints as a sin, and contends that this pious practice is a remnant of paganism. The Council of Trent, on the contrary, has decided that the bodies of the martyrs and other Saints, who were living members of Jesus Christ and temples of the Holy Ghost, are to be honored by the faithful. This decision was based upon the established usage of the earliest days of the Church, and upon the teaching of the Fathers and of the Councils. The Council orders, however, that all abuse of this devotion is to be avoided carefully, and forbids any relics to be exposed which have not been approved by the bishops, and these prelates are recommended to instruct the people faithfully in the teaching of the Church on this subject. While we regret, then, the errors of the impious and of heretics, let us profit by the advantages which we gain by hearkening to the voice of the Church.

November 9.—ST. THEODORE TYRO, Martyr.

S T. THEODORE was born of a noble family in the East, and enrolled while still a youth in the imperial army. Early in 306 the emperor put forth an edict requiring all Christians to offer sacrifice, and Theodore had just joined the legion and marched with them into Pontus, when he had to choose between apostasy and death. He declared before his commander that he was ready to be cut in pieces and offer up every limb to his Creator, Who had died for him. Wishing to conquer him by gentleness, the commander left him in peace for a while, that he might think over his resolution; but Theodore used his freedom to set on fire the great temple of Isis, and made no secret of this act. Still his judge entreated him to renounce his faith and save his life; but Theodore made the sign of the cross, and answered: " As long as I have breath, I will confess the name of Christ." After cruel torture, the judge bade him think of the shame to which Christ had brought him. " This shame," Theodore answered, " I and all who invoke His name take with joy." He was condemned to be burnt. As the flame rose, a Christian saw his soul rise like a flash of light to heaven.

Reflection.—We are enlisted in the same service as the holy martyrs, and we too must have courage and constancy if we would be perfect soldiers of Jesus Christ. Let us take our part with them in confessing the faith of Christ and despising the world, that we may have our part with them in Christ's kingdom.

November 10.—ST. ANDREW AVELLINO.

A FTER a holy youth, Lancelot Avellino was ordained priest at Naples. At the age of thirty-six he entered the Theatine Order, and took the name of Andrew, to show his love for the cross. For fifty years he was afflicted with a most painful rupture; yet he would never use a carriage. Once when he was carrying the Viaticum, and a storm had extinguished the lamps, a heavenly light encircled him, guided his steps, and sheltered him from the rain. But as a rule, his sufferings were unrelieved by God or man. On the last day of his life, St. Andrew rose to say Mass. He was in his eighty-ninth year, and so weak that he could scarcely reach the altar. He began the " Judica," and fell forward in a fit of apoplexy. Laid on a straw mattress, his whole frame was convulsed in agony, while the fiend in visible form advanced to seize his soul. Then, as his brethren prayed and wept, the voice of Mary was heard, bidding the Saint's guardian angel send the tempter back to hell. A calm and holy smile settled on the features of the dying Saint, as, with a grateful salutation to the image of Mary, he breathed forth his soul to God. His death happened on the 10th of November, 1608.

Reflection.—St. Andrew, who suffered so terrible an agony, is the special patron against sudden death. Ask him to be with you in your last hour, and to bring Jesus and Mary to your aid.

November 11.—ST. MARTIN OF TOURS.

HEN a mere boy, Martin became a Christian catechumen against his parents' wish; and at fifteen was therefore seized by his father, a pagan soldier, and enrolled in the army. One winter's day, when stationed at Amiens, he met a beggar almost naked and frozen with cold. Having no money, he cut his cloak in two and gave him the half. That night he saw Our Lord clothed in the half cloak, and heard Him say to the angels: " Martin, yet a catechumen, hath wrapped Me in this garment." This decided him to be baptized, and shortly after he left the army. He succeeded in converting his mother; but, being driven from his home by the Arians, he took shelter with St. Hilary, and founded near Poitiers the first monastery in France. In 372 he was made Bishop of Tours. His flock, though Christian in name, was still pagan in heart. Unarmed and attended only by his monks, Martin destroyed the heathen temples and groves, and completed by his preaching and miracles the conversion of the people, whence he is known as the Apostle of Gaul. His last eleven years were spent in humble toil to atone for his faults, while God made manifest by miracles the purity of his soul.

Reflection.—It was for Christ crucified that St. Martin worked. Are you working for the same Lord?

November 12.—ST. MARTIN, Pope.

ST. MARTIN, who occupied the Roman See from A. D. 649 to 655, incurred the enmity of the Byzantine court by his energetic opposition to the Monothelite heresy, and the Exarch Olympius went so far as to endeavor to procure the assassination of the Pope as he stood at the altar in the Church of St. Mary Major; but the would-be murderer was miraculously struck blind, and his master refused to have any further hand in the matter. His successor had no such scruples: he seized Martin, and conveyed him on board a vessel bound for Constantinople. After a three months' voyage the island of Naxos was reached, where the Pope was kept in confinement for a year, and finally in 654 brought in chains to the imperial city. He was then banished to the Tauric Chersonese, where he lingered on for four months, in sickness and starvation, till God released him by death on the 12th of November, 655.

Reflection.—There have been times in the history of Christianity when its truths have seemed on the verge of extinction. But there is one Church whose testimony has never failed: it is the Church of St. Peter, the Apostolic and Roman See. Put your whole trust in her teaching!

November 13.—ST. STANISLAS KOSTKA.

ST. STANISLAS was of a noble Polish family. At the age of fourteen he went with his elder brother Paul to the Jesuits' College at Vienna; and though Stanislas was ever bright and sweet-tempered, his austerities were felt as a reproach by Paul, who shamefully maltreated him. This ill-usage and his own penances brought on a dangerous illness, and, being in a Lutheran house, he was unable to send for a priest. He now remembered to have read of his patroness, St. Barbara, that she never permitted her clients to die without the Holy Viaticum: he devoutly appealed to her aid, and she appeared with two angels, who gave him the Sacred Host. He was cured of this illness by Our Lady herself, and was bidden by her to enter the Society of Jesus. To avoid his father's opposition, he was obliged to fly from Vienna; and, having proved his constancy by cheerfully performing the most menial offices, he was admitted to the novitiate at Rome. There he lived for ten short months marked by a rare piety, obedience, and devotion to his institute. He died, as he had prayed to die, on the feast of the Assumption, 1568, at the age of seventeen.

Reflection.—St. Stanislas teaches us in every trial of life, and above all in the hour of death, to have recourse to our patron Saint, and to trust without fear to his aid.

November 14.—ST. DIDACUS.

ST. DIDACUS was born in Spain, in the middle of the fifteenth century. He was remarkable from childhood for his love of solitude, and when a youth retired and led a hermit life, occupying himself with weaving mats, like the fathers of the desert. Aiming at still higher perfection, he entered the Order of St. Francis. His want of learning and his humility would not allow him to aspire to the priesthood, and he remained a lay-brother till his death, perfect in his close observance of the vows of poverty, chastity, and obedience, and mortifying his will and his senses in every way that he could contrive. At one time he was sent by his superiors to the Canary Islands, whither he went joyfully, hoping to win the crown of martyrdom. Such, however, was not God's will, and after making many conversions by his example and holy words, he was recalled to Spain. There, after a long and painful illness, he finished his days, embracing the cross, which he had so dearly loved through his life. He died with the words of the hymn "Dulce lignum" on his lips.

Reflection.—If God be in your heart, He will be also on your lips; for Christ has said, " From the abundance of the heart the mouth speaketh."

ST. LAURENCE O'TOOLE, Archbishop of Dublin.

ST. LAURENCE, it appears, was born about the year 1125. When only ten years old, his father delivered him up as a hostage to Dermod Mac Murchad, King of Leinster, who treated the child with great inhumanity, until his father obliged the tyrant to put him in the hands of the Bishop of Glendalough, in the county of Wicklow. The holy youth, by his fidelity in corresponding with the divine grace, grew to be a model of virtues. On the death of the bishop, who was also abbot of the monastery, St. Laurence was chosen abbot in 1150, though but twenty-five years old, and governed his numerous community with wonderful virtue and prudence. In 1161 St. Laurence was unanimously chosen to fill the new metropolitan See of Dublin. About the year 1171 he was obliged, for the affairs of his diocese, to go over to England to see the king, Henry II., who was then at Canterbury. The Saint was received by the Benedictine monks of Christ Church with the greatest honor and respect. On the following day, as the holy archbishop was advancing to the altar to officiate, a maniac, who had heard much of his sanctity, and who was led on by the idea of making so holy a man another St. Thomas, struck him a violent blow on the head. All present concluded that he was mortally wounded; but the Saint coming to himself, asked for some water, blessed it, and having his wound washed with it, the blood was immediately stanched, and the archbishop celebrated Mass. In 1175 Henry II. of England became offended with Roderic, the monarch of Ireland, and St. Laurence undertook another journey to England to negotiate a reconciliation between them. Henry was so moved by his piety, charity, and prudence that he granted him everything he asked, and left the whole negotiation to his discretion. Our Saint ended his journey here below on the 14th of November, 1180, and was buried in the church of the abbey at Eu, on the confines of Normandy.

November 15.—ST. GERTRUDE, Abbess.

GERTRUDE was born in the year 1263, of a noble Saxon family, and placed at the age of five for education in the Benedictine abbey of Rodelsdorf. Her strong mind was carefully cultivated, and she wrote Latin with unusual elegance and force; above all, she was perfect in humility and mortification, in obedience, and in all monastic observances. Her life was crowded with wonders. She has in obedience recorded some of her visions, in which she traces in words of indescribable beauty the intimate converse of her soul with Jesus and Mary. She was gentle to all, most gentle to sinners; filled with devotion to the Saints of God, to the souls in purgatory, and above all to the Passion of Our Lord and to His Sacred Heart. She ruled her abbey with perfect wisdom and love for forty years. Her life was one of great and almost continual suffering, and her longing to be with Jesus was not granted till 1334, when she had reached her seventy-second year.

Reflection.—No preparation for death can be better than to offer and resign ourselves anew to the Divine Will — humbly, lovingly, with unbounded confidence in the infinite mercy and goodness of God.

November 16.—ST. EDMUND OF CANTERBURY.

ST. EDMUND left his home at Abingdon, a boy of twelve years old, to study at Oxford, and there protected himself against many grievous temptations by a vow of chastity, and by espousing himself to Mary for life. He was soon called to active public life, and as treasurer of the diocese of Salisbury showed such charity to the poor that the dean said he was rather the treasure than the treasurer of their church. In 1234 he was raised to the see of Canterbury, where he fearlessly defended the rights of Church and State against the avarice and greed of Henry III.; but finding himself unable to force that monarch to relinquish the livings which he kept vacant for the benefit of the royal coffers, Edmund retired into exile sooner than appear to connive at so foul a wrong. After two years spent in solitude and prayer, he went to his reward, and the miracles wrought at his tomb at Pontigny were so numerous that he was canonized in 1246, within four years of his death.

Reflection.—The Saints were tempted even more than ourselves; but they stood where we fall, because they trusted to Mary, and not to themselves.

November 17.—ST. GREGORY THAUMATURGUS.

ST. Gregory was born in Pontus, of heathen parents. In Palestine, about the year 231, he studied philosophy under the great Origen, who led him from the pursuit of human wisdom to Christ, Who is the Wisdom of God. Not long after, he was made Bishop of Neo Cæsarea in his own country. As he lay awake one night an old man entered his room, and pointed to a lady of superhuman beauty, and radiant with heavenly light. This old man was St. John the Evangelist, and the lady told him to give Gregory the instruction he desired. Thereupon he gave St. Gregory a creed which contained in all its fulness the doctrine of the Trinity. St. Gregory set it in writing, directed all his preaching by it, and handed it down to his successors. Strong in this faith, he subdued demons; he foretold the future. At his word a rock moved from its place, a river changed its course, a lake was dried up. He converted his diocese, and strengthened those under persecution. He struck down a rising heresy; and, when he was gone, this creed preserved his flock from the Arian pest. St. Gregory died in the year 270.

Reflection.—Devotion to the blessed Mother of God is the sure protection of faith in her Divine Son. Every time that we invoke her, we renew our faith in the Incarnate God; we reverse the sin and unbelief of our first parents; we take our part with her who was blessed because she believed.

November 18.—ST. ODO OF CLUNY.

ON Christmas-eve, 877, a noble of Aquitaine implored Our Lady to grant him a son. His prayer was heard; Odo was born, and his grateful father offered him to St. Martin. Odo grew in wisdom and in virtue, and his father longed to see him shine at court. But the attraction of grace was too strong. Odo's heart was sad and his health failed, until he forsook the world and sought refuge under the shadow of St. Martin at Tours. Later on he took the habit of St. Benedict at Baume, and was compelled to become abbot of the great abbey of Cluny, which was then building. He ruled it with the hand of a master and the winningness of a Saint. The Pope sent for him often to act as peacemaker between contending princes, and it was on one of those missions of mercy that he was taken ill at Rome. At his urgent entreaty he was borne back to Tours, where he died at the feet of " his own St. Martin," in 942.

Reflection.—" It needs only," says Father Newman, " for a Catholic to show devotion to any Saint, in order to receive special benefits from his intercession."

November 19.—ST. ELIZABETH OF HUNGARY.

ELIZABETH was daughter of a king of Hungary, and niece of St. Hedwige. She was betrothed in infancy to Louis, Landgrave of Thuringia, and brought up in his father's court. Not content with receiving daily numbers of poor in her palace, and relieving all in distress, she built several hospitals, where she served the sick, dressing the most repulsive sores with her own hands. Once as she was carrying in the folds of her mantle some provisions for the poor, she met her husband returning from the chase. Astonished to see her bending under the weight of her burden, he opened the mantle which she kept pressed against her, and found in it nothing but beautiful red and white roses, although it was not the season for flowers. Bidding her pursue her way, he took one of the marvellous

roses, and kept it all his life.   On her husband's death she
was cruelly driven from her palace, and forced to wander
through the streets with her little children, a prey to hunger and cold; but she welcomed all her sufferings, and
continued to be the mother of the poor, converting many
by her holy life.   She died in 1231, at the age of twenty-
four.

Reflection.—This young and delicate princess made herself the servant and nurse of the poor.   Let her example
teach us to disregard the opinions of the world and to overcome our natural repugnances, in order to serve Christ in
the persons of His poor.

November 20.—ST. FELIX OF VALOIS.

ST. FELIX was son of the Count of Valois.   His mother
throughout his youth did all she could to cultivate
in him a spirit of charity.   The unjust divorce between his
parents matured a long-formed resolution of leaving the
world; and, confiding his mother to her pious brother,
Thibault, Count of Champagne, he took the Cistercian
habit at Clairvaux.   His rare virtues drew on him such
admiration that, with St. Bernard's consent, he fled to
Italy, where he led an austere life with an aged hermit.
At this time he was ordained priest, and his old counsellor
having died, he returned to France, and for many years
lived as a solitary at Cerfroid.   Here God inspired him
with the desire of founding an Order for the redemption of
Christian captives, and moved St. John of Matha, then a
youth, to conceive a similar wish.   Together they drew up
the rules of the Order of the Holy Trinity.   Many disciples
gathered round them; and, seeing that the time had come
for further action, the two Saints made a pilgrimage to
Rome to obtain the confirmation of the Order from Innocent III.   Their prayer was granted, and the last fifteen
years of Felix's long life were spent in organizing and de-
veloping his rapidly increasing foundations.   He died in
1213.

Reflection.—" Think how much," says St. John Chrysostom, " and how often thy mouth has sinned, and thou

wilt devote thyself entirely to the conversion of sinners. For by this one means thou wilt blot out all thy sins, in that thy mouth will become the mouth of God."

November 21.—THE PRESENTATION OF THE BLESSED VIRGIN MARY.

RELIGIOUS parents never fail by devout prayer to consecrate their children to the divine service and love, both before and after their birth. Some amongst the Jews, not content with this general consecration of their children, offered them to God in their infancy, by the hands of the priests in the Temple, to be lodged in apartments belonging to the Temple, and brought up in attending the priests and Levites in the sacred ministry. It is an ancient tradition that the Blessed Virgin Mary was thus solemnly offered to God in the Temple in her infancy. This festival of the Presentation of the Blessed Virgin the Church celebrates this day. The tender soul of Mary was then adorned with the most precious graces, an object of astonishment and praise to the angels, and of the highest complacence to the adorable Trinity; the Father looking upon her as His beloved daughter, the Son as one chosen and prepared to become His mother, and the Holy Ghost as His darling spouse. Mary was the first who set up the standard of virginity; and, by consecrating it by a perpetual vow to Our Lord, she opened the way to all virgins who have since followed her example.

Reflection.—Mary's first presentation to God was an offering most acceptable in His sight. Let our consecration of ourselves to God be made under her patronage, and assisted by her powerful intercession and the union of her merits.

November 22.—ST. CECILIA, Virgin, Martyr.

IN the evening of her wedding-day, with the music of the marriage-hymn ringing in her ears, Cecilia, a rich, beautiful, and noble Roman maiden, renewed the vow by which she had consecrated her virginity to God. " Pure be my heart and undefiled my flesh; for I have a spouse you know not of — an angel of my Lord." The heart of her young husband Valerian was moved by her words; he received Baptism, and within a few days he and his brother Tiburtius, who had been brought by him to a knowledge of the Faith, sealed their confession with their blood. Cecilia only remained. " Do you not know," was her answer to the threats of the prefect, " that I am the bride of my Lord Jesus Christ?" The death appointed for her was suffocation, and she remained a day and a night in a hot-air bath, heated seven times its wont. But " the flames had no power over her body, neither was a hair of her head singed." The lictor sent to dispatch her struck with trembling hand the three blows which the law allowed, and left her still alive. For two days and nights Cecilia lay with her head half severed on the pavement of her bath, fully sensible, and joyfully awaiting her crown; on the third the agony was over, and in 177 the virgin Saint gave back her pure spirit to Christ.

Reflection.—St. Cecilia teaches us to rejoice in every sacrifice as a pledge of our love of Christ, and to welcome sufferings and death as hastening our union with Him.

November 23.—ST. CLEMENT OF ROME

S͏T. Clement is said to have been a convert of noble birth, and to have been consecrated bishop by St. Peter himself. With the words of the apostles still ringing in his ears, he began to rule the Church of God; and thus he was among the first, as he was among the most illustrious, in the long line of those who have held the place and power of Peter. He lived at the same time and in the same city with Domitian, the persecutor of the Church; and besides external foes he had to contend with schism and rebellion from within. The Corinthian Church was torn by intestine strife, and its members set the authority of their clergy at defiance. It was then that St. Clement interfered in the plenitude of his apostolic authority, and sent his famous epistle to the Corinthians. He urged the duties of charity, and above all of submission to the clergy.

He did not speak in vain; peace and order were restored. St. Clement had done his work on earth, and shortly after sealed with his blood the Faith which he had learned from Peter and taught to the nations.

Reflection.—God rewards a simple spirit of submission to the clergy, for the honor done to them is done to Him. Your virtue is unreal, your faith in danger, if you fail in this.

November 24.—ST. JOHN OF THE CROSS.

THE father of St. John was discarded by his kindred for marrying a poor orphan, and the Saint, thus born and nurtured in poverty, chose it also for his portion. Unable to learn a trade, be became the servant of the poor in the hospital of Medina, while still pursuing his sacred studies. In 1563, being then twenty-one, he humbly offered himself as a lay-brother to the Carmelite friars, who, however, knowing his talents, had him ordained priest. He would now have exchanged to the severe Carthusian Order, had not St. Teresa, with the instinct of a Saint, persuaded him to remain and help her in the reform of his own Order. Thus he became the first prior of the Barefooted Carmelites. His reform, though approved by the general, was rejected by the elder friars, who condemned the Saint as a fugitive and apostate, and cast him into prison, whence he only escaped, after nine months' suffering, at the risk of his life. Twice again, before his death, he was shamefully persecuted by his brethren, and publicly disgraced. But his complete abandonment by creatures only deepened his interior peace and devout longing for heaven.

Reflection.—" Live in the world," said St. John, " as if God and your soul only were in it; so shall your heart be never made captive by any earthly thing."

November 25.—ST. CATHERINE OF ALEX-
ANDRIA.

CATHERINE was a noble virgin of Alexandria. Before her Baptism, it is said, she saw in vision the Blessed Virgin ask her Son to receive her among His servants, but the Divine Infant turned away. After Baptism, Catherine saw the same vision, when Jesus Christ received her with great affection, and espoused her before the court of heaven. When the impious tyrant Maximin II. came to Alexandria, fascinated by the wisdom, beauty and wealth of the Saint, he in vain urged his suit. At last in his rage and disappointment he ordered her to be stripped and scourged. She fled to the Arabian mountains, where the soldiers overtook her, and after many torments put her to death. Her body was laid on Mount Sinai, and a beautiful legend relates that Catherine having prayed that no man might see or touch her body after death, angels bore it to the grave.

Reflection.—The constancy displayed by the Saints in their glorious martyrdom cannot be isolated from their previous lives, but is their natural sequence. If we wish to emulate their perseverance, let us first imitate their fidelity to grace.

November 26.—ST. PETER OF ALEXANDRIA,
Bishop, Martyr.

ST. PETER governed the Church of Alexandria during the persecution of Diocletian. The sentence of excommunication that he was the first to pronounce against the schismatics, Melitius and Arius, and which, despite the united efforts of powerful partisans, he strenuously upheld, proves that he possessed as much sagacity as zeal and firmness. But his most constant care was employed in guarding his flocks from the dangers arising out of persecution. He never ceased repeating to them that, in order not to fear death, it was needful to begin by dying to self, renouncing our will, and detaching ourselves from all things.

St. Peter gave an example of such detachment by under-going martyrdom in the year 311.

Reflection.—" How hardly shall they that have riches enter into the kingdom of God!" says Our Saviour; because they are bound to earth by the strong ties of their riches.

November 27.—ST. MAXIMUS, Bishop.

S T. MAXIMUS, abbot of Lerins, in succession to St. Honoratus, was remarkable not only for the spirit of recollection, fervor, and piety familiar to him from very childhood, but still more for the gentleness and kindliness with which he governed the monastery which at that time contained many religious, and was famous for the learning and piety of its brethren. Exhibiting in his own person an example of the most sterling virtues, his exhortations could not fail to prove all-persuasive: loving all his religious, whom it was his delight to consider as one family, he established amongst them that sweet concord, union, and holy emulation for well-doing which render the exercise of authority needless, and makes submission a pleasure. The clergy and people of Frejus, moved by such a shining example, elected Maximus for their bishop, but he took to flight; subsequently he was compelled, however, to accept the see of Riez, where he practised virtue in all gentleness, and died in 460, regretted as the best of fathers.

Reflection.—" Masters, do to your servants that which is just and equal, knowing that you also have a Master in heaven."

November 28.—ST. JAMES OF LA MARCA OF ANCONA.

T HE small town of Montbrandon, in the Marca of Ancona, gave birth to this Saint. When young he was sent to the University of Perugia, where his progress in learning soon qualified him to be chosen preceptor to a young gentleman of Florence. Fearing that he might be ingulfed in the whirlpool of world excesses, St. James applied himself to prayer and recollection. When travelling near Assisium he went into the great Church of the Portiuncula to pray, and being animated by the fervor of the holy men who there served God, and by the example of their blessed founder St. Francis, he determined to petition in that very place for the habit of the Order. He began his spiritual war against the devil, the world, and the flesh, with assiduous prayer and extraordinary fasts and watchings. For forty years he never passed a day without taking the discipline. Being chosen Archbishop of Milan, he fled, and could not be prevailed on to accept the office. He wrought several miracles at Venice and at other places, and raised from dangerous sicknesses the Duke of Calabria and the King of Naples. The Saint died in the convent of the Holy Trinity of his Order, near Naples, on the 28th of November, in the year 1476, being ninety years old, seventy of which he had spent in a religious state.

November 29.—ST. SATURNINUS, Martyr.

SATURNINUS went from Rome, by direction of Pope Fabian, about the year 245, to preach the faith in Gaul. He fixed his episcopal see at Toulouse, and thus became the first Christian bishop of that city. There were but few Christians in the place. However, their number grew fast after the coming of the Saint; and his power was felt by the spirits of evil, who received the worship of the heathen. His power was felt the more because he had to pass daily through the capitol, the high place of the heathen worship, on the way to his own church. One day a great multitude was gathered by an altar, where a bull stood ready for the sacrifice. A man in the crowd pointed out Saturninus, who was passing by, and the people would have forced him to idolatry; but the holy bishop answered: " I know but one God, and to Him I will offer the sacrifice of praise. How can I fear gods who, as you say, are afraid of me? " On this he was fastened to the bull, which was driven down the capitol. The brains of the Saint were scattered on the steps. His mangled body was taken up and buried by two devout women.

Reflection.—When beset by the temptations of the devil, let us call upon the Saints, who reign with Christ. They were powerful during their lives against the devil and his angels. They are more powerful now that they have passed from the Church on earth to the Church triumphant.

November 30.—ST. ANDREW, Apostle.

S T. ANDREW was one of the fishermen of Bethsaida, and brother, perhaps elder brother, of St. Peter, and became a disciple of St. John Baptist. He seemed always eager to bring others into notice; when called himself by Christ on the banks of the Jordan, his first thought was to go in search of his brother, and he said, " We have found the Messias," and he brought him to Jesus. It was he again who, when Christ wished to feed the five thousand in the desert, pointed out the little lad with the five loaves and fishes. St. Andrew went forth upon his mission to plant the Faith in Scythia and Greece, and at the end of years of toil to win a martyr's crown. After suffering a cruel scourging at Patræ in Achaia, he was left, bound by cords, to die upon a cross. When St. Andrew first caught sight of the gibbet on which he was to die, he greeted the precious wood with joy. " O good cross! " he cried, " made beautiful by the limbs of Christ, so long desired, now so happily found! Receive me into thy arms and present me to my Master, that He Who redeemed me through thee may now accept me from thee." Two whole days the martyr remained hanging on this cross alive, preaching, with outstretched arms from this chair of truth, to all who came near, and entreating them not to hinder his passion.

Reflection.—If we would do good to others, we must, like St. Andrew, keep close to the cross.

December 1.—ST. ELIGIUS.

ELIGIUS, a goldsmith at Paris, was commissioned by King Clotaire to make a throne. With the gold and precious stones given him he made two. Struck by his rare honesty, the king gave him an appointment at court, and demanded an oath of fidelity sworn upon holy relics; but Eligius prayed with tears to be excused, for fear of failing in reverence to the relics of the Saints. On entering the court he fortified himself against its seductions by many austerities and continual ejaculatory prayers. He had a marvellous zeal for the redemption of captives, and for their deliverance would sell his jewels, his food, his clothes, and his very shoes, once by his prayers breaking their chains and opening their prisons. His great delight was in making rich shrines for relics. His striking virtue caused him, a layman and a goldsmith, to be made Bishop of Noyon, and his sanctity in this holy office was remarkable. He possessed the gifts of miracles and prophecy, and died in 665.

Reflection.—When God called His Saints to Himself, He might, had He so pleased, have taken their bodies also; but He willed to leave them in our charge, for our help and consolation. Be careful to imitate St. Eligius in making a good use of so great a treasure.

December 2.—ST. BIBIANA, Virgin, Martyr.

ST. BIBIANA was a native of Rome. Flavian, her father, was apprehended, burned in the face with a hot iron, and banished to Acquapendente, where he died of his wounds a few days after; and her mother, Dafrosa, was some time after beheaded. Bibiana and her sister Demetria, after the death of their parents, were stripped of all they had in the world and suffered much from poverty. Apronianus, Governor of Rome, summoned them to appear before him. Demetria, having made confession of her faith, fell down and expired at the foot of the tribunal, in the presence of the judge. Apronianus gave orders that

Bibiana should be put into the hands of a wicked woman named Rufina, who was to bring her to another way of thinking; but Bibiana, making prayer her shield, remained invincible. Apronianus, enraged at the courage and perseverance of a tender virgin, ordered her to be tied to a pillar and whipped with scourges loaded with leaden plummets till she expired. The Saint underwent this punishment cheerfully, and died in the hands of the executioners.

Reflection.—Pray for a fidelity and patience like Bibiana's under all trials, that neither convenience nor any worldly advantage may ever prevail upon you to transgress your duty.

December 3.—ST. FRANCIS XAVIER.

A YOUNG Spanish gentleman, in the dangerous days of the Reformation, was making a name for himself as a Professor of Philosophy in the University of Paris, and had seemingly no higher aim, when St. Ignatius of Loyola won him to heavenly thoughts. After a brief apostolate amongst his countrymen in Rome he was sent by St. Ignatius to the Indies, where for twelve years he was to wear himself out, bearing the Gospel to Hindostan, to Malacca, and to Japan. Thwarted by the jealousy, covetousness, and carelessness of those who should have helped and encouraged him, neither their opposition nor the difficulties of every sort which he encountered could make him slacken his labors for souls. The vast kingdom of China appealed to his charity, and he was resolved to risk his life to force an entry, when God took him to Himself, and on the 2d of December, 1552, he died, like Moses, in sight of the land of promise.

Reflection.—Some are specially called to work for souls; but there is no one who cannot help much in their salvation. Holy example, earnest intercession, the offerings of our actions in their behalf — all this needs only the spirit which animated St. Francis Xavier, the desire to make some return to God.

December 4.—ST. BARBARA, Virgin, Martyr.

Ⓢ T. Barbara was brought up a heathen. A tyrannical
father, Dioscorus, had kept her jealously secluded in
a lonely tower which he had built for the purpose. Here
in her forced solitude, she gave herself to prayer and study,
and contrived to receive instruction and Baptism by stealth
from a Christian priest. Dioscorus, on discovering his
daughter's conversion, was beside himself with rage. He
himself denounced her before the civil tribunal. Barbara
was horribly tortured, and at last was beheaded, her own
father, merciless to the last, acting as her executioner.
God, however, speedily punished her persecutors. While
her soul was being borne by angels to Paradise, a flash of
lightning struck Dioscorus, and he was hurried before the
judgment-seat of God.

Reflection.—Pray often against a sudden and unpro-
vided death; and, above all, that you may be strengthened
by the Holy Viaticum against the dangers of your last hour.

December 5.—ST. SABAS, Abbot.

Ⓢ T. Sabas, one of the most renowned patriarchs of the
monks of Palestine, was born in the year 439, near
Cæsarea. In order to settle a dispute which had arisen
between some of his relatives in regard to the administration of his estate, while still young he forsook the world
and entered a monastery, wherein he became a model of
fervor. When Sabas had been ten years in this monastery,
being eighteen years old, he went to Jerusalem to visit
the holy places, and attached himself to a monastery then
under control of St. Euthymius; but on the death of the
holy abbot our Saint sought the wilderness, where he chose
his dwelling in a cave on the top of a high mountain, at
the bottom of which ran the brook Cedron. After he had
lived here five years, several came to him, desiring to serve
God under his direction. He was at first unwilling to
consent, but finally founded a new monastery of persons
all desirous to devote themselves to praise and serve God

without interruption. His great sanctity becoming known, he was ordained priest, at the age of fifty-three, by the patriarch of Jerusalem, and made Superior-General of all the anchorites of Palestine. He lived to be ninety-four, and died on the 5th of December, 532.

December 6.—ST. NICHOLAS OF BARI.

S T. NICHOLAS, the patron Saint of Russia, was born toward the end of the third century. His uncle, the Archbishop of Myra in Lycia, ordained him priest, and appointed him abbot of a monastery; and on the death of the archbishop he was elected to the vacant see. Throughout his life he retained the bright and guileless manners of his early years, and showed himself the special protector of the innocent and the wronged. Nicholas once heard that a person who had fallen into poverty intended to abandon his three daughters to a life of sin. Determined, if possible, to save their innocence, the Saint went out by night, and, taking with him a bag of gold, flung it into the window of the sleeping father and hurried off. He, on awaking, deemed the gift a godsend, and with it dowered his eldest child. The Saint, overjoyed at his success, made like venture for the second daughter; but the third time as he stole away, the father, who was watching, overtook him and kissed his feet, saying: "Nicholas, why dost thou conceal thyself from me? Thou art my helper, and he who has delivered my soul and my daughters' from hell." St. Nicholas is usually represented by the side of a vessel, wherein a certain man had concealed the bodies of his three children whom he had killed, but who were restored to life by the Saint. He died in 342. His relics were translated in 1807, to Bari, Italy, and there, after fifteen centuries, "the manna of St. Nicholas" still flows from his bones and heals all kinds of sick.

Reflection.—Those who would enter heaven must be as little children, whose greatest glory is their innocence. Now, two things are ours to do: first, to preserve it in ourselves, or regain it by penance; secondly, to love and shield it in others.

December 7.—ST. AMBROSE, Bishop.

AMBROSE was of a noble family, and was governor of Milan in 374, when a bishop was to be chosen for that great see. As the Arian heretics were many and fierce, he was present to preserve order during the election. Though only a catechumen, it was the will of God that he should himself be chosen by acclamation; and, in spite of his utmost resistance, he was baptized and consecrated. He was unwearied in every duty of a pastor, full of sympathy and charity, gentle and condescending in things indifferent, but inflexible in matters of principle. He showed his fearless zeal in braving the anger of the Empress Justina, by resisting and foiling her impious attempt to give one of the churches of Milan to the Arians, and by rebuking and leading to penance the really great Emperor Theodosius, who in a moment of irritation had punished most cruelly a sedition of the inhabitants of Thessalonica. He was the friend and consoler of St. Monica in all her sorrows, and in 387 he had the joy of admitting to the Church her son, St. Augustine. St. Ambrose died in 397, full of years and of honors, and is revered by the Church of God as one of her greatest doctors.

Reflection.—Whence came to St. Ambrose his grandeur of mind, his clearness of insight, his intrepidity in maintaining the faith and discipline of the Church? Whence but from his contempt of the world, from his fearing God alone?

December 8.—THE FEAST OF THE IMMACU-LATE CONCEPTION.

ON this day, so dear to every Catholic heart, we celebrate, in the first place, the moment in which Almighty God showed Mary, through the distance of ages, to our first parents as the Virgin Mother of the divine Redeemer, the woman destined to crush the head of the serpent. And as by eternal decree she was miraculously exempt from all stain of original sin, and endowed with the richest treasures of grace and sanctity, it is meet that we should honor her glorious prerogatives by this special feast of the Immaculate Conception.   We should join in spirit with the blessed in heaven, and rejoice with our dear Mother, not only for her own sake, but for ours, her children, who are partakers of her glory and happiness. Secondly, we are called upon to celebrate that ever-memorable day, the 8th of December, 1854, which raised the Immaculate Conception of Our Blessed Lady from a pious belief to the dignity of a dogma of the Infallible Church, causing universal joy among the faithful.

Reflection.—Let us repeat frequently these words applied by the Church to the Blessed Virgin: " Thou art all fair, O Mary! and there is not a spot in thee " (Cant. iv. 7).

December 9.—ST. LEOCADIA, Virgin, Martyr.

S T. LEOCADIA was a native of Toledo, and was apprehended by an order of Dacian, the cruel governor under Diocletian in 304.   Hearing of the martyrdom of St. Eulalia, she prayed that God would not prolong her exile, but unite her speedily with her holy friend in His glory. Her prayer was heard, and she happily expired in prison. Three famous churches in Toledo bear her name, and she is honored as principal patroness of that city.   In one of those churches most of the councils of Toledo were held. Her relics were kept in that church with great respect, till, in the incursions of the Moors, they were conveyed to Oviedo, and some years afterward to the abbey of St. Guislain, near Mons in Hainault.   They were finally carried back to Toledo with great pomp, and placed in the great church there on the 26th of April, 1589.

Reflection.—Were we not blinded by the world and the enchantment of its follies, the near prospect of eternity, the uncertainty of the hour of our death, and the repeated precepts of Christ would produce in us the same fervent dispositions which they did in the primitive Christians.

December 10.—ST. EULALIA, Virgin, Martyr.

ST. Eulalia was a native of Merida, in Spain. She was but twelve years old when the bloody edicts of Diocletian were issued. Eulalia presented herself before the cruel judge Dacianus, and reproached him for attempting to destroy souls by compelling them to renounce the only true God. The governor commanded her to be seized, and at first tried to win her over by flattery, but failing in this, he had recourse to threats, and caused the most dreadful instruments of torture to be placed before her eyes, saying to her: "All this you shall escape if you will but touch a little salt and frankincense with the tip of your finger." Provoked at these seducing flatteries, our Saint threw down the idol, and trampled upon the cake which was laid for the sacrifice. At the judge's order, two executioners tore her tender sides with iron hooks, so as to leave the very bones bare. Next lighted torches were applied to her breasts and sides; under which torment, instead of groans, nothing was heard from her mouth but thanksgivings. The fire at length catching her hair, surrounded her head and face, and the Saint was stifled by the smoke and flame.

Reflection.—The apostles rejoiced " that they were accounted worthy to suffer reproach for the name of Jesus." Do we bear our crosses with the same spirit?

December 11.—ST. DAMASUS, Pope.

ST. Damasus was born at Rome at the beginning of the fourth century. He was archdeacon of the Roman Church in 355, when Pope Liberius was banished to Berda, and followed him into exile, but afterward returned to Rome. On the death of Liberius our Saint was chosen to succeed him. Ursinus, a competitor for the high office, incited a revolt, but the holy Pope took only such action as was becoming to the common father of the faithful. Having freed the Church of this new schism, he turned his attention to the extirpation of Arianism in the West and of Apollinarianism in the East, and for this purpose

he convened several councils.   He rebuilt the church of St.
Laurence, which to this day is known as St. Laurence *in
Damaso;* he made many valuable presents to this church,
and settled upon it houses and lands in its vicinity.   He
likewise drained all the springs of the Vatican, which ran
over the bodies that were buried there, and decorated the
sepulchres of a great number of martyrs in the cemeteries,
and adorned them with epitaphs in verse.   Having sat
eighteen years and two months, he died on the 10th of
December, in 384, being near fourscore years of age.

December 12.—ST. VALERY, Abbot.—ST. FINIAN, Bishop.

THIS Saint was born at Auvergne, in the sixth century,
and in his childhood kept his father's sheep.   He
was yet young when he took the monastic habit in the
neighboring monastery of St. Antony. Seeking the most
perfect means of advancing in the paths of all virtues, he
passed from this house to the more austere monastery of
St. Germanus of Auxerre, and finally to that of Luxeuil,
where he spent many years.   He travelled into Neustria,
where he converted many infidels, and assembled certain
fervent disciples, and laid the foundation of a monastery.
Saint Valery went to receive the recompense of his happy
perseverance on the 12th of December in 622.

St. FINIAN was a native of Leinster, was instructed in
the elements of Christian virtue by the disciples of St.
Patrick, and passed over into Wales; but about the year
520 he returned into Ireland.   To propagate the work of
God, our Saint established several monasteries and schools.
St. Finian was chosen and consecrated Bishop of Clonard.
In the love of his flock and his zeal for their salvation he
was infirm with the infirm, and wept with those that wept.
He healed the souls, and often also the bodies, of those
that applied to him.   He departed to Our Lord on the 12th
of December in 552.

December 13.—ST. LUCY, Virgin, Martyr.

THE mother of St. Lucy suffered four years from an issue of blood, and the help of man failed. St. Lucy reminded her mother that a woman in the Gospel had been healed of the same disorder. "St. Agatha," she said, "stands ever in the sight of Him for Whom she died. Only touch her sepulchre with faith, and you will be healed." They spent the night praying by the tomb, till, overcome by weariness, both fell asleep. St. Agatha appeared in vision to St. Lucy, and calling her sister, foretold her mother's recovery and her own martyrdom. That instant the cure was affected; and in her gratitude the mother allowed her daughter to distribute her wealth among the poor, and consecrate her virginity to Christ. A young man to whom she had been promised in marriage accused her as a Christian to the heathen; but Our Lord, by a special miracle, saved from outrage this virgin whom He had chosen for His own. The fire kindled around her did her no hurt. Then the sword was plunged into her heart, and the promise made at the tomb of St. Agatha was fulfilled.

Reflection.—The Saints had to bear sufferings and temptations greater far than yours. How did they overcome them? By the love of Christ. Nourish this pure love by meditating on the mysteries of Christ's life; and, above all, by devotion to the Holy Eucharist, which is the antidote against sin and the pledge of eternal life.

December 14.—ST. NICASIUS, Archbishop, and his Companions, Martyrs.

IN the fifth century an army of barbarians from Germany ravaging part of Gaul, plundered the city of Rheims. Nicasius, the holy bishop, had foretold this calamity to his flock. When he saw the enemy at the gates and in the streets, forgetting himself, and solicitous only for his spiritual children, he went from door to door encouraging all to patience and constancy, and awaking in every breast the most heroic sentiments of piety and religion. In endeavoring to save the lives of his flock he exposed himself to the swords of the infidels, who, after a thousand insults and indignities, cut off his head. Florens, his deacon, and Jocond, his lector, were massacred by his side. His sister Eutropia, a virtuous virgin, fearing she might be reserved for a fate worse than death, boldly cried out to the infidels that it was her unalterable resolution rather to sacrifice her life than her faith or her integrity and virtue. Upon which they despatched her with their cutlasses.

Reflection.—Bear patiently and sweetly bodily sufferings, and prepare for the day of trial by the courageous endurance of the daily crosses incident to your state.

December 15.—ST. MESMIN.

S T. MESMIN was a native of Verdun. The inhabitants of that place having proved disloyal to King Clovis, an uncle of our Saint's, a priest named Euspice, brought about a reconciliation between the monarch and his subjects. Clovis, appreciating the virtues of Euspice, persuaded him to take up his residence at court, and the servant of God took St. Mesmin along with him. While journeying to Orleans with Clovis he noticed at about two leagues from the city, beyond the Loire, a solitary spot called Micy, which he thought well suited for a retreat. Having asked for and obtained the place, he with Mesmin and several disciples built there a monastery, of which he took charge. At his death, which happened about two years after, our Saint was appointed abbot by Eusebius, Bishop of Orleans. During a terrible famine he fed nearly the whole city of Orleans with wheat from his monastery, without perceptibly reducing it; he also drove an enormous serpent out of the place in which he was afterwards buried. Having governed his monastery ten years, he died as he had lived, in the odor of sanctity, on the 15th of December, 520.

Reflection.—Few are called to serve God by great actions, but all are bound to strive after perfection in the ordinary actions of their daily life.

December 16.—ST. EUSEBIUS, Bishop.

ST. EUSEBIUS was born of a noble family, in the island of Sardinia, where his father is said to have died in prison for the Faith. The Saint's mother carried him and his sister, both infants, to Rome. Eusebius having been ordained, served the Church of Vercelli with such zeal that on the episcopal chair becoming vacant he was unanimously chosen, by both clergy and people, to fill it. The holy bishop saw that the best and first means to labor effectually for the edification and sanctification of his people was to have a zealous clergy. He was at the same time very careful to instruct his flock, and inspire them with the maxims of the Gospel. The force of the truth which he preached, together with his example, brought many sinners to a change of life. He courageously fought against the heretics, who had him banished to Scythopolis, and thence to Upper Thebais in Egypt, where he suffered so grievously as to win, in some of the panegyrics in his praise, the title of martyr. He died in the latter part of the year 371.

Reflection.—The routine of every-day, commonplace duties is no hindrance to a free intimacy with God. He will disclose His hidden ways to you in proportion as you follow your vocation faithfully, whether in the world or the cloister.

December 17.—ST. OLYMPIAS, Widow.

ST. OLYMPIAS, the glory of the widows in the Eastern Church, was of a noble and wealthy family. Left an orphan at a tender age, she was brought up by Theodosia, sister of St. Amphilochius, a virtuous and prudent woman. Olympias insensibly reflected the virtues of this estimable woman. She married quite young, but her husband dying within twenty days of their wedding, she modestly declined any further offer for her hand, and resolved to consecrate her life to prayer and other good works, and to devote her fortune to the poor. Nectarius, Archbishop of Constantinople, had a high esteem for the saintly widow, and made her a deaconess of his church, the duties of which were to prepare the altar linen and to attend to other matters of that sort. St. Chrysostom, who succeeded Nectarius, had no less respect than his predecessor for Olympias, but refused to attend to the distribution of her alms. Our Saint was one of the last to leave St. Chrysostom when he went into banishment on the 20th of June, 404. After his departure she suffered great persecution, and crowned a virtuous life by a saintly death, about the year 410.

Reflection.—" Lay not up to yourselves treasures on earth, but in heaven, where neither rust nor moth doth consume."

December 18.—ST. GATIAN, Bishop.

Ⓢ T. GATIAN came from Rome with St. Dionysius of Paris, about the middle of the third century, and preached the Faith principally at Tours in Gaul, where he fixed his episcopal see. The Gauls in that part were extremely addicted to the worship of their idols. But no contradictions or sufferings were able to discourage or daunt this true apostle, and by perseverance he gained several to Christ. He assembled his little flock in grots and caves, and there celebrated the divine mysteries. He was obliged often to lie hid in lurking holes a long time in order to escape a cruel death, with which the heathens frequently threatened him, and which he was always ready to receive with joy if he had fallen into their hands. Having continued his labors with unwearied zeal amidst frequent sufferings and dangers for near the space of fifty years, he died in peace, and was honored with miracles.

Reflection.—God does not ask great sacrifices from all; but in His goodness He gives us all some things to re-

nounce or to suffer for Him, and it is by our loving submission to His will that we show ourselves to be Christians.

December 19.—ST. NEMESION, Martyr.

IN the persecution of Decius, Nemesion, an Egyptian,
was apprehended at Alexandria upon an indictment
for theft.   The servant of Christ easily cleared himself of
that charge, but was immediately accused of being a Christian, and after being scourged and tormented more than
the thieves, was condemned to be burnt with the robbers
and other malefactors.   There stood at the same time near
the prefect's tribunal four soldiers and another person,
who, being Christians, boldly encouraged a confessor who
was hanging on the rack.   They were taken before the
judge, who condemned them to be beheaded, but was astonished to see the joy with which they walked to the place
of execution.   Heron, Ater, and Isidore, all Egyptians,
with Dioscorus, a youth only fifteen years old, were committed at Alexandria in the same persecution.   After en-
during the most cruel rending and disjointing of their
limbs, they were burnt alive, with the exception of Dioscorus, whom the judge discharged on account of the tenderness of his years.

Reflection.—Can we call to mind the fervor of the
Saints in laboring and suffering cheerfully for God, and
not feel a holy ardor glow in our own breasts, and our souls
strongly affected with their heroic sentiments of virtue?

December 20.—ST. PHILOGONIUS, Bishop.

ST. PHILOGONIUS was educated for the law, and appeared at the bar with great success.   He was admired for his eloquence, but still more for his integrity and
the sanctity of his life.   This was considered a sufficient
motive for dispensing with the canons, which require some
time spent among the clergy before a person be advanced
to the highest station in the Church.   Philogonius was
placed in the see of Antioch, upon the death of Vitalis in

318. When Arius broached his blasphemies at Alexandria
in 318, St. Alexander condemned him, and sent the sentence in a synodal letter to St. Philogonius, who strenuously defended the Catholic faith before the assembly of
the Council of Nice. In the storms which were raised
against the Church, first by Maximin II. and afterward by
Licinius, St. Philogonius deserved the title of Confessor;
he died in the year 322, the fifth of his episcopal dignity.

Reflection.—St. Philogonius had so perfectly renounced
the world, and crucified its inordinate desires in his heart,
that he received in this life the earnest of Christ's Spirit,
was admitted to the sacred council of the heavenly King,
and had free access to the Almighty. A soul must here
learn the heavenly spirit, and be well versed in the occupations of the blessed, that hopes to reign with them hereafter.

December 21.—ST. THOMAS, Apostle.

ST. THOMAS was one of the fishermen on the Lake of
Galilee whom Our Lord called to be His apostles.
By nature slow to believe, too apt to see difficulties, and to
look at the dark side of things, he had withal a most sym-
pathetic, loving, and courageous heart. Once when Jesus
spoke of the mansions in His Father's house, St. Thomas,
in his simplicity, asked: "Lord, we know not whither
Thou goest, and how can we know the way?" When Jesus
turned to go toward Bethany to the grave of Lazarus, the
desponding apostle at once feared the worst for his beloved
Lord, yet cried out bravely to the rest: "Let us also go
and die with Him." After the Resurrection, incredulity
again prevailed, and whilst the wounds of the crucifixion
were imprinted vividly on his affectionate mind, he would
not credit the report that Christ had indeed risen. But at
the actual sight of the pierced hands and side, and the
gentle rebuke of his Saviour, unbelief was gone forever;
and his faith and ours has ever triumphed in the joyous
utterance into which he broke: "My Lord and my God!"

Reflection.—Cast away all disquieting doubts, and learn
to triumph over old weaknesses as St. Thomas did, who

" by his ignorance hath instructed the ignorant, and by his incredulity hath served for the faith of all ages."

December 22.—ST. ISCHYRION, Martyr.

ISCHYRION was an inferior officer who attended on a magistrate of a certain city in Egypt. His master commanded him to offer sacrifice to the idols; and because he refused to commit that sacrilege, reproached him with the most abusive and threatening speeches. By giving way to passion and superstition, the officer at length worked himself up to such a degree of frenzy as to run a stake into the bowels of the meek servant of Christ, who, by his patient constancy, attained to the glory of martyrdom.

Reflection.—It is not a man's condition, but virtue, that can make him truly great or truly happy. How mean soever a person's station or circumstances may be, the road to both is open to him; and there is not a servant or slave who ought not to be enkindled with a laudable ambition of arriving at this greatness, which will set him on the same level with the rich and the most powerful.

December 23.—ST. SERVULUS.

SERVULUS was a beggar, and had been so afflicted with palsy from his infancy that he was never able to stand, sit upright, lift his hand to his mouth, or turn himself from one side to another. His mother and brother carried him into the porch of St. Clement's Church at Rome, where he lived on the alms of those that passed by. He used to entreat devout persons to read the Holy Scriptures to him, which he heard with such attention as to learn them by heart. His time he consecrated by assiduously singing hymns of praise and thanksgiving to God. After several years thus spent, his distemper having seized his vitals, he felt his end was drawing nigh. In his last moments he desired the poor and pilgrims, who had often shared in his charity, to sing sacred hymns and psalms for him. While he joined his voice with theirs, he on a sudden cried out: "Silence! do you not hear the sweet melody and praise which resound in the heavens?" Soon after he spoke these words he expired, and his soul was carried by angels into everlasting bliss, about the year 590.

Reflection.—The whole behaviour of this poor sick beggar loudly condemns those who, when blessed with good health and a plentiful fortune, neither do good works nor suffer the least cross with tolerable patience.

December 24.—ST. DELPHINUS, Bishop.—STS. THRASILLA and EMILIANA, Virgins.

LITTLE is known of St. Delphinus before his elevation to the episcopate. He assisted at the Council of Saragossa, in 330, in which the Priscillianists were condemned, and also at the Council of Bordeaux, which condemned the same schismatics. He baptized St. Paulerius in 388, and the latter, in several letters, speaks of him as his father and his master. St. Delphinus died on the 24th of December, 403.

STS. THRASILLA and EMILIANA were aunts of St. Gregory the Great. They lived in their father's house as retired as in a monastery, far removed from the conversation of men; and, exciting one another to virtue by discourse and example, soon made considerable progress in spiritual life. Thrasilla was favored one night with a vision of her uncle, St. Felix, Pope, who showed her a seat prepared for her in heaven, saying: "Come; I will receive you into this habitation of light." She fell sick of a fever the next day. When in her agony, with her eyes fixed on heaven, she cried out to those that were present: "Depart! make room! Jesus is coming." Soon after these words she breathed out her pious soul into the hands of God on the 24th of December. A few days after she appeared to her sister Emiliana, and invited her to celebrate with her the Epiphany in eternal bliss. Emiliana fell sick, and died on the 8th of January.

Reflection.—We may often think the austerities of the Saints are beyond our strength; let us, then, imitate the guard they kept over their tongue. This is within the reach of all.

December 25.—THE NATIVITY OF CHRIST, OR CHRISTMAS DAY.

THE world had subsisted about four thousand years when Jesus Christ, the eternal Son of God, having taken human flesh in the womb of the Virgin Mary, and being made man, was born of her, for the redemption of mankind, at Bethlehem of Judea.   Joseph and Mary had come up to Bethlehem to be enrolled, and, unable to find shelter elsewhere, they took refuge in a stable, and in this lowly place Jesus Christ was born.   The Blessed Virgin wrapped the divine Infant in swaddling-clothes, and laid Him in the manger.   While the sensual and the proud were asleep, an angel appeared to some poor shepherds. They were seized with great fear, but the heavenly messenger said to them: "Fear not: for behold I bring you good tidings of exceeding great joy, that shall be to all the people.   For this day is born to you a Saviour, Who is Christ the Lord, in the city of David.   And this shall be a sign to you: you shall find the Child wrapped in swaddling-clothes, and laid in a manger."   After the departure of the angel the wondering shepherds said to one another: "Let us go over to Bethlehem, and let us see the word that is come to pass, which the Lord hath shown to us." They immediately hastened thither, and found Mary and Joseph, and the Infant lying in the manger.   Bowing down they adored Him, and then returned to their flocks, glorifying and praising God.

Reflection.—Our Saviour sanctified our flesh by taking it on Himself, and with His last breath He commended us to the care of His Virgin Mother.   Day by day He still feeds us at the altar with the food of incorruption — His body and His blood.

December 26.—ST. STEPHEN, First Martyr.

THERE is good reason to believe that St. Stephen was one of the seventy-two disciples of our blessed Lord. After the Ascension he was chosen one of the seven deacons. The ministry of the seven was very fruitful; but Stephen especially, " full of grace and fortitude, did great wonders and signs among the people." Many adversaries rose up to dispute with him, but " they were not able to withstand the wisdom and the spirit that spoke." At length he was brought before the Sanhedrim, charged, like his divine Master, with blasphemy against Moses and against God. He boldly upbraided the chief priests with their hard-hearted resistance to the Holy Ghost and with the murder of the " Just One." They were stung with anger, and gnashed their teeth against him. But when, " filled with the Holy Ghost and looking up to heaven, he cried out, ' Behold, I see the heavens opened and the Son of man standing at the right hand of God,' they rushed upon him, and dragging him forth without the city, they stoned him to death."

Reflection.—If ever you are tempted to resentment, pray from your heart for him who has offended you.

December 27.—ST. JOHN, Evangelist.

ST. JOHN, the youngest of the apostles in age, was called to follow Christ on the banks of the Jordan during the first days of Our Lord's ministry. He was one of the privileged few present at the Transfiguration and the Agony in the garden. At the Last Supper his head rested on the bosom of Jesus, and in the hours of the Passion, when others fled or denied their Master, St. John kept his place by the side of Jesus, and at the last stood by the cross with Mary. From the cross the dying Saviour bequeathed His Mother to the care of the faithful apostle, who " from that hour took her to his own;" thus fitly, as St. Austin says, " to a virgin was the Virgin intrusted." After the Ascension, St. John lived first at Jerusalem, and

then at Ephesus. He was thrown by Domitian into a caldron of boiling oil, and is thus reckoned a martyr, though
miraculously preserved from hurt. Afterwards he was
banished to the isle of Patmos, where he received the
heavenly visions described in the Apocalypse. He died at
a great age, in peace, at Ephesus, in the year 100.

Reflection.—St. John is a living example of Our Lord's
saying, " Blessed are the clean of heart, for they shall see
God."

December 28.—THE HOLY INNOCENTS.

HEROD, who was reigning in Judea at the time of the
birth of Our Saviour, having heard that the Wise
Men had come from the East to Jerusalem in search of the
King of the Jews, was troubled. He called together the
chief priests, and learning that Christ was to be born in
Bethlehem, he told the Wise Men: " When you have found
Him, bring me word again, that I also may come and adore
Him." But God having warned them in a dream not to
return, they went back to their homes another way. St.
Joseph, too, was ordered in his sleep to " take the Child
and His Mother and fly into Egypt." When Herod found
that the Wise Men did not return, he was furious, and
ordered that every male child in Bethlehem and its vicinity
of the age of two and under should be slain. These innocent victims were the flowers and the first-fruits of His
martyrs, and triumphed over the world, without having
ever known it or experienced its dangers.

Reflection.—How few perhaps of these children, if
they had lived, would have escaped the dangers of the
world! What snares, what sins, what miseries were they
preserved from ! So we often lament as misfortunes many
accidents which in the designs of Heaven are the greatest
mercies.

December 29.—ST. THOMAS OF CANTERBURY.

S T. THOMAS, son of Gilbert Becket, was born in Southwark, England, in 1117. When a youth he was attached to the household of Theobald, Archbishop of Canterbury, who sent him to Paris and Bologna to study law. He became Archdeacon of Canterbury, then Lord High Chancellor of England; and in 1160, when Archbishop Theobald died, the king insisted on the consecration of St. Thomas in his stead. St. Thomas refused, warning the king that from that hour their friendship would be broken. In the end he yielded, and was consecrated. The conflict at once broke out; St. Thomas resisted the royal customs, which violated the liberties of the Church and the laws of the realm. After six years of contention, partly spent in exile, St. Thomas, with full foresight of martyrdom before him, returned as a good shepherd to his Church. On the 29th of December, 1170, just as vespers were beginning, four knights broke into the cathedral, crying: "Where is the archbishop? where is the traitor?" The monks fled, and St. Thomas might easily have escaped. But he advanced, saying: "Here I am — no traitor, but archbishop. What seek you?" "Your life," they cried. "Gladly do I give it," was the reply; and bowing his head, the invincible martyr was hacked and hewn till his soul went to God. Six months later Henry II. submitted to be publicly scourged at the Saint's shrine, and restored to the Church her full rights.

Reflection.—"Learn from St. Thomas," says Father Faber, "to fight the good fight even to the shedding of blood, or, to what men find harder, the shedding of their good name by pouring it out to waste on the earth."

December 30.—ST. SABINUS, Bishop, and his Companions, Martyrs.

T HE cruel edicts of Diocletian and Maximin against the Christians being published in the year 303, Sabinus, Bishop of Assisium, and several of his clergy, were apprehended and kept in custody till Venustianus, the Governor

of Etruria and Umbria, came thither. Upon his arrival in
that city he caused the hands of Sabinus, who had made a
glorious confession of his Faith before him, to be cut off;
and his two deacons, Marcellus and Exuperantius, to be
scourged, beaten with clubs, and torn with iron nails, under
which torments they both expired. Sabinus is said to
have cured a blind boy, and a weakness in the eyes of
Venustianus himself, who was thereupon converted, and
afterward beheaded for the Faith. Lucius, his successor,
commanded Sabinus to be beaten to death with clubs at
Spoleto. The martyr was buried a mile from that city,
but his relics have been since translated to Faënza.

Reflection.—How powerfully do the martyrs cry out to
us by their example, exhorting us to despise a false and
wicked world!

December 31.—ST. SYLVESTER, Pope.

SYLVESTER was born in Rome toward the close of the
third century. He was a young priest when the
persecution of the Christians broke out under the tyrant
Diocletian. Idols were erected at the corners of the streets,
in the market-places, and over the public fountains, so that
it was scarcely possible for a Christian to go abroad without
being put to the test of offering sacrifice, with the alterna-
tive of apostasy or death. During this fiery trial, Sylvester
strengthened the confessors and martyrs, God preserving
his life from many dangers. In 312 a new era set in.
Constantine, having triumphed under the " standard of the
Cross," declared himself the protector of the Christians,
and built them splendid churches. At this juncture Sylvester was elected to the chair of Peter, and was thus the
first of the Roman Pontiffs to rule the flock of Christ in
security and peace. He profited by these blessings to renew
the discipline of the Church, and in two great Councils
confirmed her sacred truths. In the Council of Arles he
condemned the schism of the Donatists; and in that of
Nicæa, the first general Council of the Church, he dealt
Arianism its death-blow by declaring that Jesus Christ is
the true and very God. Sylvester died A. D. 335.

Reflection.—Never forget to thank God daily for having made you a member of His undying Church, and grow daily in your attachment, devotion, and loyalty to the Vicar of Christ.

December 31.—SAINT CATHERINE LABOURE,
Virgin

AMONG the Sisters of St. Vincent de Paul at the convent in the Faubourg St. Antoine at Paris, in 1830, was one called Sister Catherine. Her name in the world was Zoe Laboure. She was born in 1806 in the village of Fain-les-Moutiers, in the Cote d'Or, not far from Dijon. Left an orphan when she was eight years old, she became at a very early age mistress of her father's house, owing to the departure of her elder sister for the Convent of St. Vincent. Poor Zoe's longing thoughts turned in the same direction, but she had many years to wait before God granted the fulfilment of her desires. At home she led a life of obedience, labor, and devotion, preparing for her future life as her Lord and Master in the humble house of Nazareth had prepared for His future ministry. At the parish church she was seen with unfailing regularity, kneeling on the flags even in the depth of winter. She fasted every Friday and Saturday in honor of Our Lord's Passion and of the Holy Mother of God, seeking with pious cunning to hide from her father her practice. But, though she loved to visit the Convent of St. Vincent at the neighboring town, and had determined, if it were God's will to enter religion, she prudently abstained from fixing on one rather than on another religious community, until the will of God was definitely made known to her by a dream, in which St. Vincent De Paul appeared to her and made known God's design that she should become one of his children in religion. In 1830 she was received into the convent at Chatillon as Sister Catherine, was clothed in 1831, and placed in a hospital attended by the Sisters of Charity, in the Faubourg St. Antoine at Paris. She was employed first in the kitchen, then in the laundry, and after this for forty years in tending the old men in the Hospice d'Enghien, and in looking after the poultry-yard. To these humble offices she devoted herself with all her heart. During the forty-six years she was in the hospital at Enghien, she was never known to say a word against charity. Her gentleness and sweetness to those placed under her were the more remarkable because she had naturally a very lively temper. She was also of a rather impulsive disposition, and for some time after she joined the Sisters of Charity, the effort to keep herself in check was manifest to all around her. Bodily sufferings were not wanting to her, in spite of her strong constitution. All her Sisters were struck with her wonderful devotion to the Holy Mother of God. She loved to pray the Rosary and deemed its daily recital a matter of great importance. Throughout her life as a Sister of Charity she was favored with many supernatural revelations and visions; the first miraculous medal was struck as a result of these visions. Our Lady appeared to her several times and made known to her the work she had to do. The most celebrated vision occurred in 1830 while Sister Catherine was at prayer with the Sisters in the chapel. The Blessed Virgin appeared to the young Sister as if in an oval frame. She was standing on the globe of the world, only half of which could be seen. She was dressed in a white robe with a blue cloak edged with silver, having as it were diamonds in Her hands, from which fell streams of golden rays upon the earth. Sister Catherine heard a voice saying: "These rays are the graces that Mary obtains for men," and saw these words written in golden characters: "O Mary, conceived without sin, pray for us who have recourse to Thee!" This prayer was in the form of a semicircle; beginning on a level with Our Lady's right hand, and passing over Her head, it terminated on a level with Her left hand. The picture then turned round, and on the reverse side the Sister saw the letter M, with a cross above it, having a crosspiece at its base, and below the letter the Hearts of Jesus and Mary, the former surrounded by a crown of thorns, and the latter pierced with a sword. Then she thought she heard these words: "A medal must be struck on this pattern; the persons who shall carry it with indulgences attached to it, and shall offer the above prayer, shall enjoy a very special protection from the Mother of God". At that instant the vision disappeared. As soon as the medal was struck it began to spread rapidly, and at once the most wonderful conversions and cures attested its miraculous efficacy. From France the devout use of the miraculous medal soon spread throughout the world and devout Catholics everywhere attest to its wonder-working power. Sister Catherine died in 1875 and was canonized by Pope Pius XII on July 27, 1947.

Reflection.—Do you think the statements of the universal efficacy of the miraculous medal incredible or exaggerated? Then give it a trial, and you will surely find by your own experience that none who trust in the Holy Mother of God shall be confounded; that she shall heap upon you treasures of joy and gladness; that "her ways are beautiful ways, and all her paths are peaceable; that she is a tree of life to them that lay hold on her; and that he who shall retain her is blessed forevermore."

APPENDIX

LIVES OF CERTAIN SAINTS

CONTAINED IN THE CALENDAR OF SPECIAL
FEASTS FOR THE UNITED STATES
AND OF SOME OTHERS RE-
CENTLY CANONIZED

February 5.—ST. PHILIP OF JESUS, Martyr, Patron of the City of Mexico.

PHILIP DE LAS CASAS was born in the city of Mexico. Brought up piously, Philip at first showed little care for the pious teaching of his parents, but at last resolved to enter the Reformed Franciscan Convent of Santa Barbara at Pueblo. He was not yet weaned from the world and soon left the novitiate. Grieved at the inconstancy of his son, de las Casas sent him to the Philippine Islands on a business errand. In vain did Philip seek to satisfy his heart with pleasure. He could not but feel that God called him to a religious life. Gaining courage by prayer, he entered the Franciscan Convent of Our Lady of the Angels at Manila, and persevered, taking his vows in 1594. The richest cargo

that he could have sent to Mexico would not have gratified
his pious father as much as the tidings that Philip was a
professed friar. Alonso de las Casas obtained from the Com-
missary of the Order directions that Philip should be sent to
Mexico. He embarked on the *St. Philip* in July, 1596, with
other religious. Storms drove the vessel to the coast of Japan,
and it was wrecked while endeavoring to enter a port. Amid
the storm Philip saw over Japan a white cross, in the shape
used in that country, which after a time became blood-red,
and remained so for some time. It was an omen of his coming victory. The commander of the vessel sent our Saint
and two other religious to the emperor to solicit permission
to continue their voyage, but they could not obtain an
audience. He then proceeded to Macao, to a house of his
Order, to seek the influence of the Fathers there; but the pilot
of the vessel by idle boasts had excited the emperor's fears
of the Christians, and the heathen ruler resolved to extermi-
nate the Catholic missionaries. In December, officers seized
a number of the Franciscan Fathers, three Jesuits, and several
of their young pupils. St. Philip was one of those arrested
and heard with holy joy that sentence of death had been
passed on them all. His left ear was cut off, and he offered
this first-fruit of his blood to God for the salvation of that
heathen land. The martyrs were taken to Nagasaki, where
crosses had been erected on a high hill. When St. Philip was
led to that on which he was to die, he knelt down and clasped
it, exclaiming: "O happy ship! O happy galleon for Philip,
lost for my gain! Loss—no loss for me, but the greatest of all
gain!" He was bound to the cross, but the rest under him
gave way, so that he was strangled by the cords. While repeating the holy name of Jesus he was the first of the happy
band to receive the death-stroke. Miracles attested the
power before God of these first martyrs of Japan. Pope
Urban VIII granted permission to say an Office and Mass in
their honor, and Pope Pius IX formally canonized them.
St. Philip died at the age of twenty-five.

Reflection.—He is an example to encourage those who
falter in the path of God's service; his prayers will aid those
who are tempted, and enable them to acquire strength to
recover lost ground and go on with renewed courage in the
narrow way of the cross.

February 27.—ST. GABRIEL OF THE SORROWFUL MOTHER

GABRIEL POSSENTI, born March 1, 1838, the eleventh of thirteen children, was reared in a home that was none the less pious because cultured. Inordinately vain and passionately devoted to the pleasures of the world, it is little wonder that his teachers and companions were incredulous when he announced that he would enter the Passionist Order immediately upon his graduation.

His life in religion was one of love throughout—joyous love, made all the sweeter by the penances prescribed by his rule, which he fulfilled to the letter. There was nothing extraordinary about him except his fidelity to prayer, his love of mortification and his joyfulness of spirit. At the age of twenty-three, just as he was finishing his studies, he was stricken with consumption, of which he died at Isola on February 27, 1862. His feast is February 27.

Reflection.—Let us in imitation of this youthful Saint, diligently ponder the sorrows of our blessed Mother, that her maternal care may insure our salvation.

March 9.—ST. DOMINIC SAVIO, Confessor.

DOMINIC SAVIO was born in Riva di Chieri on April 2, 1842. He looked so frail and puny on the morning of his birth that his father had rushed him that same evening to the parish church for baptism. As a little boy, one of Dominic's greatest joys was serving Mass. He began serving when he was five years old and was often seen at five o'clock in the morning in the front of the Church on his knees in rain or snow waiting for the doors to be opened. On the occasion of his First Holy Communion he made the resolution to prefer death rather than sin. From his earliest years he frequently expressed his determination and ambition to become a saint. The village pastor at Mondonio recognizing in Dominic a soul of rare caliber arranged to have him transferred to Don Bosco's Oratory at Turin. Don Bosco soon noted Dominic's consuming quest for sainthood and pointed out to the boy that the path to holiness is not necessarily among the hair shirts and tortures of the flesh, but in the cheerful bearing and offering up of each day's small crosses. Steering the lad away from artificial practices his master showed him that for the soul avid of penance, there is a superabundance lying around, to be had for the picking: to accept the pain which is wrapped up with the more and more perfect fulfillment of the duties of one's state of life. After a few months of life in the environment of the Oratory and under the saintly care of St. John Bosco Dominic's soul was fired with the zeal of his master whose rule of life "Give me souls; you take the rest," the boy adopted as his own. Following the example set by his master, who sought souls wherever they were to be found, in season and out of season Dominic also went after souls in the highways and byways of his own little world, especially among the boys of the Oratory. There he founded and directed the Immaculate Conception Sodality, a group of boys who by prayer, word and example carried on an apostolate among their school fellows and thus proved to be of valuable assistance to Don Bosco in his work, the Christian formation of boys. On one occasion Dominic broke up a vicious "duel with stones." Standing between the boy-duellists with dramatic suddenness he flashed a Crucifix and said: "This is Friday. Today Christ died for love of us—can you look at Him, and still hate each other?" When Dominic's health began to fail he was forced to leave the Oratory. Don Bosco and the boys were sorry to see him leave. He had been a good friend to all. Don Bosco said of him: "His cheerful character and lively disposition made him extremely popular even among those boys who were no great lovers of their Faith." His death at his home on March 9, 1857 was sweet and peaceful. Pope Pius XII canonized him on June 12, 1954.

Reflection.—Sin? I'll die first! That heart cry from the soul of Dominic is now, thanks to Don Bosco, sounding across the all but bloody fields of teen-age purity, seeking echoes in young and generous hearts.

April 11.—ST. GEMMA GALGANI, Virgin.

ST. GEMMA GALGANI was born at Camigliano in Tuscany. Her mother died when she was seven years old and from that time her life was one of continuous suffering.

These sufferings were caused partly by ill-health, partly by the poverty into which her family fell, partly by the scoffing of those who took offense at her practices of devotion, partly by what she believed to be the physical attacks of the devil. Through it all, however, she remained at peace and enjoyed constant communion with our Lord who spoke to her as if He were bodily present. She earnestly desired to be a Passionist nun, but was not accepted because of her physical infirmities. She was the subject of various extraordinary supernatural phenomena—visions, ecstasies, revelations, supernatural knowledge, visible intercourse with her guardian angel, prophecy and miracles. She also had periodically occurring stigmata between 1899 and 1901. At one time she was obsessed by the devil and during these attacks she even spat upon the crucifix and broke her confessor's rosary. She died on Holy Saturday in 1903 and was canonized in 1940.

Reflection.—Often say with St. Augustine: "Write, O most loving Saviour, Thy wounds upon my heart, that I may always read in them Thy pains and Thy love." The afflictions that God sends us are really mercies and blessings. They are the most precious talents to be improved by us to the increasing of our love and affection to God, and the exercise of the most heroic virtues of self-denial, patience. humility, resignation and penance.

April 16.—ST. BENEDICT JOSEPH LABRE,
Confessor.

ST. BENEDICT JOSEPH LABRE was born in the village of Amettes, near Boulogne-sur-Mer in France, on the 26th of March, 1748. His early education was placed in the hands of one of his uncles, who was the cure of Erin. From Benedict Joseph's earliest years he showed every sign of piety, the fulness of which began to develop and soon crowned every year of his life on earth.

After making several unsuccessful requests to enter certain monasteries, where he might serve God according to his heart's desire, he was finally received by the Cistercians in November, 1769. His happiness, however, proved to be short-lived. He was taken ill and his superiors decided that he was not called to be one of their number. Upon his recovery, he discovered God's holy will in regard to his life, "that remaining in the midst of the world, he would devoutly visit as a pilgrim the famous places of Christian devotion."

With this "holy and wholesome thought" ever before his mind, he made solitary pilgrimages to many of the great shrines of Europe. He visited the shrine of Our Lady of Loreto in Italy no less than ten different times during his life. One writer tells us that he seemed to have been destined by God to recall to men's mind the poverty of Christ. He ate nothing but the fragments he received from charity, and esteemed himself happy in suffering hunger, thirst, and the inconveniences of travel, for he had ever before his mind the mortified life of the Master and His Blessed Mother.

He loved the Church of Our Lady of the Mountains in Rome. He spent much time in this, his favorite place of devotion, and on Wednesday of Holy Week, in the year 1783, when he went to pray, he was taken suddenly ill and expired as those who attended him in his last moments said the invocation of the litany of the dying: "Holy Mary, pray for him." His feast is celebrated on April 16.

Reflection.—Let us learn from the life of St. Benedict Joseph Labre to remember that we are always in the presence of God, and particularly so when we are in church; for Jesus is really, truly, and substantially present in the Most Blessed Sacrament of the Altar.

April 21.—ST. CONRAD OF PARZHAM, Confessor.

ST. CONRAD was born at Parzham, Bavaria in 1818. He was the ninth of ten children and came from a deeply religious family. Known in the village as the "little Angel" he used to gather his schoolmates about him and say the rosary with them. He went to Mass every day and often made pilgrimages to the neighboring shrines, especially Altoetting, famous for a much venerated shrine of our Blessed Lady. He made a mission at Erring, walking the distance of twenty-four miles every day for eight days. For nine years he visited his confessor at Aigen, a distance of twenty miles, which he made on foot to and fro. Lack of talent prevented him from becoming a priest so he decided to become a lay-brother in the Capuchin Order. After his profession he was immediately stationed at Altoetting at which friary he spent more than forty years as doorkeeper. Although Altoetting was a much frequented place of pilgrimage and left the Brother Porter little leisure between the hours of six in the morning and nine at night, yet he managed to combine in a marvellous manner the contemplative and the active life. His rosary was always in his hands and his favorite saying was "The Crucifix is my book." For thirty years he took only three hours sleep; he would rise up for the midnight office and spend the rest of the night in prayer. He was remarkable for his imperturbed patience with the hundreds he met as porter, for his humility and love of his fellow-men especially children and the handicapped. He had great devotion for the Eucharist, the Passion and the Blessed Virgin. Through his exemplary life he carried on a great apostolate among the pilgrims, which bore fruit throughout Germany. He seemed to have the gift of reading hearts, and there were occasions on which he manifested a strange knowledge of the future. He died in 1894 and was canonized in 1934.

Reflection.—The life of St. Conrad is proof that no matter how busy we are, no matter how lowly our condition, we can by cooperating with the grace of God rise to great heights of sanctity, and so by good example can edify others and bring them also closer to God.

April 24.—ST. MARIE EUPHRASIA PELLETIER

ON May 2, 1940, Pope Pius XII raised to the honors of the altar a most remarkable woman, Mother Mary of St. Euphrasia Pelletier. As the solemn Te Deum swelled in gladness through the Vatican Basilica, its joyous strains were echoed and reechoed in quiet chapels hidden in every great city of the world. Almost a hundred thousand women and girls, over ten thousand white-robed Sisters in three hundred and fifty homes of charity rejoiced with their Mother. For Saint Marie Euphrasia Pelletier is the Foundress and first Mother-General of the great Congregation of Our Lady of Charity of the Good Shepherd of Angers and one of the great sociologists of the ages. Our Saint was born of pious parents on July 31, 1796 on the island of Noirmoutiers, during the terrible period of the French Revolution. So it was that Rose Virginie Pelletier began her life—a child of the sounding sea, daughter of the suffering faith of her beloved France. Because of the suppression and expulsion of religious orders, the education of the little girl had to be undertaken by her busy mother. At her knee Rose Virginie learned of God and His service. In 1814 she entered the Order of Our Lady of Charity of the Refuge at Tours. After some ten months as a postulant in this historic community at Tours, Rose Virginie received the habit and entered upon her life as a novice, September 8, 1815. At the ceremony she received the name, Sister Mary of St. Euphrasia. For two years she remained in the novitiate, training herself in the religious life, studying and absorbing the history and work of her Order. One episode of this first chapter of religious life must be told, for it is significant. Listening to the life of a saint one day she heard that he "quickly reached sanctity by his perfect obedience". "Obedience, then," reflected the young novice, "must be the best means to become holy. If only I were allowed to take the vow of obedience," and at once Sister Mary Euphrasia consulted her superiors, and was allowed to take a private vow of obedience. Sister Mary Euphrasia made her profession on September 9, 1817. Her great gifts, intelligence and ability made the young sister outstanding. In a few years her exceptional qualifications became so apparent to all that she, after having been Mistress of penitents, was elected Superior of the house. A project which had been in her mind for a long time was now made a reality. She had found in many of the penitents a real attraction for the religious life, with no desire to return to the world after their conversion. Where could they go? It was very difficult, almost impossible in most cases, to find a congregation suitable or willing to accept them. So Mother Euphrasia started a community called the Sisters Magdalens. She adapted the rule of St. Teresa, drew up a set of Constitutions, and erected the first community of Magdalens in the House of Tours. One of the greatest consolations Mother Euphrasia enjoyed in life was found in the heights of sanctity reached by so many of these religious, bound by vows to a life of prayer and penance. In 1829 she founded a refuge for penitent women at Angers which later on became the Mother-house of the New Congregation established by her with the approval of Pope Gregory XVI. During the thirty years she lived as Superior-General Mother Euphrasia sent her sisters out to found one hundred and ten houses, in every land beneath the sun; sisters inflamed with her own zeal, trained at her hands. She died at Angers in her seventy-second year having welcomed death with the faith and serenity which marked her whole life.

Reflection.—Someone has written: "Of all great hearts, the greatest is still the heart of a saint. For it wants to contain, not only its neighbor, strangers, all suffering, sinful, worrying humanity, but God Himself". Mother Euphrasia's was such a heart; and it could only be so all-embracing in its love for the unfortunate because that heart through its perfect charity did embrace God Himself.

April 27.—ST. TURRIBIUS, Archbishop of Lima.

TURRIBIUS ALPHONSUS MOGROBEJO, whose feast the Church honors on April 27th, was born on the 6th of November, 1538, at Mayorga in the kingdom of Leon in Spain. Brought up in a pious family where devotion was hereditary, his youth was a model to all who knew him. All his leisure was given to devotion or to works of charity. His austerities were great, and he frequently made long pilgrimages on foot. The fame of Turribius as a master of canon and civil law soon reached the ears of King Philip II, who made him judge of Granada. About that time the see of Lima, in Peru, fell vacant, and among those proposed Philip found no one who seemed better endowed than our Saint with all the qualities that were required at that city, where much was to be done for religion. He sent to Rome the name of the holy judge, and the Sovereign Pontiff confirmed his choice. Turribius in vain sought to avoid the honor. The Pope, in reply, directed him to prepare to receive Holy Orders and be consecrated. Yielding at last by direction of his confessor, he was ordained priest and consecrated. He arrived at Lima in 1587, and entered on his duties. All was soon edification and order in his episcopal city. A model of all virtue himself, he confessed daily and prepared for Mass by long meditation. St. Turribius then began a visitation of his vast diocese, which he traversed three times, his first visitation lasting seven years and his second four. He held provincial councils, framing decrees of such wisdom that his regulations were adopted in many countries. Almost his entire revenues were bestowed on his creditors, as he styled the poor. While discharging with zeal his duties he was seized with a fatal illness during his third visitation, and died on the 23d of March, 1666, at Santa, exclaiming, as he received the sacred Viaticum: "I rejoiced in the things that were said to me: 'We shall go into the house of the Lord.'" The proofs of his holy life and of the favors granted through his intercession induced Pope Innocent XI to beatify him, and he was canonized by Pope Benedict XIII in the year 1726.

Reflection.—Saint Turribius was a model for all states— as a holy youth, as a pious and zealous layman, as a great and exemplary bishop.

May 22.—ST. RITA OF CASCIA, Widow.

ST. RITA OF CASCIA, whose feast is celebrated on May 22, was born at Rocca Porena, Italy, about the year 1386, and died at Cascia in the year 1456. Her parents opposed her desire to become a nun, and persuaded her to marry a man who, in a short time, lost his reputation on account of his cruelty. After being converted from his wicked ways, he was murdered by an enemy. Rita's two sons then resolved to take revenge, but through her prayers they repented. After their death, she applied several times for admission into the Augustinian Convent at Cascia. Repeatedly refused until God Himself cleared away all obstacles, she entered the convent, made her profession and lived the life of a holy and devout Religious for forty-two years, "a shining example of every Christian virtue, pure as a lily, simple as a dove, and obedient as an angel." That "God is wonderful in His Saints" is easily proved in the life of St. Rita, and, owing to her great number of miracles, she is often styled "The Saint of the Impossible." The Church has placed her stamp of approval on these miracles of St. Rita and has raised her to the dignity of the altar by canonizing her a saint of God on the 24th of May, 1900.

Reflection.—Let us learn from the life of St. Rita to pray frequently for the conversion of sinners.   There is no prayer more pleasing to God than that which has for its object the conversion of those who lead lives of sin, particularly sins against faith, such as leaving the one true Church and prac- tising a false religion, wilful doubt, disbelief, denial, ignorance, and those who commit sin by exposing their faith to danger.

May 23.—ST. JOHN BAPTIST DE ROSSI,
Confessor.

ST. JOHN BAPTIST DE ROSSI is the first instance in modern times of the canonization as Confessor of a priest be- longing to no Religious Order or Congregation.   He was born at Voltaggio, a little town north of Genoa, February 22, 1698. From the first he was distinguished for his piety and purity. The parish church was his favorite resort and thither he would hasten after the early morning class to serve as many Masses as he could.

When our saint was ten years old, a wealthy couple, at- tracted by the unaffected piety and winning ways of the boy, obtained from his parents permission to adopt him.   After a residence of three years in Genoa, he began attending the lower classes of the Roman College and there was no more in- dustrious or saintly student to be found.   At the age of eigh- teen he received the Tonsure and the following year Minor Orders.   When he was twenty-three years old he was ordained priest.   The first shape his charity assumed was an active interest in the young students who flocked to Rome from every part of the Catholic world.   He organized special serv- ices for them, preached sermons specially suited for them and gathered them about him on his visits to the hospital to assist him in soothing and relieving the sick and the dying.   In February, 1735, much against his own inclination, he was ap- pointed assistant to his cousin, who was growing feeble, and when, two years after, that good man died, his property and canonry were left to him.   Within a fortnight our saint had got rid of a great part of the property.   He entered upon the duties of his new office at once and soon gathered round him crowds of devout worshipers. His confessional was besieged by eager penitents, but always the poorest and most ignorant. The rich and noble he managed to put off, saying that they could find confessors in plenty.

His devotion to the poor and ignorant was remarkable. He sought out the most abject and abandoned people and pursued this work of Christian charity with such zeal as to merit the title *"Venator Animarum"*—the hunter of souls.

The endless labor and the severe penances which the saint imposed on himself finally told on his delicate frame, and on May 23, 1764, a stroke of apoplexy ended his mortal life and brought him the endless bliss of the presence of God for which his soul had so long yearned. His feast is celebrated on May 23.

Reflection.—Let us learn from the consideration of the life of St. John Baptist de Rossi that the pomp and riches of the world are as nothing in the sight of God; and that whatever service we do the poor will not go unrewarded.

May 25.—ST. MADELEINE SOPHIE BARAT,
Virgin.

ℳADELEINE SOPHIE BARAT was born at Joigny, Yonne, France, December 12, 1779, at a time when her country was just recovering from the ravages of the Revolution. At the age of sixteen she was brought to Paris for her education and came under the direction of Father Joseph Varin. He had long cherished a desire to found a Congregation of women devoted to the Sacred Heart and dedicated to the education of girls, and beheld in her the instrument of God's will. Though she was only twenty-one, she set about to establish the society and was soon joined by a few companions. In the course of her sixty-three years as Superior General of the Society of the Sacred Heart, she built 105 houses of the Order in the principal countries of the world. When houses in France were suppressed through inimical legislation, she opened up new ones elsewhere. She exhorted her Reilgious at all times to seek the glory of the Heart of Jesus in laboring for the sanctification of souls. Meekness and humility were to be the characteristics of her spiritual daughters; "Those who see one of ours, ought to be able to say: 'That is a Religious of the Sacred Heart; we know her by her meekness and humility.' " Her unfailing serenity and sweetness cheered and encouraged all who came in contact with her. "To suffer myself and not to make others suffer" was one of her favorite mottoes. The Saint died at Paris, May 25, 1865; was beatified May 24, 1908, and was canonized May 24, 1925.

Reflection.—Let us implore the Sacred Heart of Jesus to make us grow in that humility and love which advanced St. Madeleine Sophie Barat to eternal glory in heaven.

May 30.—ST. JOAN OF ARC, Virgin.

AT Domremy, on the Upper Meuse, was born on January 6, 1412, of pious parentage, the illustrious heroine of all time, St. Joan of Arc. Taught by her mother from earliest years to pray each night "O God, save France," she could not help but conceive that ardent love for her country which later consumed her life. While the English were overrunning the north of France, their future conqueror, untutored in worldly wisdom, was peacefully tending her flock, and learning the wisdom of God at a wayside shrine. But hearing Voices from heaven and bidden by St. Michael, who appeared to her, to deliver her country from the enemy, she hastened to the King and convinced him of her divine mission. Scarcely did her banner, inscribed "Jesus, Mary," appear on the battlefield than she raised the siege of Orleans and led Charles VII to be crowned at Rheims. Later, abandoned by her King, she fell into the hands of the English, who gave her a mock trial and burned her as a heretic. But the Maid of Orleans has at last come into her own, for with greater pomp than ever a king was crowned, and amid the acclamations of the whole world, on May 13, 1920, Pope Benedict XV proclaimed her St. Joan of Arc.

Reflection.—To few has it been vouchsafed to be so set apart for God's instrument in the fulfillment of His decrees. But each and all can within the limits of their calling, follow in the footsteps of one whose virtues are those which may shine and blossom in every Christian soul.

May 31.—ST. ANGELA MERICI, Virgin.

ANGELA MERICI was born at Desenzano, in the territory of Venice. From her earliest years, she kept the strictest guard over the lily of her virginity, which she had resolved should never be taken from her. Hating all feminine adornments, she made a point of making the beauty of her features and her attractive hair unsightly, that she might find no favor save with the heavenly Spouse of souls. While yet in the bloom of her youth, she lost her parents, and tried to retire into a desert, that she might lead a life of penance; but being prevented by an uncle, she fulfilled at home what she was not permitted to do in a wilderness. She frequently wore a hairshirt, and took the discipline. She never ate meat, except in case of sickness; she never tasted wine, except on the feasts of the Lord's Nativity and Resurrection; and, at times, she would pass whole days without taking any food. Devoted to prayer, she took her very short rests on the ground. When the devil sought to beguile her in the form of an angel of light, she quickly detected him, and put him to flight. At length, having resigned the fortune left by her father, she accepted the habit and rule of the Third Order of St. Francis. At Brescia, being commanded by a voice from heaven and by a vision, she founded a new society of virgins, under a fixed discipline and holy rules of life. She put them under the title and patronage of St. Ursula, the brave leader of virgins. She foretold, shortly before her death, that this institute would last to the end of the world. She died in 1540 and was canonized in 1807.

Reflection.—To will is for us; to accomplish for God, who chooses the times and the means. After Angela's death her order grew and spread throughout the world.

July 9.—ST. JOHN FISHER, Martyr.

SAINT JOHN FISHER, born at Beverley, Yorkshire, England in 1469, was the son of a draper. He was educated at Cambridge and thereafter was always connected with the life of the university. He was appointed Bishop of Rochester in 1504 and in the same year was elected Chancellor of Cambridge University, to which post he was reelected annually for ten years and then appointed for life. When the question of the divorce of Henry VIII from Queen Catherine arose, Fisher became the queen's chief supporter and most trusted counsellor. In this capacity he appeared on the queen's behalf in the legates' court, where he startled his hearers by the directness of his language and most of all by declaring that, like St. John the Baptist, he was ready to die on behalf of the indissolubility of marriage. He was arrested several times because of his opposition to the king and finally in 1534 was sent to the Tower of London for refusing to take the oath of supremacy. In May 1535 Pope Paul III created Fisher Cardinal Priest of St. Vitalis, his motive being apparently to induce Henry by this mark of esteem to treat the bishop less severely. The effect was precisely the reverse. Henry forbade the cardinal's hat to be brought into England, declaring that he would send the head to Rome for it instead. In June a special commission for Fisher's trial was issued, and on June 17 he was arraigned in Westminster Hall on a charge of treason, in that he had denied the king to be supreme head of the Church. He was declared guilty, and condemned to be hanged, drawn, and quartered at Tyburn, but the mode of execution was changed, and instead he was beheaded on Tower Hill. The martyr's last moments were thoroughly in keeping with his previous life. He met death with a calm dignified courage which profoundly impressed all present. His headless body was stripped and left on the scaffold till evening, when it was thrown naked into a grave in the churchyard of Allhallows, Barking. Thence it was removed a fortnight later and laid beside that of Sir Thomas More in the church of St. Peter ad Vincula by the Tower. His head was stuck upon a pole on London Bridge, but its ruddy and lifelike appearance excited so much attention that, after a fortnight, it was thrown into the Thames, its place being taken by that of Sir Thomas More, whose martydom occurred a few weeks later, July 6. John Fisher died with the Te Deum on his lips and was canonized 1935.

Reflection.—St. John Fisher, by suffering and death, acquires the crown of martyrdom. In reproving iniquity he loses his life for justice sake, but he secures the possession of immortal glory. Have you never endangered your salvation by flattering the vices, or weakly condescending to the disorders of those whom you might or ought to have charitably admonished, forfeiting everlasting happiness through human respect?

July 22.—ST. LAURENCE OF BRINDISI,
Confessor.

T̶HIS saint was born July 22, 1559, and from an early age showed an inclination for a monastic life. To encourage this his pious parents placed him in the Franciscan Convent at Brindisi. Being left an orphan when quite young, he went to Venice, where his uncle, a man of great learning, was superior of the College of St. Mark. When not quite sixteen, Laurence was attracted to the Capuchins and on February 18, 1575, he joined the Order. So great was the harvest of souls gained by his preaching that Pope Clement VIII called him to Rome for the conversion of the Jews. In 1596 Laurence was named Definitor-General and was about to make a visitation of the Capuchin houses throughout Sicily when Pope Clement VIII ordered him to Germany, there to found houses of his Order, in hope of stemming the tide of heresy then deluging the kingdom. In this, as in his other good works, Laurence was eminently successful and within a year had founded houses in Vienna, Prague, and Gratz.

About this time the Turks, smarting to avenge their defeat at Lepanto, threatened to overrun and capture Hungary, and it seemed as if no power could stop them. Their armies, numbering from eighty to ninety thousand men, crossed the Danube and confronted the Christian army, which it was decided dare not risk an attack. But Laurence so fired the hearts of the soldiers that they were eager for the battle. Cross in hand, the holy monk advanced before the Christian army and, although greatly outnumbered, before nightfall victory perched on their banner.

His military service ended, Laurence returned to Italy. When Easter came, he went to Rome and assisted at the General Chapter held there; and when the election for General took place, he found, to his great dismay, that, although not fifty-three years of age, he had been elected Superior-General, the highest office in his Order. In June, 1618, Laurence intended to visit Brindisi, which he had not seen since childhood. On his way he stopped at Naples and at the urgent request of the Cardinal he undertook a mission to King Philip, who was at Lisbon. He had hardly reached that place when he was taken ill and on July 22, 1619, his busy life was brought to a close and he was enabled to enjoy the rest he had so long yearned for.

Reflection.—The militant Christianity of St. Laurence should remind us that we are all soldiers of Christ, that our banner is the Cross, and that our life here on earth is a continual warfare against the armies of Satan.

July 24.—ST. FRANCIS SOLANO, Confessor.

THE diocese of Cordova, in Spain, was the birthplace of this Saint, who won many thousands of souls to God. From his earliest years he was characterized by a modest behavior, prudent silence, and edifying meekness. His education was entrusted to the Jesuit Fathers, and later he entered the Order of St. Francis. Soon he excelled every one in the house in humility, obedience, fervor in prayer, and self-denial. In 1589 he sailed for South America to preach the Gospel to the Indians in Peru. While near shore the ship struck rocks, and there was danger of drowning. The captain hurried the officers and principal passengers into the only boat there was, and tried to induce the missionary to accompany them; but he refused to do so. Consoling the remaining passengers, he prayed fervently and alone kept up his hope in God's mercy. At last rescuers arrived and all were taken off in safety. The missionary did not confine his ministry to Lima. He visited the forests and deserts inhabited by the Indians, and by degrees he won their trust and in this way baptized nine thousand Indians. He was then recalled to Lima, which at that time was like a godless Ninive. Francis preached to the hardened sinners, and the whole city became converted. Finally after a painful sickness his last words being, "God be praised!" his soul departed this earth on July 14, 1610. He was declared *Blessed* by Pope Clement X in 1675, and canonized by Benedict XIII in 1726. St. Francis' feast is held July 24th.

Reflection.—St. Francis Solano was an apostle of charity

and peace. He stopped the duels and healed the feuds of the Spanish settlers, and taught them forbearance to the conquered race. This then is perfect charity, to make peace between those who are enemies, and to do this for the sake of Christ, who is our peace.

July 25.—ST. CHRISTOPHER, Martyr.

ALTHOUGH ST. CHRISTOPHER is one of the most popular saints in the East and the West, nothing certain is known about his life or death. The Roman Martyrology makes him a martyr under the Emperor Decius. According to an ancient legend he was the son of a heathen king who gave him the name Offerus. Acquiring in time gigantic stature and great strength, Offerus resolved to serve only the strongest and bravest. He bound himself successively to a mighty king and to Satan, but he found both lacking in courage, the former dreading even the name of the devil, and the latter frightened at the sight of a cross by the roadside. For a time his search for a new master was in vain, but at last he found a hermit who told him to offer his allegiance to Christ, instructed him in the Faith, and baptized him. Christopher, as he was now called, would not promise to do any fasting or praying, but willingly accepted the task of carrying people, for God's sake, across a raging stream. One day he was carrying a child who continually grew heavier, so that it seemed to him as if he had the whole world on his shoulders. The child, on inquiry, made himself known as the Creator and Redeemer of the world. To prove his statement the child ordered Christopher to fix his staff in the ground. The next morning it had grown into a palm-tree bearing fruit. Thereafter he promised to serve the Lord faithfully and became a zealous preacher of the Gospel, converting many to the Faith. On his missionary journeys he came to Lycia, where, after his first sermon, eighteen thousand heathens requested baptism. This excited the rage of Emperor Decius who had him cast into prison, and after many cruel torments, beheaded.

Reflection.—We ought all to be Christbearers, by preserving in our hearts faith, hope and charity, and by receiving our Lord worthily in Holy Communion.

August 15.—ST. TARCISIUS, Martyr.

THE holy acolyte and martyr Tarcisius suffered at Rome in the persecution of Valerian and Gallienus about the middle of the third century. In those days the office of conveying the Blessed Sacrament to the imprisoned confessors of the faith was often intrusted to inferior ministers of the Church, and indeed it was frequently given into the keeping of the faithful laity, who were permitted to communicate themselves. When Tarcisius was one day bearing the Holy Eucharist he was stopped by a fierce pagan mob, who pressed him to show them what he was carrying. Mindful of our Lord's injunction not to give that which is holy to dogs, nor to cast pearls before swine, the brave boy stoutly resisted their entreaties, and soon fell beneath a shower of blows and stones. His constancy was rewarded. When his persecutors searched his lifeless remains they could not find, either in his hands or in his garments, any vestige of the Blessed Sacrament, which God had miraculously preserved from desecration. The heathen fled in terror at this sign of Divine power, and the Christians, taking up the body, buried it in the cemetery of Callistus on August 15. The tomb was afterwards decorated with an inscription by Pope Damasus, in which he states that St. Tarcisius, "carrying the Sacraments of Christ, chose rather to suffer death than to betray the heavenly Body to profane mad dogs."

Reflection.—Have reverence for the Blassed Sacrament. It is food "that must not be thrown to dogs". Concerning the reception of this Sacrament St. Augustine has this to say: "Wouldst thou receive the life? change, then, thine own. For otherwise thou wouldst receive life to condemnation, and wouldst obtain thereby, not health, but corruption; not life, but death."

August 16.—ST. ROCH, Confessor.

THE date of the birth of St. Roch can not be determined with exactness, but it is said that he was born about 1295, at Montpellier. His father held a position of power and influence in the city. After the death of his parents, when he was about twenty years of age, the young man had

no inclination to take his father's position, but handed over
the government to his uncle. He then distributed his wealth
to the poor and set out on a journey to Italy. At that time
many people were afflicted with the plague, and the young
man, dressed as a pilgrim, devoted his time, energy, and
prayers to the care of those who had been stricken. Wherever
he went the plague disappeared before him, due to the fact
that God gave him the power of working miracles in behalf
of those who were suffering from the terrible disease. Having
contracted the malady himself, from which he recovered in
the course of time, the young man went back to his own city
in the year 1322. Not wishing to make himself known, he
was cast into prison as a spy and died there five years later
in the year 1327. When his identity became known from
some papers in his possession, he was accorded a public
funeral, which was the occasion of numerous miracles.

The relics of St. Roch are venerated at Venice, and the
Church has established an arch-confraternity in his house.
His feast is celebrated on the 16th of August.

Reflection.—Considering the great and miraculous power
of St. Roch during his life, and through his intercession after
his death, let us remember to call upon him in the time of need.

August 17.—ST. HYACINTH, Confessor.

HYACINTH, the glorious apostle of Poland and Russia, was
born of noble parents in Poland, about the year 1185.
In 1218, being already Canon of Cracow, he accompanied
his uncle, the bishop of that place, to Rome. There he met
St. Dominic, and received the habit of the Friar Preachers
from the patriarch himself, of whom he became a living copy.
So wonderful was his progress in virtue that within a year
Dominic sent him to preach and plant the Order in Poland,
where he founded two houses. His apostolic journeys extended over numerous regions. Austria, Bohemia, Livonia,
the shores of the Black Sea, Tartary, and Northern China on
the east, and Sweden and Norway to the west, were evangelized by him, and he is said to have visited Scotland. Everywhere multitudes were converted, churches and convents
were built; one hundred and twenty thousand pagans and

infidels were baptized by his hands. He worked numerous miracles, and at Cracow raised a dead youth to life. He had inherited from St. Dominic a most filial confidence in the Mother of God; to her he ascribed his success, and to her aid he looked for his salvation. When St. Hyacinth was at Kiev the Tartars sacked the town, but it was only as he finished Mass that the Saint heard of the danger. Without waiting to unvest, he took the ciborium in his hands, and was leaving the church. As he passed by an image of Mary a voice said: "Hyacinth, my son, why dost thou leave me behind? Take me with thee, and leave me not to mine enemies." The statue was of heavy alabaster, but when Hyacinth took it in his arms it was light as a reed. With the Blessed Sacrament and the image he came to the river Dnieper, and walked dry-shod over the surface of the waters. On the eve of the Assumption he was warned of his coming death. In spite of a wasting fever, he celebrated Mass on the feast, and communicated as a dying man. He was anointed at the foot of the altar, and died the same day, A.D. 1257.

Reflection.—St. Hyacinth teaches us to employ every effort in the service of God, and to rely for success not on our own industry, but on the prayer of His Immaculate Mother.

August 17.—ST. CLARE OF MONTEFALCO, Virgin.

THIS devoted Religious, who, many centuries after her death, was canonized a saint of God, was born at Montefalco about the year 1268. In her early life she was very pious. With her sister and other friends of her own age, she became a member of the Third Order of St. Francis, established for people living in the world. When she arrived at the proper age, and found that she was called by God to the religious state, she sought the advice of the bishop of Spoleto, and he gave her and others, including her sister, the rule of the Third Order of St. Augustine. In the course of time, her sister was selected for the abbess of the community. After her sister's death, in 1295, Clare was chosen to fill the vacancy, despite her objections. Her life as superior of her Order was most exemplary in every regard, particularly in the heroic practice of those great virtues by which she secured for herself the favor of God and canonization as a saint of

God's Church by Pope Leo XIII in the year 1881. Her feast is celebrated on August 17.

Reflection.—Let us ask Almighty God, as the Church does on the feast of St. Clare, to remember the bitterness of the Passion of Our Divine Lord, that we may enjoy the glories of the Blessed Trinity in heaven.

September 3. — ST. PIUS X, Pope.

BORN Joseph Melchior Sarto on June 2, 1835, this remark- able man described himself in his will, "I was born poor, I lived in poverty, I wish to die poor." His place of birth was the little village of Riese in Upper Italy. His parents had nine other children, two of whom died as infants. When the father, a cobbler, died, the mother supported herself and the children by the work of sewing and the products of the small farm. Joseph Sarto after attending high school went on to the seminary at Padua and was ordained September 18, 1858.

He was successively village curate in Tombolo where he instituted a night school for adults, a parish priest in Salzano, chancellor of the Diocese of Treviso, then Bishop of Mantua and finally Cardinal Patriarch of Venice in 1893. After ten years, he was elected Pope to succeed Leo XIII. As Pope he labored for the renovation of the Christian spirit in keep- ing with his motto, "To restore all things in Christ."

Among the outstanding works of his pontificate was the permission for children to approach the Eucharist at a tender age, and the general encouragement given to all with the proper dispositions to go to daily Communion. From his tender years, throughout his Papacy and unto his dying hour, his life of deep inner prayer reflected in his countenance and won the reverence and affection of all.

His life as Pope lasted until 1914 when at the outbreak of the World War which he had foreseen, he went peacefully to his reward. At once, he was revered by priests and people alike as a saint. Finally, the almost universal acclaim of his holiness brought his beatification through the usual process in 1951 and he was canonized by Pope Pius XII on May 29, 1954.

Reflection.—Our Christian life is centered about the

Eucharist. If we bring to Holy Communion the spirit of piety of Saint Pius X, this source of grace will be for us a veritable tree of life, providing health, nourishment and strength for our souls.

September 26.—ST. ISAAC JOGUES AND COMPANIONS, Martyrs.

THE following holy Jesuit missionaries are the first martyrs in North America: Isaac Jogues, John de Brebeuf, Noel Chabanel, Anthony Daniel, Charles Garnier, Gabriel Lalemant, priests; and Rene Goupil and John Lalande. They were beatified by Pope Pius XI in 1925 and were canonized by the same Pontiff five years later.

Saint Isaac Jogues was born at Orleans, France, January 19, 1607. After entering the Society of Jesus, he was appointed professor of literature at Rouen, and later was sent as a missioner to "New France," now Canada. His zeal for converting the Indians led him amid continual hardships to penetrate as far as Sault Ste. Marie. As they were extremely superstitious and attributed the blighting of the crops or the advent of sickness to the presence of the missionaries, the latter were in constant danger of death. One time he and some companions were captured near Three Rivers, New York; Saint Goupil was slain, and the others after severe tortures were condemned to death. But while preparations for their slaughter were in progress, they escaped, and Jogues returned to France. Though several of his fingers were mutilated, the Pope gave him permission to say Mass. In a few months, he returned to Canada and as a delegate arranged peace with the Indians. On his subsequent arrival among them, however, the crops were bad and the blame was put upon him. They stripped and slashed and finally tomahawked him, October 18, 1646, at the town of Auriesville, New York, now a popular place of pilgrimage. Shortly after his death 3,000 Huron Indians were converted, much to the distress of the Iroquois. The latter therefore seized his remaining companions and, after torturing them with arrows, boiling water and hot irons, put them to death.

Reflection.—Some are especially called to work for souls;

but there is no one who cannot help much in their salvation by holy example, earnest intercession and the offering of actions in their behalf.

October 3.—ST. TERESA OF THE INFANT JESUS, Virgin.

ARIE-FRANCOISE-THERESE MARTIN, known as "The Little Flower of Jesus," was born at Alencon, France, on January 2nd, 1873. Reared in a home of comfort and surrounded by refinements that would have spoiled an ordinary child, Teresa's intelligence had an early dawning which enabled her to comprehend the Divine Goodness far in advance of her tender years. Our Lord visited upon the child a severe trial—a strange malady from which there seemed no recovery. Her implicit confidence in God, however, overcame her infirmity and she progressed rapidly toward sanctity. Teresa adopted flowers as the symbol of her love for her Divine Saviour and offered her practices in virtue, sacrifice, and mortification as flowers at the feet of Jesus. At fifteen she entered the Carmelite Convent at Lisieux, France, where she distinguished herself by punctual observance of the rule, burning love for God and wonderful trust in Him. Before she died, this "lily of delicious perfume"—as Pope Pius X called her—revealed to the superiors her life story in pages of rarest beauty. She died in the odor of sanctity on September 30th, 1897, at the age of 24. Since her death countless graces have been attributed to her intercession. Pope Benedict XV in 1921 opened the way for the process of her beatification and she was declared *Blessed* by Pope Pius XI on April 29, 1923, and was canonized on May 17, 1925.

Reflection.—"For one pain endured with joy, we shall love the Good God more forever."—The Little Flower.

November 5.—BLESSED MARTIN DE PORRES.

HAT the truth is stranger than fiction is verified in the life of this holy man who was born on December 9, 1579, and died on November 3, 1639. He was the son of Don Juan de Porres, a Spanish adventurer and nobleman, and Ana Velasquez, a freed Negro woman of Panama. Martin's father arranged for some sort of schooling and then had him apprenticed to a barber-surgeon from whom he learned the rudiments of medical practice.   This elementary study of the healing arts enabled him to set bones, dress wounds, give doses for the cure of fever and be the good Samaritan for years in Lima, Peru.   Wishing to dedicate himself entirely and freely to the service of others, he became a Tertiary of the Dominican order.   While never a professed religious, he lived as a Third Order member of their convent at Lima, Peru, and from it as headquarters went forth to a daily life of utter self-sacrifice for the needy.   The stories of his marvels of healing and the countless works of wonder that he did remind one of the early days of Christianity.   Incredible though they sound, they are attested to by reliable witnesses and account, in some way, for the constant devotion to him in South America and the more recent cult to him in North America.   All the works of mercy found him their ready minister.   Such practical acts of kindness as getting marriage dowries for young girls and establishing orphanages and shelter for bereaved children were part of his beneficent program.   His father, who in time became Governor of Panama never aided him but in fact, attempted to prevent his ambition to lead the religious life.   Behind these self-effacing and charitable enterprises was a life of profound prayer, furthered by heroic penances.   Martin de Porres was beatified in 1837.

Reflection.—"There is neither Jew nor Greek, neither bond nor free; you are all one in Christ Jesus" said Saint Paul.   Therefore the union of the Christian soul with Christ Jesus blossoms into an active charity towards all, particularly those in the greatest need.

November 16.—ST. GERTRUDE, Abbess.

GERTRUDE was born in the year 1263, of a noble Saxon family, and placed at the age of five for education in the Benedictine abbey of Rodelsdorf.   Her strong mind was carefully cultivated, and she wrote Latin with unusual elegance and force; above all, she was perfect in humility and mortification, in obedience, and in all monastic observances. Her life was crowded with wonders.   She has in obedience recorded some of her visions, in which she traces in words of indescribable beauty the intimate converse of her soul ,with Jesus and Mary. She was gentle to all, most gentle to sinners; filled with devotion to the Saints of God, to the souls in purgatory, and above all to the Passion of Our Lord and to His Sacred Heart. She ruled her abbey with perfect wisdom and love for forty years. Her life was one of great and almost continual suffering, and her longing to be with Jesus was not granted till A.D. 1334, when she had reached her seventy-second year.

Reflection.—No preparation for death can be better than to offer and resign ourselves anew to the Divine Will— humbly, lovingly, with unbounded confidence in the infinite mercy and goodness of God.

November 26.—ST. LEONARD OF PORT MAURICE, Confessor.

ST. LEONARD OF PORT MAURICE was born on the 20th of December, 1676, at Porto Maurizio, Italy. His family name was Casanova. His early studies were made in a Jesuit college in the city of Rome. Knowing that his vocation was to serve God as a Religious, he joined the Riformella, a society similar to the Friars Minor, introduced into Italy by Blessed Bonaventure of Barcelona in 1662. He received the habit in 1697, and after making his notiviate was sent to the principal house at Rome to complete his studies. After his ordination he suffered from ill health for a period of four years, during which time his superiors kept him in a monastery of the Franciscan Observants in his native city. Upon his recovery, he began the work of giving missions, which he continued throughout his life. His first missions were given in his native city. From there he went into Tuscany, and his efforts in recalling sinners to penance were blessed by God with many noted and remarkable conversions. His missionary labors took him to all parts of Italy and the islands, and on many occasions he was compelled to preach outside the churches, on account of the immense crowds of people who came to hear him. He encouraged the people to lead pure and upright lives, and recommended to them in particular the adoration of the most Blessed Sacrament, and the devotion of the Way of the Cross.

Besides engaging in the work of the missions, St. Leonard found time to write a great many works, made up mostly of sermons, letters, books on the spiritual life, and devotional works of various kinds for the benefit of priests and people. Viewed from the exterior, we can see that he devoted his entire time to working in the vineyard of the Lord. From the interior, we can see him as the true man of God. Severe with himself by fasting, discipline, and prayer, he raised himself, through the power of God's grace, to an eminent degree of sanctity. He died in Rome on November 26, 1751. He was beatified by Pius VI and canonized by Pius IX on the 29th of June, 1867. His feast is celebrated on November 26.

Reflection.—Let us ask Almighty God, through the intercession of St. Leonard of Port Maurice, who was powerful in word and work in bending the hearts of obstinate sinners to penance, to bring about the conversion of those who have fallen away from the one true Church of Jesus Christ, and in doing so are living in sin.

December 22.—ST. FRANCES XAVIER CABRINI[1]

SAINT FRANCES XAVIER CABRINI was born at St. Angelo on July 15, 1850. A few hours after her birth a flock of white doves alighted in the courtyard, in which her father had spread the grain to dry. Fearing that the doves might damage the grain, he drove them away, but vainly so. They returned again and again—it was a happy omen! When seven, she was confirmed, and at ten she received first holy Communion. As a child, she was so modest and amiable that she was named "the little Saint." She liked to play with dolls dressed as Nuns, whom she ruled as a little abbess, and making small paper boats, she would fill them with violets, and placing them on the water, she imagined she was sending Missionaries to pagan lands. She received her early education from her Sister Rose, a licensed teacher. When

---

[1] Adapted from the English translation of the Pastoral Letter by His Excellency, Pietro Calchi Novati, Bishop of Lodi, with permission of the Missionary Sisters of the Sacred Heart of Jesus, New York.

thirteen, she entered the school of the Daughters of the
Sacred Heart at Arluno, and at eighteen, having succeeded
brilliantly in her studies, was granted a normal school cer-
tificate.   Then she went home, losing her parents through
death in the following years.   At that time Don Bassano
Dede, parish priest of St. Angelo, needed aid in his pastoral
work.   Frances gladly helped him, teaching Christian doctrine
to the children, visiting the sick and helping the poor.   Later
she taught school in a nearby town.   All this time she felt
strongly drawn to the Religious life and performed many
acts of self-denial.   Thus she slept on two boards in place of
a mattress.   Several times she applied for admission to
different Religious Communities, but in vain.   Some time
later when asked to supervise an orphanage in Cadogno, she
at first refused, because she still hoped to become a Religious.
Finally, she consented to try it for fifteen days.   Those
fifteen days became six years, and in 1880, she was still
directing this work, surrounded by a group of young women,
who also were desirous of dedicating themselves to the
Missions.   That same year, the Bishop of Lodi commissioned
her to found a Missionary Institute.   Frances and her companions took over an ancient Franciscan Convent, and a few
days later, Holy Mass was celebrated and Holy Communion
was distributed to the new community.   Then an Academy
was opened, which was soon filled to capacity.   Then Frances
was elected Mother General of the Missionaries of the Sacred
Heart.   The Community grew and new houses sprang up
quickly, among them two in the Papal City, Rome.   On
March 12, 1888 the Holy See approved the Institute of the
Missionary Sisters of the Sacred Heart.   One day, Bishop
Scalabrini, the founder of the Missionaries of Emigration,
told her of the difficulties and misery of Italian emigrants in
America, and suggested that Frances establish her Community in New York.   Saint Cabrini did not immediately
act on this suggestion.   But when in an audience, Pope Leo
XIII said to her, "Not to the East, but to the West.   Go to
the United States," Saint Cabrini no longer hesitated.   She
landed in America on March 31, 1889, and immediately set
to work, a work that lasted until her death.   For the Italian
children she erected schools, kindergartens, orphanages, hospitals and free dispensaries. She became active in all kinds

of social welfare work. In 37 years she erected 67 houses in Europe and America. At her death, her Community numbered five hundred Sisters, there were five thousand children in her schools, orphanages, etc. Her hospitals took care of almost one hundred thousand sick. Saint Cabrini died in Chicago on December 22, 1917, at the age of 67. One November 13, 1938, she was declared "Blessed" by Pope Pius XI and was canonized by Pope Pius XII in 1946. Her relics are preserved in the Chapel of the Mother Cabrini High School, New York.

Reflection.—"Therefore I endure all things for the sake of the elect, that they also may obtain the salvation which is in Christ Jesus, with heavenly glory." (2 Tim. 2, 10)

December 28.—ST. GASPAR DEL BUFALO, Confessor.

SAINT GASPAR DEL BUFALO was born in Rome, January 6, 1786. He passed his youth in study and in works of charity and piety. When only fifteen years of age he received minor orders and already began to preach in Rome with remarkable success. He was ordained in 1808 and shortly afterwards was exiled to Piacenza for refusing to swear allegiance to Napoleon. The period of exile told on his health and in 1810 he became so sick that he was expected to die. It was then that his spiritual director, Father Albertini, told him a prophecy of a certain holy nun, Sister Mary Agnes of the Incarnate Word, concerning a young man who would found a new congregation of missionary priests under the title of the Divine Blood, for the reform of morals and the salvation of souls and as an ornament to the secular clergy. Albertini, convinced that this prophecy referred to del Bufalo, bade him pray for recovery and offer to God the Father the Most Precious Blood of His Son for this purpose. Gaspar harkened to the voice of his director and his prayer for recovery was heard. On the Feast of the Assumption in 1815 at Giano, diocese of Spoletto, he organized a group of priests to bring God and peace into a world torn by irreligion and unrest in the wake of the Napoleonic wars. The new society and especially its founder, worked wonders. Great was the fruit of Gaspar's missionizing. Innumerable sinners were brought to penance, some of whom joined strict religious communities to atone for their past. Anticlericals, free-masons, apostates, atheists were won over. Public reconcilia-tion of enemies, destruction of weapons, and burning of bad books gave striking proof of the real effect of his sermons. The Society of the Precious Blood spread through Italy and into Switzerland, Germany and the United States. On the evening of December 28, 1837, Blessed Vincent Palotti, hastened to the bedside of his dying friend, Gaspar del Bufalo. "I come," he said, "to assist at the death of a saint." Saint Gaspar died that night and it is said that Blessed Vincent saw his soul like a beautiful star going up to heaven. Many miracles were worked through the intercession of Gaspar del Bufalo after his death. He was beatified by St. Pius X on August 29, 1904, and was canonized by Pope Pius XII on June 12, 1954. His feast is celebrated Decem-ber 28th.

Reflection.—Imitate the zeal of St. Gaspar who exhorts us to repeat always with Francis de Sales: "If I knew that one thought of my mind, one affection of my heart, one work of my hands would not be entirely for God, I should not choose to possess mind or heart or hand."

INDEX

A